An introduction to
reasoning

An introduction to
reasoning

Second Edition

Stephen Toulmin
Richard Rieke
Allan Janik

Macmillan Publishing Co., Inc.
New York
Collier Macmillan Publishers
London

Macmillan Publishing Company
866 Third Avenue, New York, New York 10022
Collier Macmillan Canada, Inc.

Library of Congress Cataloging in Publication Data

Toulmin, Stephen Edelston.
  An introduction to reasoning.

  Includes index.
  1. Reasoning. I. Rieke, Richard D. II. Janik, Allan.
III. Title.
BC177.T59 1984   160   83-16196
ISBN 0-02-421160-5

Printing: 10 11 12 13 14 15 16   Year: 3 4 5 6 7

ISBN   0-02-421160-5

Preface

In recent years the study of practical reasoning and argumentation has begun to play a larger part in college courses, especially at the introductory level. On this level, it is taught not just in philosophy departments, but also in departments of communication and English, as well as in professional schools of law and business. The resulting field of analysis and instruction goes by different names in different contexts: "informal logic" and "rhetoric" among many others. *An Introduction to Reasoning* has been written with an eye to the needs of all the current types of courses, and is designed to serve as a general introduction to them. The book presupposes no familiarity with formal logic, and is intended to provide an introduction to ideas about rationality and criticism without requiring a mastery of any particular logical formalism.

The "basic pattern of analysis" set out in Parts II and III of this book is suitable for application to arguments of all types and in all fields. By contrast, the chapters in part VI discuss the special features associated with practical reasoning in different fields of argumentation—law, science, fine arts, management, and ethics, respectively. Parts IV and V deal with a number of general issues connected with the rational criticism of arguments as viewed from the standpoints of philosophy, communication, and other disciplines: they include a discussion of *fallacies* as nonformal failures in the *process* of reasoning, rather than as blunders in the mechanics of argumentation.

In planning courses for particular purposes, it will probably be convenient for the instructor to select those parts of the book best adapted to the interests of the classes in question. All students will need a basic grasp of the material in Parts

II and III, but the various chapters in Parts IV, V and VI can be regarded as "electives," dependent upon time and interests.

The exercises included in the text are designed to test the reader's grasp of the material. In one respect, of course, the practical criticism of arguments differs significantly from formal logic: there are no uniquely "right" or "wrong" solutions to problems as there are in algebra. This has made it impracticable to design "true or false" tests of a multiple choice type. And, rather than pretend to a greater degree of formalism than the nature of our subject matter allows, we have chosen to provide questions that allow for some exercise of the reader's judgment and understanding.

Finally, in this text we have attempted to discuss practical argumentation in a wide variety of fields and disciplines. In preparing this second, revised edition, we have profited greatly from the comments and criticisms of instructors who have used the book in different kinds of classes, and we shall welcome further reactions from our colleagues. In a rapidly developing field of teaching and study, we all need to pool our experience, if we are to develop a well-founded tradition of teaching and a common body of understanding about practical reasoning and argumentation.

S.E.T.
R.D.R.
A.S.J.

Contents

Part III
Second level of analysis: the strength of arguments ⎯⎯⎯⎯⎯⎯⎯⎯⎯ 79

Part IV
Fallacies: how arguments go wrong ⎯⎯⎯⎯⎯⎯⎯⎯⎯ 129

Part V
Critical practice   199

Part VI
Special fields of reasoning   269

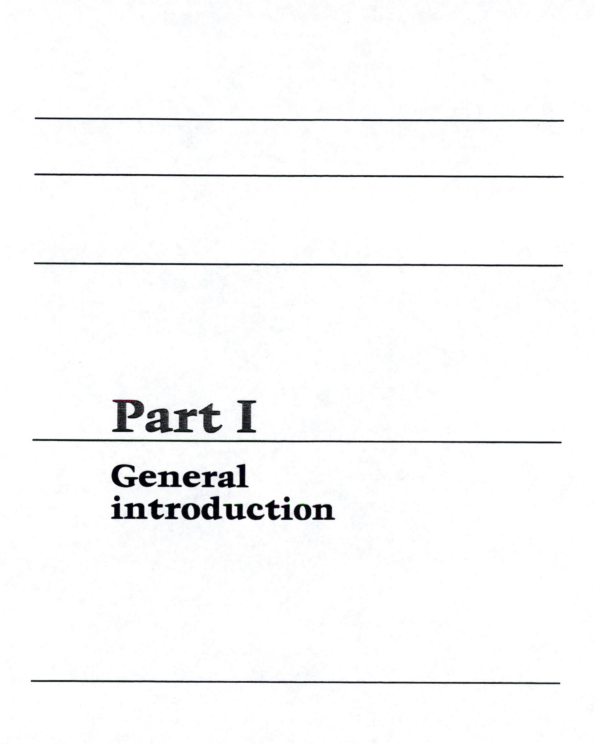

Part I

General introduction

1

Reasoning
and
its
goals

"Porsches are superior to any sports car made in the United States," says the auto salesman, "if for no other reason than the well-known fact that German automotive engineering is the best in the world." Is that a reasonable thing to say?

"On election day, the voters should return me to office again," declares the political candidate: "During my current term the rate of inflation has fallen from 11 percent to 6 percent, the real gross national product is up 5 percent, more people are working than ever before, and the United States is not at war." Does this candidate make sense?

"If you know what's good for you, you'll major in business," a college counselor is heard to say. "Employers are turning away from liberal arts majors to seek out graduates with marketable skills." Is that advice sound?

"It's crazy to make it illegal for people under 18 to buy contraceptives," writes a young man to the newspaper advice column. "Kids are going to have sex anyway, and this law will just mean more unwanted pregnancies." Does he offer a good argument?

"You should study your family's medical history," says the physician, "for epidemiological studies indicate that a family history of lung, breast, or abdominal cancer increases your chances of developing that same cancer from two to four times." Is the M.D. making a logical argument?

What does it mean to ask if someone's statement or argument or advice is sensible or well reasoned, sound or logical? Do we expect all the things that people say or do to be reasonable? What do these demands for "good reasons" and "sound arguments" amount to? And how are we to judge this kind of goodness and soundness? That is what this book is all about.

If you listen carefully to the comments people make around you or look closely at the written matter to which we are all exposed, you will find such terms as these in widespread use. Alongside them, too, are such other words and phrases as *because, therefore, it follows, it's reasonable to assume, thus, my conclusion is,* and so on. Evidently reasoning—or at least the giving of reasons—is pervasive in our society. The practice of providing reasons for what we do, or think, or tell others we believe is built firmly into our accepted patterns of behavior. This is so much the case that situations in which people fail to supply voluntarily the reasons we are expecting can be shocking or humorous. For example, a guest professor was directing a seminar when a student asked him, "Professor Black, the statement you just made is quite different from what you said this morning. Aren't you contradicting yourself?" The professor simply answered, "No," and proceeded to relight his pipe. The students waited, expecting him to add reasons in support of this negative response as soon as the pipe was going again. Instead the professor looked up and remained silent, as if waiting for the next question. The group shuffled nervously, and finally there was embarrassed laughter. Later on, the student who asked the question was heard to say he felt that the professor had put him down. He was angry. The professor had violated a strong social demand requiring him to provide reasons for disagreeing with his questioner.

THE VARIED USES OF LANGUAGE

People put language to use in innumerable ways and for innumerable purposes, and not all of these by any means involve the offering and evaluation of "reasons." We use language to move, persuade, or convince one another; to exchange and compare perceptions, information, or reactions; to command, greet, woo, or insult one another; to sue and seek redress from, or to negotiate and arrive at understandings with, one another; to unburden our own hearts or enchant one another's ears; and so on.

There are thousands of these human transactions in everyday life—exchanging greetings in the morning, small talk about the weather, or items of information about routine procedures; singing, making love, daydreaming out loud; dancing, listening to records together, reporting interesting events of the day, or commenting on last night's movie—that often put little, if any, emphasis on the giving and evaluating of reasons. And that lack of attention to "reasons" and "reasoning" is usually not missed.

So even though we put a high priority for many purposes on being able to supply reasons for claims, there are plenty of situations in which that demand is set aside. If someone learns that I meditate and asks me why I do so, I may answer simply, "It seems to help me." That's not much of a reason. If they pursue the subject, I may reply, "I have found a path to health and happiness through TM." If I am then asked to prove that meditation does what it claims, I may decline to engage in any further argument: "It is enough that I believe in it, and I do not care if you do." We treat many sensitive subjects in a similar way. Typically we do not ask why two friends love each other. If they are happy, that is all that matters: their love does not have to be further supported by reasons. And there are familar and accepted ways of brushing aside the demand for reasons in such cases, with a noncommittal response—with a "I can't say," or "I don't know," or "No special reason."

To start with, we may distinguish between *instrumental* and *argumentative* uses of language. By *instrumental* uses we mean those utterances that are supposed to achieve their purpose directly, as they stand, without the need to produce any additional "reasons" or "supporting arguments." We give orders, shout for joy, greet our friends, complain of a headache, ask for a pound of coffee, and so on, and the things we say in these cases either work or fail to work, either achieve their purpose or fall flat, either have their intended effect or go astray, without giving rise to any debate or argument. By *argumentative* uses, in contrast, we mean those utterances that succeed or fail only to the extent that they can be "supported" by arguments, reasons, evidence, or the like and that are able to carry the reader or the hearer along with them only because they have such a "rational foundation."

An order or a command, for instance, achieves its intended effect if it is obeyed and fails if it is disobeyed or ignored. It gives the people to whom it is addressed only two options: either they can accept it and go along with it, or else they can reject it and/or disregard it. Their understanding of it, and assent to it, are shown in their direct response. A command represents an exercise of power through the use of language and takes the right to have that power for granted. A command does not, as it stands, have to be "proved."

When is an argument not an argument?

Much of the language we hear and read does not contain any *arguments* at all. It is not intended to *convince* us of anything; all it aims to do is to describe a situation, report an event, tell a story, or express a personal attitude. Therefore, the first thing we need to learn is to recognize when people are using language with the intent to convince us: that is, to rely on facts we already agree about, in order to show us that we should accept other claims or assertions as well.

This is not always easy to do. Some small words often serve as clues to a speaker's or writer's intentions: among these are *so, because,* and especially *therefore*. Think of the sentence, "He was born abroad, *so* he may well not be a citizen." But these clues are not a hundred percent reliable. Think of the sentence, "He felt a headache coming on, *so* he took an aspirin." Nor is the line between persuading and convincing a hard and fast one. A friend may say, "Do come to the party! There will be lots to drink and good music and friendly people, *so* you will have a fine time." In this case, it is not wholly clear whether we should say that he wants to convince us that we should do ourselves a good turn by going with him, or whether he is just twisting our arms.

By contrast, when people make most kinds of assertions or claims—scientific, political, ethical, or artistic—they do not expect to convince other people directly. Instead they usually appeal to the hearers' understanding and agreement by providing additional "support" for the original claims, and they seek in this way to enlist voluntary assent or compliance. When occasion requires—when the desired agreement is not forthcoming at once—the initial utterance must be followed up and reinforced by further exchanges. The initial claim will be agreed to only if it is further explained and justified through the production of additional considerations, arguments, or other "reasoning."

Claims and assertions of the latter, argumentative kind give rise to the "trains of reasoning" whose nature and criticism are the central topic of discussion in the present book. We aim to achieve one or another goal of a kind that involves changing other people's minds, for example:

— To pass on a piece of news.
— To stake a legal claim.
— To object to some new company policy.
— To comment on a musical performance.
— To put forward a new scientific hypothesis.
— To support a candidate for a job.

Such goals cannot usually be accomplished by a bare assertion, or "unsupported" claim:

— We produce reasons.
— We are cross-questioned about the strength and relevance of those reasons.

— We meet objections.
— We perhaps modify or qualify the original assertion.

And only after such an exchange—such a train, or sequence, of reasoning—do we normally complete the task we embarked on with the original claim. (Of course, we may not bring it off: our arguments may not be strong enough to achieve their purposes. But by putting forward the strongest case we can, we have done what is rationally required of us in an "argumentative" situation.) The train of reasoning may thus have to be pursued at some length before the initial difference of view between the speaker and the hearer is either resolved or else sharply enough defined to make it clear that the difference is in fact irreconcilable.

In practice, we shall also find that utterances lie along a spectrum, from the *purely* instrumental to the *purely* argumentative. Even an order may occasionally give rise to an argument, if the person to whom it is addressed is prepared to challenge the speaker's authority or purposes—by asking, for instance, "Who are you, to order me about like that?" or "What do you think you are after, with that order?" (In an extreme case, this is known as being "insubordinate.") In this way, what began as a linguistic exercise of undisputed power, based on the assumption of "well-founded" authority, can turn into an argument. In the face of such a challenge, even this supposed authority may need to be "rationally justified" before it can be exercised. Instead of being taken for granted, its "foundation" must now be exposed to critical scrutiny.

Claims and discoveries

Arguments have several kinds of goals. Often, one person uses an argument to convince another person about something he himself was clearly convinced of in advance. In these cases, as we put it, the first person makes a *claim* which he then uses the argument to justify or establish. On other occasions, people start off with questions to which they have at first no clear answers, and use argumentation as a way of arriving at answers. They begin with *problems,* and their arguments lead them to *discoveries.*

Here, we shall distinguish between *inquiry,* the kind of reasoning designed to lead to a novel discovery, and *advocacy,* the kind of reasoning designed to support a previous claim.

Once again, the line between these two kinds of reasoning is not always in practice a hard and fast one. Sometimes, we make claims about which, as the conversation goes along, our arguments turn out to be weaker than we thought, so that a discussion that began as advocacy turns into inquiry. This should not worry us. It is a mark of intellectual honesty if you are prepared to admit, halfway through an argument, that your reasoning is not as strong as you had previously thought.

More generally, in what follows, our central concern will be to consider these questions:

— How are claims to be supported by *reasons?*
— How are those reasons themselves to be evaluated?
— What makes some arguments, such as trains of reasoning, better and others worse?

We shall be looking to see how "argumentative" utterances initiate trains of reasoning; how those subsequent discussions either succeed in supporting or fail adequately to support the initial utterances; and how the methods of setting out, appraising, and judging arguments in different fields of human activity have become codified into regular procedures that can be taught and learned, for example, in the course of professional training. In this way, we shall move from simple everyday beginnings to the point at which we shall see how "reasoning" and the criticism of reasoning play a central part in such enterprises as law, science, and business management.

REASONING VARIES WITH SITUATIONS

The trains of reasoning that it is appropriate to use vary from situation to situation. As we move from the lunch counter to the executive conference table, from the science laboratory to the law courts, the "forum" of discussion changes profoundly. The kind of involvement that the participants have with the outcome of the reasoning is entirely different in the different situations and so also will be the ways in which possible outcomes of the argument are tested and judged.

Notice how what looks at first glance like a single unchanging issue may be transformed as we go from one situation to another. A friend tells me, in the course of a casual conversation, that our acquaintance, Alex Avery, has decided to drop out of college and join the air force. Although I don't know Avery very well, I still ask why he is doing that. The reply: "Avery isn't making any money going to school, and they will pay him to learn a trade in the air force." At most, I raise my eyebrows. "That way," continues the answer, "he can afford to buy a car and some new clothes and still get an education."

My overall response is likely to be " You don't say." There is little occasion for me to spend time and energy testing seriously the plans of Alex Avery: they are none of my concern. But if my friend then goes on to make a more general claim—for example, "It makes sense to forget about college and let Uncle Sam set you up in business"—I may have somewhat more interest in testing it. In fact, I may reply that my friend is stupid to say this, and we may exhaust our remaining free time debating the issue, only to forget all about it by nightfall.

A further change of situation may raise the same issue for me again in another way. To my surprise, I find myself assigned to write a term paper evaluating the relative merits of various forms of career preparation, including attending college and engaging in military training. My situation has now changed in several ways. The person for whom I must construct arguments is a professor rather than a friend; my arguments will be closely scrutinized, and weaknesses will be publicly exposed; my grade in the course will be influenced by this test; my arguments will be written and turned in without my having a chance to hear critical responses and revise my own arguments. I must make the first effort my best.

Still later, after receiving the grade on my term paper, I may find myself in a conversation with my family. Now the issue has become directly personal: whether or not I myself should drop out of college and enter the military. Again the situation is changed. I know more about my ability to succeed in college; my reasoning involves all sorts of considerations and motives that were irrelevant in the context of a college term paper but that may now be highly relevant; and, not least, there is no immediate deadline for concluding the reasoning—my family and I can talk about the issue again and again, revising our arguments as we go along.

However, all these varied discussions, in all these varied situations, do have certain general features in common. In themselves, *claims* are not "freestanding" or self-supporting. When I make an assertion, offer an hypothesis, present a legal claim, advance a moral objection, or hazard an aesthetic opinion, my readers or hearers can always ask further questions before they decide whether to assent or disagree. Their assent or disagreement will then reflect and depend upon my capacity to offer "reasons" relevant to this situation to support the initial claim and will be conditional on their recognizing or disputing the "solidity" of those reasons. It is as though the initial claim itself resembled a kind of "building" whose reliability depends upon its being "supported" by sufficiently solid and secure "foundations."

In all these different kinds of situations, in dealing with different kinds of problems, the same set of questions can therefore be raised:

— What does the *giving of reasons* achieve?
— How do the different statements embodied in any train of argumentation succeed in *supporting* one another?
— What makes certain reasons or considerations *relevant* in supporting any particular claim, while other considerations would be *beside the point?*
— How is it that some supporting reasons are *strong,* while others are shaky?

This family of questions defines the topics involved in the critical study of argumentation or reasoning, with which this book is concerned. Our task is to see what kinds of features make some arguments strong, well founded, and persuasive, while others are weak, unconvincing, or baseless. And we also ask how we should embark on the task of setting out any such "argument" for analysis, so that we can recognize for ourselves:

1. How it is put together—what elements it is composed of, or how these different elements are related to one another; and
2. What bearing, if any, those relations have, either on the strength of the entire argument or on the acceptability of the claim under criticism.

REASONING AS A CRITICAL TRANSACTION

Notice that from our point of view, the essential locus of reasoning is a public, interpersonal, or social one. Wherever an idea or a thought may come from, it can be examined and criticized "rationally"—by the standards of "reason"—only if it is put into a position where it is open to public, collective criticism. Typically, reasoning is less a way of *hitting on new ideas*—for that, we have to use our imaginations—than it is a way of *testing and sifting ideas critically*. It is concerned with how people share their ideas and thoughts in situations that raise the question of whether those ideas are worth sharing. It is a collective and continuing human transaction, in which we present ideas or claims to particular sets of people within particular situations or contexts and offer the appropriate kinds of "reasons" in their support.

Reasoning thus involves dealing with claims with an eye to their contexts, to competing claims, and to the people who hold them. It calls for the critical evaluation of these ideas by shared standards; a readiness to modify claims in response to criticism; and a continuing critical scrutiny both of the claims provisionally accepted and of any new ones that may be put forward subsequently. A "reasoned" judgment is thus a judgment in defense of which adequate and appropriate reasons can be produced.

To say all this is not, however, to take it for granted that the standards by which the appropriateness and adequacy of those reasons are judged are universal and eternal. One of the central questions in our whole inquiry will be just how far, and in just what respects, we can hope to state general or universal standards of judgment for telling the validity, relevance, and strength or weakness of "reasons" or "arguments"; just how far, and in just what respects, these standards will inevitably vary in time or differ according to the context and circumstances of the judgment.

Certainly some degree of variety and variation in our standards of judgment is familiar from everyday life. Consider, for instance, a series of similar judgments that we are required to make in the course of growing up, for example, about the kinds of sex roles we are to follow. At the outset, we commonly take our parents' word as sufficient reason for us to accept a particular view of this role, for example, "You're a boy—boys don't cry." If Dad assures us of this, surely that will be enough for most of us. But later on, as adults, we may come to quite a different view about male tears, so that we may end by saying, "It takes real courage in our society for a man to let himself show his grief in actual tears." Now Father's views will no longer be accepted as final or authoritative but will be reappraised with an eye to a much more complex body of experience and ideas.

What goes for parents and children goes also for different groups of adults. Reasons and arguments that appear quite acceptable and proper to one group may be successfully challenged when discussed within other groups. Consider what happens to the cultural truisms of one group when they are subjected to challenge by outsiders. For example, many of our social and religious beliefs may be sincerely held by every member of our immediate family and social group, yet these beliefs may be rejected by members of some other social group that is in other ways quite similar to our own. We all agree that it is sound and reasonable to believe, perhaps, that we ought to brush our teeth after every meal, believe in God, and cover selected parts of our bodies when in public. But just because these ideas are so strongly shared by all those with whom we are in immediate contact, we may not have needed to generate any very substantial body of reasons in support of them. It is sufficient that those whom we respect have advocated them. What happens, the psychologists ask, to those who leave the shelter of this protective group with which the ideas are shared and enter a foreign environment, for example, on going away to college?

Such collective truisms have been found by researchers to be easy prey to attack. If a roommate challenges one of them, we may find that we have no very solid reasons to offer in its support—we have never had, before now, to go beyond the fact that "everybody believes it." Since our roommate will find this statement neither true nor sufficient, we shall need other reasons that may not be readily available. The result, according to the social psychologists, is that we are liable either to abandon the position rather quickly for lack of appropriate reasons or to fall back on some inflexibly dogmatic position. If we want to hold on to the beliefs in a critically defensible way, we must now provide ourselves with "reasons" of a new kind, more appropriate to this time and context. In fact (the psychologists suggest), a suitable process of "inoculation," by which we expose our most cherished ideas to systematic attack and begin on the task of building up a more adequate body of reasons in advance of a serious challenge, may allow us to develop our own critical faculties in a way that prepares us to deal more robustly with future attacks on our beliefs.

Reasoning, then, comes into play as a means of providing support for our ideas when they are open to challenge and criticism. This is not to say that procedures of reasoning always take place later in time than the formation of the ideas that call them forth. Since reasoning (or the providing of good reasons) plays so important and widespread a part in our culture, we often begin to test our ideas in a critical manner and think over the available reasons for or against them as soon as we first have the ideas. In a form of thinking that might be called *intrapersonal communication,* we imagine ourselves sharing an idea with other people and rehearse the questions they might ask and the challenges they might make to our supporting reasons.

In the course of this rehearsal, we may be able to refine and improve on the reasons in support of the idea, and so we finally arrive at a point where we can "go public," confident in our ability to justify it. Or alternatively, we may find ourselves recognizing so many arguments against the idea that we decide to forget it altogether or never to make it public. In either case, the "transactive" character of reasoning is preserved, at any rate to the extent that we criticize it with an eye to its "viability" within a collective debate—in terms either of how certain specific people would respond to it or in terms of some more overall picture of the kinds of people who might attack the idea. (Will our argument have to be presented to a jury, to a group of professional scientists, to a political meeting, or to whom?) Once again, the standards for judging even this "intrapersonal" reasoning must respect the claims of the forum in which it will eventually have to make its way.

THE STRUCTURE OF ARGUMENTS

Our first task here is to recognize how *arguments*, or *trains of reasoning*, are constructed out of their constituent parts: *claims, reasons,* and the rest. For instance, consider the following example. Two pro football buffs are discussing the prospects for the coming season:

> One of them says, "I'm laying a bundle on Dallas this year: the Cowboys are a certainty for the Super Bowl."
> His companion raises his eyebrows: "Why do you say that?"
> The first man assumes an air of great confidence: "Look at their strength—they're solid right through both squads—defensive and offensive both."
> His friend is not yet convinced: "Are they so unique?"
> The first man persists: "Ah, but look at the opposition! The Raiders have crumbled the last two seasons; the Steelers are brittle on the defense; the Dolphins will start with a flourish, but crack under pressure; the Vikings are strong on defense, but they just don't have the heavy artillery—take away their first string quarterback, and where are you? . . . I just don't see anyone who can touch the Cowboys."
> "Yeah," concedes his companion, "I get the argument; but I'm just not sure you can afford to rely on past performance that much."

By considering the successive steps, or procedures, followed in this conversation, we can make explicit the matters at issue at each stage in the exchange. In brief:

— The Dallas Cowboys enthusiast begins by issuing his central claim, namely, that the Cowboys are such a certainty for the Super Bowl that he plans to bet heavily on their success.

— His hearer, in reply, sets about probing the foundations of this claim. Through a succession of questions, he brings to light other more specific associated beliefs, by appeal to which the Dallas fan supports and attempts to justify his initial confident claim.

— At the end of the conversation, the two parties may part with their differences of opinion unresolved. But at any rate, they can now understand more clearly what those disagreements rest on, for instance, their differing assessments of other pro football teams, and their differing degrees of confidence in the reliability of past performance as a guide to pro football results.

When we analyze a conversation in these terms—as an exchange of opinions accompanied by a probing of the foundations of those opinions—we are able to scrutinize and criticize the *rational merits* of the arguments presented. In this way, we investigate and consider the relevance, adequacy, and soundness of the considerations that each of the two parties puts forward at any particular point in the conversation as his contribution to the argumentative interchange between them.

Evidently the rational procedures followed in our sample conversation pass through a succession of distinct phases:

— At the outset, the Dallas supporter puts forward his initial claim about the Super Bowl.

— His friend then questions him about the "grounds" on which he can give "rational support" to this prediction.

— In this way, two points are brought to light: first, the reliance of the claim on a belief about the *general kinds* of teams that win the Super Bowl and, second, a collection of detailed judgments about the *specific strengths and weaknesses* of the main rival pro football teams.

— Then the solidity, reliability, and relevance of those beliefs are each tested in turn.

— And so on.

The "rational merits" of the successive steps through which the participants go in the course of this conversation have to do with the reliability and trustworthiness both of the facts, grounds, evidence, testimony, and so on put forward as contributions to the argument and also of the links between the different elements in the argument. In a well-conducted argument, we do not just have to produce enough "reasons": we must also produce those reasons at the right point in the argument, if they are to do the job they are required to do. (We all know people who cannot get their thoughts together and who sprinkle their conversations with afterthoughts: "Oh, and there's another thing . . . !") The considerations that are going to be powerful at any point in an argument thus depend both on the general issue under discussion and also on how far the exchange of reasons has proceeded.

SOME DEFINITIONS

It is time to explain the use of the key terms that will appear in this book:

— The term *argumentation* will be used to refer to the whole activity of making claims, challenging them, backing them up by producing reasons, criticizing those reasons, rebutting those criticisms, and so on.

— The term *reasoning* will be used, more narrowly, for the central activity of presenting the reasons in support of a claim, so as to show how those reasons succeed in giving strength to the claim.

— An *argument,* in the sense of a *train of reasoning,* is the sequence of interlinked claims and reasons that, between them, establish the content and force of the position for which a particular speaker is arguing.

— Anyone participating in an argument shows his *rationality,* or lack of it, by the manner in which he handles and responds to the offering of reasons for or against claims. If he is "open to argument," he will either acknowledge the force of those reasons or seek to reply to them, and either way he will deal with them in a "rational" manner. If he is "deaf to argument," by contrast, he may either ignore contrary reasons or reply to them with dogmatic assertions, and either way he fails to deal with the issues "rationally."

With most of these terms, we shall be following everyday usage pretty closely. But special care is needed in one case. The word *argument* has two distinct colloquial senses: it can refer either to a "train of reasoning" (as here) or, alternatively, to a shouting match or other human dispute. For instance, we may talk about the *argument* that Pythagoras put forward in classical times in support of his famous theorem about the squares on the different sides of the right-angled triangle—that is, the intellectual steps that make up his "proof." Or else we may talk about the *exchange of views* that took place between Pythagoras and his associates when he set about presenting them with his theorem. And this latter is also, sometimes, referred to in everyday English as an *argument:*

> When Pythagoras put forward his theorem, was there much of an *argument* about it? Or did his pupils catch on to the proof straight away? How did they react to his pronouncement? Was there a dispute? Did the discovery make them angry or joyful? Or did it leave them cold?

In the first sense, Pythagoras' "argument" is a matter for geometers, and we can still set it out today in just about the same form that he presumably discovered. In the second sense, however, we know next to nothing about Pythagoras' "argument." No historical reports have come down to us, so we lack any reliable information about the human interactions between the master and his pupils.

In the first sense then, "arguments" are *trains of reasoning* lifted out of their original human contexts and considered apart from them. In the second sense, "arguments" are *human interactions* through which such trains of reasoning are formulated, debated, and/or thrashed out:

— In the first sense, arguments are strong or weak, well supported or flimsy, thoroughly convincing or initially implausible, concise or complex; but they are not—in themselves—friendly or violent, calm or noisy, amiably drunken or colored with hidden malice.
— In the second sense, arguments are something that people become involved in, persist in, carry through doggedly, lose patience with, and, on occasion, fight their way out of.

Understood in this latter sense, an argument may comprise quiet and careful speech, shouts, or whispers; complex blackboard calculations, slaps on the back, or bloody noses; convinced agreements, bitter partings, or exhausted concessions—as contrasted with the sound or shaky inferences, valid or fallacious deductions, rigorous or faulty proofs, and powerful or frail reasons typical of an "argument" in the first, train-of-reasoning sense.

Can we always distinguish between "arguing" in these two senses? In one respect, yes. A train of reasoning can always be set out as a sequence of statements linked together rationally, as evidence, grounds, rules, and so on. By contrast, a complete personal exchange of views, a bargaining session, or a noisy brawl cannot be presented in full simply by reporting the statements made in the course of it. On one level, therefore, the distinction between trains of reasoning and argumentative human interactions is clear enough. However, there is the same risk of ambiguity about some instances of human argumentation in practice that there is about the difference between persuading and convincing. We may begin by trying to convince a friend that her hairdresser has given her a poor haircut; but it may turn out that she herself chose the styling deliberately; and, instead of backing down and withdrawing the original claim, we may find ourselves drawn into a shouting match. That is to say, what begins as the presentation of an "argument" (in the first sense) may gradually turn into a disagreeable "argument" (in the second sense).

When this happens, it is helpful—as well as intellectually honest—to sit down cooly afterwards, and figure out what happened. We can then ascertain how the weakness of our original reasoning made it easy for us to slide into verbal armtwisting, or even personal abuse.

THE FORUMS OF ARGUMENTATION

One last introductory remark is necessary before we start our basic analysis of the structure of arguments. Arguments (trains of reasoning) are put forward for discussion and critical scrutiny, and arguments (human interactions) are accordingly initiated and carried through to completion in all sorts of different locations, or *forums*. This can happen in bars or at the breakfast table; on street corners or in the law courts; at scientific meetings or in hospital wards; on television talk shows or in congressional debates. (The list is a long one.) Furthermore, the ways in which arguments are judged always require the participants to have an eye to the "forums" in which they are occurring, and to this extent, the separation between the two senses of the term *argument*—trains of reasoning and their human working-through—can never be absolute or complete.

The typical "forums of argumentation" include

— Law courts.
— Professional scientific meetings.
— Corporation board meetings.
— Medical consultations.
— University seminars.
— Congressional committee hearings.
— Engineering design conferences.

Each forum involves its own types of discussion. These are organized and conducted so as to ensure the clear statement and public criticism of the corresponding arguments—whether legal or scientific, financial, medical or political. Because the kinds of issues raised in each forum are of such different sorts, the procedures used in the resulting discussions are different, and the manner in which claims and arguments have to be presented and defended also varies. These variations from forum to forum are a direct consequence of the *functional* differences between the needs of the enterprises concerned, for example, law or science, business or medicine.

The business of the courts, for instance, is with rendering *judgments*. Rival parties come before a court, present their respective "cases" (i.e., claims and supporting arguments), and depend on the judge or the jury to decide between them. The business of a scientific meeting is to discuss *intellectual problems*. A scientist commonly presents a hypothesis, or experimental study, and puts forward ideas and arguments for critical debate among his colleagues. He usually does not expect immediate agreement or disagreement from them; the needs of the case do not make any such immediate judgment necessary; it may be enough for him that he has the opportunity to put his ideas into circulation. The business of a board meeting or a medical consultation will commonly be to work out a *policy*. This may have to do with investment possibilities or alternatively with possible ways of treating a sick patient, but in either case, the matter usually cannot wait.

Human argumentation thus has a whole range of distinct functions. For example, the quality of legal reasoning is judged by its relevance and its power to support a judgment on behalf of a given charge or defense; the quality of business reasoning is determined by its power to guide policy discussions; and so on.

While certain very broad rules of "rational procedure" apply to arguments in all these forums, many of the more specific rules of procedure (or "due process") that govern arguments in one area or another are relevant only to, say, the proceedings in a law court rather than a scientific meeting, or the other way around. One of the main aims of this book will in fact be to show the difference between

— Those universal ("field-invariant") rules of procedure that apply to rational criticism in all fields and forums, and
— Those particular ("field-dependent") rules that are appropriate in law, or science, or business, but not everywhere.

Differences of subject and differences of reasoning

Everyone at school or college has the chance to check out these likenesses and differences. Think about the different ways in which you are expected to present your arguments (i.e., through trains of reasoning) in the subjects that you study. Writing an essay about Shakespeare's *Merchant of Venice* for your English literature class is one thing; writing up a laboratory report in chemistry class is another; while solving a problem in trigonometry is yet a third.

In the following chapters, we shall investigate a whole string of ideas and distinctions that link together—yet at the same time help us to distinguish—the intellectual and practical concerns of different school subjects, and also the concerns of the larger human activities for which they are a preparation. Many people find it helpful to use the patterns of analysis that we shall be setting out here as a way of clarifying their reasoning for themselves, and even as a way of planning essays and arguments in other school subjects. It will be worth your while to think, as we go along, how you can apply these methods of analysis to your other studies. For instance, ask yourself what kinds of *fallacies* are most frequent in scientific, or historical, or literary reasoning; or what kinds of *rules* or *laws* are relied on to justify claims and discoveries in different subjects.

CONCLUSION

We have said that reasoning varies from situation to situation and from forum to forum. Furthermore, not all situations call for reasoning. In the main body of this book, we shall show how trains of reasoning, or arguments, are employed and criticized in practical life. We shall describe practical reasoning as it occurs in daily use, in the hope of understanding better its actual assumptions and potentialities. Rather than abandon decision making to whim, power, or the effects of unreasoned persuasion, we shall describe the critical procedures through which ideas are examined in competition with each other and judged by relevant criteria so as to make it possible for us to arrive at reasonable choices.

It is impossible in the last resort to divorce the criticism of *reasoning* and *decision making* entirely from an understanding of the people giving the reasons and making the decisions. It is people who make choices, and their involvement cannot be eliminated. Reasons and decisions must be considered in terms of the ways in which people employ language to present their reasons and to justify their decisions.

There is a certain advantage to be gained from standing back and looking directly at things that we otherwise do unthinkingly. By reflecting on these "obvious" things, we can come to understand ourselves and our activities in ways that help us protect ourselves from certain confusions. The hero of Molière's play *The Bourgeois Gentleman* was surprised to learn from his grammar teacher that he had been "talking prose for forty years." People who begin studying logic or argumentation or rhetoric in adult life today must often feel something of the same surprise. Yet, in fact, the use of language for the purposes of reasoning or argumentation plays a major part in our lives, and it is natural and proper that we should set about trying to understand this particular use of language—and so become self-aware also about the arts of speaking and writing, communicating and expressing ourselves, presenting "claims" and supporting them with "arguments."

A fable

Let us end with a story. This will serve as a reminder about the general ways in which inquiry and advocacy, claims and discoveries, and persuading and convincing work together in real life—that is, how *reasoning* serves human purposes.

Some years ago, there was an advertising specialist in New York City who used to pass the time folding paper airplanes. That was his hobby and he was good at it. One day he folded a new plane that flew better than any he had ever made. In particular, it did not stall. Unlike most airplanes—whether paper models or of full size—which fall abruptly when their angle of ascent becomes too sharp, this particular paper plane did not do so. Instead, when the "angle of attack" at which the wing met the air reached a maximum, the plane leveled off and continued to fly, rather than losing speed and falling as planes with conventional wings are apt to do. The advertising man's friend, a pilot, was so impressed with this plane that he convinced the man to patent it. So it was that the so-called Kline-Fogleman wing came to be invented.

The two men next wrote to various organizations and companies, hoping to convince others that the new wing was a major discovery. They got little response until their idea was reported on a network TV program. Then they received letters expressing interest—from a toy manufacturer and from the National Aeronautics and Space Administration, among others.

Now began some critical tests. The questions under examination varied from whether the wing could be used in a toy that children would enjoy and would buy, to whether fighter airplanes could better engage in war if built with such a wing, to whether rocket-propelled vehicles designed to go into space and then return to earth could better complete their missions with this wing, and so on. In each case, rather different criteria were relevant, and the claims for the wing had to be justified with an eye to different demands. Thus, whether this invention was accepted as "good" depended on the people doing the reasoning and on the circumstances in which they were functioning.

The toy manufacturer quickly decided that the invention was "good" and has launched a new line of toy planes. (If these do not fly well, they will not sell, and the company will lose money. Depending on the sales, they will either continue making the toy or stop.) The Department of Defense is still conducting secret tests and will have to justify the cost of a new line of war planes to a money-conscious Congress and the novelty of the new design to the pilots who will risk their lives in it. (If it fails to fly as predicted, people will die and the country could suffer battle losses. In either case, great amounts of money will have been spent.) NASA is also testing whether the wing will help space flight. Unlike the toy makers and the fighter plane manufacturers, they must work on problems of flight in and out of the Earth's atmosphere. An "antistall" wing may or may not be a good move for them, if it proves to have weaknesses when used outside the atmosphere.

Is this an unusual story? Not so, says one aeronautical specialist who now teaches in a university and once worked at NASA. Technical ideas of this kind often come from quite unexpected sources, like a grown man playing with paper airplanes. The origin of the new ideas is not the point: what matters, from the standpoint of rationality, is that we should take the novel idea and subject it to critical tests. Reasoning (he might have said) does not create ideas and does not answer once and for all whether those ideas are good or bad, true or false. Rather, the task of reasoning in each situation is to enable the questioner to make the best decision about a particular issue, in particular circumstances, within a particular forum and enterprise. How the critical functions of different trains of reasoning can best be analyzed and understood, with an eye to the forum and the context involved, is the question to which we must now turn.

Exercises

I. Bring to class an example of reasoning that you have encountered and be prepared to discuss how it differs from "ordinary discourse,"

II. Which among the following contain arguments? Discuss the reasoning in each passage:

1. ROLLIE: Trends, Zonker! that's where I'm at these days! Roone's very concerned that ABC news have its own mood man! So that's why I was hoping you might be able to turn me on to any new trends here in your neck of the woods.

   ZONKER: Well, I'm not sure that I can help you there.

   ROLLIE: To tell you the truth, the problem is one of overkill. There're so many trends sweeping the nation these days, it's hard to find one to really call your own! Take your magazines, for instance. During the same week recently "Time" and "Newsweek" ran cover stories on the cooking craze and the dieting craze . . . in other words according to our major newsweeklies, the two hottest trends in the country are eating and not eating! So who knows? Lately I've been thinking of just striking out on my own.

ROLLIE: Good plan, I hear more and more people are doing that these days.

G. B. Trudeau, *Doonesbury*

2.   **THE NEW CHEVROLET**

Its beauty is in the eyes, the legs, the hands and the heart of the beholder.

The New Chevrolet can make you feel good in many different ways. Which is probably why so many people have been buying it. Clean, crisp styling that stands proudly apart. A bright spacious interior with more headroom and more rear-seat legroom than in the larger full size 1976 Chevrolet it replaced. (More trunk room too.) That nice "Chevy feel" when you take the wheel. A level of interior quiet we urge you to experience for yourself. And if the rational side of you recoils at this talk of pleasure, please remember: the New Chevrolet was designed for efficiency. For a car so roomy it does surprisingly well in the mileage department. EPA estimates are 24 mpg. highway 17 city with the standard 250 Cu. In. engine and automatic transmission. Estimates lower in California. Actual mileage may vary depending on how and where you drive, your car's condition and equipment. (The New Chevrolet is equipped with GM built engines produced by various divisions. See your dealer for details.) Like we said, it's a car that can make you feel good in many different ways. A test drive will quickly confirm it.

Chevrolet Ad, *Business Week*

3.   Joshu asked the teacher Nansen, "What is the true Way?"
Nansen answered, "The everyday way is the true Way."
Joshu asked, "Can I study it?"
Nansen answered, "The more you study, the further you are from the Way."
Joshu asked, "If I don't study it, how can I know it?"
Nansen answered, "The Way does not belong to things seen: nor to things unseen. It does not belong to things known: nor to things unknown. Do not seek it, study it or name it. To find yourself on it, open yourself wide as the sky."

Zen Buddhism (Peter Pauper Press)

4.   The primroses were over. Towards the edge of the wood, where the ground became open and sloped down to an old fence and a brambly ditch beyond, only a few fading patches of pale yellow still showed

among the dog's mercury and oak-tree roots. On the other side of the fence, the upper part of the field was full of rabbit holes. In places where the grass was gone altogether and everywhere there were clusters of dry droppings, through which nothing but the ragwort would grow. A hundred yards away, at the bottom of the slope, ran the brook, no more than three feet wide, half-choked with king-cups, watercress and blue brook lime. The cart track crossed by a brick culvert and climbed the opposite slope to a five-barred gate in the thorn hedge. The gate led into the lane.

Richard Adams, *Watership Down*

5. Real truths are those that have to be invented.

Penalties serve to deter those who are not inclined to commit any crimes.

Medicine: "your money and your life."

In case of doubt decide in favor of what is correct.

One of the most widespread diseases is diagnosis.

Karl Kraus (Zohn translation, Engendra Press)

III. Be prepared to discuss your colloquial understanding of reasoning. Where do you normally encounter reasoning, persuading, and convincing situations? Are reasoning, persuading, and convincing the same sort of thing, or are they different from one another?

IV. Discuss some of the contexts in which we disagree with one another. What role does reasoning play in resolving disagreements? How do we come to change our minds when we do change them?

Part II

**First
level
of
analysis:
the soundness of
arguments**

2

Introduction

At this point, we must provide ourselves with a pattern of analysis and a vocabulary for identifying and describing the strengths and weaknesses of arguments. These are the basic instruments we shall need in order to understand what is involved in the rational criticism of arguments. The following questions are important:

— What is the natural "starting point" of an argument?
— What is its proper "destination"?
— What kinds of procedures must it follow?
— What sequences of stages will an argument pass through, and what are the relations between successive stages?
— What kinds of questions must we ask, and what kinds of tests must we employ, in checking whether a particular argument is fully reasoned through?

THE ELEMENTS OF ANY ARGUMENT

In Chapters 3–6, we shall take up four sets of questions in turn. We shall look, in succession, at four elements that can be found in any wholly explicit argument. These are (1) claims and discoveries, (2) grounds, (3) warrants and rules, and (4) backings. Let us briefly explain what these four kinds of elements are, and how they are connected.

1. *Claims*. When we embark on an argument, there is always some "destination" which we may arrive at for ourselves as a discovery, or else may be invited to arrive at by somebody else, as an assertion; and the first step in analyzing and criticizing the argument is to understand the precise character of that destination. The first set of questions is

   What exactly are we discussing? Where precisely are we to stand on this issue? And what position must we consider agreeing to as the outcome of the argument?

2. *Grounds.* Having clarified the claim, we must consider what kind of underlying foundation is required if a claim of this particular kind is to be accepted as solid and reliable. The next set of questions will therefore have to do with these foundations:

    What information are you going on? What grounds is your claim based on? Where must we ourselves begin if we are to see whether we can take the step you propose and so end by agreeing to your claim?

    Depending on the kind of claim under discussion, these grounds may comprise experimental observations, matters of common knowledge, statistical data, personal testimony, previously established claims, or other comparable "factual data." But in any case, the claim under discussion can be no stronger than the grounds that provide its foundation.

3. *Warrants.* Knowing on what grounds a claim is founded is, however, only the first step toward judging its solidity and reliability. Next we must check whether these grounds really do provide genuine support for this particular claim and are not just irrelevant information having nothing to do with the claim in question—designed to "pull the wool over our eyes," for instance. The next set of questions is

    Given that starting point, how do you justify the move from these grounds to that claim? What road do you take to get from this starting point to that destination?

    Once again, the type of answers we may expect to this further set of questions will depend on the kind of claim under discussion. Steps from grounds to claims are "warranted" in different ways in law, in science, in politics, and elsewhere. The resulting warrants take the form of laws of nature, legal principles and statutes, rules of thumb, engineering formulas, and so on. But in any practical case, some appropriate warrant will be needed if the step from grounds to claim is to be trustworthy.

4. *Backing.* Warrants themselves cannot be taken wholly on trust. Once we know what rule or law, formula or principle, is being relied on in any argument, the next set of questions can be raised:

    Is this really a safe move to make? Does this route take us to the required destination securely and reliably? And what other general information do you have to back up your trust in this particular warrant?

    The warrants relied on to authorize arguments in different fields of reasoning require correspondingly different kinds of backing: legal statutes must have been validly legislated; scientific laws must have been thoroughly checked out; and so on. Aside from the particular facts that serve as grounds in any given argument, we therefore need to find out the general body of information, or backing, that is presupposed by the warrant appealed to in the argument.

The claims involved in real-life arguments are, accordingly, well founded only if sufficient grounds of an appropriate and relevant kind can be offered in their support. These grounds must be connected to the claims by reliable, applicable warrants, capable in turn of being justified by appeal to sufficient backing of the relevant kind. In the remaining chapters of Part II, we shall be concerned with elaborating these questions and definitions.

A first sample argument

To summarize the general ways in which claims and grounds, warrants and backing enter into our arguments (and "hang together" within them), consider the following statement:

> It's Monday already, and last Thursday was Thanksgiving. By law, Thanksgiving can never fall before November 23rd. *So,* there are less than thirty days left to do our Christmas shopping.

Here, a final *claim*—namely,

> There are less than thirty shopping days left—

is supported, first, by pointing out particular facts, or *grounds,* which are relevant to it—for example,

> It's Monday after Thanksgiving today—

next, by drawing attention to a generalization which connects those grounds, to the claim, and serves as a *warrant* for using one and support for the other—

> Thanksgiving can never be before November 23rd—

and lastly, by indicating the underlying basis, or *backing,* on which the reliability of that general warrant depends—

> The date of Thanksgiving is established by Act of Congress.

In the next four chapters, we shall look at each of these elements (claims, grounds, warrants, and backing) in turn, to see how they join together to form arguments that can be accepted as *sound*.

3

Claims
and
discoveries

"The San Francisco 49'rs are a certainty for the Super Bowl this year."

"This new version of King Kong makes more psychological sense than the original."

"The epidemic was caused by a bacterial infection carried from ward to ward on food-service equipment."

"The company's best interim policy is to put this money into short-term municipal bonds."

All of these are "claims," that is, assertions put forward publicly for general acceptance. They contain the implications that there are underlying "reasons" that could show them to be "well founded" and therefore entitled to be generally accepted.

The first element that we can identify in any argument, then, is the element we have been calling a claim. When we analyze the force and procedure of any argument, the relevant claim defines both the starting point and the destination of our procedures:

— At the outset, the task of the *assertor* or *claimant* (whom we may refer to as *A*) is to present a well-defined position for her hearers to consider and discuss. In this way, she gives her audience or *interrogators* (whom we may refer to as *I*) the occasion to elicit the additional material normally required before other people can judge for themselves the justice and/or acceptability of that claim, and so be properly convinced of its correctness.

— Later on, when all the necessary material has been brought to light, *I* and *A* will end up with an argument that is fully reasoned through. The claim or *hypothesis* that originally formed the unsupported starting point for discussion now becomes—after critical analysis—a more-or-less adequately supported destination, discovery or conclusion.

Whereas *A* first put forward a claim simply as her own opinion, that opinion is now either established or discredited, and practical or theoretical consequences may flow from it as a result, depending upon the precise nature of the particular claim. If the claim was a legal one, the original plea now becomes a verdict, and its consequences will take the form of some judicial order or sentence. If the claim was a medical one, the original hypothesis now becomes an established diagnosis, and its consequences will be the recommendation of some specific course of therapy. If the claim concerned a business decision, what began as *A*'s opinion may end by becoming the company's agreed policy. If the initial claim was a scientific one, then the original suggestion is entitled—once properly established—to take its place in the corpus of knowledge about this branch of science.

THE NATURE OF CLAIMS

The word *claim* has a long history. One of its primary uses refers to legal rights and entitlements—specifically, in disputes about property rights. Recall how in Gold Rush days miners used to "stake a claim." This meant marking out an area within which their exclusive rights of digging were to be respected. Naturally, they did not expect other miners to leave such claims unchallenged, so they accepted it as necessary to be able to *defend them* publicly. By establishing a proper "title" over an area, they could create a legal position. The result was that other miners had to refrain from digging within that area. To "argue" a claim meant doing whatever was needed—producing documentary evidence and oral testimony before the magistrate or the title registry—to convert the bare demand for rights into a well-established, enforceable title, which other miners were obliged to concede.

For our purposes here, "arguing a claim," in this legal sense, is one extreme case in the spectrum of arguments that we shall be examining. As we move along the spectrum toward other less pragmatic kinds of cases, the matters at stake become less tangible and more theoretical. Suppose that your scientific colleagues acknowledge that you have put forward a "well-founded" argument for some scientific hypothesis and go on to incorporate your ideas into their ways of thinking about beetles or glaciers or mesons. The consequences will be less obviously dramatic and lucrative than the consequences of persuading the Yukon police that they should prevent other miners from trespassing on your digging rights. Still, in its own property context, "intellectual property" has as solid a status as real property or digging rights. Within scientific forums, the business of establishing "intellectual claims" is no less exacting and significant than the business of establishing property rights before a court of law.

In their detailed substance, of course, the procedures we are required to follow in making good claims of different kinds will be very different:

— In establishing our property rights over a stolen bicycle.
— In winning the prospects for the Super Bowl.
— In convincing others to have respect for our critical opinion about the merits of a movie.
— In giving a firm basis to our ideas about the causes of the aurora borealis.

Between the general procedures to be followed in supporting all these claims, however, there is much less difference. In each case, our business is a three-fold one:

— To draw attention to the generally accepted and relevant facts (grounds) on which the claim is to be based.
— To indicate what general rules, laws, or principles (warrants) make these facts relevant to the claim.
— To make it clear just how the available grounds and support provide a basis for the present claim rather than any alternative or rival claim.

CLAIMS THAT ARE AMBIGUOUS OR UNCLEAR

It is not always a simple matter to satisfy ourselves that a claim is properly stated in the first place. Often enough, the particular words in which an assertor (A) first presents a claim will not be wholly clear. The chosen words may contain unresolved ambiguities and may lend themselves to alternative interpretations. These ambiguities must be resolved before criticism of the claim in question can even begin.

Suppose that in the course of an everyday conversation, A casually remarks that his brother James is "mad." At first, we may not know exactly how to take this assertion:

Does he mean mad only in a colloquial sense? Does he mean that Jim is temporarily infuriated, so that we should watch our step in dealing with him, leave him to simmer down, or try to pacify him?

Does he mean, more gravely, that Jim's behavior has become seriously confused, so that he can no longer manage his own life and property, and that the time has come to have his affairs placed in legal guardianship?

Or does this mean that Jim is experiencing a psychotic episode, and needs to spend some time in a mental institution?

The actual situation within which a claim is put forward—in a judge's chambers, a doctor's office, or whatever—will often enable us to decide between these alternative interpretations. When one is talking to a judge, *mad* presumably means "legally incompetent." When one is talking to a psychiatrist, it presumably means "psychotic." Such ambiguities are seriously harmful only when the claims in question are put forward without any clear context, that is, in a conversation from which all situational clues are missing. When this happens, our very first critical task—even before we ask for "grounds"—is to sort out the initial ambiguity. This means asking any additional questions that are needed in order to put the claim into its proper context and so to clarify its implications:

Just what are you saying? Do you mean that Jim is legally incompetent, or taking a rest in a mental clinic, or just infuriated? Tell me that first, so that I don't get hold of the wrong end of the stick at the very outset!

These ambiguities in our claims are connected with some other ambiguities that we noticed earlier: in those between persuading and convincing, and between the two kinds of "arguments." The more clearly and unambiguously a claim or hypothesis is stated at the outset, the easier it is to avoid having it degenerate into a confused string of disagreements. In everyday discussion, it is clear enough how our arguments fall apart. But it is worth noticing that the same thing can happen, just as well, in more serious and professional debates. In the present case, for instance, the ambiguities built into a word like *mad* do not cause trouble only for ordinary people. Lawyers and psychiatrists, also, often end at cross purposes when they discuss the relevance of insanity to questions of criminal responsibility— think of the passionate debates prompted by the Hinckley verdict in which a young man who shot President Reagan was sent to a hospital rather than a prison.

Exercises

In the following the student should:

a. Distinguish the claim from the grounds adduced to support it.
b. Identify the question that the arguments are intended to resolve.
c. Reformulate the grounds more specifically or precisely where possible.

1. Anderson is a good neighbor because he maintains his property conscientiously.
2. Prince Charles is the next in line to be king of England because he is the eldest male descendant of the reigning monarch.

3. The Cardinals have a weak pitching staff; therefore, they will have a slim chance of getting into the playoffs.

4. July is a bad month for trout fishing because trout feed on the fry of other fish during that month.

5. Frost in the coffee-growing regions of the world, short supply in the largest consuming nations, and a desire to flex their economic muscles on the part of the producers will bring about a doubling of the price of coffee in the world market in the next six months.

6. Cheating on exams can sometimes be justified because not all courses are part of a student's major program nor related to the student's career plans; besides, it is just as important to have a high grade-point average as it is to be competent in one's area of specialization.

7. Mitchell committed the murder. After all, his fingerprints were on the weapon, he had ample opportunity to slip into the house unobserved, and he was known to have borne a grudge against the victim for several years.

8. It's not that Jones isn't honest enough to be the secretary-treasurer of our club; rather it's that he's simply too unreliable to fill the post.

9. Today is a day for using "red" wax on our cross-country skis because the temperature is 36 degrees and the snow is powdery.

10. One route to energy conservation would be to impose a high tax on gasoline. Americans consume an enormous part of their energy in the form of gasoline, and a high tax on gas would cut consumption quite a lot.

11. The notion that health, like nutrition, may be a factor in juvenile delinquency and school failure is significant because it implies a new approach to treatment of these profound social problems. It is easier to improve a person's health than to improve many of the other aspects of his environment. If each factor (usually in combination with other factors) contributes to antisocial behavior, simply improving health and reducing malnutrition could make profound changes in American social illness.

New England (Boston *Globe* Sunday Magazine)

12. Despite all the turmoil and intense personality conflicts that kept the Yankees from playing their best until late August last year, they managed to capture their divisional title with a 100–62 record. With a healthier pitching staff, Gossage added to Lyle in the bullpen, and some tranquility in the locker room, New York should be able to withstand the powerful Red Sox challenge in the 1978 season.

Baseball Forecast

13. Business doesn't draw up a contract with the government; it tries to get the best deal it can in an increasingly coercive society. There is no such thing as voluntary planning. It compels somebody to do something he otherwise wouldn't do.

[Objection from *Skeptic* magazine interviewer]: What if we vote for it?

It's still coercion. You can call it Nazism, or you can call it Communism. You vote away my minority rights to disagree; I don't find that anything but coercion. Majority rule is coercion if it tramples on minority rights.

Robert M. Bleiberg, Editor *Barron's,* in an interview with *Skeptic* magazine

14. The boy is trained for his career in many subtle ways; one of the most important is rugged (masculine) team sports. His achievement, his stardom, is being part of a winning team. He learns at an early age that he needs other players to make a team and that teammates are valued not on the basis of personal relationships, but on the team's need to win. He also learns to accept team members who do not perform at top level as long as they don't pull him down. This emotional detachment and criteria for selection will be transferred to the corporate management team later in life. . . . For little girls the story is quite different. For those sports and activities (frequently individual not team games) in which she is encouraged to participate, it is not winning that counts, but the quality of the performance. Carried into corporate life these patterns serve to hinder a woman's progress.

MS. magazine

15. Why didn't the psychological establishment challenge Burt's research [which argued that heredity was *by far* the most important factor in determining intelligence and was extremely influential until the evidence was shown to have been "rigged"], which was full of inconsistencies? Because, the psychologists admit, Burt was "enormously powerful." In short, they were afraid of him.

But there was another reason, Kamin says. Burt's data wasn't [*sic*] challenged because "every professor knew that his child was brighter than the ditchdigger's child, so what was there to challenge?"

The moral of the tale, says Kamin, is "the people who buy social science should remember that those who have collected the data may have axes to grind."

It is well to remember that this applies to parapsychologists as well as those who criticize them.

Fate magazine

16. Unless the government screws things up—and that's always a possibility— *the next twenty years will be as revolutionary as any period ever.* Technology will burst about our ears throughout the period, and the car will emerge profoundly changed.

Already we have the rotary as an alternative to the gas-fired piston engine, and the diesel is most certainly gaining ground, not to mention turbocharging. When the next two decades have passed, still other alternatives will have been offered to the public.

And the revolution will extend to other automotive systems, as well: electronics; fuel delivery systems; suspension and even basic structural materials.

George Weir, *Four Wheeler* magazine

17. The Finance Committee would give parents a tax credit of half the tuition they pay up to $1000. That's $500, and a tax credit is the same thing as a cash grant. The subsidy is big enough to start a rapid growth of every kind of private school. The Carter administration points out that by contrast federal aid to public schools comes to only $128 per pupil. The administration adamantly opposes the whole idea of this credit, and so will anyone else who values the public schools.

Albert Shanker, New York *Daily News*

18. Despite impressive evidence of the incident at Kinross Air Force Base, many UFO researchers are uncomfortable in discussing it. In fact, there are numerous UFO cases in which it is apparent that the UFOs exhibit hostility toward humans, even to the point of causing injury and death!

We may not want to even consider the possibility, but we could be in a war against alien forces beyond our comprehension.

Argosy, UFO edition

19. There is a strange *sameness* about the darker occult rituals, whether originating in ancient China, practiced by early Babylonians, by primitive witch doctors or used by witches and warlocks during the middle ages. The alarming fact is that they have been often able to sneak in to our society in disguise—eventually upsetting the psychic and spiritual equilibrium of the less wary. To the latter group, the initial illusion is sweet but the inevitable stakes are high!

Argosy, UFO edition

20. We did research that showed women in the sun-belt, leisure environments and southern California tested more poorly than men. They were less authoritative. Men overshadowed women tremendously.

In the traditional strict environment—the Boston-banking, darksuit, conservative kind of world—women were at an advantage to the point where strong women overshadowed weak men. I'm not sure of all the reasons, but I think part of it involves the "non-verbal communicants"—the clothes, the appearance. And all studies on verbal and nonverbal communicants show the nonverbal are stronger. Women in these areas tended to adopt the conservative look and assumed part of the authority that goes with it.

TWA AMBASSADOR magazine

4

Grounds

"The San Francisco 49'rs are a certainty for the Super Bowl this year."

"What makes you say that?"

"Just compare them with the opposition! None of the other teams has such a combination of offensive and defensive strength."

"This new version of King Kong at any rate makes some sort of psychological sense."

"What do you have in mind?"

"Well, the girl doesn't just scream and run: she has some kind of a developing interchange with Kong—she shows real personal feelings for him."

"The infection was carried by food-service equipment."

"How do you know?"

"Our tests ruled out everything else, and we finally located a defect in the canteen washing-equipment."

"The best interim investment is short-term municipal bonds."

"Why is that?"

"They're easily traded and bring in decent interest, and the income is free of federal tax."

Here each of the claims is supported by grounds, that is, statements specifying particular facts about a situation. These facts are already accepted as true, and can therefore be relied on to clarify and make good the previous claim, or—in the best case—to establish its *truth, correctness,* or *soundness,* in turn.

Suppose that *I* is satisfied that he has ironed out any confusions and so understands the nature and significance of *A*'s claim. What happens next? At this stage, his first task is to ask about the nature of *A*'s "grounds" for that claim. The question at issue at this stage is

What do you have to go on?

As a first step toward establishing his claim, *A* is now required to place in discussion whatever detailed assemblage of facts, observations, statistical data, previous conclusions, or other specific information he is relying on as the immediate support for his specific claim.

The term *grounds* refers to the *specific* facts relied on to support a given claim. For instance:

What exactly is it about your brother's behavior that makes you think he is going mad?

What precisely about the strengths and weaknesses of the teams makes you so sure that the 49'rs are a certainty this year?

What specifically in the new version of *King Kong* do you regard as psychologically subtler than the original version?

What particular observations about the spread of infection through the hospital point the finger of blame at the food-service equipment?

In each case, *I*'s demand for grounds is not a request for general theories. The time for such general considerations comes at a later stage. It is a request to be shown the specific features that mark off *this* precise situation from others and so point toward *this* specific claim or conclusion rather than others. More precisely, it is a request for *A* to put into discussion the specific "facts of the case" that can be agreed on as a secure starting point acceptable to both sides, and so "not in dispute."

Facts as common ground

If two people wish to argue effectively, the first thing they can usefully do is to discover how much common ground they already share: that is, what things they are both prepared to accept as not needing to be questioned or established, at least for the purposes of their present argument. Indeed, until they reach this first agreement about the "facts" of the present case, they are in no position to frame any clear argument at all.

To quote a striking and well-known recent example: in the trial of John Hinckley for the attempted assassination of President Reagan, very little of what actually happened on the day of the crime was in dispute. Both the prosecution and the defense agreed that Hinckley was indeed present at the scene of the crime, that he had a gun with him, that it was he who fired the bullets that injured the President and three other people. All of these statements were accepted as "facts" by both sides—as lawyers say, the facts were "stipulated" and so not in dispute. In this way, the trial was focused on the more specific question of Hinckley's state of mind in acting as he did when he did, and the relevance that state of mind had to his criminal responsibility for what he did.

Notice how this preliminary procedure, of agreeing about what is *not* in dispute, makes it possible for us to bring into sharp focus exactly what *is* in dispute. By this means, we establish the nature of the *common ground* on which we are both prepared to stand, and which we both accept as a shared starting point. This is not only a useful procedure; it is also a necessary one in any honest argument. For once an argument is under way, it is a kind of cheating for us to go back and start questioning facts that were already stipulated before the argument began, without admitting what we are doing. If we begin to suspect halfway through an argument that our original starting point (or "common ground") was not as secure as we at first thought, we can go back to challenge it only by changing the subject, thereby initiating a new and different argument.

The necessity for this procedure is connected with the function of reasoning as a means of establishing *truth*. Trains of reasoning are intended to carry us from truths we already accept to new truths. If we have second thoughts about the truth of the "facts" that were our starting point, those second thoughts will affect any conclusions we may subsequently arrive at from that starting point. The computer engineers have a saying, "Garbage in, garbage out." In the same way, we can say, "Falsehoods in, falsehoods out."

Of course, not all the statements that *A* initially offers as "grounds" need be considered as unquestioned "facts" also. Some of the specific items that *A* introduces as grounds for his claim may be questionable for *I*:

> Is the Miami Dolphins' defense really all that shaky?
>
> Were the washing machines in the hospital checked out as fully as the food-service equipment?
>
> Did the map you deposited at the claims office in support of your goldmining claim show the exact boundaries of your proposed diggings?

As a result, a substantial amount of time may be spent in the early stages of any argument going over the material initially offered by *A* as supporting "facts," for *I* must decide which of *A*'s grounds to accept as data; that is, which of them cannot be called into dispute before he goes any further. The question to look at here is, accordingly:

> What makes one particular set of grounds or facts acceptable and relevant for the purposes of this or that specific claim?

A FIRST PATTERN OF ANALYSIS

In developing an overall pattern for use in the analysis of arguments, let us begin by setting down the grounds in support of any particular claim (G) alongside the claim itself (C), and let us indicate the relationship between them by the use of an arrow (Figure 4–1).

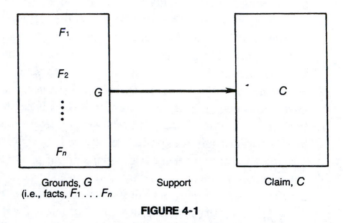

Grounds, G Support   Claim, C
(i.e., facts, $F_1 \ldots F_n$

FIGURE 4-1

Having registered a claim, C, the assertor, A, has taken the first step toward *establishing* it. A has done this by placing in discussion the specific set of factual grounds, G, on the basis of which he is prepared to justify the claim:

"G, therefore C."

Correspondingly, in subjecting A's claim to rational criticism, I's first step is to assess the relevance and/or sufficiency of those grounds:

Maybe, the facts A offers as grounds are *too few or too slight*. In this case, I is entitled to object to A's argument—in colloquial terms—as being too "slim."

Alternatively it may be doubtful whether A's grounds are really as *relevant* as he declares. In this case, I can object to the argument—in colloquial terms—as being too "shaky."

If A's argument is both slim and shaky—if the facts offered as grounds strike I both as too few and as irrelevant—I may even sweep A's claim aside at this opening stage with the bare comment, "No case!" This happens quite regularly in the law courts. At the end of the opening statement by the plaintiff or the prosecutor, the defending attorney may convince the judge that the entire proceedings should come to an end on the spot. To do this, he must convince the judge that the opposing attorney, who acts in this context as assertor, has given the defense *no case to answer:*

Plaintiff's attorney claims that my client slandered him by accusing him of dishonest business dealings and casting doubt on his paternity. Granted; my client has a short temper and may well have uttered some offensive personal remarks to the plaintiff when they were alone together or when they were on the telephone. But there is no suggestion that any third party overheard these conversations, so plaintiff's public reputation has in no way been at risk. A defamation uttered by a defendant to a plaintiff alone is not actionable.

For lack of any evidence that the defamation was ever "published," I therefore submit that no question of "slander" even arises and that there is no case to answer.

Similar situations arise in less august forums of argument also. In any argument, the assertor must begin by producing at least minimal grounds for his claim in the form of some first set of undisputed facts that is neither hopelessly slim nor irredeemably shaky. Unless he can satisfy this initial requirement, he has not fulfilled the requirement of what is called *burden of proof*. We shall discuss this requirement in Chapter 11. The argument may come to an abrupt halt at this point, since he has simply failed to present an opening claim worth discussing and criticizing at all. Rather than being a rationally defensible claim, his initial opinion may thus be dismissed as untenable.

"Spring is coming early this year.

"Really?"

"Yes: I saw three squirrels scampering around in the snow this afternoon. They must know something we don't know."

"'Fraid not. Squirrels don't fully hibernate—a good January thaw and they'll frisk around for a couple of days. But the next Arctic blast and they'll be fast asleep again—you'll see."

THE VARIETY OF GROUNDS

Just what kinds of information or "facts" will *A* have to produce in support of claims in different fields of enterprise? That depends on the nature of the enterprise concerned and on the particular contexts of the arguments themselves. To give some samples:

Joe was born in Cincinnati, and his father was certainly an American: *so,* he should be a United States citizen all right.

The wind has veered from southwest to northwest and the rain has stopped: *so,* we can expect the weather to be clearer and cooler tomorrow.

Both the Dolphins and the Cowboys have lost their leading quarterbacks by retirement: *so,* the 49'rs have a better chance than ever.

The laundry equipment was free of contamination when checked this week: *so,* the food-service equipment is still the prime suspect.

Woody Allen's movie *Annie Hall* remains credible throughout and avoids the sense of caricature in his earlier efforts: *so,* this is his most successful film to date.

To consider these examples in order:

1. A claim to legal status depends on establishing that the relevant statutory conditions are fulfilled. A person's citizenship is legally determined by a set of requirements involving place of birth, parentage, and subsequent life history. These requirements are laid down in part by the U.S. Constitution, in part by current legislation. If these facts about the individual are not disputed, the question of citizenship can be settled quickly and with confidence, even certainty.

2. A straightforward prediction calls for rather different grounds, whether it has to do with a natural phenomenon like the weather or with a human activity such as football. Forecasts of either sort need to be supported by other factual information that can be relied upon to serve as a pointer to the particular future event being forecast. If the wind veers and the rain stops, that indicates the passage of a "cold front," hence the weather forecast. Similarly the departure of talented quarterbacks from two rival outfits clearly enhances a strong football team's own prospects.

In these latter cases, grounds and claim are connected not by legal statute (as with a citizenship issue) but rather on the basis of accumulated experience—we have become familiar with the ways of cold fronts and team sports:

3. The aesthetic merits of a movie have to be illustrated by yet other kinds of facts. To argue convincingly about them, we must have some idea about what the director intended to convey, what means she chose to employ, and how well she succeeded in getting her ideas across. If we can draw attention to relevant features of the movie that others are ready to acknowledge, we can then make a good case for our critical assessment of the film under consideration.

This is not to say that there is just *one* kind of grounds relevant to all kinds of legal claims, *one* kind relevant to all kinds of aesthetic claims, and so on. The actual position is a good deal more complicated than that! There are numerous different kinds of scientific argument, medical argument, business argument, or whatever in which the claims being made need different kinds of supporting facts in order to be established. (We shall return to this kind of variety and variability in Part VI.)

Notice at the outset, also, that one discussion's claim may become another discussion's ground. Having convinced I that one claim (C_1) is correct and well-founded, A may at once go on to make another consequential claim:

"Well then, in that case, C_2."

When I raises her eyebrows at this further step, A may produce as the basis (G_2) for his new claim (C_2) the statement just agreed to (as C_1):

> You agreed, after all, that both of the 49'rs chief rivals had lost their best quarterbacks: *so, . . .*
>
> You agreed that the laundry equipment had been checked out last week and found to be free of contamination: *so, . . .*

Figure 4–2 illustrates this process.

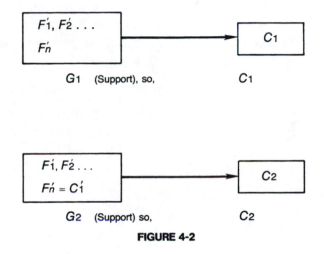

FIGURE 4-2

In this manner substantial chains of arguments may be linked together in such a way that large, difficult, and initially implausible claims can be made convincing. The case for accepting these larger claims is broken down into a number of parts, and the audience is taken through the entire case by a succession of smaller steps. Think, for instance, how an attorney often presents her case to a jury. She offers them a sequence of argumentative steps, each of which is fairly easy to take and which among them "add up" to a powerful argument in favor of the large conclusion.

Nor does the information we produce as grounds have to comprise only newly established pieces of factual evidence—newly discovered "facts," that is. There is a wide range of sorts of information that are capable of supporting one or another specific sort of claim: oral testimony, matters of common knowledge, well-known truisms or commonsense observations, reminders of things easily overlooked, historical reports, precise statements of legal precedent, and so on:

> If you want to give your children a first rate private education, you had better not take up full-time public-interest law. (*Q:* Why?) Well, there's not much of a living to be got out of it these days, and you will be better off doing commercial law.

We can't ignore that Jack is a possible suspect in the case, because we know that he was at Mary's place earlier in the evening. (*Q:* How do you know that?) Well, we have Mary's word for it that he was there, and she has no evident motive for lying about it.

It begins to look as though Bill may be thinking of giving up his job. (*Q:* Why do you say that?) Well, you must have noticed that he's been getting restless and inattentive lately, and there's no smoke without fire, I always say.

While on a few rare occasions brand-new and freshly discovered "evidence" may make a spectacular difference to an argument, the majority of claims are supported by factual grounds that come as no particular surprise to anyone. (In this respect, Perry Mason's last-minute "mystery witnesses" give a false impression of what *winning a case* chiefly depends on.)

5
Warrants and rules

"I get what you're saying about the 49'rs, and there's certainly something in it. But is a combination of offense and defense really the crucial thing to look for in a Super Bowl winner?"

"Maybe there's a bit of an emotional relationship between King Kong and the girl. But how does that weigh up against all the implausible anti-business nonsense in the second half of the movie?"

"Don't you need to tell us something more about the food-service problem? Is defective dish-washing equipment the sort of thing that could account for an epidemic of this proportion?"

"That doesn't strike me as much of an argument—surely, we could obtain a much higher interest rate from private bonds without much loss of liquidity?"

Now the questioner asks for warrants, that is, statements indicating how the facts on which we agree *are connected to* the claim or conclusion now being offered. These connecting statements draw attention to the *previously agreed general* ways of arguing applied in the particular case, and so are implicitly relied on as ones whose trustworthiness is well established.

Let us assume that *A* has produced a substantial and significant body of factual material as grounds (*G*) and presents this as being all the "support" needed in order to establish his initial claim (*C*). Once this stage is reached, *I*'s critical attention shifts away from the grounds themselves and begins to focus instead on the nature of this step from *G* to *C*; that is, on the implications hidden within the word *therefore* in the statement "*G*, therefore *C*."

Put colloquially, the central question is now no longer "What do you have to go on?" and has become instead "How do you get there?" The interrogator, *I*, must now inquire about the general rule or procedure that the assertor, *A*, is relying on in presenting the step from *G* to *C* as a trustworthy step that we can safely follow him in taking. Notice two things:

1. The assertor's task is normally to convince us not just that it was legitimate for him to adopt the initial claim *for himself* but also that we should share it and so rely on it *ourselves*. In a phrase, he argues his case because he wants us to *go along with him*.

2. While the claim he puts forward (*C*) and the set of grounds he produces in its support (*G*) are quite particular and specific—he talks, for instance about chances for this year and about the current form of this or that other specific football team—he will normally have to justify the step *from G to C* by producing some more general considerations, for example, how things tend to go for football teams in general, not just *this* year but *any* year.

THE NATURE OF WARRANTS

At this point, let us consider the new term *warrant*, which we shall use here in discussing the step from grounds to claims. Consider the following simple exchange:

A: I should choose the ice cream today!
Q: Why do you say that?
A: Jack chose yesterday, and Jill the day before.
Q: So?
A: Everyone should have a turn at choosing.

In this exchange, the assertor, *A*, first backs up her original claim, *C* ("It's my turn!"), by producing her specific factual ground, *G* ("Jack chose yesterday, and Jill the day before"); and then, when the questioner, *I*, raises his eyebrows, *A* goes on to offer a further additional statement of a more general kind: "Everyone should choose in turn." This last statement has the effect of authorizing the step from *G* (the turn) to *C* (the choice). We can in fact read it as meaning "Wherever someone's turn comes around, it can be concluded that it is time for them to act." Such a general, step-authorizing statement is called a warrant.

Kinds of warrants

In different areas of discussion, the warrants on which our arguments rely are of different sorts, and go by different names. In practical subjects, we may talk of them as (for instance) rules of thumb, "In costing out office space in the city center, you can reckon on $100 a square foot." In more theoretical areas, we talk of principles, or in some cases about laws of nature. Elsewhere, we appeal to accepted values, customs, or procedures.

As a first hint, if a complete argument is designed to produce a particular result, then the facts or grounds which go into the argument are like the *ingredients* of a cake or casserole. The warrant is then the general *recipe* used to combine those ingredients into the finished product.

This comparison has two merits. Firstly, it helps us to see that whenever we produce an argument we put to use a procedure, or way of arguing, about the general reliability of which we are already confident. The warrant of our argument is what entitles us to be confident that, in this particular case, the step from grounds to claim is a step of a generally reliable sort. In this respect, it is like the instructions in a recipe, which are intended to apply to *any* batch of eggs or *any* bag of white sugar.

Secondly, this comparison helps us to see that our choice of facts to use as grounds for supporting a particular claim is always selective. As we say, facts have to be *relevant* if they are to support a claim at all. Therefore, when we set about constructing an argument, the things we already know are like the contents of our kitchen cupboard. We have to know what *kind* of an argument we need to construct before deciding which of all those facts to bring forward and put to work as grounds. That is to say, the character of the *general* ways of arguing that we rely on determines the relevance of particular facts to particular claims.

Warrants as general procedures

How we can argue safely, then, depends on the general ideas we have already mastered in the field of discussion concerned. We approach all situations with prior conceptions about the kind of matter at hand: about how we can argue, think about, interpret, and/or deal with such things. The general ways of thinking and acting that we carry with us to new situations thus commit us to accepting certain warrants as defining the established ways of arguing in such areas.

In other words, the difference between grounds and warrants (facts and rules) is a *functional* difference. This difference is sometimes concealed, because we use the word *all* in both contexts, and do so in rather different ways. For example, at the beginning of the school year questions arise about whether the children entering first grade have had the necessary vaccinations. I may then report, as a matter of fact, that *all* the children in my family have been vaccinated: that is to say, that *each and every* child has been vaccinated. The school nurse on the other hand, is concerned—as a general matter—that all the new school children are to be vaccinated: that is to say, that *any* child must have been vaccinated to be admitted to school. No doubt, general rules that apply to *any* child are supposed to apply to *each particular* child. But there remains a functional difference between the way in which we understand the word *all* within a general rule, and the way we understand it in a report about the members of a collectivity.

In looking at the idea of grounds, we noticed how necessary it is, in constructing an effective argument, to decide in advance what facts we are prepared to commit ourselves to, at least for the purposes of that argument. What is true of the particular facts that serve as the ingredients of the argument is true also of the general procedures we rely on for the purposes of the argument. We can construct an effective argument only if we already know what general ways of arguing we are going to rely on, and employ, in this particular case.

Warrants as licenses

As with *claims* and *grounds,* the term *warrant* is a natural and familiar enough one to use in this context. Historically speaking, the term has always had close associations both with the notion of a *license* or *permit* and also with that of a *warranty* or *guarantee.* When a medieval monarch conferred on one of his subjects some noble rank or position of power, the document authorizing that individual to perform the functions of his office was called a *royal warrant.* And the continuing use of the term *warrant* in the familiar sense of an "arrest warrant," issued to the police by a judge in the name of the State, is one surviving vestige of this old practice. In this respect, the meaning of the term, as used in police work, indicates what is involved in showing that the step from *G* to *C* is a rationally defensible one, for its effect is to point out what "authorizes" or "legitimates" the step in question. ("Given smoke, *you are entitled to* infer fire.")

Notice how our colloquial ways of talking already make use of some related words. For instances, people commonly object to a claim as being *unwarranted:*

WIFE TO JEALOUS HUSBAND: "You only saw me walking to the bus stop with one of the men from my office, and you at once jumped to the conclusion that I was having a clandestine affair: that inference was quite *unwarranted.*"

Here the wife uses the absence of a satisfactory "warrant" as her reason for objecting to the husband's argument. His one ground, *G* ("She is walking along the street with a man I do not recognize"), is quite insufficient to legitimate the conclusion, *C* ("She is having a clandestine affair with this man"). So the step from *G* to *C* is plainly "unwarranted," if not downright irrational. For when we analyze the actual content of the argument, we find that it relies on an implicit but transparently implausible warrant:

"If a woman is seen walking down the street with a man whom her husband does not know, *it may be concluded that* she is having a clandestine affair with that man."

Why do we say that the husband's implicit warrant is *transparently* implausible? Or to put the same question more generally, how do we tell those warrants for arguing from G to C that are trustworthy and reliable from those that are worthless and implausible? That general question will be our concern in the next chapter, where we shall consider the notion of *backing*. For the moment, our immediate business is to consider how different kinds of warrants play their parts in practical argumentation within different types of human enterprises and arguments.

EXTENDING THE PATTERN OF ANALYSIS

We can fix the essential task of a warrant within the framework of argumentation most clearly by adding one feature to the preliminary pattern of analysis introduced in our previous chapter. There we simply showed the assertor's claim, C, as linked to his grounds, G, by a simple arrow. Now, we may indicate also that the step from G to C is being taken in the manner authorized by the warrant, W (Figure 5–1).

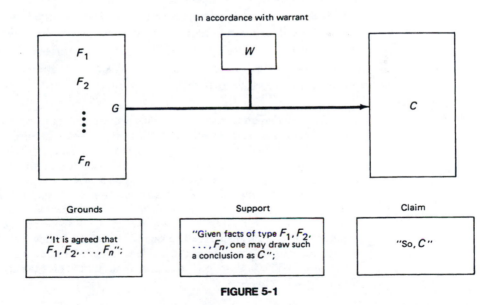

FIGURE 5-1

The question is this: Within the varied contexts of different human enterprises, what kinds of general statements may be appealed to as providing the "rational authority" needed to connect any specific set of grounds, G, to the correspondingly specific claim or conclusion, C? Once our assertor, A, has presented his particular set of grounds, *G,* what else must he produce in response to *Q*'s critical questioning if he is to show that his conclusion, *C,* is *warranted*?

SOME TYPICAL WARRANTS

Let us look at the ways in which warrants function in various different fields of argument. We looked already at one colloquial use of such warrants in the context of everyday conversation.

"It's my turn" (*A*)—"The one whose turn it is should choose" (*W*)—"So I should choose" (*C*).

A warrant of this kind gives us, of course, only a rough and ready rule or procedure; and we may expect to find much stronger rules and connections in other kinds of cases. We looked at the difference between fully reliable, universal warrants and approximate, rough-and-ready generalizations, and that might lead us to consider at this point the force of such qualifying phrases as *very likely, in all probability,* and *presumably.* This is a topic to which we shall return in Part III.

In science and engineering

It will be convenient to concentrate first on cases in which the warrants are both reliable and exact. Such examples can most easily be found in such professional fields of argumentation as natural science and the law. Scientists and engineers, for instance, often employ exact and general mathematical formulas, with the help of which they calculate the values of unknown magnitudes from the values of other related variables that they already know:

Suppose that an engineer is designing a bridge that must be capable of carrying twenty-ton trucks. He will need to figure out what size girders of a given material are required to support the roadbed of the bridge. For this purpose, he has at his disposal certain established equations linking the dimensions of steel girders of various shapes to their breaking strength, or shear.

So, when the engineer presents his conclusion, *C*—"We must use standard I-section girders at least three feet tall"—he will support that claim in two different kinds of ways. He will cite the relevant specific facts about the location of the required bridge and its materials as grounds, *G,* and in addition, he will appeal to the general formula that relates the breaking strain of a girder to its shape and dimensions, and he will use this formula as a warrant (*W*) for the argument from *G* to *C*. (See Figure 5–2.)

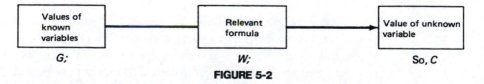

| Values of known variables | Relevant formula | Value of unknown variable |
| *G;* | *W;* | So, *C* |

FIGURE 5-2

In law and ethics

The situations that arise in the legal field give us examples of a similar kind. Suppose the "facts" in a particular case are not in dispute:

> You left your car in a parking space next to a meter while you went into the store for a carton of milk. But instead of feeding coins into the meter, you simply set your hazard lights flashing. There was a line at the checkout, and your errand took you much longer than you expected. As a result, by the time you got out of the store, the traffic cop was already writing you a ticket.

You ask a lawyer friend whether there is any point in fighting the charge. He explains, regretfully, that there is no real way out:

> The quarter you saved on that meter was a false economy. Given those facts, any traffic court is going to have to find you guilty.

If you press him, he can at this stage show you the statutes governing parking violations and point out that the wording of the relevant clauses is quite unambiguous:

> There is no exception in the statute for people who leave their cars unattended in a parking space, even for a very short time, with the hazard lights flashing.
>
> If you had merely gone into the store for a moment to change a dollar bill and had come out at once, coin in hand, to operate the parking meter, you might have had a case. The courts must allow you reasonable time and opportunity to put a coin in the meter. As matters stand, however, the facts are all against you, and there is no way of fighting the ticket. (See Figure 5–3.)

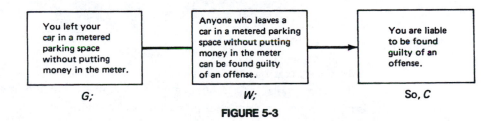

FIGURE 5-3

More precisely, the argument in this example can be written, "*G*; *W*; so presumably *C*." As your lawyer friend explains, this presumption could be met, or rebutted, in case you had left the car for only long enough to get change and put money in the meter. But in your actual situation, no such rebuttal or "excuse" is available by way of defense.

When laws are well framed and the judicial system is working properly, it will in general be clear what legal conclusions are warranted in most typical situations. Indeed much of the knowledge that law students master during their professional training has to do with learning to recognize what general statements of law will serve as satisfactory warrants to legitimate—or alternatively to refute—some particular legal claim, *C*, given a particular set of specific facts, *G*.

Again, in some straightforward, everyday cases, the role of "moral principles" in ethical discussion is similar to that of legal statutes and rules in judicial argument (see Figure 5–4).

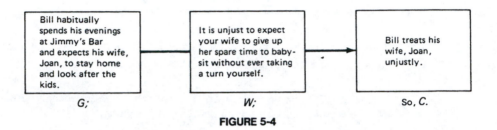

FIGURE 5-4

Once again, of course, the conclusion *C* in such a case is only "presumptive." If there is nothing more to the relations between Bill and Joan, then the facts quoted indicate that Bill's behavior is highly unfair. But a closer understanding of the ways in which Bill and Joan have chosen to live their life together might possibly "rebut" that presumption.

Notice one thing about this ethical example. As it stands, nothing about its structure and procedures marks it off from an argument in law, or science, or elsewhere. In this respect, the fact that ethical issues and claims involve "values" does nothing, by itself, to take them out of the realm of rationally debatable issues and rationally defensible claims. The basic pattern—"*G*; *W*; so, *C*"—applies here just as well as anywhere else.

THE SCOPE OF WARRANTS

In some areas of human activity and inquiry, exact and reliable decision procedures are available for validating conclusions or for defending claims on the basis of some given body of undisputed data, or grounds. Law, science, and engineering are three familiar enterprises within which this is normally the case, but they are not the only ones. Wherever a fully established and articulated body of knowledge exists that can be transmitted by teachers to novices through apprenticeship—as is widely the case in the arts and sciences—we commonly find such warrants recognized and put to use.

In other fields, however, it may be harder to articulate all the warrants employed in argument, in the form of explicit laws, rules, or principles. Let us consider two rather different examples of this difficulty.

In medicine

The art of clinical medicine is not as easily reduced to formulas as is the business of civil engineering. From a position at the bedside of a sick patient, the physician may pick up minute signs or pointers on which he or she is justified in relying as clues to what is troubling the patient. Yet the doctor may not be able to relate the meaning of those small signs to any general principle of a sort that might figure in a medical handbook or textbook. In such a situation, it will not be surprising to find the physician saying, "In my experience, that kind of pallor around the temples *can mean* some sort of viral infection, and in this particular kind of case, I am inclined to think that it does." Just what exact "kind" of pallor and "kind" of case he is pointing to, the physician may not be able to explain any further; to that extent, therefore, the argument may be incomplete.

Failing any established explanations or tests for telling cases in which pallor around the temples is produced by a virus from those in which it is not, doctors have simply to rely on their own accumulated but inarticulate "experience" (see Figure 5–5).

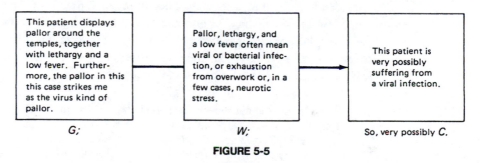

This patient displays pallor around the temples, together with lethargy and a low fever. Furthermore, the pallor in this this case strikes me as the virus kind of pallor.

G;

Pallor, lethargy, and a low fever often mean viral or bacterial infection, or exhaustion from overwork or, in a few cases, neurotic stress.

W;

This patient is very possibly suffering from a viral infection.

So, very possibly *C.*

FIGURE 5-5

In this situation, some people might of course question whether the physician really does have "good" reasons—let alone a "solid" argument—for concluding that this patient has a viral infection. Certainly if two physicians familiar with the particular patient "read" the pallor around the temples differently, there may be no way in which one of them can convince the other to change his or her mind. And often enough, individual physicians may concede that their diagnoses are indeed based on hunches—on how cases "smell" to them—so that we may prefer to reserve judgment, rather than letting ourselves be convinced merely by this ambiguous pallor around the temples.

If Dr. Bernard has a hunch that this is the *virus* kind of pallor rather than the *overwork* kind, then *you can take it that* it's probably a virus.

Such a warrant is not as compelling as those we are accustomed to in law or engineering, yet it may be quite sufficient to justify us in going along with the conclusion concerned (see Figure 5–6).

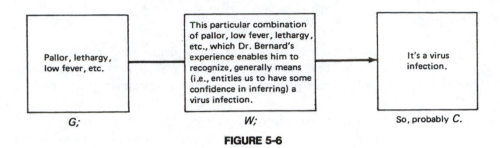

FIGURE 5-6

In aesthetics and psychology

In some other fields of discussion and argumentation, there is even less scope for formulating exact warrants. In aesthetic discussions, for instance, we do not point to undisputed data, facts, or grounds to support our aesthetic claims with any expectation of connecting *G* to *C* by any strict formula or calculation. In criticizing works of art, our aim is rather to clarify the implications of the claim itself. In this way, we may hope to justify our claims by showing how they are grounded in a discriminating perception of relevant details of the work itself.

Anyone who claims, for instance, that the 1976 version of *King Kong* treats the psychological relations between Kong and the kidnapped girl, Dwan, more subtly and convincingly than the original version can be challenged to produce reasons for this judgment. For instance, one might say:

> In the original version, the heroine has only a single, stereotyped reaction to King Kong. Whenever he appears, she screams and runs. In the new version, Dwan responds to Kong in a wide variety of ways—initially in terror, of course, but later on playfully and sympathetically, at times even taking on the role of a favorite daughter.
>
> As a result, the relations between the protagonists develop quite genuinely and plausibly as the movie goes along. In particular, when King Kong is finally killed, the heroine's grief becomes an intelligible outcome of the whole plot.

Explaining the basis of the original claim ("The new version is psychologically more subtle") here means *showing* the subtleties rather than *inferring* them. Accordingly, in aesthetic discussions, the normal task of *A*'s grounds or reasons will *not* be to draw attention to features of (facts about) the movie in question of which *I* was previously unaware. Rather, these grounds will usually remind *I* of things she already knows, even though she may not have seen them as significant. In accepting the features in question as reasons in support of the original claim, *I* may therefore reply by saying, not "I didn't *know* that before" but rather "I now see what you *mean*"—not "I see now that your claim *was well warranted*" but rather "I see now that your claim *makes a lot of sense.*"

Some everyday psychological claims and arguments share this feature of aesthetic claims and arguments. Suppose that *A* makes an assertion about some-body's character, intentions, or state of mind. Once again, *I* may challenge it—"What reasons do you have to say that he's selfish and lazy?"—and *A* can meet this demand for "reasons" by reminding the questioner of relevant features (or "facts") in the person's past behavior or present attitudes. As in aesthetic criticism, these features will be cited as supporting the claim under discussion by *exemplifying* its detailed application.

Consider, for instance, the following scenario:

A: Jack's pose of total conscientiousness really is a bit suspect.

Q: How can you call it a pose? After all, he's been working very hard at his job these last months—even years.

A: I grant you that. But don't you see how selective he's been in the things he's *chosen* to work so hard at? They're always things from which he gets some special honor or glory, not just the actual satisfaction of doing his job. Put him in a position in which he had to do his own nuts-and-bolts work—to say nothing of real drudgery—and it would be another story. When did you last see him offering to help out when the rest of the staff was under pressure, for instance? He certainly isn't much of a one for doing good by stealth!

Q: Well, I see what you mean. Maybe, he's fooled me and I've been giving him too much credit. (See Figure 5–7.)

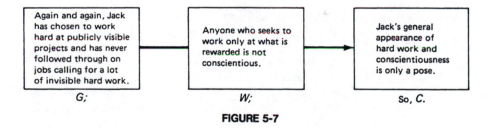

Again and again, Jack has chosen to work hard at publicly visible projects and has never followed through on jobs calling for a lot of invisible hard work.	Anyone who seeks to work only at what is rewarded is not conscientious.	Jack's general appearance of hard work and conscientiousness is only a pose.
G;	*W;*	So, *C.*

FIGURE 5-7

In this dialogue, some of the facts to which *A* draws *I*'s attention may have been unknown previously, but the force of the argument does not depend on this being the case. On the contrary, in this situation *A*'s primary task is to establish the existence of a systematic *pattern* in Jack's conduct, and the facts he points to serve as illustrations of this pattern: he uses that pattern to give all the facts in question a new significance. So even if *I* has previously known about them all, it is still possible for *A* to connect them together in a new way. This lends conviction to the original claim by highlighting the pattern in question. That being the case, it will once again be natural (as in aesthetics) for *I* to concede the original claim by saying, not "I didn't know that" or "That's a valid proof," but rather "Now I see what you mean" or "That makes a lot of sense."

SUMMARY

In conclusion, we may briefly sum up this initial discussion of *warrants*. In moving from one rational enterprise and forum of reasoning to another, or from one type of argument to another, we find many different kinds of general statements serving the function of warrants. Many kinds of general statements, that is, authorize the inferences by which different collections of specific information (data, relevant facts, known variables, significant features, and so on) are put forward as rational support for claims.

In the natural sciences, this function is performed by general laws of nature and the like. In judicial contexts, it is performed by statutes, precedents, and rules. In medicine, it is performed by diagnostic descriptions, and so on in other fields. We shall study the most significant features of the warrants used in different enterprises and forums later on, in Part VI.

For the moment, our concern is with the similarities between them, that is, with the shared roles that these different kinds of general statements perform in one type of argument or another. They all license or require us to accept specific kinds of claims, such as *C,* as following from—or at the very least, as finding support in—an initial collection of information, such as *G,* produced as reasons or grounds for the claims.

Exercises

I. Identify the warrants that are appealed to in the following arguments. They are not all explicit in the arguments themselves.

1. For some periods, as between 1936–1939, and 1949–1953, it is insufficient to describe the U.S.S.R. as totalitarian—it was in fact what could be called a terror-society, where no citizen, regardless of his position or the degree of loyalty to the regime, could feel safe.

    The landscape of Soviet politics reminded one of a surrealist painting; it became crowded with phantasmagoric figures of traitors, saboteurs and class enemies.

    The once leading personages of the party, government, and the armed forces were "unmasked," and in many cases were coerced to admit publicly having been agents of Hitler, the Japanese militarists, the British Intelligence or (following the war) of the American imperialists and Zionists.

    Boston *Globe*

2. The harder some people work the less they seem to accomplish. This is not an axiom but a fact. You know the men and women who are conscientious, energetic, anxious. Their production instead of being profitable, however, is either just enough to take care of their needs and obligations, or they are at the brink of economic collapse.

No Answer?

Some of the great minds in the world have grappled with this subject and have been unable to devise a specific formula that would help a willing worker to build up a foolproof financial competence. The trouble is that social and economic formulas do not take into consideration the complex structure of the human soul, whereas Astrology does. And if Astrology were allowed to solve some of the social and economic riddles of the world today perhaps there would be a whole lot fewer of them.

The answer to almost any problem is written in the sky, and until a simpler and more accurate method is found, why not analyze your problem according to Astrology?

Horoscope Guide magazine

bigga is better because 1 way winning is drawn

3. The Knight Fold is a fool proof system for increasing your chances of winning in the drawings and raffles that are always being run by charities. Since perfecting my technique, I've won a case of liquor (twice), a bottle of liquor, a child's game, and, most recently, a $50 bill. In baseball parlance, I'm 5 for 7. . . . The mechanics of the Fold are even simpler than the mathematics of the draw. You merely fold the ticket [diagonally] and drop it in the box, having previously packed your bags for the ever-popular trip to Paris for two you are hoping to win. The reason the Fold works is that your ticket occupies a larger area in the box than the other tickets and is therefore more likely to be drawn.

Thomas S. Knight, Jr., *Money* magazine

C

4. Though most economists are predicting more inflation for the U.S. economy this year, not all signs point in the same direction. Clifton B. Luttrell and Niel A. Stevens, staff economists at the Federal Reserve Bank of St. Louis, a monetarist bastion that is not known for its optimism about inflation, see essentially stable wholesale agricultural *-g* prices for the remainder of 1978. And they believe that a boost in food production will keep the increase in supermarket prices at close to last *g* year's 4%, despite sharp increases in the cost of food production and marketing.

Pointing to a level of carryover stocks that is at a record for the decade, the St. Louis economists expect cereal prices to be stable this year. And the filling of California's reservoirs could hold down vegetable prices for a long time to come.

Business Week magazine

with it many it works

5. Bus drivers have used biorhythm with significant decreases in accidents. A major airline has used biorhythms on their pilots for greater efficiency. Professional athletes have used these same rhythms to greatly improve their games. Biorhythm can even predict the sex of a pregnant woman's child with 75% accuracy. If the woman is physically high when she conceives she has a 75% chance of delivering a boy. If she is emotionally high when giving birth, the chances are that baby will be a girl.

Forewarned is forearmed: When you know the dates of your bad days, you can be extra careful and avoid costly mistakes. On your good days, you can tackle those important things in life with a greater chance of success. Biorhythm is for students, business executives, hunters, athletes, housewives, factory workers, drivers, employees, children, and grandparents. Everyone will benefit from a biorhythm chart.

Ad for Bio-Institute

6. Carew's season was phenomenal. Not only did he hit 24 points higher than ever before and flirt with a .400 batting average, but he also drove in 100 runs and scored 128. He had an all time high 38 doubles and smashed 16 triples.

Baseball Illustrated magazine

7. Larry J. Hillis, of Altus, Okla., reported to the National Highway Traffic Safety Administration that, in a distance of 20,623 miles his new car has been shod with 11 Uniroyal steel-belted radials. One blowout three days after he bought the car; two more replaced within 12,000 miles; four tires cracked and split in the sidewalls and rim.

"All the time with the tires it has been the same problem," Hillis wrote, "cracking and splitting around the rims, rounding on the edges and wearing improperly."

He insisted that he kept the tires "properly inflated and rotated, balanced and aligned." We feel there is a defect somewhere.

Boston *Globe,* automotive section

8. Swiss ski-resort operators, mindful of the dollar's recent schuss, are telling Americans that the time to ski Switzerland is in the spring—when days are longer and the rates are lower.

From mid-March until the end of the ski season, all-inclusive deals run 15% to 20% less than early-winter prices, except during the Easter holidays. This year some good skiing is expected in the Alps after Easter.

Business Week magazine

9. Supertankers are an appropriate symbol for the last quarter of this century. They are the inevitable and indispensable answer to the energy needs of the world. Japan, whose situation is direst, has no oil of its own and what it gets must be transported thousands of miles from the Persian Gulf. Tankers are the only way to get it there. So the superships are as important to the industrialized, oil-consuming nations as they are to the millionaire shipowners. Environmentalists with whom I have spoken concede that tankers are necessary. And that makes safety and environmental issues all the more important to resolve.

Skeptic magazine

10. It's a rare person who doesn't feel better after a good cry, because it's one of the basic forms of self-expression—both of joy and sadness. Psychologists tell us that people who continually repress their urge to cry can actually become sick. Some psychiatrists say asthma and other allergic reactions can surface in children who are constantly told not to cry.

Glamour magazine

II. Discuss the following warrants. What topics will they typically be concerned with? Construct arguments based upon appeal to them.

1. Keeping promises is the first requirement of ethical behavior.
2. The United States strategic forces exist for the purpose of deterring war. (How might this statement function in a discussion of the development of new and costly weapons systems?)
3. All religions must be allowed freedom of expression in a democracy. (How might this rule function in a discussion of the activities of, say, the Moon church?)
4. The club pool is restricted to members and their guests.
5. Choosing one's own life-style is what freedom means.
6. People who are so upset that they will murder will not long be deterred by lack of a handgun.
7. God made people to have children; it's natural to have them.
8. Left-handed pitchers are more effective against right-handed hitters.
9. The aim of punishment of criminals is deterrence of crime.
10. Fifteen miles per hour is the speed limit in thickly settled areas.

6

Backing

"Your hesitations about the 49'rs show that you haven't learned the lessons of history; in fact, *every single* Super Bowl winner *has had* a well-balanced mixture of offense and defense.

"I'm not saying anything about De Larentiis's politics or social ideas; all I'm saying is that *he does pay attention* to the psychology of the relationship between Kong and the heroine."

"Sure, I can give you a fuller account of what supports our conclusion about the food-service equipment; it's a *technical matter* of bacteriology and epidemiology—but here goes. . . ."

"How you choose an investment depends on *when and how you want* your money back; when you are soon going to need access to it at very short notice, you must be prepared to sacrifice a point or two on the rate of interest."

Here the assertor responds by indicating her "backing," that is, generalizations making explicit the body of experience relied on to establish the trustworthiness of the ways of arguing applied in any particular case. *Simple*

We now move on to the next phase of argumentation. Suppose that our interrogator, *I*, has obliged the assertor, *A*, to produce and place on the table not merely the grounds (*G*) for his claim but also the warrant (*W*) connecting *G* to *C*, by which the step from *G* to *C* is supposedly authorized. And suppose that *I* understands perfectly well what specific facts about the present situation A is relying on as grounds and how he proposes to legitimate the move from those facts to his conclusion. Even so, something remains to be done. It is one thing to state a warrant, but it is quite another thing to show that it can be relied on as sound, relevant, and weighty. This is particularly the case, if there are several possible ways to connect G and C, which support conflicting claims. How, then, can A hope to carry I with him over this further hurdle? In particular, how can A show that his warrant (W) is superior to other conflicting ones?

THE NATURE OF BACKING

The questions to be faced at this next stage do not have to do with the truth or the falsity of A's factual basis (G) for the claim, C. They have to do, rather, with the facts supporting his way of arguing, as expressed in the warrant W:

> "OK, it's your turn all right. Nobody is disputing that. But do you have to insist on taking your turn?"

Does relying on the general warrant "If it's my turn, I should choose" really provide you with the only sound way of arguing?

To put the problem in a nutshell, *warrants are not self-validating.* Our warrants and the modes of reasoning they authorize normally draw their strength and solidity from further, substantial supporting considerations. So instead of letting A's warrant (W) pass without question, it is open to I to call that appeal into question and subject it to further examination and scrutiny. That is to say, I can now go on to ask either or both of two further questions:

1. "Is that warrant reliable at all?"
2. "Does that warrant really apply to the present specific case?"

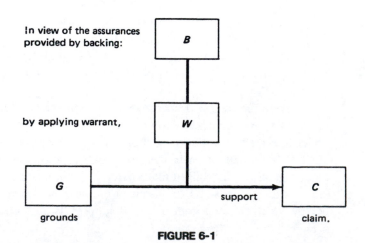

FIGURE 6-1

An argument will carry real weight and give its conclusions solid support only if the warrants relied on in the course of it are both sound (i.e., reliable or trust-worthy) and also to the point (i.e., relevant to the particular case under examination).

To mark off this new phase in *I*'s questioning, we introduce one more technical term. When *I* challenges *A* to produce "further substantial support, all considerations"—and so demonstrate that his warrant is sound and relevant—*I* requires *A* to provide that warrant with backing. We can indicate the role of backing, *B*, by adding one further element to our basic diagram (see Figure 6–1).

SOME SAMPLES OF BACKING

If we compare enterprises of different kinds—moving from natural science to sports predictions, from medicine to the law courts, from art criticism to business decision making, and so on—how are the different kinds of warrants we appeal to *backed up* when their reliability and relevance are challenged? And what overall similarities exist in the ways that backing operates, despite the differences between these fields and forums?

1. Let us begin by looking at our applied-science example. After the hospital epidemic inquiry, someone may still doubt whether the investigator's report really makes its point. Is it really the case that freshly washed food-service equipment can still transmit bacterial infections in the ways he suggests? Are the warrants (i.e., scientific generalizations) that he appeals to in his report really as solid, trustworthy, and to the point as he evidently supposes?

    Confronted by this further challenge, the investigator may have to amplify his earlier account. He may have to spell out the underlying theories and hypotheses on which his warrants rely for their deeper foundation. And he may have to summarize also the scientific evidence justifying us in accepting those theories and hypotheses.

    In this way, the particular warrants on which the investigator's argument depends will be given their required *backing* through being put in a larger scientific context and so given the theoretical and experimental foundation they need. (See Figure 6–2.)

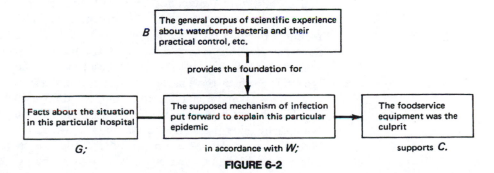

FIGURE 6-2

2. For contrast, let us consider an example from the law. In the course of a lawsuit, the attorney for one of the parties may appeal to a statute or precedent as a warrant for an argument on her client's behalf. The rival attorney may now challenge this warrant, *either* by questioning whether the statute or precedent in question is still binding *or else* by submitting that it was never meant to cover a case like the present one.

   If her warrant is challenged in this way, the first attorney must now go behind her original, unsupported warrant and introduce additional evidence designed to establish the current status and the binding force of the law or precedent. She will commonly do this by making a historical report—citing the relevant act of the appropriate legislature or else the previous judicial ruling by which the court is bound in the present instance.

   If she does this in a well-documented manner, her warrant is then properly backed. It is in this way, giving the statutory or other backing required, she counters the objections of the other party. Thus the foundation on which the authority of the challenged warrant rests will be confirmed. (See Figure 6–3.)

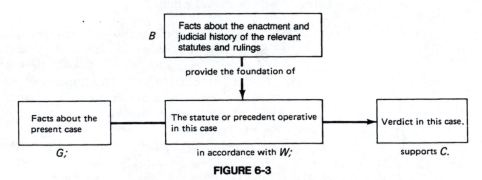

FIGURE 6-3

   To give a particular example: The grounds, *G,* may comprise a set of facts illustrating how a plaintiff was discriminated against, because she was black and female; the warrant, *W,* will then be the Fourteenth Amendment to the United States Constitution; and the conclusion, *C,* will be the claim that the plaintiff is entitled to legal redress. The relevant backing, *B,* will then comprise the whole relevant judicial history of the application of the Fourteenth Amendment in situations that were similar to the present case. Notice that, in the nature of things, a full statement of *backing* will always be longer and more complex than a simple recital of grounds or a statement of the rule on which the present argument relies. Indeed, a judicial history of the way in which the Fourteenth Amendment has been applied in cases of sexual and racial discrimination could fill a whole book.

3. Similar patterns hold also in other, less formal situations. Our sports fan initially takes it for granted that only a pro football team solid in both offense and defense can be considered a serious contender for the Super Bowl; he sees no reason at first to underline this fact.

Under pressure of further questioning, he may be obliged to reconsider that assumption and examine its foundations more critically. He may be compelled to go back over the actual records in order to see how far previous form in the Super Bowl bears out the assumption he has been making.

Does such an analysis of past form really confirm his assumption that any team weak in one or the other department has always fallen by the wayside long before the Super Bowl game? Once again, it may take a long time to assemble all the relevant backing in this case. And people like Jimmy the Greek make money from having a fuller and more complete "book" than the people who lay bets with them. If that does turn out to be the case, he will have given his warrant the backing that the nature of this case requires. (See Figure 6–4.)

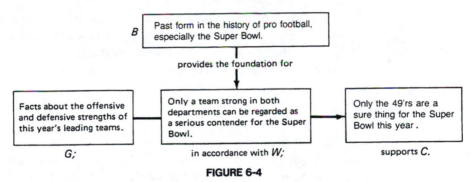

FIGURE 6-4

In all these examples, warrants of the form "*G*, therefore *C*" are at first offered without any explicit foundation. There is, of course, no objection, provided the soundness and relevance of the warrants in question are "obvious" matters of "common knowledge" and so need no spelling out. But, where the questioner challenges the initial assertor, it is necessary to provide additional information so as to determine whether the warrant in question (together with all arguments that rely on it) rests on an adequate foundation.

THE GENERALITY OF THEORIES

Any given body of scientific theory, any given set of sporting records, any given corpus of legal statutes provides backing not just for one but for many different warrants and arguments. The kinds of information that serve as backing or foundation for our warrants are in this respect broader and more general than the individual warrants themselves:

A complete scientific theory may cover a whole branch of physics in a general and comprehensive manner. That being so, it will be relevant to specific scientific arguments of many different kinds and in many different contexts.

A complete legal statute may deal with commercial transactions of all kinds in comprehensive terms, so it will lend its authority to many different kinds of specific arguments . . . and so on.

Thus, as we move from the specific facts relevant to any particular argument to those more general aspects of experience on which our confidence in that argument is ultimately based, we move from particular to general in two successive steps. First, we look and see what more general warrant, or way of arguing (W), covers the step from this particular set of grounds (G) to this specific claim (C). For example:

> "Anyone born of American parents in the United States will normally be an American citizen."

Then we go on and inquire, more generally again, on what broader foundation that warrant itself rests. What broader body of knowledge and experience (e.g., the laws and constitutional provisions about citizenship) is presupposed by anyone who accepts this warrant as a trustworthy guide in argumentation?

Choosing between warrants

In many situations, we find ourselves having to choose between a number of different ways of arguing, each with its own warrants, which point us in different directions. As we say, we have to "weigh" conflicting arguments against one another. For example, in recent years American law has paid increasing attention both to the right of access to many kinds of information as well as to rights of privacy. As a result, the courts have been attempting at one and the same time to protect our ability to find out when government agencies or private corporations are doing things that affect our interests, and also our ability to preserve our persons, homes, and private affairs against the intrusion of others. This balance is hard to strike. One person's right to know is another's unwarranted intrusion. In cases of this general kind, our problem is not to find a generally reliable warrant, but to choose between *several* such warrants.

How are we to do this? Nothing in the warrant itself guarantees its final authority in any particular case. We can make our choice only by going behind the warrant and looking to see on what basis its authority rests. In legal arguments, for instance, it is necessary to show what general kinds of backing underlie each of the conflicting warrants (e.g., the right of privacy versus free access to information). Only then can we begin to judge which of the warrants carries more weight in a particular case.

In formal law cases, this is a comparatively straightforward task. In the less formal arguments of everyday life, it is not always so easy to do. We grow up in a culture that forms our initial values, attitudes, and expectations. It equips us also with ways of thinking and reasoning whose underlying basis or backing is not always made explicit. We sometimes find ourselves drawn into arguments that appear more straightforward than they really are. Different people may apparently agree on the need to take into account "the common good" or "national security," yet disagree about their implications. Although they both accept the same words, they do not, after all, really share the same conceptions: the common good includes for one person demands which his or her opponent does not accept. As a result, political arguments may turn from rational exchanges into shouting matches, simply because of mutual misunderstandings. Each side takes it for granted that the other party understands words and phrases in the same sense; and the ambiguities of those words and phrases make it look as though both opponents are pigheaded.

An important part of sound reasoning therefore consists of "critical thinking," and this involves being prepared to ask questions about the underlying backing for those ways of thinking and reasoning our culture has drilled into us and normally takes for granted. It is no good being mesmerized by slogans. Even the best intentioned phrases, such as "the right to life," have a force and relevance that depends on the experience out of which they grow; they give strength to our arguments only if we use them as human beings rather than as parrots. To mention here a distinction which we shall look at carefully in Part VI, we may call arguments in which the accepted rules, warrants, or procedures are applied unquestioningly "regular" arguments, and contrast them with "critical" arguments in which the rules themselves are challenged and refined.

Finally, the backing we shall appeal to in any particular situation will depend on whom we are arguing with. If I am betting on the Super Bowl with a friend, my arguments for supporting the 49'rs need only be stated in general terms. But if I am betting against Jimmy the Greek, I shall need to be much surer of my ground, since Jimmy the Greek has the fullest records on the form of all the teams—after all, he "keeps the book" on them.

THE VARIED KINDS OF BACKING

A warrant and its backing are related in very similar ways in many different contexts of argumentation. But the kinds of substantive considerations that actually support our warrants vary greatly between different enterprises and fields of argument: in scientific, medical, and legal arguments, in discussions about sport, art or business, in abstract discussions of pure mathematics, and in the practical judgments of everyday life. In all these fields, our warrants derive their foundation and authority from backing of quite different sorts. Hence the colloquial point of the phrase "in the nature of the case."

In a judicial context, for instance, the basic question will be

> Can we find proper support for this warrant in the common law, statutes, administrative regulations, codes and so on currently accepted as valid, binding, and authoritative ("in force") within the relevant jurisdiction?

In a scientific context, by contrast, the basic question will be, rather:

> Can we find support for this way of arguing in currently accepted theories that rest on adequate experimental evidence or other observations and are in proper accord with our long-established ideas about the general workings of nature?

In the legal case, we are finally driven back to specific historical facts about certain human decisions. We have to identify the formal acts of the legislature that passed a particular statute, or the court rulings by which a particular legal precedent was established. In the scientific case, we have to bring to light the relevant body of experience by which our theoretical concepts and hypotheses have been squared with the result of observation and experiment.

Certain types of warrants thus rely for their soundness and relevance (as in statute law) on deliberate collective human decisions. Others (as in natural science) rely on our recognition of general patterns in the world of nature. Others (as in much of our everyday understanding of human actions and motives) rely on familiar, recognized regularities in human affairs. In the last resort, how far arguments of any particular type depend on backing of one kind or another—how far on collective decisions, how far on discoveries about nature, how far on familiarity with human affairs—is something that varies greatly from one context of argumentation to another.

BACKING AND EXPERIENCE

What ways of thinking and reasoning we can use with understanding depend on what experience we have had, and how far we have reflected on it. One of the most important things that people have to master when they enter any profession—science or engineering, law or medicine, for example—is the ways of thinking which that profession puts to use, the types of situations to which each of the associated warrants applies, and the backing on which the authority of that warrant rests.

To understand science includes understanding how the establishment of general theories lends authority to particular ways of arguing in particular situations we may encounter in the future. It is this that validates our scientific explanations. To understand the law involves understanding how the general acts, rulings, and decisions of legislatures and courts determine which arguments will stand up to criticism in different legal contexts: that is what gives our legal judgments a firm foundation. Similarly, in business and medicine it is by reflecting on the relevance of theory (economic or physiological theory, as the case may be) to our practical experience in novel situations that we legitimate the day-to-day rules by which our decisions are guided: it is this reflection that gives us the understanding we need to take those decisions with reasoned confidence.

In each case, professional training and experience help the apprentice to recognize the deeper sources from which the ways of reasoning typical of her profession draw their power. How, for instance, do our general theories about nature support specific explanations of particular phenomena? This is what one comes to recognize in the course of a scientific training. How do legislative acts and judicial precedents affect future legal decisions? That is one of the things learned in law school and the early years of legal practice. Thus, expertise in any field weds general understanding with particular skills. The experienced professional has to be familiar *both* with current general principles, *and also* with how these general principles apply in practice to fresh problems and situations.

Exercises* Backing ⇒ Proof = of Warrent

I. The following assertions may be assumed to be warrants. What kinds of information would go into backing them?

1. All religions must be allowed freedom of expression in a democratic state.
2. People who are so upset that they will murder will not long be deterred by the lack of a handgun.
3. The United States has an obligation to defend human rights throughout the world.
4. "The only thing that gives you equal status with other musicians is your musicianship. Period." Linda Ronstadt quoted in *New Woman*.
5. "For all but the most skillful drivers, front-drive cars are probably safer than rear-drive." *Money* magazine.

II. What considerations would go into backing these arguments, some of which have been discussed in previous chapters? In some cases it will be necessary to supply the implicit warrant before turning to the question of determining the appropriate backing.

1. There is a strange *sameness* about the darker occult rituals, whether originating in ancient China, practiced by early Babylonians, by primitive witch doctors or used by witches and warlocks during the middle ages. The alarming fact is that they have been often able to sneak in to our society in disguise—eventually upsetting the psychic and spiritual equilibrium of the less wary. To the latter group, the initial illusion is sweet but the inevitable stakes are high!

Argosy, UFO edition

*Several of these exercises take up examples already used in the exercises for earlier chapters. It will be helpful in dealing with them here *first* to give your answers in terms of the ideas discussed in the present chapter and *afterwards* to look back at the earlier chapters and consider the relationship of backing to claims, grounds, and warrants.

2. Despite all the turmoil and intense personality conflicts that kept the Yankees from playing their best until late August last year, they managed to capture their divisional title with a 100–62 record. With a healthier pitching staff, Gossage added to Lyle in the bullpen, and some tranquility in the locker room, New York should be able to withstand the powerful Red Sox challenge in the 1978 season.

Baseball Forecast

3. For some periods, as between 1936–1939, and 1949–1953, it is insufficient to describe the U.S.S.R. as totalitarian—it was in fact what could be called a terror-society, where no citizen, regardless of his position or the degree of loyalty to the regime, could feel safe.

   The landscape of Soviet politics reminded one of a surrealist painting; it became crowded with phantasmagoric figures of traitors, saboteurs and class enemies.

   The once leading personages of the party, government, and the armed forces were "unmasked," and in many cases were coerced to admit publicly having been agents of Hitler, the Japanese militarists, the British Intelligence or (following the war) of the American imperialists and Zionists.

Boston *Globe*

4. Business doesn't draw up a contract with the government; it tries to get the best deal it can in an increasingly coercive society. There is no such thing as voluntary planning. It compels somebody to do something he otherwise wouldn't do.

   [Objection from *Skeptic* magazine interviewer]: What if we vote for it?

   It's still coercion. You can call it Nazism, or you can call it Communism. You vote away my minority rights to disagree; I don't find that anything but coercion. Majority rule is coercion if it tramples on minority rights.

Robert M. Bleiberg, Editor, *Barron's,* in an interview with *Skeptic* magazine

5. Why didn't the psychological establishment challenge Burt's research [which argued that heredity was *by far* the most important factor in determining intelligence and was extremely influential until the evidence was shown to have been "rigged"], which was full of inconsistencies? Because, the psychologists admit, Burt was "enormously powerful." In short, they were afraid of him.

   But there was another reason, Kamin says, Burt's data wasn't [*sic*] challenged because "every professor knew that his child was brighter than the ditchdigger's child, so what was there to challenge?"

   The moral of the tale, says Kamin, is "the people who buy social science should remember that those who have collected the data may have axes to grind."

   It is well to remember that this applies to parapsychologists as well as those who criticize them.

Fate magazine

6. I regard the death penalty as a savage and immoral institution which undermines the moral and legal foundations of a society. A state, in the person of its functionaries, who like all people are inclined to make superficial conclusions, who like all people are subject to influences, connections, prejudices and egocentric motivations for their behavior, takes upon itself the right to the most terrible and irreversible act—the deprivation of life. Such a state cannot expect an improvement of the moral atmosphere in its country. I reject the notion that the death penalty has any essential deterrent effect on potential offenders. I am convinced that the contrary is true—that savagery begets savagery.

Andrei Sakharov, *Matchbox* (the *Amnesty International* magazine)

7. Most of our universities have long since abandoned as hopeless their responsibility for the moral development of their students.

Rampant cheating is a case in point—from the copying of answers to the purchase of term papers. Unwilling to punish the cheats or to demand hard work and excellence, many educators have rationalized that tests are unimportant. Therefore, they have degraded grades, first by passing out A's and B's indiscriminately, then by doing away with real grading altogether.

Thus, many students are proclaiming that they cannot or will not measure up to the standards that were required in the past. And many adults are saying that, instead of insisting on good work, we shall make these students the norm. We will lower our standards and throw out the tests. Meanwhile, one out of six college students receiving government-backed tuition loans turns out to be a deadbeat, sponging off taxpayers.

Jack Anderson, *Parade* magazine

8. The World War II GI Bill paid a veteran's tuition, whatever it was, and on top of that it gave him a monthly subsistence allowance. The Vietnam-era Bill provides just one flat monthly sum. This has effectively prevented all but the wealthy Vietnam veterans from attending expensive private institutions. Lump-sum payments favor veterans who come from states such as California where tuition rates at public institutions tend to be low. Veterans from the South and the West have used almost 50 percent more GI Bill money than their counterparts from the "high-tuition" states of the Midwest and the Northeast. Timing has also made a difference. The assistance Jones received in 1977 is at least vaguely in line with the benefits provided a World War II veteran. But in 1966, when President Johnson grudgingly signed the Vietnam-era GI Bill into law, benefits were pegged at a lower level in absolute dollars than they had been after the Korean War. From 1966 to 1974, in the years when the men who served in Vietnam needed educational assistance most, the new GI Bill was clearly inadequate compared to the World War II one. Moreover, it was incompetently administered. Throughout the sixties and early seventies the VA grew famous for misplacing GI Bill checks. Some veterans had to drop out of school for lack

of cash, because their checks did not arrive in time. Just how many quit school for this or other reasons isn't known. The VA's PR men like to point out that 64 percent of all Vietnam-era veterans have used some part of their forty-two months of GI Bill benefits, about 10 percent more than the World War II Bill attracted, but this seems a hollow boast, because the VA has no idea how many veterans have actually completed their courses of study.

The Atlantic Monthly

9. NEW TECHNOLOGY DOES MORE WITH LESS

Another area in which the Bell System is effecting savings is in power for switching and transmission equipment. Constantly, new energy-saving technology is being added to the system. *Item:* Over two billion power-saving transistors, diodes and integrated circuits have been put into use. *Item:* Light Emitting Diodes (LEDs) are replacing incandescent bulbs in switch boards and telephones, and saving over 90 per cent of the previously required power. *Item:* A new microprocessor called MAC-8 is less than one tenth the size of a postage stamp yet contains the equivalent of over 7,000 transistors. The MAC-8 can execute several hundred electronic "thinking" functions, yet it will operate on only one tenth of a watt of power.

Ad for the Bell System

10. No doubt *Close Encounters* is a vulgar, silly movie, ridiculous in its pretentions and adolescent in its conceptions; it is also a splendid piece of entertainment, rooted in the best American tradition of carnival ballyhoo *cum* Electric Theater under Black Top. For Ward to measure the film against the standards implicit in his review is equivalent to measuring Disneyland against the standards of the British Museum.

Letter to the Editor, *The Atlantic Monthly*

7

Chains
of
arguments

Thus far, we have been considering single arguments, taken one at a time, and we have looked at the various elements that make up any such single argument. But in practice, of course, any argument is liable to become the starting point for a further argument; this second argument tends to become the starting point for a third argument, and so on. In this way, arguments become connected together in *chains*.

From any one claim, chain reasoning can proceed either forward or backward. At times, we may be so confident in our acceptance of a claim that we will want to think forward quickly to its next reasonable implication just as we sometimes jump to the punch line of a joke as soon as we see where it is going. At other times, we may develop serious doubts about the claim at hand and decide to look back at its foundation claims—those upon which it was built—to see if we may have moved too far too quickly. In this sense, any claim being considered can be seen as the product of a series of preceding claims and the potential grounds for still more claims in the future.

Suppose, for instance, that we are discussing the politics of pollution. As time goes on, we discover more and more about the variety of gases and liquids that are released into the atmosphere and the ground from industrial plants. In addition, we develop instruments capable of detecting the presence of such substances with greater and greater sensitivity. The question then arises as to "How far can we insist on eliminating every last one of these emitted substances, or reducing it below the present level of detectability?" At this point, the general argument may either move further in the same direction, or else turn back on itself. Those whose commitment to clean air and pure water is absolute will want to press forward at any cost. Those whose commitment is more limited will want to turn the argument back on itself, and ask whether the price of 100 percent purity is one which we can afford to pay. The radical conservationists will thus follow the chain of argument forward wherever it leads, whereas more hesitant pragmatists will retrace this chain of argument back, so as to discover what pre-suppositions it took for granted.

Loners and Brainstormers

Chains of argument also enter into our thinking and reasoning in two different kinds of situation. In some cases, a single individual pursuing a train of thought in isolation may follow out such a sequence of arguments either forwards or backwards, and so discover either the consequences and implications of the initial argument, or the concealed assumptions on which that first argument had relied. In other cases, a number of people engaged in a joint discussion may be able, in collaboration, to pursue the chains of argument further than any one of them could have done while thinking alone.

This is the essence of the *brainstorming* method of making discoveries. A group of computer engineers, for instance, may hit on ways of developing new and more powerful programs by pooling their ideas and reacting to each others' suggestions, and in this way come up with possibilities none of them would have arrived at in isolation—or at least not have done so in so short a time. When this happens, the argument that emerges as the product of their collective discussion acquires (so to say) a life of its own. It ceases to be "Joe's argument" or "Bill's argument" and becomes "*the* argument"—or rather, "the argument which led to the new program."

To this extent, a complex argument will, in practice, often have features that cannot be fully captured simply by writing down the *sentences* of the argument on a sheet of paper. The rational power of the argument, for instance, may be derived in part from the fact that everybody involved in the brainstorming session was able to go along with it happily, as it developed out of the collective discussion. The very fact that it was the product of a team effort, rather than of a solitary train of thought, will mean that it has been exposed to a significant amount of critical scrutiny in the very course of being formulated.

AN EXAMPLE

Suppose, for instance, that we find ourselves involved in a discussion about the Vietnam war. One party to the discussion claims that the United States ought never to have intervened in that conflict in the first place. When that claim is challenged, he replies by producing three statements as his "grounds":

> Let's face it. The war was a civil war in the first place; its outcome had little bearing on our national interests overseas; and America's involvement only caused inflation and civil disorder at home.

How are we to deal with such a response? Two kinds of critical examinations are called for. In the first place, we can examine the implied connection between the three statements he is now making—"It was a civil war," "It had little bearing on our interest," and "It caused inflation and disorder at home"—and the original claim that America should have kept out. Even if we accept those statements without further examination, the first question is "Will they settle the matter?" This first question raises the issues about warrants and backing which we looked at in earlier chapters.

In the second place, however, we may wish to call in question the further statements that he produces as the *grounds* for his claim. Was it, after all, just a civil war? Were our interests as a nation really so little involved, and so on? That is to say, we can go behind the original argument and treat each of the grounds presented as representing, in turn, a further *claim* whose foundation can also be scrutinized. In this way, each of the constituent statements in the original argument will become the starting point for a further argument.

As a result, we can analyze the content of this argument, and the assumptions on which it rests, in a way that shows how all its different elements connect together. In addition to the original argument, we shall then obtain three *sub-arguments*, each of which is linked to the original argument by way of one or another of the three "grounds" in that argument.

We can set this whole pattern of connections out in the form of a series of diagrams. The point here is *not* whether we agree or disagree with the conclusion of the argument, or whether we accept the truth of the statements offered in support of the conclusion. The point is that we can effectively explain *in what respects and for what reasons* we agree or disagree, only if we take the trouble to examine all the assumptions and connections implicit in the argument, and face the question honestly, whether or not all the facts are as stated, and whether or not they really have the implications the original speaker claims. Figures 7–1 through 7–5 illustrate this.

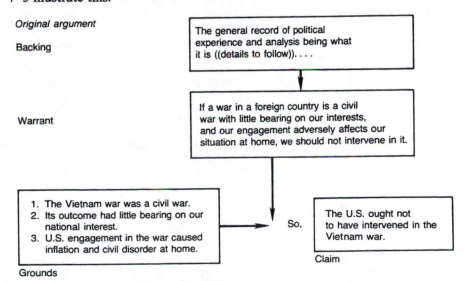

FIGURE 7-1

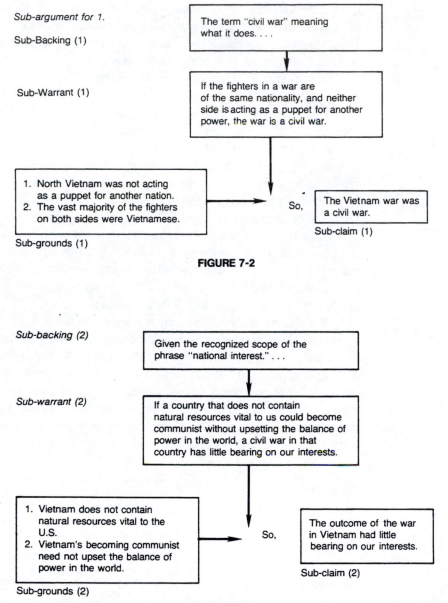

FIGURE 7-2

FIGURE 7-3

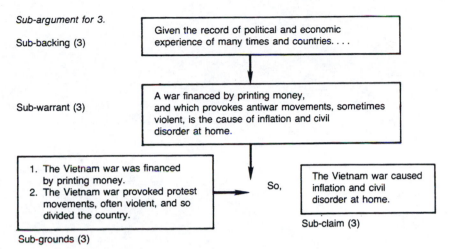

Sub-argument for 3.

Sub-backing (3)

Given the record of political and economic experience of many times and countries. . . .

Sub-warrant (3)

A war financed by printing money, and which provokes antiwar movements, sometimes violent, is the cause of inflation and civil disorder at home.

1. The Vietnam war was financed by printing money.
2. The Vietnam war provoked protest movements, often violent, and so divided the country.

So,

The Vietnam war caused inflation and civil disorder at home.

Sub-claim (3)

Sub-grounds (3)

FIGURE 7-4

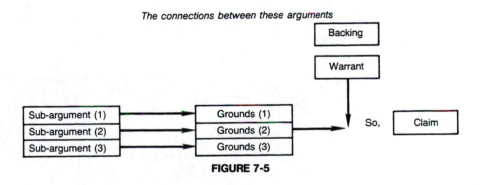

The connections between these arguments

Backing

Warrant

Sub-argument (1)	Grounds (1)
Sub-argument (2)	Grounds (2)
Sub-argument (3)	Grounds (3)

So,

Claim

FIGURE 7-5

Part III

Second level of analysis: the strength of arguments

8

Introduction

The relationships we examined in Part II have to do, in one way or another, with the question "How do the parts of this argument hang together?" Whether or not an argument is *sound* depends on whether or not the required connections between the parts of that argument are or are not present *at all*. A conclusion which is groundless, or an inference which is unwarranted, or a warrant which is baseless, is *no* conclusion, inference or warrant. The arguments embodying it will be wholly unsound.

Once the presence of the required connections has been demonstrated, however, a further set of questions can then be raised. These further questions have to do with the *strength* of the connections on which the argument depends. Granted that we have constructed an argument that is *sound* enough, so far as it goes, how much *weight* will it bear? From what has been said so far, one might get the impression that all rationally based arguments are either *totally and unconditionally* sound or shaky. It may seem as though the supporting material presented in the arguments must either be *totally and unconditionally* sufficient to support the claim, or else must entirely fail to support it.

Yet separating questions of *soundness* from questions of *strength,* as we have done here, is never more than a first simplification. Clearly, in real life, the "warrants" in our arguments do not authorize the steps from particular "grounds" to particular "claims" absolutely. In many situations we have to deal with claims, arguments, and trains of reasoning in which reliability is somewhat less than absolute. Only within the abstract arguments of pure mathematics can our statements be linked together by relations of "absolute necessity": in all practical realms, the connections that we have to deal with are more or less *qualified,* and more or less *conditional.* If we always waited until absolutely rigorous arguments could be constructed before we acted with reasoned confidence, we would be overtaken by events before we had occasion to act. In practice, therefore, it is often reasonable to base our conclusions on something less than absolutely perfect evidence. We then put forward our claims, not as being *formally* irrefutable, but rather as being *practically* strong or reliable.

Even where the connections embodied in our arguments are sound in themselves, we may often be justified in relying on those arguments only *generally,* not necessarily or invariably, or else *on certain conditions,* rather than absolutely and unconditionally.

How, then, do we think and talk about the strength of arguments, as contrasted with their soundness? In Part III, we shall be looking at four groups of issues. We shall begin by considering the *qualifying* phrases that are commonly employed to mark the degree and kind of certainty that attaches to different claims. Some warrants lead us to the required conclusion invariably; others do so frequently, but not with 100 percent reliability; others again do so more often than not; and so on. We accordingly present some conclusions as *certainly* the case, others as *probably* the case, others again as *very possibly* so. There is a whole string of adverbs and adverbial phrases that have characteristic functions in different types of practical arguments.

Secondly, we shall consider how *conditions* and *exceptions* are allowed for, in the critical presentation and discussion of claims or arguments. Some warrants lead us to the required conclusions unconditionally, others do so in all normal cases, others again do so only in exceptional circumstances. Correspondingly, we present our conclusions as *presumably* the case, as *normally* the case, or as *occasionally* so. Once again, there is a whole string of terms and phrases that have characteristic uses; these indicate how the strength of our arguments depends on the circumstances and conditions of their presentation. In particular, we shall have to pay special attention to the notion of *rebuttal.* Very often, we present arguments which we have reason to believe are strong arguments, but we do not state explicitly all of the conditions and assumptions on which that confidence rests. Just because we have reason to believe that the conditions hold, we are entitled to *presume* that the conclusion of our argument holds true. If someone is now able to demonstrate that one of our assumptions is, in fact, incorrect, she may then be able to upset our conclusions simply by pointing out that fact. (As we may say, her objection *rebuts* our original presumption.)

Thirdly, we shall consider the connected ideas of *burden of proof* and *quandaries.* In many practical situations, we need to take decisions in a rationally defensible way, either in the absence of sufficient information, or even in the presence of information that points us in conflicting directions. Where the evidence is insufficient, it may yet be irrational to suspend judgment, because urgent practical priorities may demand prompt and timely action. It is often reasonable to start by assuming one particular conclusion in the absence of evidence to the contrary. Similarly, where the evidence is conflicting, it is often reasonable to start by assuming one of two possible positions until these conflicts have been resolved.

Finally, we shall have to consider, in more general terms, how practical arguments fit into the contexts of their use, and what is meant by talking of their "relevance." The critical analysis of particular arguments (we shall find) leads us back, in the end, to an examination of the different human enterprises whose common purposes those arguments serve. In the last resort, we shall best understand what gives practical argumentation its rational force and power only by investigating how it serves the purposes both of specialized professional activities like law and science and of our everyday nonprofessional lives and "common-sense" needs.

AN EXAMPLE

A patient turns up at the doctor's office with a sore throat, a headache, and a running nose that just will not clear up. The physician recognizes the symptoms as frequently associated with a bacterial infection of the upper respiratory tract, and her first inclination is to prescribe penicillin. Why? Because penicillin has frequently been found to be effective against the general run of upper respiratory infections. There is implicit in the physician's prescription the following argument:

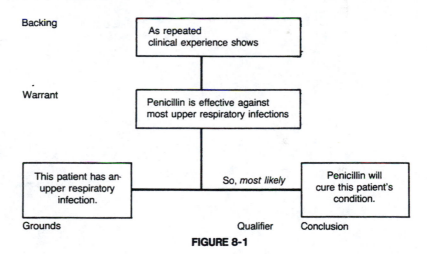

FIGURE 8-1

However, as is well known, a small proportion of patients are penicillin-sensitive; that is, if they take penicillin they are liable to suffer a severe or even fatal reaction to the drug. Even if penicillin kills the bacteria responsible for the infection, it would in that case do serious damage to the patient. The physician therefore has to ask her patient whether he has any past history of reactions to antibiotics. With this inquiry, the physician's argument takes on a further aspect:

In Figure 8–1, the phrase *most likely* illustrates the kind of qualifying phrase that we use to register the strength of our conclusions. In Figure 8–2, the word *presumably* illustrates the conditional character of the conclusion, while the further reference to penicillin-sensitivity indicates the circumstances under which the conclusion would be *rebutted*.

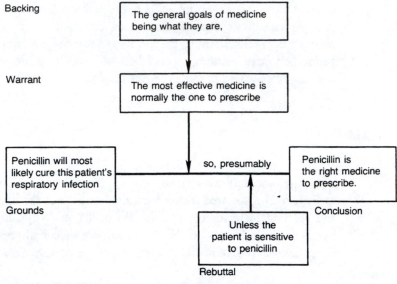

Backing

The general goals of medicine being what they are,

Warrant

The most effective medicine is normally the one to prescribe

Penicillin will most likely cure this patient's respiratory infection

Grounds

so, presumably

Penicillin is the right medicine to prescribe.

Conclusion

Unless the patient is sensitive to penicillin

Rebuttal

FIGURE 8-2

9

Qualified claims and tentative discoveries

"So certainly—if anything in sports can ever be certain—the 49'rs should make it to the Super Bowl this year."

"So evidently enough—granted the triviality of the overall plot—the new King Kong makes more psychological sense than the original."

"So presumably—within the limits of our bacteriological test procedures— the food service equipment was the source of infections."

"So on the face of it—the market being what it is at present—municipal bonds are our best bet."

Here the strengths and limitations of the initial claims are indicated by the addition of qualifiers. These are phrases that show what kind and degree of reliance is to be placed on the conclusions, given the arguments available to support them.

At this point, the interrogator, I, can direct fresh critical questions at the assertor, A, to bring to light the precise strength of A's supporting argument. Even after A has placed on the table all the grounds, warrants, and backing on which she is relying, two further sets of questions can still be raised. These have to do (1) with the strengths, and (2) with the conditions of relevance of the proposed argument. They represent the strengths, and conditions of relevance, of the link between the original claim (*C*) on the one hand and the entire body of supporting material (*G, W,* and *B*) on the other.

THE NATURE OF QUALIFIERS

We may begin, once again, by noting some colloquial phrases. Suppose that the questioner, *I,* asks the assertor, *A,* "How strong is your claim?" *I* may expand the question as follows:

> "I mean—are you making this claim unconditionally and without qualification? Are you saying that it's certainly and necessarily so, or only that it's probably, very likely, or quite possibly the case?"

In a word, every argument has a certain kind of strength. Any claim is presented with a certain strength or weakness, conditions, and/or limitations. We possess a familiar set of colloquial adverbs and adverbial phrases that are customarily used to mark these qualifications. Their function is to indicate the kind of rational strength to be attributed to *C* on the basis of its relationship to *G, W,* and *B.* Such adverbs and adverbial phrases include the following:

— Necessarily
— Certainly
— Presumably
— In all probability
— So far as the evidence goes
— For all that we can tell
— Very likely
— Very possibly
— Maybe
— Apparently
— Plausibly
— Or so it seems

Grammatically all these phrases have one feature in common. They can all be inserted into the statement "*G,* so *C*" immediately after the word *so.* In this way, they yield such modally qualified statements as the following:

— *G,* so in all probability *C.*
— *G,* so certainly *C.*
— *G,* so apparently *C.*

In each case, this addition of the adverb or the adverbial phrase has the effect of indicating what *sort* of reliance the supporting material entitles us to place on the claim, *C*.

At one extreme, consider a situation in which (1) we have all the grounds we could reasonably need, (2) our warrant is unambiguous and clearly relevant, and (3) the solidity of its backing is unchallenged. In that event, it may be legitimate to advance our claim emphatically and unconditionally:

> "*G*, so *certainly C*."

Alternatively we may be in a weaker position. Either the available grounds may point toward *C* strongly but not conclusively, or else the backing for our warrant may indicate a strong rather than a 100 percent correlation between the relevant facts and the present claim. In that event, we can appropriately state the argument in a less emphatic, more qualified manner:

> "*G*, so *probably C*."

Again the warrant may be one that applies in cases like the present one *only* in certain conditions. That is to say, there may be certain exceptions or disqualifications that would invalidate the application of the warrant—even though, in the present situation, they are assumed *not* to do so. This kind of case too can be indicated by the use of the appropriate qualification:

> "*G*, so *presumably C*."

Thus, in general, we may extend our basic pattern of analysis to include "modal qualifiers" as in Figure 9–1.

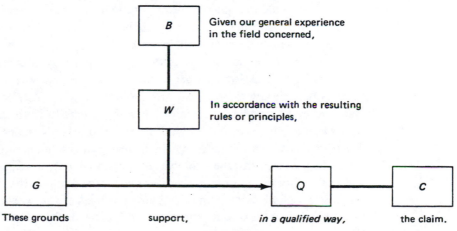

FIGURE 9-1

The letter Q will be used to indicate the particular modal qualifier used in any argument.

THE USES OF QUALIFIERS

In law

The degree of strength and certainty that any legal claim is entitled to depends on two things: the quality of the evidence available and the precise force of the relevant legal statutes or precedents. In legal arguments, modal qualifiers can be used to do either of two things: to reflect how good the evidence is or to register limitations on the relevant legal provisions.

Take an example: George has died without leaving a known will, and the question arises, "What will happen to his widow, Mary?" (See Figure 9–2.)

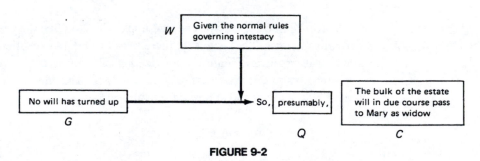

FIGURE 9-2

Here, the modal term *presumably* marks the fact that the claim, C, is less than absolutely certain and makes that claim *conditional*.

Why should this qualifier be necessary? It can be for either of two reasons. *Either* a more thorough search may yet bring a will to light. In that event, the existence of new evidence (G) will inevitably oblige us to reconsider the claim (C). *Or else,* a more careful scrutiny of the relevant law may affect the reliability of the warrant (W). Although when a husband or wife dies without leaving a will most American jurisdictions deal with the rights of the widow or widower in the same general way, there is some variation in the details. Until these finer points of difference have been looked into, the extent of Mary's right to inherit in the absence of a proven will must remain unclear. Still, as an initial position, we can reasonably assume that the available facts support our qualified conclusion, failing *either* the discovery of new documents *or else* some quirks in the local inheritance laws, either of which may upset it. Those are the kinds of possibilities we guard against by using the modal term *presumably* instead of *certainly*.

In science

In fields such as medicine and natural science, also, we may find ourselves similarly placed, with something less powerful by way of an argument than we would prefer. This may happen either through lack of a theoretical understanding of the events in question or through an insufficiency of factual evidence. In each case, we can register this fact by presenting our claims as *provisional* and therefore *uncertain*. On the one hand, there may be no doubt what theoretical arguments are relevant to a particular case, and so what warrants are applicable. But the quantity of relevant factual information at our disposal may be inadequate. On the other hand, we may have a substantial body of factual data in our possession. But this evidence may not indicate unambiguously just what theoretical considerations are relevant in the present case.

As an illustration of the first situation:

A physician is treating a hitherto fatal disease with a new drug. This drug has been strikingly effective in preliminary clinical trials, but the statistics from this testing program are still fragmentary. In these circumstances, the physician cannot say, "This treatment *will* work." Rather, all that he can conclude is "The drug has shown some signs of effectiveness, so *there is a real possibility that* it will work in this case."

As an illustration of the second situation:

Faced with a new phenomenon, a physicist is in some initial uncertainty. Is this a matter for the theory of gravitation, for electromagnetic theory, or what? If the factual evidence gathered so far suggests that the phenomenon is gravitational but does so only tentatively, the physicist will be limited to a conditional conclusion: "On the supposition that this is a purely gravitational effect, *G*, so *presumably C*."

For just so long as the gravitational hypothesis remains acceptable, the relevant theoretical statement will warrant the inference "*G*, so presumably *C*." But, if that initial presumption falls, the inference will—correspondingly—be undercut entirely. Once we are sure that the phenomenon is not after all a gravitational one, conclusions drawn from gravitation theory cease even to be "very possible," far less "likely."

And in everyday life

The use of such qualifying phrases is not, of course, limited to technical fields such as law, medicine, and science. On the contrary, we can hedge our claims in similar ways in all kinds of situations and all types of argumentation. Whatever other differences there are between the modes of argumentation appropriate to our different activities and enterprises, we frequently have occasion

1. To present our claims tentatively, without staking our whole credit on them.
2. To put them into debate in an uncommitted way, merely for purposes of discussion.
3. To treat them as serious but conditional conclusions.
4. To offer them simply as a good bet.

As a result, the relevant modal qualifiers—*probably, possibly, presumably, very likely,* and so on—have a part to play in all kinds of arguments.

Indeed the technical uses of these qualifiers are best understood as special cases of the more general uses. The meaning of adverbs like *probably* is entirely familiar to us from everyday life and provides a basis for moving on to more abstract technical terms, such as the noun *probability* itself. For instance, when the weather service reports that "the probability of precipitation is 30 percent," this means the same kind of thing as "The odds that it will rain or snow are 100 to 30 against." Even within the exact theoretical discussions of such sophisticated sciences as quantum mechanics, the link between *probabilities* and *reasonable expectations*—as contrasted with scientific certainties and solidly founded predictions—remains the same as it is in ordinary life. No doubt, the scientific statement "The probability of such an event's occurring by chance is 0.081" can serve as the warrant in much more exact inferences than the everyday statement "That kind of thing is very unlikely to happen," but the meaning of the two statements is very similar. This is just one of those cases in which we should try to avoid being flabbergasted by figures.

Not all forms of argumentation are as tightly organized as the proceedings in a law court or the transactions of a scientific academy. Where less hangs on the outcome of our arguments, we may speculate more freely and speak more loosely. So in casual conversation, we often put forward claims that are extremely tentative—or even only half serious—in order to see how far the available arguments will take us:

"It sometimes seems to me as though . . ."
"I sometimes think that . . ."

In doing so, of course, we run the risk of being misunderstood. So we put our more general credit at risk if we do not pepper our statements with the appropriate qualifying phrases. Instead of presenting our claims in unqualified terms—as though we were equally certain about them all—we find it natural, in consequence, to throw in plenty of such phrases as "it looks as though" and "I imagine that" or, alternatively, such qualifying adverbs as *apparently* and *normally*. In this way, we *cover* ourselves and guard against the charge of thinking carelessly, talking loosely, and shooting from the hip.

Exercises*

Qualifiers & what are their limits?

I. What sorts of restrictions are pertinent to the following statements, if we assume that they are warrants? Try to be as precise as possible in the formulation of the restrictions (modals) and rebuttals as you can. Both restrictions and rebuttals may not be required of all of them.

1. Water should be thrown upon burning materials to extinguish them.
2. Raising the price of gasoline will help to take the edge off the energy crunch.
3. "Avoid caffeine, especially in the first trimester of pregnancy, since it has been associated with birth defects in animals." *Mother Jones* magazine.
4. "We should choose energy policies that are consistent with market forces." Henry Ford II, *New York Times*.
5. Two parts hydrogen combine with one part oxygen to form water.
6. Municipal bonds are safe low-yield investments.
7. "Your birthdate number was selected for you by Fate and it will allow use of your assets to achieve the highest in destiny when you are aware of its significance." *Horoscope Forecast* magazine.
8. Quality speakers are the crucial elements in a first-rate stereo system.
9. The only thing you can count on in life is that people will be invariably treacherous when they think that they will escape prosecution.
10. Left-handed pitchers are most effective against right-handed hitters.
11. Supertankers are an appropriate symbol for the last quarter of this century. They are the inevitable and indispensable answer to the energy needs of the world. Japan, whose situation is direst, has no oil of its own and what it gets must be transported thousands of miles from the Persian Gulf. Tankers are the only way to get it there. So the superships are as important to the industrialized, oil-consuming nations as they are to the millionaire shipowners. Environmentalists with whom I have spoken concede that tankers are necessary. And that makes safety and environmental issues all the more important to resolve.

    Skeptic magazine

12. Carew's season was phenomenal. Not only did he hit 24 points higher than ever before and flirt with a .400 batting average, but he also drove in 100 runs and scored 128. He had an all time high 38 doubles and smashed 16 triples.

    Baseball Illustrated magazine

*Several of these exercises take up examples already used in the exercises for earlier chapters. It will be helpful in dealing with them here *first* to give your answers in terms of the ideas discussed in the present chapter and *afterwards* to look back at the earlier chapters and consider the relationship of modalities and rebuttals to backing, claims, grounds, and warrants.

13. Unless the government screws things up—and that's always a possibility—*the next twenty years will be as revolutionary as any period ever.* Technology will burst about our ears throughout the period, and the car will emerge profoundly changed.

   Already we have the rotary as an alternative to the gas-fired piston engine, and the diesel is most certainly gaining ground, not to mention turbocharging. When the next two decades have passed, still other alternatives will have been offered to the public.

   And the revolution will extend to other automotive systems, as well: electronics; fuel delivery systems; suspension and even basic structural materials.

   George Weir, *Four Wheeler* magazine

14. The notion that health, like nutrition, may be a factor in juvenile delinquency and school failure is significant because it implies a new approach to treatment of these profound social problems. It is easier to improve a person's health than to improve many of the other aspects of his environment. If each factor (usually in combination with other factors) contributes to antisocial behavior, simply improving health and reducing malnutrition could make profound changes in American social illness.

   New England. (Boston *Globe* Sunday Magazine)

15. Business doesn't draw up a contract with the government; it tries to get the best deal it can in an increasingly coercive society. There is no such thing as voluntary planning. It compels somebody to do something he otherwise wouldn't do. [Objection from *Skeptic* magazine interviewer]: What if we vote for it?

   It's still coercion. You can call it Nazism, or you can call it Communism. You vote away my minority rights to disagree; I don't find that anything but coercion. Majority rule is coercion if it tramples on minority rights.

   Robert M. Bleiberg, Editor, *Barron's,* in an interview with *Skeptic* magazine

16. American parapsychologists believe most everybody's got it to one degree or another. Though most people claim they've never had an ESP experience, they usually can come up with a sister who "did this funny thing one time," or a mother who "has this weird way of knowing . . . " Men call it a "hunch," which sounds masculine rather than mystical. Women usually have no problem falling back on "female intuition."

   New Times magazine

17. The placebo, then, is not so much a pill as a process. The process works not because of any magic in the tablet but because the most successful prescriptions are those filled by the human body itself. The placebo is powerful not because it "fools" the body but because it translates the will to live into a physical reality by triggering specific biochemical changes in the body. Thus the placebo is proof that there is no real sep-

aration between mind and body. Illness is always an interaction between both. Attempts to treat most mental diseases as though they were completely free of physical causes and attempts to treat most bodily diseases as though the mind were in no way involved must be considered archaic in the light of new evidence about the way the human body functions.

Reader's Digest (originally *Saturday Review*)

18. As a photography critic, I was glad to see *Ms.* Magazine's December, 1977, arts issue. Too often, feminism has been used as an excuse for the exhibition and publication of mediocre or unresolved work; there's been too much back-patting, and not enough criticism. Women merely patronize each other if they allow bad work to go uncriticized under the guise of ideology. The search for a "women's art" has led, in some cases, to the creation of exclusionary guidelines about art that are at least as constricting as the dictates of the male-dominated power structures in the art world. Women can hardly be praised for imitating the patterns that oppressed them, even if they make up a new set of rules.

Ms. magazine

19. *No-fault may make it harder for women to get a fair financial settlement.* Formerly, a wife whose husband "wanted out" had some negotiating power. She could bargain about money, trade his freedom for reasonable alimony and a fair property division. Under no-fault, women have lost much of that leverage. For wives with young children, or for middle-aged women with few job skills, the result can be financial hardship.

Reader's Digest

20. In the wake of controversy over the sanctioned death by starvation of the Down's Syndrome baby, Johns Hopkins Hospital established a committee to work with physicians and parents facing similar problems. Such committees are often proposed as a solution to the problem of subjectivity in medicine's ethical decision-making. Employing a variety of specialists—doctors, nurses, social workers, psychologists, clerics, etc.— an ethics committee would, in theory, decide each situation from a humane but socially utilitarian point of view. In fact, there are dangers inherent in such committees.

"Typically, committee members are socially elite persons," says Dr. Duff. "Therefore they are distant from the lives of most people. . . . Remember too that these persons are quite powerful, and they often seek more power. This tends to corrupt. . . . They may seek advantages from their colleagues more than an enlightened policy to guide decision-making."

To Dr. Duff, committees are " . . . very close to the German model in Nazi times. . . . [They] would be one step away from agony. On the surface it would seem to relieve people of the need to face agonizing choices, but the moment you do that, you surrender autonomy and control. Once you surrender them and they become institutionalized . . . it becomes impossible for the citizenry ever to get them back."

Actually, the citizenry has never had rightful control when it comes to terminating treatment for babies. Dr. Stahlman was correct: Informed consent is, at least legally, a farce. "Discussions of who should decide to withhold treatment presupposes the question that someone has the right to let the infant die," states Michael Shapiro, professor of law at the University of Southern California. "To permit a baby to die is a form of homicide; it's as simple as that."

The law makes no judgments about the worth or quality of life for any human, including infants. There is legally no difference between denying treatment to a handicapped newborn or a handicapped adult; both are protected equally.

New Times magazine

10

Rebuttals and exceptions

"So, certainly—*barring* accidents, unforeseeable injuries, or a more than usual degree of managerial incompetence—the Raiders should make it."

"So evidently enough—*unless* there's some hidden wisdom about the earlier version that we've missed—the new *Kong* makes more psychological sense than the old one."

"So presumably—*unless* there is some other factor that our tests didn't reveal or *unless* our bacteriological ideas are generally haywire—the food-service equipment is the villain of the piece."

"So on the face of it—*absent* some quite new kind of investment opportunity that the bank may give us a line on—municipals are the thing to go for."

Here, with final caution and modesty, the conclusions are provided with possible *rebuttals,* that is, the *extraordinary or exceptional circumstances* that might *undermine the force* of the supporting arguments.

As we have seen, there are two distinct reasons why claims often have to be presented as somewhat less than definite or certain:

— *Either*, because *G*, *W*, and *B* lend their support to *C* only partly or, weakly.
— *Or else*, because they support *C* only in certain conditions.

In the first event, we typically qualify the statement of our argument in a way that indicates its incomplete strength—by saying, for example, "*G*, so *probably C*." In the second event, we do so in a way that indicates its conditional character—by using the alternative form, "*G*, so *presumably C*."

The special force of the qualifier used in this second type of case *(presumably)* is directly connected with the idea of *rebuttals*. It registers the fact that the inference is warranted—that the claim is directly supported by the grounds—only *in the absence of some particular exceptional condition*, which would undercut (i.e., withdraw the authority of the warrant for) the inference.

Consider a sample scenario. At a New England town meeting, a closely fought motion is about to be voted upon. The question then arises who is (or is not) entitled to vote on the issue. It looks as though Hannah Smith may be the tie breaker. She asserts her right to participate in the vote, but this right is challenged.

A: I'm a taxpayer like everyone else here (*G*), so presumably (*Q*) I'm entitled to vote (*C*). You recall the well-established American principle: No taxation without representation!

Q: But what's your citizenship?

A: I have a Canadian passport, but I'm permanent U.S. resident.

Q: That's unfortunate for you. Though, in general, every local taxpayer is entitled to vote at the town meeting (*W*), the law specifically makes an exception that rules out those persons who are not full citizens.

To put the point concisely, being a local taxpayer creates the presumption that Hannah Smith can vote since that is the general rule, but her not being a U.S. citizen rebuts that presumption.

The term rebuttal (*R*) has an established use in all similar cases: it applies wherever a general presumption is set aside in the light of certain exceptional facts. An argument that would normally have been sound is invalidated as a result of the discovery of those special circumstances. Figure 10–1 completes our diagrammatic representation of the resulting argument.

A similar pattern is found in other kinds of cases. For example, a physician is prescribing for a new patient who is complaining of a sore throat and fever:

A: It's an upper respiratory infection (*G*), so a couple of days off work and a four-day course of penicillin will presumably (*Q*) get you back to normal health quickly enough (*C*).

Q: Are you sure that won't do more harm than good? I'm allergic to penicillin (*R*).

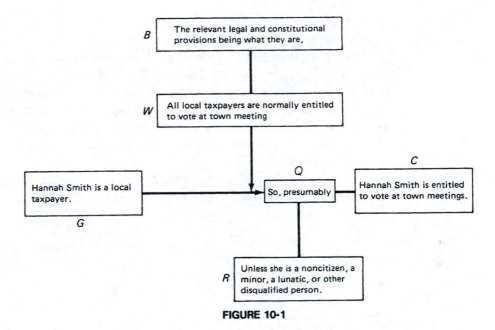

FIGURE 10-1

A: Are you indeed? In that case, I take back what I said. It's tetracycline, not penicillin, for you . . . and I strongly advise you to wear a Medicalert tag in the future, so that your medical attendants won't inadvertently kill you.

The well-proven effectiveness of penicillin against normal infections of the upper respiratory tract creates a general "presumption" about the treatment of any new infections of this kind, but the additional information about the patient's allergic reaction once again *rebuts* that presumption. The rule of thumb warrant "Upper respiratory infections call for (i.e., *are to be* treated with) a short course of peni-

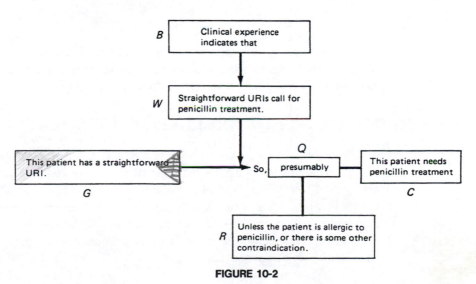

FIGURE 10-2

cillin" may certainly hold good as *a general rule,* but it does so only subject to certain *specific exceptions and exclusions.* (See Figure 10–2.)

When we encounter exceptional cases involving resident aliens, penicillin-sensitive patients, and so on, the "general rules" that serve us as sound warrants in standard situations may cease to apply. What is generally true of local taxpayers or run-of-the mill upper respiratory infections no longer holds good in these exceptional instances. The general rule creates a presumption in favor of the normal conclusion; the exceptional facts about a particular case serve as a rebuttal of that presumption.

To allow for this last element, accordingly, we have added one final feature to our basic analytical diagram (see Figure 10–3).

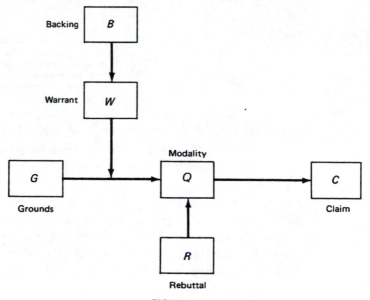

FIGURE 10-3

"Given grounds, *G,* we may appeal to warrant, *W* (which rests on backing, *B*), to justify the claim that *C*—or, at any rate, the presumption (*Q*) that *C*—in the absence of some specific rebuttal or disqualification (*R*)."

HOW TO TELL THE NORMAL FROM THE EXCEPTIONAL

Accordingly, *I*'s critical interrogation of *A* raises the topic of possible rebuttals at the point where *I* asks *A* such questions as "Are you sure you can always argue that?" or "What sort of information might undercut your argument?" Notice that we use the words *might undercut* rather than *would undercut* because statements of the form "*G,* so presumably *C*" and "*G,* so the presumption is that *C*" are properly used only when we have *no prior reason* to suppose that we are dealing with an exceptional case.

Once exceptions become so frequent that we continually find ourselves having to make allowances for them—as is beginning to be the case, by now, with penicillin-sensitivity—it is more appropriate to present our argument in another form. In that case, we take care to make the character of the possible rebuttals explicit:

"*G*, so *very possibly C,* but that depends on whether or not *R.*"

"It's a normal URI, so *very possibly* you should take penicillin, but that depends on whether or not you are allergic to it."

Going further, if the situation develops to a point at which *no* standing presumption can be securely established in the first place, there will be nothing left to rebut. Instead, we shall then have to work with two alternative parallel arguments and apply one or the other of them in any particular case, depending upon which of the alternative conditions holds good:

"*On the one hand*, if the patient is not allergic to it, penicillin may be safely and effectively prescribed for upper respiratory infections. *On the other hand*, in cases of penicillin sensitivity, some other broad-spectrum antibiotic should be prescribed, such as tetracycline."

That is, where the "exceptions" are not truly *exceptional*, we cannot present the conclusions of our arguments as being "presumably" sound, subject only to a possible rebuttal. Instead we do better to restate our warrants, explicitly, as holding good only *on condition that* certain specific conditions are satisfied.

Finally, we may go to the opposite extreme. Supposing that penicillin-sensitivity became almost universal rather than remaining an exception, physicians might even be justified in regarding penicillin less as a medicine than as a poison. True, it would be a poison that had valuable therapeutic properties for the lucky minority of patients immune to its toxic effects, but it would be a poison nonetheless. (Something of this kind is already true, with suitable dosages, of strychnine.) And somewhere along the spectrum of changes that runs from penicillin-allergy's being genuinely exceptional to its being frequent, or almost universal, physicians face a decision point: a point beyond which allergic reactions become too serious and frequent to count as *merely exceptional*, so that a short course of penicillin can no longer be regarded as *the normal treatment* for upper respiratory infections.

Just where are they to draw the line? At just what point should one begin treating "exceptions" as perfectly "normal" and so stop treating the standard case as creating a "presumption" at all? No general answer can be given to that question. Rather, the task of drawing this line raises *pragmatic* issues—decisions of policy to be decided collaboratively between professional experts and the public's representatives.

THE BASIC PRESUPPOSITIONS OF EVERYDAY ARGUMENT

We are here entering the world of "small print." Very few sound practical arguments are *absolutely* incapable of leading us astray. When, for instance, we "read" the behavior and intentions of our fellow humans, we mobilize a whole range of presuppositions about their normal day-to-day capacities and susceptibilities, needs, and interests. The general knowledge that we all possess about the tendencies and habits of our fellow human beings leads us gravely astray only in comparatively rare cases. Yet many types of familiar everyday argumentation on which we currently rely as sound would immediately become *shaky* if any of those presuppositions ceased to hold good. Television series like *Wonder Woman* and *Six Million Dollar Man* take advantage of this fact to entertain us by giving their protagonists properties and abilities that ordinary humans do not possess.

If we were to insist that all our "general knowledge" should be accepted as reliable only if it were actually *infallible,* it is doubtful whether we should end up with any general knowledge at all. As the history of philosophy makes abundantly clear, the more we are tempted to insist that all genuine "knowledge" be absolutely certain, the more we drive ourselves in the direction of skepticism. For instance, those philosophers who have argued that all our knowledge must be as rigorous as pure geometry have encountered repeated disappointments, as one type of knowledge after another has failed that test. Having let themselves be seduced by that initial but delusory hope, they have ended by concluding that—geometry apart—there is nothing else left for human beings to *know,* except perhaps their particular "sense impressions" of the present moment.

Even without going to this philosophical extreme, however, we should recognize that in certain crucial respects, the overall soundness of all practical argumentation does depend on the continuing correctness of certain very general assumptions, preconditions, or presuppositions. In their most general form, these presuppositions can be stated in such broad phrases as the following:

> "Provided the writ of Congress still runs . . ."
> "Provided the phenomena of nature still follow regular laws . . ."
> "So long as human beings remain what they now are . . ."

Naturally it would be a waste of time and energy to bother recording these wholly general presuppositions explicitly in every actual case by writing them into the particular warrants on which our practical argumentation relies. Nor may it in fact be practicable to enumerate all these general assumptions exhaustively in advance of encountering the very rare exceptions that bring them to light.

For both theoretical and practical reasons therefore, it is helpful to think of most practical warrants as holding *in general* rather than *necessarily.* Where good practical reasons exist for enumerating explicitly the specific (though rare) exceptions and exclusions that limit the application of such a warrant, we can legitimately state the resulting claim as a presumption, setting the exceptions and exclusions on one side to be dealt with separately as rebuttals when and only when they arise.

Yet to make it a general practice to reject the use of small print entirely would mean, in return, depriving ourselves of the chance to present "normal" or "typical" conclusions concisely and intelligibly. This alternative would involve stating all our general warrants in ways that spelled out all the rare, though possible, rebuttals or exclusions explicitly on every single occasion that we invoked the warrant—however "typical" that case might be. And that, of course, will naturally invite the counterobjection of "legal gobbledygook."

So this discussion of the role of presumptions and rebuttals in everyday argumentation once again faces us with a pragmatic choice. Once we fully understand the complexities of practical affairs and decisions and recognize the functions that everyday argumentation performs in their service, it is apparent that we have to strike a balance. To avoid an excess of small print, we must spell out at sufficient length the particular kind of exceptions, exclusions, and other rebuttals that limit the force of our arguments. To avoid gobbledygook, we must prevent this recital of exceptions from getting too long and banish the rarest and least significant exceptions to the small print. Where is this line to be drawn? That decision can be made only when we know enough about the audience (e.g., laymen or attorneys), the forum of argumentation (e.g., law court or office), and the general purpose of the particular discussion in question.

Exercises

Suggest as many possible rebuttals or exceptions as you can think of for each of the following arguments.

1. The Soviet Union should allow Pentecostals to leave their country without undue difficulty. To do otherwise would violate their freedom of religion.
2. The floods along the Colorado River in the Spring of 1983 caused extensive damage to homes and farms, but the people hurt have only themselves to blame because they built homes and businesses within the river's floodplain.
3. Food and Drug Administration officials have found dioxin levels in fish recently caught in Saginaw Bay reduced to 20 to 24 parts per thousand billion. Since levels below 25 are considered safe for human consumption, it is reasonable to conclude that the bay is getting better.
4. Concern over police brutality toward blacks in New York City should be reduced by the appointment of a black captain for the 28th Precinct.
5. While the situation in Central America is at a critical point, it is still possible to achieve U.S. objectives without use of our troops if we increase our military

aid by 40 percent. It is money, not troops, that the local governments need in order to resist the revolutionary activity, because the majority of the people in each country oppose revolution.

6. The Soviet Union made some minor concessions at the Madrid conference on European security. In the absence of major diplomatic activity, such concessions may constitute a signal that East–West relations are improving.

7. The Congress should support development and deployment of the MX missile system if for no other reason than the fact that it will give the administration an important bargaining chip in future negotiations.

8. Continued government deficits threaten economic health because deficits will raise interest rates and high interest rates will discourage economic activity.

11

Presumptions and quandaries

We have said a good deal about the ways in which arguments can be set out and analyzed, once they have got started. But we have not yet looked carefully at how arguments begin—what sort of situations trigger them off and how they get going in the first place. This will mean looking more carefully at the factors that give rise to arguments and the ways in which one party to a discussion may come to find himself on the defensive, obliged to produce a "justification" of his beliefs, attitudes, or actions.

GROUNDS FOR DOUBT AND OCCASIONS FOR ARGUMENT

Notice, first of all, that there is not always a basis for raising an "issue"—whether a scientific, legal, ethical, or other kind of issue. There has to be something about a situation that provides an "occasion" for challenging somebody's statements; there has, that is, to be something in the situation that gives rise to a doubt about the claims made in those statements. Unless we can point to the factors that create these grounds for doubt, we may simply find the people whose views or actions we are challenging sweeping our questions aside and replying that there is nothing to explain, apologize about, or justify. And they may, in many cases, be entitled to respond in just that way.

What, then, is involved in deciding whether an issue really arises at all, in the first place? Regardless of the context and type of argumentation, the question can always be raised,

"Why does this particular position need to be justified?"

And unless that question can be met—unless a genuine ground for challenging it can be recognized—the challenge, as such, will fail in advance of any critical discussion about its merits. The need for rational argumentation is established only *after* a genuine ground for questioning has been isolated and some reasons have become apparent for taking the proposed issue seriously.

Recall the colloquial phrases we commonly use to stop an argument from beginning:

"What are you complaining about? I'm not breaking any law."

"You don't have to be puzzled. This kind of weather is an everyday occurrence around here."

"Why are you worried? It's a perfectly healthful food, isn't it?"

"There's nothing to get anxious about. That's quite a normal way for a five-year-old child to react."

"Don't fuss! That much administrative hassle is par for this particular course."

All of these remarks are ways of short-circuiting argument by denying that there is really anything to argue about—legal, scientific, medical, psychological, and so on:

" . . . So don't trouble to ask 'Why?' or 'What?' or 'How?' The question does not arise!"

The purpose of such phrases is to cut off argument before it gets started. As the respondent sees the matter, there is really no issue and so nothing to argue about—nothing substantial for the challenger to prove and so no counterarguments for him to think up. And until it has been demonstrated that some real matter of substance exists, there is no occasion for getting an argument started. As we say, the challenger has not discharged his "initial burden of proof." And for so long as that remains the case, the rest of the world is entitled to go its own way without taking any notice of his questions.

This "burden" is not confined to cases in which the issues involved are technical ones. In familiar everyday situations, we may find our questions ignored or swept aside for lack of "occasion":

"Why do you ask, will I really come and pick you up after school? I've *told* you I will, haven't I?"

"What do you mean, is this really a cucumber? What sort of a question is that? Don't you trust your own eyes?"

In the situation that *precedes* the actual presentation of an "argument," the various parties involved are not all on the same footing. The potential challenger, who wishes to raise the issue, has an initial task to perform before the potential respondent is obliged to say anything in reply. The burden is on the challenger to "show cause" for his challenge:

"Don't you see? By filling that job vacancy without advertising it and so giving women and minority candidates no chance to apply, you were probably contravening their civil rights under affirmative action. How do you meet the charge of discrimination?"

"Look, this is really very odd. Meteorologically speaking, we shouldn't be getting both heavy rain and thick fog at the same time, so just what is going on? Is the fog really industrial pollution, or what?"

"Take care! Not all supermarket products are as safe as they may seem. Are you sure the artificial coloring and other additives in this particular product are approved by the Food and Drug Administration (FDA)?"

"Well, last week you said you would pick me up and you didn't."

"It looks to me more like an odd kind of melon than a cucumber."

It is only when enough has been said to create a *genuine and specific ground for doubt*—about the legality of an action, the naturalness of a phenomenon, the safety of a food product, or whatever—that there exists an occasion for rational discussion. And only at that point need the respondent begin to collect and marshal the relevant arguments in "justifying" his particular position.

Burden of proof and policy considerations

To see the full subtlety of *burden of proof,* let us consider the food-additive example in greater detail. The question "What food additives are dangerous?" may not look like a question about burden of proof but rather like a straightforwardly technical question of a sort that medical research scientists alone can investigate and answer:

> "Has this or that particular preservative or coloring agent ever been shown, in fact, to increase the rate of stomach cancer in experimental animals? If so, by how much, and for what dosage?"

Yet that is too simple a view. What does the term *food additive* cover anyway? Does it mean only "commercially developed food additives introduced since 1930" or something like that? Almost everything that passes our lips, including salt, sugar, and coffee—to say nothing of alcohol—can have pathological effects on living creatures of one kind or another, if taken in a large enough dosage. So the question of just what food- and drug-licensing procedures should be used to protect the public is a question of practical decisions as well as biomedical science.

True, without information from scientific research we cannot arrive at an "informed" decision about such issues. But taken by itself, this information is rarely unambiguous enough to settle the policy matter by itself. For example, we do not need to be warned against treating strychnine as a "food." The risks are too clear. By contrast, recall the current debate about the perils and blessings of saccharine. There the balance of pros and cons is much harder to strike. In most practical cases, therefore, we must weigh all the available *scientific* evidence, and then ask the *policy*-relevant question:

Not "Are there any risks?" but rather "Just what risks are to be tolerated?"

To go further, in situations like this, just what actual risks we are prepared to tolerate will depend in part on what procedures exist for protecting us against various risks. Putting Red Dye #2 on the list of unacceptable food additives is administratively feasible, but banishing sugar from the nation's kitchens or alcohol from its living rooms probably is not. Yet scientifically speaking, sugar and alcohol very likely do more harm to more people than Red Dye #2 ever will.

Thus the simple-looking inquiry "What food additives are dangerous?" transforms itself on closer inquiry into the practical question.

"What food additives should be brought under administrative regulation?"

And this question, in turn, rapidly transforms itself into the *burden-of-proof* question:

"To what extent should commercial food processors be free to use whatever additives they please, without regulation by the Food and Drug Administration? And in what respects should such practices be subject to challenge and regulation?"

Let us fill in the background of this example. The enterprise of commercial food-processing provided no particular occasions for legal challenge—beyond those normally covered by personal injury suits and the law of tort (broken glass in the bread, for example)—until it began to create significant risks to which consumers could not effectively respond on an individual basis. (As individuals, we can tell if there is broken glass in the bread but not if there are risky preservatives in it.) So it was only when those risks were judged to be "significant" in specific cases—by both technical and political standards—that the occasion arose for challenging the manufacturing processes involved. For only then was the "presumed" harmlessness of food, and food processing, put in genuine doubt. Only then had the first step been taken by which the "burden of proof" was shifted so that instead of the FDA's having to show that there was a risk demanding regulation, it was up to the processors themselves to show that the "risk" was in fact negligible.

The first practical problem in launching a rational discussion of such a problem is, thus, to make it clear *who* exactly needs to establish *what*, that is, what "presumptions" govern the discussion and when "rebuttals" may therefore be called for.

Q: Should you really be using that dye in your food processing?

A: It's a standard preservative that has been in routine use for many years, so *presumably* there's no objection to using it.

Q: That's no longer so clear. There is now a real suspicion that it may pose a genuine health hazard.

A: If the FDA were to substantiate your fears, that would of course change matters. But you should not let yourself be worried by the scaremongers. Rumors are only rumors. So as matters stand, this really isn't a serious practical issue for the food industry.

Q: Maybe that's how you see it now. But you had better keep a sharp lookout for adverse research reports. Otherwise you could have the FDA breathing down your neck.

The practical discussion of such an issue thus has two closely interlinked aspects: (1) On the one hand, the food processor is entitled to continue with a long-established practice, arguing that the longstanding, routine use of this preservative indicates that it is *presumably* free from significant toxicity, lacking solid evidence to *rebut* that indication. (2) Procedurally speaking, on the other hand, the practical issues involve questions about *burden of proof*. Should commercial food processors have been in the position, all along, of having to justify their use of particular additives in advance of actually using them? Or was the initial burden, rather, on biomedical scientists and the FDA to "show cause" by producing specific evidence of risk?

Such questions as these have to be dealt with in practice before any question arises of raising an issue for rational discussion and critical argumentation. It is these questions and presuppositions that set the stage on which subsequent debate and criticism are performed and against which they must be judged.

THE NEED FOR INITIAL PRESUMPTIONS

In all practical affairs, we begin with some general ideas about:

1. What position it is reasonable to accept, failing a strong enough argument for doing otherwise.

2. Whose task it is in such a situation to make out the "strong enough argument" without which we are entitled to stand by our original views.

In practical affairs, the task of argumentation is not so much to *give* the hearer an opinion about some topic he had no opinion about before as to *change* his opinion by producing reasons for him to give up his former opinion in favor of a new one. Correspondingly, an opinion is not *in itself* "rational" or "irrational."

Rather, it is someone's argumentative *conduct* that is "rational" or "irrational"—to the extent that he either is prepared to change his opinion when offered good reasons for doing so or else refuses to change it despite those reasons.

Those opinions that it is in general reasonable to adopt, in the absence of solid arguments to the contrary, we may call *initial presumptions*. We can find out a good deal about our various rational enterprises by looking to see what initial presumptions are operative within them and how those presumptions change from one situation to another or from one historical epoch to another. To begin with examples from science and law:

1.   Within a natural science, we can normally identify the "established body of knowledge" in the field concerned—that is, the ideas and beliefs that are currently presumed as the basis for scientific argument.

     If a scientist suspects that one or another of these ideas and beliefs is unreliable or misleading, it is *up to him* to make out the case for changing it. The established ideas and beliefs thus serve as collective intellectual benchmarks against which novel ideas and beliefs have to be measured and justified, to the extent that they would require us to *move* those benchmarks.

2.   Similarly, in the law courts, some initial presumption is always operative at the moment a trial begins. There is always a clear understanding not only about the standard of proof relevant in arguing a particular case but also about who bears the prime responsibility for making out this argument. Most often, this burden rests on the prosecutor or complainant. The defendant can initially rely on her right to be free of arbitrary arrest or financial exactions, unless the charges or complaints made against her have been supported.

So, in general, the practical demands of everyday argumentation make it unavoidable that we should rely on "initial presumptions," "prior probabilities," and the like. In most practical fields, the claims, decisions, and problems that we have to make up our minds about cannot wait indefinitely for the collection of further material. A moment arrives at which a balance must be struck. After that time, it will be *more* unreasonable *not* to reach some conclusion, on the basis of our admittedly imperfect material, than to delay a decision while collecting still further information, on the off chance that something will eventually turn up to change our minds.

> In the world of business decisions, we often have to take action with much less evidence than we should like about the prospects to be expected from different courses of action. Suppose that after a large-scale deal, a business corporation finds itself with an unforeseen windfall—namely, an uninvested cash balance of perhaps $1 million. This windfall has been sitting in the firm's current account at the bank since yesterday morning; so what is to be done with it?
>
> In this case, even to do *nothing* is—from a managerial point of view—to do

something. Leaving $1 million cash in a current bank account amounts, in effect, to "investing it at low interest." Something has to be done—and done *today*—if the affairs of the corporation are to be carried on in a reasonable and responsible manner. And this action has frequently to be taken *in advance of* full information about the alternative courses of action open to the firm.

Does this mean that business decisions have to be taken in an "irrational" manner? Not at all. One might certainly criticize a businessman who habitually took decisions without even attempting to collect the information readily obtainable within the time constraints of his situation. To act always in that way would indeed be to run the business in an irrational—because *needlessly and willfully* uninformed—manner. But it would be equally irrational for him to persist in delaying and to refuse to make up his mind simply because he had not collected *absolutely all* the information relevant to his decision.

The *rational* or *reasonable* way of reaching a conclusion is therefore also the *timely* way of reaching that conclusion. We have to choose between the need to spend time collecting more grounds (evidence, testimony, factual material) and the need to settle the matter at issue promptly. Hence the practical question is not so much how to achieve "absolute certainty" in our arguments but how to set them "beyond a reasonable doubt" within the time available and to ensure that they have "all the weight they need," given the nature of the case.

We have to weigh the arguments that are offered in favor of changing our ideas and be ready to accept or reject those arguments when the time to do so arrives. But until the time comes for making up our minds, we may reasonably stand by our previously established positions, treating them as "initial presumptions" that continue to hold good until a case is built up for changing or abandoning them.

QUANDARIES AND PUZZLES

Even when we have overcome this preliminary hurdle and are satisfied that a real *question* arises, a further difficulty may face us before we can get down to the business of collecting, marshalling, and criticizing the arguments for and against some particular *answer* to that question.

Ideally, it would be nice if "logic" or "rational criticism" could provide us with a completely effective method. It would be nice, that is to say, if we always found ourselves with only *one* plausible answer to any given question, and so needed to ask ourselves only:

"Is there a good argument in favor of this particular answer?"

Unfortunately, many of the real-life situations we find ourselves in are ones to which this ideal model is irrelevant. All too often, we begin either with *too many* possible and plausible answers to our initial question or else with *none at all*. Rather than having all the relevant facts needed to pick on one and only one correct and certain way of settling an issue, we are frequently unable to justify even moderately reliable answers to our most pressing questions and problems.

In this way, the posing of a problem may at first put us in a *quandary*. That is to say, we may find ourselves with no clear and satisfactory way of resolving the problem. Such quandaries arise in two forms. Suppose that two incompatible views, C_1 and C_2, are offered as answers to a question or solutions to a problem. On the one hand, it may be that *both* of these claims are apparently supported by strong and convincing arguments. Or alternatively, it may be that *neither* of the two claims can be adequately supported by solid and convincing arguments. Think, for instance, of the position of the jury in many criminal trials:

> First, the prosecutor makes the guilt of the accused (C_1) appear thoroughly convincing. But immediately afterwards, the defense presents an equally attractive counterargument, absolving the accused from guilt (C_2).
>
> Alternatively, the prosecutor may put forward a somewhat weak and unconvincing case (C_1) and then the defense attorney also presents a feeble answer (C_2) to the charge on the defendant's behalf.

How are we to deal with these quandaries? Where there are two strongly supported but incompatible positions, how are we to choose between them?

> If *both* sets of arguments are strong and convincing, why should we prefer *one or the other* conclusion?

Where there is no strong support for either position, what are we to do?

> If *neither* set of arguments carries conviction, how can we accept *any* conclusion?

By purely logical standards, the only legitimate course in either case would be to throw up our hands in skeptic despair. By these standards, it would be "irrational" to accept either of the two positions. Failing a clear and convincing choice in favor of C_1 rather than C_2, the only "rational" thing for us to do in either situation would be to accept neither!

In actual, practical situations, that response is no help. In dealing with practical problems, we are often obliged to give "working answers" to countless questions that cannot be conclusively settled on the basis of strong and convincing arguments. Life does not permit us to leave our minds idling like weathercocks until the wind picks up enough to blow us in one unambiguous direction. Instead the practical needs of our enterprises often oblige us to make up our minds even in the absence of clear and convincing arguments.

As a result, wherever something substantial is at stake—someone's life or liberty, the fruits of a political policy, a massive investment decision, or whatever—there are general practical guidelines for resolving our quandaries. By relying on these guidelines, we can move ahead in a reasonable, rationally defensible manner. For instance:

> When a criminal case goes to the jury, the judge will instruct the jury that it is their task to decide whether or not the prosecution has produced evidence and arguments that make out the truth of the charge "beyond a reasonable doubt." They are not required to ask themselves *either* whether that evidence "absolutely proves" the truth of the charge *or* whether the evidence and arguments of the prosecution and the defense are equally strong.
>
> If the prosecutor fully meets the reasonable-doubt requirement, the jury may disregard the defense arguments as having failed to shake the prosecutor's case. If the prosecutor fails to meet that requirement, the fact that the defense arguments as well may be rather feeble does not matter. The charge has not been adequately made out, and the defendant is entitled to an acquittal.

Instead of listening to the two attorneys with weathercock minds, it is the jury's business to *presume* the innocence of the accused until a case has been made out against him to the required reasonable-doubt standard.

Similar guidelines and standards of proof are recognized in other forums of argument where substantial interests are at stake.

Exercises

In the following situations, explain with reasons what you believe ought to be presumed and what would be necessary to advance the burden of proof necessary to create doubt.

1. The County Treasurer was charged with violating the law by using his office personnel to conduct private business during regular working hours and on public salary. The court found the treasurer not guilty of illegal activity, but stated the behavior was unethical. The treasurer now wants to resume his job from which he was suspended when criminal charges were made. The Chair of the County Commission believes he should not be allowed to return to the position.
2. You have fallen while skiing and are experiencing extreme pain in your left knee. The Ski Patrol has taken you to a medical station in the ski lodge, and a person identifying herself as an orthopedic surgeon has examined you. She announces you need immediate surgery which she is able to perform here at the ski lodge. If you wait even a day you risk permanent damage to the knee. You feel uneasy about agreeing to allow the surgery.

3. Your stock broker has called to announce a forthcoming new issue of common stock by a young but rapidly growing firm manufacturing electronic medical devices such as pacemakers. You have been with the broker for several years and his advice has generally been sound although you have taken the usual number of losses. In order to take advantage of the new issue, you must make a commitment of purchase within twenty-four hours, but you are not sure this is a time to buy common stock as the market has been unsteady for the past two months.

12

Relevance and the contexts of argument

Even after considering qualifications, rebuttals, and presumptions, however, this question still remains:

> What are the deeper sources from which arguments of different types—and the considerations on which they rest—derive their strength in actual practice?

Why is it that in, for example, legal or scientific arguments, medical or artistic ones, we start with the particular initial presumptions we do? Why do we in each case qualify our conclusions and claims in the particular ways we do, recognize those exceptions and rebuttals, or find ourselves caught in quandaries as and when we do? In order to answer those questions, we have to go beyond the *structure* or *pattern* of the arguments in question; it is not sufficient to investigate only the ways in which the particular grounds or warrants *hang together*. Instead, we have to discover how the arguments *function* within the larger human enterprises whose purposes they serve.

THE STRENGTH OF ARGUMENTS

What gives judicial arguments their strength, in the context of actual court proceedings? Evidently, this does not come from the simple coherence, or "hanging together," of the parts of the argument alone. In a properly pleaded case, the

113

arguments on both sides will hang together successfully: any trial attorney had better take care to present a *coherent* argument, for fear of being accused of incompetence, or even downright "malpractice."

Nor does the strength of a judicial argument come merely from ensuring that the proceedings are conducted in strict accord with the rules of order, or "due process." Those rules are important, and we may generally rely on them to help in the achievement of justice; but we all know that, on occasion, an impeccably conducted trial results in a "miscarriage of justice." The strength of such an argument is substantive, not procedural; so our question becomes "From what *substantive* source—as contrasted with coherence and due process—does the strength of a judicial argument derive?"

To press the question home, we can go still further: in all cases that come before the U.S. Supreme Court (as the jurist Karl Llewellyn used to argue) both sides typically present arguments that are not just coherent in form, but also strong in their substantive claims. Indeed, only those cases that are well balanced in both structure and substance are likely to reach the U.S. Supreme Court at all, since the Court normally *accepts* the cases it will hear as "worth hearing," and is free to refuse to hear cases that do not raise points of law of sufficient legal ambiguity or social importance.

This means that if an argument is to be both *sound* and *strong* it must serve the proper purposes of the relevant human enterprise. The status and force of *judicial* arguments, for instance, can be understood fully only if we put them back into their practical contexts, and ask what purposes they serve in the actual conduct of our legal institutions.

In a scientific discussion, likewise, the evidence and laws relied on in an argument must be set out in an orderly and relevant manner, if the initial claims or conclusions are to be open to understanding and rational criticism by all concerned. To this extent, the formal *pattern* of the argument helps to make it *sound* rather than *shaky*. But what finally gives such an argument its force—what makes it "strong" rather than "weak"—is, once again, something more than its structure and order. Its scientific force and standing can be understood fully only by putting it back into its practical context, and recognizing how it contributes to the larger enterprise of natural science. Just as judicial arguments are *strong* only to the extent that they serve the deeper goals of the legal process, scientific arguments are *strong* only to the extent that they serve the deeper goal of improving our scientific understanding.

The same is true in other fields. We understand the fundamental force of medical arguments only to the extent that we understand the enterprise of medicine itself. Conversely, the differences between physicians and Christian Science healers lie not just in their respective ability (or inability) to follow physiological arguments or diagnoses. At bottom, they lie in the different conceptions held about the nature of "illness," and about the human activities for relieving pain and suffering: one side focuses on changing the state of the patient's body, the other on changing the sufferer's attitudes. (Notice: the words "patient" and "sufferer" initially meant the same thing, but have since acquired specialized meanings, through the differentiation of the activities in which they figure.)

The same holds true for business, politics, and any other field. In all these activities, reasoning and argumentation find a place as central elements within a larger human enterprise. To mark this similar feature—the fact that all these activities place reliance on the presentation and critical assessment of "arguments" and "reasons"—we shall refer to them as *rational* enterprises.

Typically, then, arguments of any given type find the place and function they do—and acquire the *strength* they do—by virtue of their places in the corresponding rational enterprises. They carry weight, function, and they "ring a bell" only when presented to the appropriate audience, in an appropriate forum: legal arguments to a jury in court, or scientific arguments to readers of a relevant specialized journal. The larger activities of the rational enterprise serve as a kind of "energizing field," like the electromagnetic field that surrounds the armature of an electric motor, and so provide the ultimate source of the argument's force and power. How this works out in practice, in representative human enterprises, is a topic we shall return to in Part VI.

THE INTERDEPENDENCE OF THE ELEMENTS

One crucial step in judging the strength of any argument is that of recognizing the *relevance* or *irrelevance* of the various elements that are put forward in it. When a dispute breaks out between two neighbors over their respective water rights, the exact boundaries between their properties, or the barking of the family dog, both sides will often begin by pouring out a whole stream of "facts," all of which may be true, and based on correct information. But an outsider who is brought in to arbitrate between the disputants may, at first, be simply overwhelmed by all this talk:

"One thing at a time," he will plead. "Let's begin by getting this thing sorted out."

In other words, he cannot possibly judge the rights and wrongs of the dispute until he has first sorted out all the complaints and matched up all the "facts" against them, so as to see which (if any) of the "facts" are genuinely *relevant* to which (if any) of the points at issue between the two sides.

In judging the relevance of any factual information (such as "grounds") offered in any argument, however, we cannot look merely at the facts and at the claim or conclusion they are used to support. We also need to know what general rules or principles of other "warrants" are available for connecting the facts and the claims. Questions of relevance raise issues about the *interdependence* of the different elements in an argument. We cannot be sure that the facts offered in any argument have any "bearing" on the conclusion or claim, unless we have some idea about the warrants available for connecting them, and the solidity of the backing for those warrants:

Q: If it's *fire* you are interested in, then why all this talk about *smoke?*
A: There's causal connection between them.

Or else:

Q: Who cares where Jack was born anyway? He's a real full-blooded American, isn't he?
A: Legally speaking, the crucial conditions for citizenship are birthplace and parentage.

Similarly, we cannot always be confident about the *applicability* of a warrant until we have looked into the backing on which it rests. Having carefully read the actual statute on which some legal rule is based, for instance, we may be forced to restate it so as to make its wording more precise and allow for certain exclusions and exceptions.

Q: Yeah, but Sam Lee here was born in Philadelphia, and he's only a resident alien.
A: It has to be *both* birthplace *and* parentage. Both of Sam's parents are Chinese nationals, so his citizenship is not automatic.

Finally, until we discover what degree of certainty is being attached to a conclusion, some residual questions will remain about all the other elements: grounds, warrant, and backing alike. It will make a considerable difference whether the claim is put forward as "a necessary conclusion," as "a reliable presumption," as "a high probability," as "a mere possibility, " or whatever. A necessary conclusion, for instance, calls for a more rigorously formal argument, in which the backing of the warrant meets more demanding standards than does a practical presumption or a mere possibility.

The functional interdependence of the various elements within an entire argument thus links them together in a dozen ways. There will be no question, for instance, of completing the scrutiny of grounds entirely before we have gone on to look at warrants, backing, and all the rest. Our critical judgment on the acceptability of any one element will remain only provisional until the whole argument has been set out explicitly and we have had the chance of checking back on the bearing of possible rebuttals, on the relevance of the grounds, and on the applicability of the warrant:

Q: Oh, you're only saying that penicillin is a good *general* treatment for URIs, are you? I was wondering what you were going to say about penicillin-sensitive patients.

A: Sure. I was excluding allergic patients from the argument at this stage.

RELEVANCE AND EXPERTISE

In certain respects, the *conditions of relevance* of grounds are fully intelligible only when we take into account the larger demands of the rational enterprise within which *A*'s claim is presented. What precisely is involved in the advancing of a scientific hypothesis or in comments on a movie or in an application for a judicial injunction? All those who present genuine claims and enter into serious discussion about their justification within science or the law, for example, have to have some general understanding of the defining features of those enterprises. The participants in any such discussion have at their fingertips a flood of information or "data"—significant and insignificant—and out of all these data they need, for the purposes of the present discussion, to select those specific items that bear on the conclusion they are interested in establishing or criticizing. So the precise status of *A*'s claim (as a scientific hypothesis, a criminal indictment, or a medical diagnosis, say) will determine the criteria by which he can select certain items of information as being *to the point* for scientific (or legal or medical) purposes, while setting others aside as being *beside the point* and having nothing to do with the case.

Accordingly, *relevance* is a substantive matter, to be discussed in science by scientists, in law by lawyers, and so on. There are very few "conditions of relevance" of an entirely general kind that hold good in all fields and forums and apply to all types of arguments. On the contrary, the professional training involved in learning how to operate in any rational enterprise consists largely in learning to recognize what kinds of information will serve as relevant supporting facts in making a case for one or another specific claim:

What precisely makes you think that this sudden rise in the patient's temperature is a sign of pneumonia?

How exactly are we do demonstrate malicious intent, as we need to do if we are to support a charge of slander?

Just what should we be looking for in the Raiders' lineup in order to form a good idea about their chances for this season?

Student lawyers, physicians in-training, budding sportswriters, young scientists—people in "apprentice" roles—are all engaged in amassing the knowledge and experience they will need in order to develop a good eye for the symptoms, clues, indicators, track records, testimony—or any other "factual material"—that can serve as *relevant grounds,* in law or medicine or sportswriting or science or whatever.

After all, the reason we are ready to pay professionals to give us judgments or opinions about problems in their field is that it is their professional business to "know what's what," that is, to have a keen eye for the crucial "facts" that bear on claims and problems arising within the bailiwick of their particular professions.

COMMON SENSE

This does not, of course, mean that effective reasoning and argumentation are possible *only* within specialized and technical fields, and for highly qualified professionals. Enterprises such as medicine and business, or physics and law, have their own special aims and methods; and we can learn something about "reasoning" in general by looking to see how argumentation proceeds in the professional forums and contexts characteristic of these enterprises. But there are other very broad fields of experience in which we all stand on the same footing, and in which we can all reason in the same ways and to the same effect.

We may not all understand what precisely is involved when a physician arrives at the exact diagnosis of a patient's illness, or at a particular prescription for its treatment. Nor do we all understand the "small print" in an insurance contract, or the precise reasons for which the company may be entitled to refuse payment—at least, we may not understand this without the advice of a lawyer. But we *do* all understand what is involved when, for example, we promise to meet friends for lunch, and then stand them up. And we *do* all understand the difference between a promise made "dead seriously," and one made idly, in a context where our words were clearly meant as a joke. ("You *knew* I had to be out of town that day, so what are you complaining about?") In the affairs of everyday life, that is to say, we rely on a commonly shared body of understanding about how we shall act in various familiar situations (and so what "warrants" we shall recognize), and about how seriously our words are to be taken (and so what "exceptions" we are entitled to plead). See Figure 12-1.

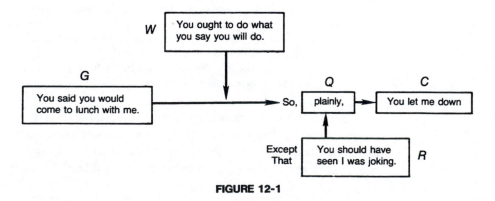

FIGURE 12-1

These factors are part of what we call *common sense*. To join in the activities of our society or culture as effectively as we do is largely a tribute to the success of our education. In the course of childhood, for instance, we spend a good deal of time learning to tell which people's words and actions we can put real weight on from those we should ignore. ("Don't take any notice of Uncle Harry: can't you see he's pulling your leg?") And we all know what happens to those people who "lack common sense"—people who either take everything too seriously or nothing seriously enough, or people who either insist on their "rights" even where others would not make a fuss, or else plead "excuses" or "exceptions" even where others would let things pass.

This kind of "common sense" covers a broad range of kinds of experience, and creates the foundation from which more technical enterprises branch off as a result of specialization. When a doctor deals with a patient, for instance, she can usually rely on the patient's understanding advice in a "common sense" way: understanding that he is meant to take his "diet" *instead of,* not *in addition to,* his regular meals:

DOCTOR: "But I thought I put you on a diet, Mr. Jones. . . ."
PATIENT: "Oh yes, doctor: I've had my diet, and now I'm having my dinner!"

When we deal with the world around us, likewise, we all have a certain general grasp of "the way things happen." Our knowledge does not really amount to *physics,* but it provides a natural way to comprehend the physical sciences. Remember the kinds of simple "experiments" a school science teacher can think up, using quite simple bits and pieces: for example, floating a needle on water to demonstrate "surface tension." (This is the kind of situation people mean when they refer to science as "organized common sense".)

Though we are not all professional attorneys, we similarly ask that technical matters of *law* make sense to us, when explained in everyday terms; and, when they fail to do so, we are tempted—and entitled—to respond, "But that's *crazy!*" (In this respect, the ideas and arguments of the law should "organize" our commonsense ideas and arguments about human relations, as those of science do those about natural events.) In general, therefore, the familiar world of common sense and everyday experience underlies and provides a basis for the technical—and at first sight mysterious—worlds of professional expertise and argumentation.

Most important, *common sense*—the sifted and digested experience of sensible, reflective people—underlies, and serves as the final *backing* for, methods of argument that should carry conviction with hearers from any background. To the extent that all human beings have similar needs, and live similar lives, they share the foundation they need for using and understanding similar methods of reasoning.

The technical reasoning of science and other professions may not be clear to the rest of us in detail and with full force. Arguments about the merits of a pop song may not make sense to a classical music lover, or *vice versa*. Discussions about political tactics may be intelligible only to people who already know what the underlying political strategy and goals are. All the same, once matters of taste and goals have been spelled out openly, reasoning and argumentation of all kinds can be led back to their roots in common sense and common experience. To that extent, the force and backing of the arguments in question can—at least, in sufficiently general terms—be made intelligible to people from quite different backgrounds.

As a result, the world of argumentation and reasoning is not split up into so many noncommunicating groups, each with its own distinct ways of thinking and reasoning. Instead we are all members of a common "rational community," and so part of the jury by which the soundness of argumentation is finally to be decided.

Exercises

In the following argument written by former Senator Sam J. Ervin, Jr. and published in the *Congressional Record* on July 28, 1983 as an open letter to President Reagan, tuition tax credits are charged with being (1) unwise, (2) unjust, and (3) unconstitutional. The charge that the credits are unwise is broken into three subordinate claims: (1) it is repugnant to good government, (2) repugnant to sound economics, and (3) repugnant to true religion.

Working with each claim and subordinate claim individually, cast each into the standard pattern of analysis which has been explained in Parts II and III. When necessary, insert implied elements in the pattern and enclose them in brackets.

Then, prepare your own argument in which you describe the context in which this argument was written, identify what you believe to be relevant and irrelevant considerations, and suggest the common sense elements of Ervin's argument in contrast to those you believe to be specialized in relation to law and politics. End this exercise by presenting your own common sense argument either agreeing or disagreeing with Ervin.

When they send their children to parochial and private schools which teach religion, parents are primarily motivated by their understandable desire to have them instructed in the religious faith of their churches.

No matter how worthy your motive for urging it may be, the proposal that Congress grant these parents credit on their federal income taxes for the tuition they pay to these schools is indefensible for three reasons. It is unwise; it is unjust; it is unconstitutional.

WHY THE PROPOSAL IS UNWISE

The proposal is unwise because it is repugnant to good government, sound economics, and true religion.

Government owes the people specific obligations, which require substantial taxes to finance them. The teaching or the financing of the teaching of religion is not one of them. But public education is.

Apart from its constitutional infirmities, the tax credit proposal is repugnant to good government.

The government's financial resources are limited. It has none beyond what it can exact from taxpayers without impoverishing them or crippling the economy.

Government should never dissipate its limited financial resources to finance nongovernment obligations. When it does, it offends both good government and sound economics because it impairs its capacity to perform its own obligations in an acceptable way.

If it should approve the tax credit proposal, Congress would diminish the nation's ability to finance the public schools, and public education would suffer accordingly.

This observation is always true. Its importance is much magnified, nowadays, however, because the nation is staggering under a national debt in excess of a trillion dollars, and is anticipating a deficit in the coming fiscal year exceeding one hundred billion dollars. It is no time for government to increase the deficit by financing a non-governmental and constitutionally forbidden undertaking.

Furthermore, the tax credit proposal is repugnant to true religion. Under God's plan, religion is dependent for its support on the persuasive power of the truth it proclaims, and not on the coercive power of governmental taxation.

The Man of Galilee affirmed this to be so when he said, "Ye shall know the truth, and the truth shall make you free" (John, c. viii, v. 32), and "render, therefore unto Caesar the things which are Caesar's, and unto God the things that are God's" (Matthew c. xxii, vs. 15–22).

Government is contemptuous of true religion when it confiscates the taxes of Caesar to finance the things of God.

If it is to be faithful to itself, religion must look to the voluntary contributions of its adherents and not to the involuntary taxes of Caesar for its support. Churches merit no praise for undertakings if members are unable or unwilling to finance them.

WHY THE PROPOSAL IS UNJUST

It is unjust for government to compel one taxpayer to pay taxes and to exempt another, either in whole or in part, from paying like taxes. Yet that is exactly what the tax credit proposal, if approved by Congress, would do.

Moreover, it would do this with a vengeance. While every man receiving as income the bare pittance which subjects him to federal income taxes would be compelled by it to pay his income taxes in full, the proposal would grant special exemptions from taxation, in whole or in part, to parents for tuition paid by them to schools teaching religion, even though their incomes total $75,000 a year.

Taxation to support the established church in Virginia was abolished by Thomas Jefferson's Statute of Virginia for Religious Freedom.

This Statute declares that it is both sinful and tyrannical for government to compel men to make contributions of tax moneys for the propagation of religious opinions they disbelieve.

It is just as sinful and tyrannical for government to do this in 1982 as it was in Thomas Jefferson's day.

Yet that is exactly what the tax credit proposal, if adopted by Congress, would do. Protestants and Jews and all other Americans who do not send their children to parochial and private schools for religious instruction would be compelled to pay taxes to propagate the religious doctrines these schools teach, even if they disbelieve them.

This is so because these Protestants, Jews, and other Americans would be compelled by law to supply the deficiency in treasury receipts the tax credit would occasion.

WHY THE PROPOSAL IS UNCONSTITUTIONAL

In times past government imprisoned the minds and spirits of men and women in intellectual and spiritual jails. It did so by denying them freedom of religion, and by compelling them to pay taxes to support churches established by it, even if they disbelieved the doctrines the churches proclaimed.

The Founding Fathers knew the history of these governmental tyrannies, and were determined that they would not be repeated in our land. They staked the very existence of America as a free Republic on their abiding conviction that the state must keep its hands off religion, and religion must keep its hands off the state in general and the public purse in particular.

To this end, they added the First Amendment to the Constitution, and thus forbade government to make any law "respecting an establishment of religion, or prohibiting the free exercise thereof."

The tax credit proposal is repugnant to both prohibitions of the First Amendment.

If it were adopted by Congress, the tuition tax credit would be a law "respecting an establishment of religion" because it would indirectly supply to parochial and private schools tax credits to aid them to teach religion.

If it were approved by Congress, the tuition tax credit would also be a law "prohibiting the free exercise of religion" because it would tax Americans who do not send their children to parochial and private schools for religious instruction to supply the deficiency in treasury receipts arising out of the tax credits to those who do. . . .

13

Summary and conclusions

In Parts I and II, we looked first at the elements required if an argument is to hang together at all (if it is to be "sound")—these parts include grounds, warrants and backing. Next, we investigated the considerations that show what weight the argument either claims, or in fact possesses (how "strong" it is)—these factors consist of qualifications, possible exceptions and rebuttals. Finally, we observed the contextual features that determine the relevance of all these elements.

Up to now, we have presented these elements as though they were always encountered in the same order: the claim first, then the grounds for the claim, next the warrant connecting these grounds to the claim, and after that (in due sequence) the backing for the warrant, the qualifications of the resulting conclusion, and any rebuttals that might possibly overturn it. This procedure was of course only a matter of convenience. We now can see that this apparent sequence was to some degree artificial.

It is true that in some cases we may take an argument apart and criticize it in a way that follows this suggested order of steps. But things need not—and do not always—happen in the same order. Once we see how all the elements connect and relate to one another, we can recognize that they are *interdependent:* we cannot always be finally satisfied about the relevance of the grounds to some claim unless we have first checked the solidity of the backing for the warrant that would make those grounds *relevant*. Observe the situation set out in Figure 13-1.

"You ought not to be walking on the grass!"
"What do you mean? Is there a law against it?"

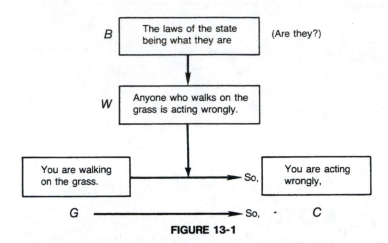

FIGURE 13-1

The true object of critical analysis is, then, the *complete argument,* with all its elements in place, and considered within its practical context.

SOME FINAL EXAMPLES

To bring together the results of this analysis of the structure and procedures of argumentation, we may assemble a few sample arguments and set them out fully and explicitly in conformity with our basic pattern of analysis (Figures 13–2 through 13–5). It would be entirely possible to do this for *all* the arguments

1. A familiar meterological illustration: "The weather will be clearing and cooler by tomorrow morning."

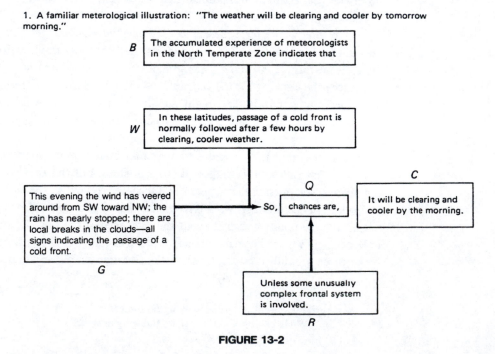

FIGURE 13-2

2. A comparable sporting prediction: "San Francisco is a shoo-in for the Super Bowl."

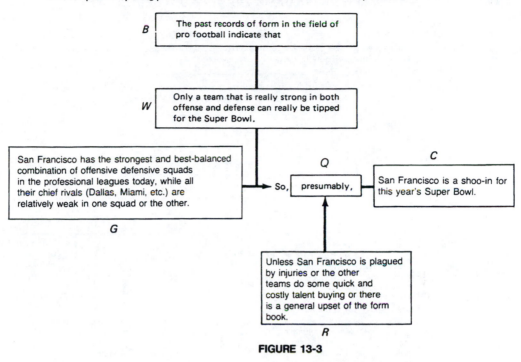

FIGURE 13-3

3. An ethical argument, for a change: "Jim treats Betty unfairly and inconsiderately."

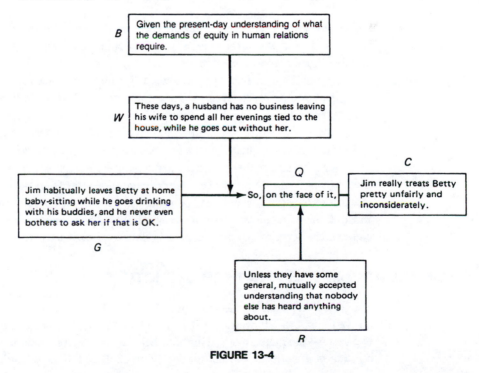

FIGURE 13-4

4. A somewhat more challenging example from pure mathematics, for purposes of comparison: "There are five, and only five, regular convex solids."

B | Given the axioms, postulates, and definitions of three-dimensional Euclidean geometry,

W | Any regular convex solid has equilateral plane figures as its faces, and the angles at any vertex will add up to less than 360°.

G | In the *tetrahedron*, the faces joining at each vertex are 3 equilateral triangles, with angles totalling 3 × 60° = 180°; in the (8-faced) *octahedron*, 4 equilateral triangles, totalling 4 × 60° = 240°; in the (20-faced) *eicosahedron*, 5, totalling 5 × 60° = 300°. In the *cube*, they are 3 squares, with angles totalling 3 × 90° = 270°, and in the (12-faced) *dodecahedron*, they are three pentagons, totalling 3 × 108° = 324°. No other set of equal angles at the vertex of a solid adds up to less than 360°.

So, | Q | with strict geometrical necessity,

C | There are five and only five regular convex solids.

No rebuttals or exceptions available within the formal system of Euclidean geometry.

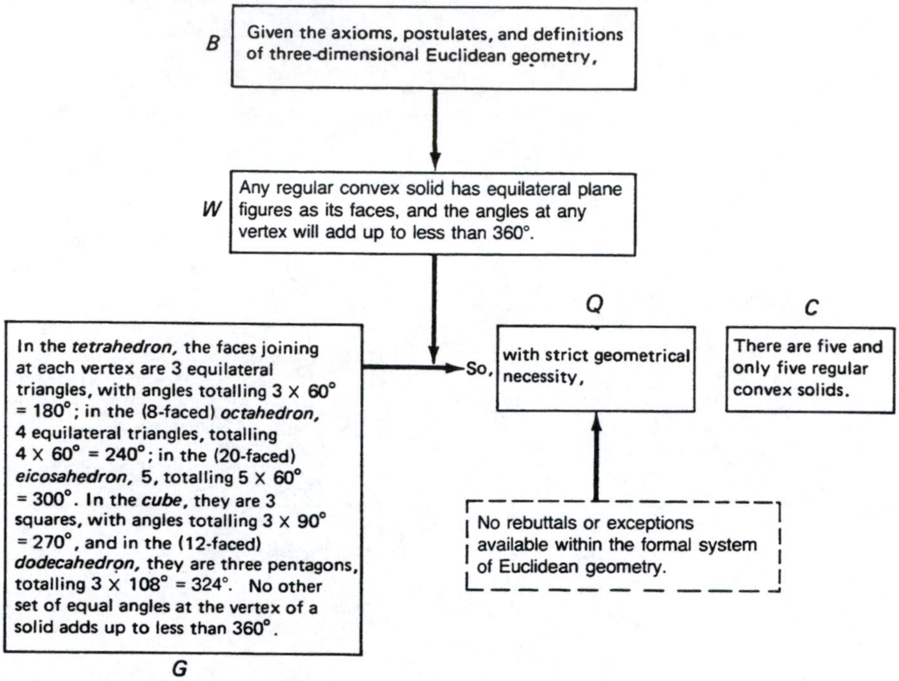

FIGURE 13-5

looked at in these chapters. But four contrasted illustrations will be enough to show the way in which the general pattern applies, and the other arguments can be left for the reader to treat as exercises.

Figure 13–5 is included because of its historical interest. It represents a novel geometrical proof given by Theaetetus in Plato's own lifetime, which gave Plato a great impression of the "rational power" of geometrical argumentation. Here at last—it seemed—was an argument in which strict necessity was achieved, while establishing a quite unforeseen conclusion about the world we live in.

As they stand, these four illustrations present arguments in isolation from their larger forums, or contexts, of argumentation. But from what has been said in earlier chapters, it should not be difficult to construct appropriate contexts for most of the arguments. It has to be remembered that, aside from *some* specific context, the force of any argument is in danger of evaporating.

FORMAL ARGUMENTS AND THEIR STRUCTURE

This last example has one special feature. Look at ways in which the backing (*B*) supports the warrant (*W*) in each of the sample arguments. In the first two cases—the meteorological and football cases—we are concerned with general matters of experience, so the relation between *B* and *W* is *factual*. The backing

B "gives us reason to believe" that the warrant *W* is generally true, and/or a reliable guide to future cases. In the third case, we are again concerned with a matter of experience, but the relation is no longer purely factual. The experience in question is the experience of living a life among (and interacting with) our fellow human beings, and the backing *B* lends *moral* support to the general rule of family life captured in the warrant *W*.

If we had given an example from the law, the relation would have been different; for instance, the backing *B* might have specified a statute (a law passed by the relevant legislative assembly, or parliament) or a judicial precedent (a previous binding case), and the warrant *W* would have stated the general rule that derives its legal authority from that statute or precedent. We may call this relation "a matter of experience," if we please; but the experience in question is neither a simple matter of observed fact nor a matter of moral decision. Rather, it is a matter of *professional* experience: of having learned what existing laws and precedents are relevant in a case such as the one currently under discussion.

In our final example, the relation between *B* and *W* is different yet again. The support any given mathematical statement derives from the axioms, postulates, and definitions of the formal system in which it belongs can scarcely be described as "a matter of experience." True, we have to *recognize* the link between the given statement and the underlying axioms; but the link we see between them is a *formal* one, and holds good because of the general character of the entire mathematical system. It is not the sort of connection which "just happens" to be the case, or which we are free to establish or suspend, either by our own moral decision, or by (perhaps) an Act of Congress.

We might alternatively have phrased the argument in the following manner. Given as backing (*B*) the assumption

"The system of three-dimensional Euclidean geometry being as it is. . . ."

we can define a "regular convex solid" in the way specified in the warrant (*W*); and we can then apply that definition to *prove*—as a matter of formal structure— that the theorem (*C*) has a proper place in the entire geometrical system.

With this final illustration in mind, we can come back to a distinction remarked on at the beginning of this book. The term *argument* is used in colloquial speech in two ways: to refer, either, to formal trains of propositions and the ways in which they are implicated with one another, or to the interactions between human beings in the course of which opinions are presented, criticized and/or defended. Our chief concern in this book is with the latter ("human-interaction") sense of the term *argument,* and with the ways in which arguments—as so understood—derive their strength and solidity from the ways in which they enter into human life.

Nevertheless, the other, more formal sense of the term "argument" also has its place. Using the term in this other sense, there are occasions when it can be helpful to set aside for the time being all those considerations that have to do with the factual experience and contextual aspects involved in the case at issue, and instead to abstract out the propositions under examination and focus solely on the formal connections that hold between the propositions themselves. That is what is done in such branches of pure mathematics as Euclidean geometry, and it is also done in all the theoretical sciences—in theoretical economics quite as much as in physical theory and other natural sciences. And it is on this kind of occasion that the language of formal "proof," "deduction," and "demonstration" takes over from the language of "support," "backing," and "establishment."

When considering arguments in such fields as economics, which have both a formal, theoretical aspect, and also are concerned with matters of practical experience, we need to move with caution. We must take care to be clear in our minds whether the current argument is to be considered from the *formal* stand-point—so that we are asking whether the conclusion of the argument really "follows deductively from," and so can be *proved* within, for example the theory of imperfect competition—or whether the matter at issue is one of *experience*—whether this case is one in which the theory of imperfect competition can properly be regarded as *relevant*.

In short, the rational criticism of an argument requires us to pay attention to questions of two rather different sorts. On some occasions, the question is one about the *internal structure* of the argument:

> "Am I arguing *right?* Are all the connections among the various statements in the argument *impeccable?*"

On other occasions, the question is one about the argument's *external relevance:*

> "Am I using the *right* argument? Is this practical situation one in which an argument of this particular form carries any *weight?*"

We shall see in the following sections, when we look at the ways in which arguments can go wrong, that trains of reasoning can get us into trouble, in practice, in either or both of these respects at once.

Part IV

**Fallacies:
how
arguments
go
wrong**

14

Introduction

Just as certain widely accepted ways of construing arguments are recognized as sound across a wide range of fields, so too *certain modes of procedure in argumentation have been traditionally recognized as unsound*. These modes are termed *fallacies*. No discussion of practical reasoning is complete that does not consider some representative examples of fallacies and inquire into the question of what makes them fallacious.

Three preliminary cautions are required:

1. Many fallacies result from inappropriate or untimely use of the rational strategies, or procedures of argument. So the catalog of fallacies will forever remain incomplete. (People can always invent new ways of going astray in their reasoning!) Thus students should not expect that our discussion of fallacies will exhaust what can be said about unsound modes of arguing. Nor should the student expect that the difficult subject can be mastered in a mechanical way, for fallacies are complex—sometimes to the point of being ingenious—and varied.

2. Furthermore, fallacies do not lend themselves to neat and tidy classification. We shall simply proceed here to discuss and provide illustrations of various sorts of fallacies, without offering any systematic account of their classes and sub-classes. This is because nearly every such effort ends up being more confusing than helpful. We shall instead present a collection of modes of arguing that have been persistently acknowledged by students of reasoning as unsound.

3. Most disturbingly to some people, arguments that are fallacious in one context may turn out to be sound in another context. Therefore, we shall not be able to identify any intrinsically fallacious forms of arguing. Instead we shall try to indicate why certain kinds of argument are, in practice, fallacious in one or another kind of context.

In what follows, therefore, we shall emphasize how by paying proper attention to the grounds and warrants we use in our arguments and being on the lookout for ambiguity in the terms employed in arguing we may hope to circumvent fallacious argumentation.

The study of fallacies can be thought of as a kind of sensitivity-training in reasoning. It should attune the student to the omnipresent dangers to which we are exposed as a consequence of employing imprecise expressions—vague, ambiguous, or misdefined terms. Students should also be alert to unarticulated assumptions and presumptions as well as to inadequate grounding in arguments.

FIVE TYPES OF FALLACIES

Fallacies are arguments that can seem persuasive despite being unsound. Their power of persuasion arises from their superficial resemblance to sound forms of reasoning. This similarity lends them a bogus air of plausibility. It is very important to bear in mind from the outset that fallacies may be either accidental or deliberate, either honest or dishonest mistakes. This distinction is crucial because we will want to respond quite differently to dishonest than to honest errors. We normally do not blame people for being misled, but we find efforts to mislead us repugnant. We simply require of those who make honest mistakes in reasoning that they reformulate their arguments in ways that eliminate the mistakes in question. By contrast, if we discover that a fallacy has been deliberately committed (such fallacies are sometimes referred to as sophisms)—if we discover that the speaker is trying to put one over on us—we may be inclined to question whether there is any point to further discussion.

Fallacies divide into five broad types according to our model:

1. Fallacies that result from missing grounds;
2. Fallacies that result from irrelevant grounds;
3. Fallacies that result from defective grounds;
4. Fallacies that result from unwarranted assumptions; and
5. Fallacies that result from ambiguities in our arguments.

Fallacies that result from missing grounds are pseudo-arguments, for no real evidence is presented on behalf of the claim. Fallacies that result from defective grounds present evidence for a claim of the right sort of establishing the claim in question but which are insufficient for establishing the claim in question. These fallacies involve relevant but inadequate grounds. Fallacies resulting from irrelevant grounds simply offer the wrong type of evidence. The data in question do not pertain to the claim being pressed. Fallacies resulting from unwarranted assumptions involve the presumption that you can move from grounds to claim when you really cannot. They usually involve an assumption that there is widespread consensus concerning the applicability of a warrant, when in fact there is not. Fallacies resulting from ambiguity occur when some term in our argument can be construed in more than one way. This fifth class of fallacies differs from the first four in that fallacies of ambiguity concern the meaning of terms or assertions within our arguments rather than structural problems in our inferences.

In the case of the fallacies that result from improper grounding or unwarranted assumptions we shall discover that the problem in the argument involves seeing how the chief elements in our model, grounds, warrants, and backing all work together to establish a claim. Paradoxically, this is perhaps clearest when our argument is defective. In many cases we can only discover that there is something wrong with our grounds once we have (1) made our warrant explicit, and (2) raised the question of how that warrant would be backed. In effect, to ask if an argument is fallacious is to question the whole *procedure* of moving from grounds to claim (this process always implicitly involves warrants and backing). In sound argumentation we are normally more or less disinclined to probe further beyond accepting a claim as grounded; in contrast, when we suspect fallacious reasoning we tend to be more concerned about warrants and backing. The point is that, even if a fallacy is principally a matter of inadequate grounds, explaining just what is fallacious in the argument will almost inevitably raise questions about warrants and backing (these questions are implicit in any rational procedure). It is for this reason that we emphasize that our discussion of fallacies is not intended to be the prelude to a mechanical process of memorizing definitions that permit neat classification of errors in reasoning. Rather, our discussion teaches attunement to reasoning as a complex procedure involving the interaction of all the elements in our model. The fallacies presented in this Part are thus not intended to exhaust but to *typify* the ways in which reasoning can go astray.

15

Missing grounds

It might seem strange to speak of arguments that lack grounds, but they do occur. They are the least sound arguments of all, for to lack grounds for assertions is to fail the first test for rational adequacy in argumentation. An argument that misses grounds is nothing other than a bare-faced assertion, no real evidence is presented for the claim in question. Because no reasons are actually offered for making an assertion, we can designate such efforts as pseudo-arguments. Perhaps the best example of such pseudo-argumentation traditionally recognized by students of reasoning is embodied in the fallacy of *begging the question*.

Begging the question

We commit this fallacy when we make a claim and then argue on its behalf by advancing "grounds" whose meaning is simply equivalent to that of the original claim. We seem to be asserting *C* and offering additional grounds, *G*, in its support, but actually *C* and *G* turn out to mean exactly the same things—though this fact may be concealed because they are phrased in different terms.

A: Smith is telling the truth.
Q: Why do you say that?
A: He wouldn't lie to me about this.

If "he wouldn't lie" is understood to mean "is not on this occasion lying," *A*'s second statement is nothing more than a disguised restatement of his first statement; it adds nothing to it. The two statements differ only in that one is stated in positive, the other in negative, terms.

As with many other fallacies, begging the question becomes easier and more deceptive in larger and more extended arguments:

A: Pablo Picasso is the greatest painter of this century.

Q: How do you know that?

A: People who know about art admire Picasso above all other twentieth-century artists.

Thus far there is nothing to object to about this argument. But it can quickly become question-begging if our assertor is asked to expand on his grounds:

Q: Just who are these people who know so much about art?

A: The people who know about twentieth-century art are people who understand Picasso's work well enough to admire him above all other painters of the present century.

In this second case, we are more likely to overlook the "circularity" because we so rarely insist that people spell out their arguments in detail. Yet the demand that our arguments be based upon reasons that can be articulated (and must be articulated, if a questioner requires clarification) implies that we should in every case be prepared to spell out the whole of our reasoning on a given subject. This will become clearer if we look at Figures 15–1 and 15–2:

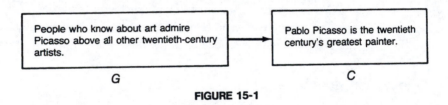

FIGURE 15-1

So far this looks like a legitimate argument. However, when we add the step that allegedly warrants this move, as we do in Figure 15–2, we find the following result:

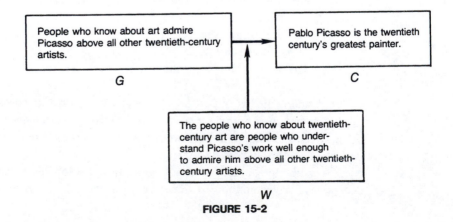

FIGURE 15-2

Once we articulate the warrant we discover that we have not really moved at all in our apparent passage from grounds to claim. The warrant simply asserts that knowing about art is tantamount to insisting that Picasso is the greatest twentieth-century painter. As soon as we ask how we would go about backing such a warrant we realize that it would involve establishing *exactly* the same claim as our original grounds attempted to establish. Our argument has not advanced in the least. Though we have stated grounds, we have not really performed *the grounding procedure.*

Question-begging also occurs in definitions. *The so-called circular definition actually begs the question involved in defining the term under discussion.* Consider the following definitions:

— A cat is a feline animal.
— A cause is anything that produces an effect.
— Distillation is the operation of distilling.

Each of these formulations presupposes an understanding of the term to be defined. Nobody who does not already know what a cat is can have any idea what it means to be feline. Nor can someone who does not already understand what a cause is grasp the notion of an effect. Nor, for that matter, is it likely that someone who has no idea of what distillation is will know what distilling is. The last instance is an example of defining by synonym—a typical feature of vest-pocket dictionaries (this is one of the reasons teachers discourage students from using such dictionaries).

Question-begging amounts to a failure to advance substantial evidence in support of a claim. What appears to be offered as evidence is in fact merely a restatement of the claim itself. Nevertheless, question-begging is never by itself fatal to an argument. Although nothing substantive has been added to the original claim, nothing has been done to discredit it either. If the assertor has a position that can be defended—if grounds are available on which we can build the claim—he must merely start anew and approach the subject from another direction.

Question-begging epithets. Another frequent source of fallacies is the use of question-begging epithets. *These are phrases that are either fallaciously circular or else permit complex questions to enter into arguments.* Terms such as "naive optimist," "bleeding-heart liberal," "foolhardy radical," "cowardly pacifist," "dangerous atheist," "mindless Fundamentalist," "obscurantist conservative," and the like may in a few cases be perfectly apt descriptions of the individuals concerned. But the use of such phrases can quickly become a dangerous habit. Each is a complex description, in which the modifying epithet ("naive," "mindless," and so on) comes to be treated as a universal feature of all who belong to the group designated by the corresponding noun ("optimist," "Fundamentalist," and so on). Yet all optimists need not be naive, even if it were true that the majority were. Nor is it a foregone conclusion that radicals must be foolhardy, pacifists cowardly, atheists dangerous, Fundamentalists mindless, or conservatives obscurantist. The question-begging character of most clichés and stereotypical ideas makes appeals to them objectionable in most rational arguments.

Accordingly, when someone is accused of being a "cowardly pacifist," he can respond by distinguishing the complex question implied in the epithet:

"Yes, a pacifist I am; but I deny that I am cowardly."

Whenever we encounter derogatory adjectives modifying class terms, like those listed here, we should always be on the lookout for question-begging epithets. They are one of the commonest features of political rhetoric.

Phrases like *cowardly pacifist* become circular whenever the suppressed assumption (that anyone who is a pacifist must be a coward) is left uncriticized. The element of question-begging accordingly involves also something of the fallacy of poisoning the wells: there may be no evidence that is capable of falsifying the allegation implied in the epithet. Question-begging epithets are insidious precisely because they are so easily overlooked, unless we keep our eyes skinned for them. A short phrase, carelessly introduced, can thus undermine an otherwise sound argument.

There are also a large number of similar phrases that express qualities generally admired in our society. Using these terms, or their opposites, can color our arguments to the point at which those arguments become fallacious. We all want to be thought sincere, spontaneous, tolerant, authentic, and so on, and few of us really want to be thought of as impractical or aloof. Similarly, writers and speakers regularly use certain words to embellish their points; for example, *evident and obvious, certain* and *precise.* Yet these terms are frequently misused. We are expected to acquiesce in the arguments concerned just because the assertor presents views in this way. Yet what is asserted as "evident" or "obvious" is in fact often far from being so. (It pays to be on the lookout for such question-begging terms also; they are insidious precisely because they so easily pass unnoticed.)

The basic step involved in question-begging is common to a number of fallacies that we shall discuss in detail in subsequent chapters. In a sense, any argument in which the grounds are irrelevant to the conclusion—any situation in which we might be agreed about the facts of the case but may dispute whether they are the right *type* of facts—we beg the question in the wide sense. However, we can do this in so many ways that each of those traditionally identified as a fallacy of relevance merits special discussion for the insight they give us into various aspects of fallaciousness. It is to these fallacies that we shall turn in the next chapter. Two fallacies that deserve special attention as arguments with missing grounds are *evading the issue* and *poisoning the wells.* It is to the first of these as a model of arguments with irrelevant grounds that we shall now turn.

16

Fallacies resulting from irrelevant grounds

In addition to arguments that go wrong because they miss grounds, there is a larger and more insidious group of arguments that go wrong not because they fail to produce grounds for the assertions they advance but because they advance the wrong sorts of grounds for establishing their claims. *These fallacies occur when the evidence we present for our claim is not directly relevant to that claim.* It is important to emphasize that evidence may be relevant to a claim without being *directly* relevant to it. For example, it may or may not be fallacious to argue that someone should be barred from government work on the grounds that she had once been a Communist. If the person in question is applying for a position as a letter carrier, her Communist past is hardly directly relevant to the capacity to deliver mail. However, it might be a very important consideration in deciding whether she is fit for a State Department job. Everything depends upon what is at stake: the nature of the claim and the warrants which determine what is and what is not justifiably asserted regarding the subject of the claim. This will become clearer as we examine some of the classic instances of irrelevant efforts to ground claims. The fallacy of evading the issue is the simplest instance of irrelevance, so we shall begin with it.

Evading the Issue

We evade the issue when we attempt to ground our claims on evidence not directly relevant to the issues at stake. We can do this in a number of ways. In some instances, we introduce the wrong sort of data purely and simply; in other cases, the data is only tenuously linked to our assertion; and in yet other instances we may evade the issue by sidestepping a question addressed to us. The fallaciousness of such arguments usually becomes apparent when we articulate the warrants upon which they have been constructed.

Figure 16–1 presents an argument in which the claim rests upon grounds that are loosely relevant and that are generally the sorts of considerations to which most members of a typical American community would agree. However, the argument is fallacious because the considerations advanced as grounds do not allow us to infer a claim as specific as the one being made.

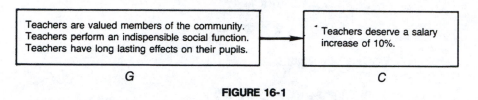

FIGURE 16-1

This becomes clear when we spell out the warrant that would be implicitly appealed to in such an argument as in Figure 16–2:

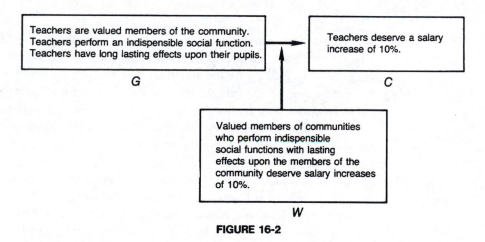

FIGURE 16-2

There can be little doubt that this argument would have a certain force in the abstract. However, if we conceive of it as occurring at a session—perhaps of a New England Town Meeting devoted to fiscal affairs—it will not be difficult to see that the warrant or rule at stake is not one that we could profitably rely upon. In fiscal matters we have a fixed amount of money for budgets. Considerations such as those advanced in our argument certainly have *some* bearing upon how we ought to allocate community resources, but they are not the sorts of information that will allow us to determine whether or not teachers deserve *10 percent* as a salary increase in the coming year. To determine that, we would have to know such things as the current salary scale for teachers, how they had fared in the battle with inflation, their comparative salaries with respect to other comparable school districts, and community employees, as well as the community's fiscal priorities short- and long-term. All of these considerations are more *directly* relevant to the question of teachers' salary increases than the considerations which were advanced in the argument in Figure 16–1.

Another mode of evading the issue focuses upon our response to questions. We can also evade the issue fallaciously when we attempt to sidestep rather than to answer a question. Politicians use this tactic in order to avoid divulging their true opinions about controversial bills. A Congressman may be asked, for example, how he intends to vote on an upcoming bill that would raise benefits for Social Security recipients. He may reply by saying that he considers the elderly a very important segment of the community, that he has fought vigorously on their behalf in the past, and that he deplores the ill treatment of the aged. However noble and highsounding these sentiments may be, none of them in fact answers the question posed. These considerations may, in the end, be of some relevance to answering the question posed—they might, for example contain significant hints to the Congressman's opinion of the bill—but as stated they are not *directly* relevant to the question. If he deliberately confines his answer to general statements of this kind in order to conceal the fact that he intends to vote against the bill, he is certainly evading the issue fallaciously.

Two types of diversionary tactics in argumentation deserve mention as part of our discussion. These are the *red herring* and the *straw man.*

To introduce a *red herring* into an argument is to misdirect the discussion by bringing up a topic whose bearing is tangential to the main point under dispute. For example, in an argument about the compatibility of socialism and democracy as abstract concepts (a philosophical discussion within political theory), someone might bring up Stalin's purges as evidence that socialism is essentially undemocratic. This consideration is certainly germane to any discussion of the compatibility of socialism and democracy in the concrete, but it is unclear to what extent we can illuminate the abstract issues involved in examining the issue by looking at one episode in the development of socialism in one country (any more than the Vietnam War illustrates something about the *concept* of democracy).

The *straw-man argument* is another diversionary tactic in which someone ends up making a case for or against a position that nobody in fact holds. Typically, straw-man arguments oversimplify issues, though it is not impossible to produce a straw-man argument that overcomplicates an issue. To introduce a straw man is similar to introducing a red herring into the discussion in that it has a diversionary function in the argument; however, the way in which the diversion takes place allows us to distinguish the two. A red herring takes the whole discussion off on a different track. The straw man, on the other hand, represents an attempt to refute another's position by restating it in such a way that it can be easily rejected. The problem in this is that a straw man typically involves a distorted or oversimplified restatement so that the refutation that is so easily accomplished simply does not address real issues. For example, consider that we are arguing against someone who believes that abortion on demand should not be legal. In the course of that argument we produce a statement that murder is and ought to be illegal. This statement is intended to show that our opponent really is in agreement with us. To establish that murder ought to be a crime is to say nothing about abortion until it has been established that abortion is murder (a considerably more difficult stance to prove). To show that murder is a crime is not utterly irrelevant to the claim that abortion should be prosecuted as murder, but it by no means establishes the moral and legal character of abortion. To argue that it does is to argue with a position not held by any of the participants. We consequently evade the issue by erecting a straw figure that is easily blown over (hence the name).

Of course, not all evasions of the issue are necessarily fallacious. Questioners, for example, do not always have the right to the information they request. Students do not have the right to ask their teachers which questions will appear on their examinations. Similarly, national security demands that the military classify certain information (which is not to say that it should be entirely unobtainable to anybody except the military). These situations are significantly different from our earlier example of the politician who is queried by his constitutents, for it is the Congressman's sworn duty to represent his constituents in Congress. Here, as elsewhere, the issue of whether the argumentative procedure in question is fallacious or not can depend upon the situation in which it is employed.

Appeals to authority

Authority is one of the familiar and traditional topics around which sound arguments can be constructed. Such *appeals to authority become fallacious at the point where authority is invoked as the last word on a given topic. The opinion of that authority is taken as closing off discussion of the matter in question.* No further evidence is considered; the authority's opinion has settled the matter once and for all.

The classic case in which authority was supposedly invoked to counter other, more directly relevant evidence was that of the Aristotelian scientists who refused to look through Galileo's telescope. They refused in the conviction that Aristotle's opinion could not possibly be wrong, so that no observation could possibly—as Galileo alleged—run contrary to what Aristotle had taught. The argument ran roughly as set out in Figure 16–3. This argument alleges that Aristotle's testi-

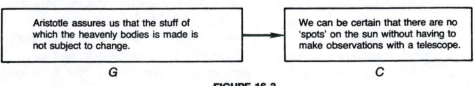

Aristotle assures us that the stuff of which the heavenly bodies is made is not subject to change.	We can be certain that there are no 'spots' on the sun without having to make observations with a telescope.
G	*C*

FIGURE 16-3

mony is adequate to making the claim that there are no "spots" on the sun. The irrelevance of these grounds can be established when we spell out the warrant upon which they depend, as we do in Figure 16–4.

The reliability of that warrant could be established only if we could produce, as backing, evidence that Aristotle's views on scientific matters were infallible.

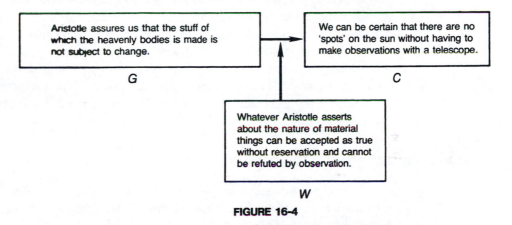

FIGURE 16-4

In this example, the fallacy arises because the supposed grounds (i.e., Aristotle's views about the nature of matter) are simply *irrelevant* to the question at issue (i.e., just what can, or cannot, be observed on the sun). The data used to support the initial claim are simply unrelated to the issue that has to be decided.

Some other fallacious appeals to authority are closer to our everyday experience. Consider the endorsements that film stars, athletes, and other celebrities make in advertisements of various products. Madison Avenue is well aware that fame, by itself, carries with it an aura of authority, and they use this mystique of the famous to sell us stockings or mufflers, whiskey or razor blades. Here again, the fallacy lies in the fact that the mere endorsement—which may not even represent the true personal opinion of the celebrity about the product in question—is just *irrelevant* to questions about the quality of the stockings or razor blades so endorsed.

Another fallacious variety of appeals to authority relies on taking the authority out of her field. Thus someone might attempt to argue in support of Zionism by pointing out that Albert Einstein was a Zionist. This argument rests on the implied warrant that Einstein's position on political matters can be taken seriously, just because he was an acknowledged expert on physics—a warrant that itself needs to be critically examined. It could well be asked whether an eminent scientist is any more of an authority on political matters than a baseball player is an authority on the merits of auto mufflers. (Our final answer may be "Yes, he is!"; but at any rate the question must be asked.)

This, of course, is not to suggest that *all* references to authority are irrelevant to the justification of claims and the resolution of debates. On the contrary, the increasing specialization of all our knowledge obliges lay people to seek the opinions of specialists having expert knowledge in particular fields for the information needed in the resolution of disputes. So the opinion of, say, Einstein on a question in physics might well be definitive. It is only when the authoritative character of his opinion is generalized in an unwarranted manner—when his expertness in physics is assumed to rub off onto all his opinions—that *fallacy* begins.

Similarly, appeals to authority become fallacious only when expert opinion is invoked in an argument precisely to stifle further inquiry rather than to illuminate the issue in question. Even in those cases where the appeal to authority may be in order, we should be prepared to justify our particular choice of experts. (Why choose Albert Einstein rather than Nils Bohr?) This will involve making explicit just who our chosen authority is and what his or her status actually is in the field concerned.

The argument against the person

The argument against the person is the fallacy of rejecting the claims a person advances simply on the basis of derogatory facts (real or alleged) about the person making the claim. Such a procedure takes for granted that the substance or content of a *claim* is essentially connected with the character or situation of the *claimant*. The most blatant forms of this fallacy reduce to nothing better than name calling—and it is an unfortunate fact that we are all of us apt to take such tactics seriously when we are on the opposite side of an argument from the claimant in question.

Suppose, for instance, that the point at issue is the Carter administration's advocacy of human rights in the Soviet Union. Some people will challenge this policy on the grounds that its advocates within the administration were either stupid or hypocritical. Yet even if that were clearly the case, would that really discredit the policy itself? Evidently, arguing against the person in this kind of way can serve as a powerful method of distracting attention from—and so evading—a thorny issue.

There are, however, more subtle variations on the same theme. Another way of arguing against the person rather than against his or her claim, for instance, is sometimes referred to as attributing *"guilt by association."* Here we try to refute a claim by associating the claimant with a discredited *group* of persons; if the claimant is a Red, say, then he or she cannot be trusted to tell the truth. Smith's claim that unemployment is a graver problem than inflation, for example, may be countered on the grounds that Smith is a Communist. The presumed warrant is that the opinions of Communists on such matters are *always* biased. Furthermore it is presumed that this generalization is *obviously* true. This is where the difficulty begins. Just because someone is a Communist—or, for that matter, a Jew or an ex-convict or a redneck, an intellectual or a liberal or a woman—does not *by itself* imply that what the person says about any issue is false, unjustified, or gravely biased. Even the most misguided of people occasionally put forward true claims—if only by accident!

A third type of argument against the person assumes that all members of any group are interchangeable, so that there will be no significant difference between individuals within the group. Further, it is assumed that by the very nature of the group, anyone who belongs to it simply cannot—with all the good-will in the world—treat the given question objectively.

Thus it may be argued that a certain historian's interpretation of Luther is incorrect merely by virtue of the fact that the historian happens to be a Roman Catholic. This argument assumes that Roman Catholics are incapable of viewing the Protestant Reformation (more specifically, Luther) without bias. The person whose views are being argued against is said to "have a blind spot": something about his social or economic, ethnic or religious backround disqualifies him from seeing the given subject objectively.

This may as a matter of fact sometimes be the case. But we should be aware that it does not have to be so. It is an open question whether any individual will or will not be able to view any subject disinterestedly. Until they are supported by relevant evidence about the individual concerned, charges of bias such as these amount to no more than accusations of guilt by association.

The argument from ignorance

The argument from ignorance is a fallacy that we are apt to commit when we erroneously reason from opposites—or, to be more precise, when we erroneously argue that a claim is justified simply because its opposite cannot be proved.

The classic illustration of such an appeal to ignorance is that of an atheist who claims that God does not exist simply on the grounds that no one has ever proved beyond doubt that He does exist. Granted, the fact that no one has ever proved the existence of God beyond doubt may well seem to lessen the probability that there is a God. But that is not a sufficient basis for asserting that the issue is resolved against God's existence, once and for all. To put it simply, *on the basis only of what has* not *been proved about something, we cannot certainly infer* anything at all.

A similar appeal to ignorance underlies many people's credulity toward astrology:

- c: The stars seem to hold the key to our destiny.
- G: No one has ever demonstrated conclusively that the stars do *not* hold the key to our destiny.
- w: When a hypothesis has not been conclusively disproved, that lack of proof by itself can be taken as *evidence for* the hypothesis.

To provide backing for such a warrant, we should have to argue that *lack of proof* is itself a kind of evidence, and this would trivialize the concept of *evidence* beyond recognition. If that were true, we would no longer need to establish any substantive connections between grounds and claims—which is still the primary question at issue in any area of rational thought and investigation.

(Notice that this assertion is *not* in contradiction with what we said in Chapter 11 about standing presumptions, for example, the presumption of innocence in a criminal trial under Anglo-American jurisprudence. There the standing presumption is justified by specific *functional* considerations. It is not just a general license to think as we please in the absence of *contrary* evidence.)

The appeal to the people

The appeal to the people refers to fallacious attempts to justify a claim on the basis of its supposed popularity. The fact that many members of a given group hold some belief is offered as evidence that this belief is true. Class or national, religious or professional identity is substituted for the evidence that would be genuinely relevant to the truth of the claim.

Such fallacies are committed by political propagandists, for example, when they endeavor to win support for a policy of heavy taxation by reminding us that *real* Americans have always possessed enough pioneer spirit to withstand belt tightening. (Think of the sacrifices that the heroes of the Revolution made in order to free the country from British tyranny, and so on.) Hitler's propaganda machine continually made use of such arguments, disarming opposition by calling on "true Germans" to fall in line behind his efforts to redeem the fatherland from its disgrace at the ignoble hands of international Jewry, and so on.

In democratic societies the fallacy of the appeal to the people can take the form of confusing popular opinions with constitutionally guaranteed freedoms. It is not mere popularity but the choice of the people as expressed in the form of a vote which makes the will of the people binding. Even then, John Stuart Mill, one of democracy's foremost defenders, warned against the possibility of the sentiments of the majority creating a "tyranny of the majority" which might obliterate minority rights. Protection of certain basic rights such as those guaranteed by the first ten amendments to our constitution for all people, including nonconformist minorities, is of the very essence of democracy. It is only the pseudo-democrat who converts the predominant popular feeling into the ultimate court of appeal. We do not have to approve of homosexuality to defend the constitutional rights of homosexuals. Popular disapproval of homosexuality can never justify abrogation of the constitutional rights of this or any other minority. To argue that it would is to commit the fallacy of the appeal to the people. Similarly, it is only the pseudo-conservative who simply bases reasoning on an uncritical acceptance of the status quo. This is because the status quo does not have to represent traditional wisdom. Indeed, it is possible for the status quo to be the result of ignoring tradition. Unfortunately this can become confusing because it is possible to ignore tradition in the name of tradition. To do this is to commit the fallacy of the appeal to authority. But these are not the only fallacious appeals to popular sentiment. Thus, appeals to tradition, like appeals to authority, can function rationally as well as irrationally. The authority of genuine traditions can indeed be a legitimate source of grounds for justifying claims. However, tradition can be appealed to in such a way as to preclude rational discussion of a topic. It is these latter unquestioning appeals to tradition that are fallacious.

Advertisers use a similar tactic when they appeal to consumers to buy products by associating them with an image of "the ideal American." Television commercials for breakfast cereals present a blissful family scene; the implication is that your family will become like this one—happy, bright, respected, admired—when you switch to their brand of cereal. Others play on our conformity or on our snobbishness instead of giving us real information about the quality of the product. The implied warrant encourages us to trust the product (or belief) in question, not on account of any demonstrated merits but simply because other people supposedly do so.

The appeal to compassion

The appeal to compassion is the traditional name for a fallacious "sob story." Sob stories are not necessarily fallacious. They become so only when they are used to obscure an issue.

The appeal to compassion is an argument that plays upon our feeling of human sympathy in situations where we are required to make rational decisions. Defense lawyers in criminal cases will often resort to this tactic, if not to convince the jury that their clients are innocent, at least to lessen their sentences. Thus, in defending a young car thief, a lawyer may underline the facts that her client came from a home where he was insecure and continually lonely; that his parents abused him, and he ran away from home to avoid this; that he fell prey to the influence of hardened criminals, who were the first persons to treat him with any appearance of kindness—and ask the court to take all the facts into consideration before pronouncing too heavy a sentence.

This argument can be schematized as follows:

C: This young man should not be sentenced according to the full severity of the law.
G: He has had a miserable childhood.

Implicit in this argument is a warrant:

W: When we are deeply moved by the early sufferings of a young car thief, we should let those emotions be our guide in determining the appropriate punishment.

Formulated as a general rule, this warrant appears somewhat ludicrous. Certainly it would be hard to provide adequate backing for such a warrant having anything to do with the facts of the case, that is, how many cars were stolen, under what circumstances, and so on.

Can any sensible person ever fall for such tactics? According to some reports, just such considerations led President Ford to issue his controversial pardon of Richard Nixon. As the story goes, Ford was told that Nixon was in such bad physical and psychological shape that he might commit suicide within months of resigning the presidency. Yet did these considerations have anything whatsoever to do with Nixon's guilt or innocence in the Watergate affair or the subsequent cover-up? Or would it be correct to conclude that in pardoning his predecessor, President Ford was distracted by the appeal to compassion from paying attention to the questions really at issue?

The appeal to force

Traditionally, an appeal to force is included among the fallacies of unwarranted assumption. Strictly speaking, however, such an argument is hardly a *fallacy* at all. It leads to compliance rather than conviction in a hearer, and the speaker who resorts to such arguments is scarcely self-deceived.

Appeals to force are simply threats, *which imply that the individual will be harmed in some way unless she does or says (or refrains from saying or doing) whatever the assertor requires by way of agreeing with his claim.* The principle—or warrant—by which such an argument is enforced is the notion that "might makes right," that is, that those who have strength cannot only make and enforce claims but can also justify them.

The threats need not, of course, be physical; they can be moral or psychological. The preacher who promises us damnation if we do not stop sinning *threatens* us as surely as the criminal who promises us that our family will be injured if we testify about his misdeeds in a court of law. There is no doubt that such "arguments" are persuasive, but they only persuade us to act or speak in the required way *against our wills and personal convictions.* We do not come away from such threats convinced that just because we comply with these demands they are *justified.* We come away intimidated rather than deceived.

At the same time, there are certain perfectly sound "arguments of expediency" that people use when they resort to threats. Consider the argument in Figure 16–5. The implied warrant is shown in Figure 16–6. For this warrant, there is all too much backing available in the form of knowledge about the sufferings of those who are old and sick, poor and dependent on charity.

As every scriptwriter knows, those who threaten force often in fact produce mock warrants sounding just like the one in Figure 16–7 as added "persuasion" to enforce their threats. But in this case, a new kind of circularity is introduced into the argument, for the only backing available in the case of an appeal to force

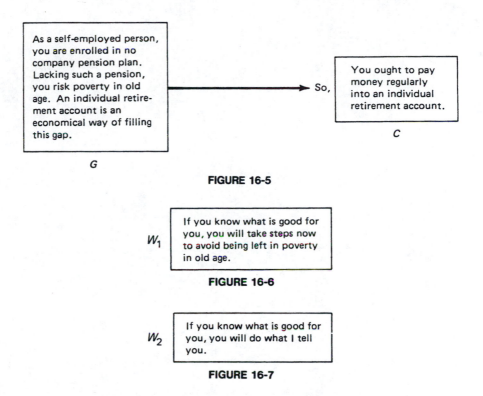

As a self-employed person, you are enrolled in no company pension plan. Lacking such a pension, you risk poverty in old age. An individual retirement account is an economical way of filling this gap.

G

So,

You ought to pay money regularly into an individual retirement account.

C

FIGURE 16-5

W_1

If you know what is good for you, you will take steps now to avoid being left in poverty in old age.

FIGURE 16-6

W_2

If you know what is good for you, you will do what I tell you.

FIGURE 16-7

is the very threat that we started from. All that is produced as "justifying" you in accepting the assertor's original claim is a second-order threat, namely, that if you do not agree, the original threat will be carried out.

In this respect, no doubt, a hellfire sermon differs from a straightforward criminal assault; where both preacher and congregation are convinced believers in hell and damnation, the prospect of eternal punishment after death can provide as powerful a "reason" for virtue in this life as the prospect of poverty in old age can provide for regular saving during your working years. The question that remains in this case has to do with the solidity of the *backing* for the associated "warrant" (see Figure 16–8).

W_3

If you know what is good for you, you will take steps now to avoid eternal punishment by hellfire.

FIGURE 16-8

The list of fallacies of relevance which we have presented to this point makes no claim to being exhaustive. These are the kinds of arguments that have been traditionally recognized as presenting irrelevant grounding. The careful student is bound to discover many more.

17

Fallacies resulting from defective grounds

It is possible that the grounds offered in support of a given claim can be of the right sort but nevertheless can be inadequate for establishing the specific claim in question. These fallacies are called *fallacies of defective grounds*. In this chapter we shall consider three types of arguments in which the reasons offered for accepting an assertion are of the relevant type but remain less than adequate to the task of establishing that assertion.

Hasty generalization

The name that students of reasoning give to the everyday phenomenon of "jumping to conclusions" is *fallacies of hasty generalization. We commit fallacies of hasty generalization when we:*

1. *Draw a general conclusion from* too few *specific instances,* for example, basing the general statement "All Audis are lemons" on a few individual reports from friends who have happened to have trouble with their own Audis.

or, alternatively, when we:

2. *Draw a general conclusion from* untypical *examples,* for example, concluding that we do not care for Woody Allen movies (which are nor-

mally comedies) on the basis of our reaction to *The Front* (one of the rare serious films in which Allen acted).

Thus we jump to conclusions when we *either* fail to take note of a sufficiently large sample of cases *or else* select as our grounds some individual case that is atypical of the class in question.

Inadequate samples. We sometimes encounter this kind of hasty generalization in arguments about racial or national stereotypes. Someone may argue, for example, that Poles are unintelligent on the grounds that the thirty-odd Poles he has worked with over the years have all appeared to him to be on the dull side. If we ask such a person to spell out the warrant (W) he employs and then to provide appropriate backing (B) for it, the irrationality of his position quickly becomes obvious. His argument will be something like that in Figure 17–1:

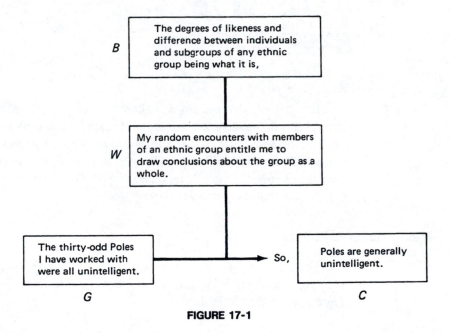

FIGURE 17-1

Once we attempt to support the warrant implicitly appealed to in such an argument, the difficulties involved in such generalizations are evident. The warrant on which our hypothetical bigot relies—"My thirty random encounters with members of this ethnic group entitled me to form judgments about the group as a whole"—is open to a devastating rebuttal, for both the total number of Polish-Americans in the U.S. population and variety of individuals and subgroups among them clearly establish the inadequacy of the original sample of thirty. Though the relevance of the data to the claim being made is beyond question, there simply isn't enough data available for making the sweeping claim that is alleged to follow from the data.

Atypical examples   The other kind of fallacy of hasty generalization occurs when we take as our evidence examples that are unrepresentative of the given phenomenon and base a general conclusion upon that atypical evidence.

Thus we cannot draw any general conclusions about Woody Allen's films on the basis of *The Front,* in the way that we could perhaps do on the basis of *Everything You Always Wanted to Know About Sex* or *Annie Hall.* (The latter two movies are more "typical" than the first). Someone who had seen only *The Front* might argue, for instance:

> C: People make too much fuss about Woody Allen's film performances.

And he might support this claim by saying

> G: In *The Front,* Woody Allen played a role that could be clearly classified neither as straight nor as comic. The result was merely confusing and gave no evidence of Allen's competence as an actor.

In this case, the step from *G* to *C* evidently rests on an assumed warrant (see Figure 17–2).

> W: *The Front* can be taken as typical of the films in which Woody Allen has acted.

The presumed conclusion of this argument, is, of course, immediately subject to the objection:

> R: Neither was *The Front* directed by Allen, nor was it a comedy like most of his films, nor was it even particularly well directed. In short, his performance in *The Front* is in no way typical of his movie performances.

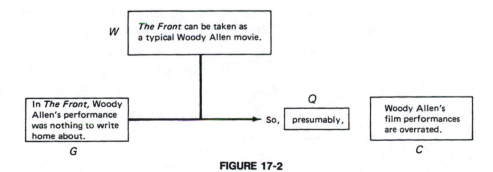

FIGURE 17-2

This rebuttal (*R*) introduces evidence that clearly invalidates appeals to *The Front* as irrelevant to any discussion of Woody Allen's *general* merits as a movie actor.

Taking these two kinds of hasty generalizations together, we can already see something about *what makes fallacies fallacious*. This is that the most insidiously deceptive things about unsound arguments spring from their *abbreviation,* that is, from the omission of indispensable elements. If we are forced to spell out the warrants on which our arguments rely and the backing on which those warrants depend, it will usually become clear at once when our grounds are based on *too small* a sample of cases or on examples that are quite *untypical*.

Accident

The *fallacy of accident occurs when someone bases an argument on a rule that is valid* in general *but fails to consider whether the case in question may not fall under one of the* exceptions *to that rule.* The person who commits the fallacy of accident fails to acknowledge that some particular aspect of the present situation makes the general rule inapplicable to it. For example, a student working in a college library might want to charge a professor from another university a fee for use of library facilities on the grounds that the professor is not a member of the college community. The student is thereby appealing to the general rule that anyone who is not a member of the college community must pay such a fee. However, upon appealing to the head librarian it could happen that the normal rule covering such situations was waived in the case of scholars visiting the area for the specific purpose of utilizing the library holdings for a short period of time, provided that the scholar's residence was more than one hundred miles from the library. Given these exceptional circumstances, normal procedure did not obtain. The general rule admitted of exceptions. Unaware of this, the student who first denied the visiting professor access to the library's facilities committed the fallacy of accident.

Accident, then, is the converse fallacy of hasty generalization. In the fallacy of hasty generalization our grounds are defective in that they are quantitatively insufficient or so atypical to warrant inferring the alleged claim from them. In fallacies of accident, our grounds are defective in that they fail to take into account some specific circumstance in a particular case which renders a general rule inapplicable.

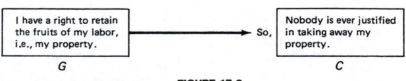

FIGURE 17-3

One frequent illustration of this fallacy is to be seen in the way in which some people argue about their right to their own property, as though property rights were absolute and could never be suspended under any circumstances (see Figure 17–3).

Here the all-important warrant relied on is seen in Figure 17–4.

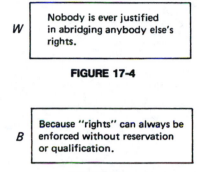

W | Nobody is ever justified in abridging anybody else's rights.

FIGURE 17-4

B | Because "rights" can always be enforced without reservation or qualification.

FIGURE 17-5

And this in turn requires for its backing the statement in Figure 17–5, which is plainly untrue.

Two things need to be noted here:

1. The implicit warrant, *W,* involves the specific moral and legal term *rights* and uses it in a way that runs counter to common usage and experience.
2. This departure from common usage could be defended only by the elaboration of a full-scale, absolutist "theory of rights."

The difficulty that arises in this case springs from the arguer's refusal to recognize that there can be any but universal rules—from the assumption that where there are *rules,* there can be no *exceptions:*

> Imagine someone's arguing that fire engines and funeral processions ought not to go through stop signs without stopping, because there is a rule that all vehicles must come to a full stop at all such intersections.

These arguments illustrate how quickly and easily we may find ourselves moving, in the course of argumentation, *from* the familiar and concrete *to* the abstract and general.

Further, the fallacy of accident, like the fallacy of hasty generalization, illustrates how easily the fallaciousness of bad reasoning can be detected once we get into the habits of asking for the rule or warrant on which the argument relies and looking for the justification or backing by which that warrant is supported.

18

Fallacies of unwarranted assumption

Fallacies of unwarranted assumption occur when there is a presumption that it is possible to make the move from grounds to conclusion on the basis of a warrant shared by most or all members of the community when in fact the warrant in question is not commonly accepted. The fallaciousness of such a move often derives from the fact that the warrant concerning which consensus is assumed is not made explicit in the argument. When the warrant is made explicit it usually becomes clear that the principle upon which the argument rests is dubious even though it did not originally appear to be.

Complex question

Fallacies of complex question occur when we are asked to respond to what is in actuality two questions as if they were a single issue. For example, someone might ask, "Have you ceased to abuse drugs?" Like all complex questions, this question is "loaded" in that it is impossible to answer it without committing yourself to something that incriminates you. In this case, whether you answer *yes* or *no,* you end up admitting that you abuse drugs. Thus, the person who asks you such a question is putting words in your mouth. The classic example of this fallacy is the old chestnut, "Have you stopped beating your wife?" However, the fallacy of complex question may take other forms. One of the most widely discussed problems in twentieth-century Anglo-Saxon philosophy was generated over the complex question "Is the present King of France bald?" Since there was no King of France at the time the question was posed, an answer of *yes* or *no* was unacceptable because it committed the respondent to the existence, real or imaginary, of such a monarch. The first step to solving the problem is to recognize that it is in fact not one but two separate questions for which a single answer is inappropriate. Politicians often pose complex questions to their constituents, with a view to suggesting the answers to the questions they pose to them beforehand. For example, a candidate for office might have asked whether we are committed to further deterioration of the American family by supporting the Equal Rights Amendment (ERA). This question suggests fallaciously that it is impossible to be in favor of equal rights for women without being at the same time in favor of a radical transformation of family life that would threaten traditional values. Here we have as many as three distinct issues suggested under a single question.

> It is one thing whether or not I favor equal rights; another whether or not I favor a radical transformation of the family; a third whether such a radical transformation is necessarily an evil thing.

There are thus several ways in which this question can be answered. It is possible to be pro-ERA and pro-family, but it is equally possible to be pro-ERA and stand in opposition to the values embodied in the traditional family structure. Further, it is possible to advocate a radical change in the family structure without assuming that the evils it may embody are the results of a plot to keep women subjugated. Similarly, it is possible to believe that there are evils in the family structure without being committed to the ERA as the solution to our problems relating to family life.

The fallacy of complex question tends to reflect a simplistic approach to complex problems. In a desire to drive to the heart of the matter, for example, someone may dismiss abruptly all subtle considerations and claim a question to be one of friend or enemy, guilt or innocence, right or wrong. This behavior is also frequently associated with dogmatism: there can be no middle ground; there can be no extenuating circumstances. Sometimes the nature of the decision may actually call for such a simplistic consideration: when a tornado is almost upon you, there is no room for discussing subtle alternatives. However, few of the questions facing us will benefit from such a dogmatic approach that makes unwarranted assumptions and does not allow the examination of slight shadings of difference. Most reasoning will improve as questions are broken down into single-issue consideration and broad assumptions are brought under critical scrutiny.

False cause

The fallacy of false cause occurs:

1. *When we confuse temporal succession with causal sequence,* that is, when we take one event to be the cause of another simply because the one event *happened before* the other.
2. *When we mistakenly take one event to be the cause of another,* that is,

when we assert that the one event is the cause of the other and are simply *wrong*.

There are two ways of misusing the topic *cause* in argumentation, which we will consider in turn.

Temporal succession and causation.   To illustrate the first type of fallacy of false cause, suppose that a customer appears at an all-night lunchroom late on a Saturday morning and complains that a sandwich he ate there in the early hours made him nauseous at 5 A.M. The implicit argument in this case is as follows:

C: Your sandwich made me nauseous at 5 A.M.
G: Your sandwich was the last thing I ate before going to bed last night.
W: The last thing that I ate was presumably the cause of my nausea.

The manager of the lunchroom—if he knows his customer—may ask in reply whether by any chance the customer had drunk anything alcoholic before eating the sandwich. The customer replies that he had only a dozen or so cans of beer, to which the lunchroom manager is entitled to respond:

"Did it never occur to you that the beer might have made you nauseous?"

He thereby questions the backing for the customer's warrant.

The source of the customer's nausea must be determined by a consideration of the *normal causes* of such disorders, that is, the kinds of thing that bring them on in the normal course of events. It is always possible that an overrich or stale sandwich was the culprit; we know enough about the workings of the stomach and the effects of spicy food and bacteria upon those processes to recognize that an ill-timed sandwich could bring on a stomach disorder. Even so, it could not be identified as the cause simply because it was the last thing the customer ate before the sickness occurred. Knowing what we do about the effects of beer and observing that nobody else had been made ill by the lunchroom food last night, we might find it safer to conclude that the beer had got to him.

The central point here is that *causality* normally involves more than *temporal succession* alone. The answers to questions about causes always rest on assumptions about general explanatory mechanisms and processes, for example, about how beer decomposes into stomach acid. It is these general assumptions that allow us to establish substantive connections between the two events in question. The grounds, in short, must be *causally relevant* to the claim.

To cite another example, politicians often take credit for economic upswings that take place *after* their party gets into office without indicating what it was about their policies that brought about this improvement. The risk of committing the fallacy of false cause should warn us not to make the simpleminded leap to the conclusion that the later event (the upswing) was *brought about by* the earlier event (the change of administration) merely because it came after it. In this case, decisions taken in quite another part of the world may have been chiefly responsible for the current prosperity here in ways that can be analyzed adequately only in economic, rather than political, terms. Alternatively, the true cause of the improvement may be that the sound (but unpopular) policies of the previous administration are now bearing fruit at last!

Such examples as these indicate the complexities surrounding causal claims and explanations, in both the natural and the social sciences. There is, indeed, a mountain of literature about causality in the philosophy of science that attests to the manifold difficulties that surround the concept.

Mistaken cause.   Our second type of false-cause fallacy occurs when we are simply mistaken *about a given phenomenon.* The history of science abounds with such false attributions of causality; for example, the notion that lower animals are generated spontaneously in rotting matter, accepted by thinkers as different as Albertus Magnus and Francis Bacon.

Not all false attributions of causality need, of course, be labeled as fallacies. In the time of Albertus Magnus, for instance, no alternative explanation was available to account for the appearance of maggots in rotten meat. So it would be as harsh to fault Albert the Great for his false belief in this case as it would be to fault medieval astronomers for accepting Ptolemaic astronomy, with its Earth-centered picture of the universe. We may properly speak of the fallacy of false cause only when the arguer is himself responsible for his own lack of information on the given subject.

Statistical correlations often serve as the basis for fallacious causal reasoning of this second type. Consider the example in Figure 18–1.

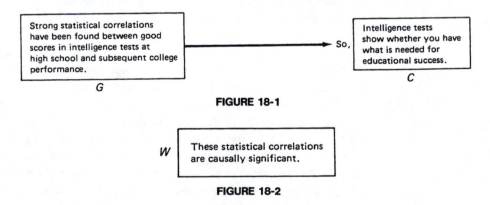

FIGURE 18-1

FIGURE 18-2

This argument relies on the implicit warrant in Figure 18–2. And we can hardly accept this warrant without further, more detailed investigation of *this particular case.*

Clearly, statistical reasoning is afflicted by all sorts of pitfalls. It might, for example, prove possible to correlate success in college with a student's choice of breakfast cereal or even with the baby food that her mother fed her—which would delight the cereal and baby food producers! But we would view any such discovery with serious suspicion so long as it was based on statistical evidence *alone*. Evidently the *causal relevance* of statistical considerations has to be established by other arguments just as much as the causal relevance of temporal succession.

There is, in any case, a further difficulty. For may not "success in high school intelligence tests" itself be, in part, a *cause* of "success in higher education"? What, for instance, if those who do well on these tests are preferred by institutions of higher learning *just because* they do well on those tests? In that case, the statistical correlations themselves may not be measuring intelligence so much as providing a justification for preserving the existing structure—and biases—of our institutions. In that case, the argument would no longer illustrate the fallacy of false cause; rather, we would now be faced by a "self-fulfilling prophecy."

We must be particularly cautious in dealing with claims based solely upon statistical evidence, not because "probability" has no place in reasoning but because so many different *kinds* of correlations are present in any given situation—only one of which might claim to be the one and only cause. Statistical correlations have the same sort of relation to causal assertions that a series of points on a graph have to the curve a scientist draws through them. Many different curves may be used to link the points together, and we must have good outside reasons for choosing one rather than another.

A final note of warning: the task of assigning causes to given events is rarely simple and straightforward. So the real danger behind the fallacy of false cause is the danger of *oversimplification*. In ordinary discourse, we often do not stop to articulate our warrants, let alone to scrutinize our backing and modal qualifiers. By paying closer attention to these other elements, we can help to avoid the fallacy altogether or else reformulate our arguments in such a way that it is easy to recognize and guard against.

False analogy

Hardly any type of argument exposes us to the risk of fallacy more often than analogy. Analogies are comparisons that enrich our language and have the power to enlighten our understanding—when they are appropriate and successful. Sometimes they work on us through similes or metaphors. Think of likening the lion to a king in the phrase "king of beasts," or the state to a ship in the phrase "the ship of state," or the German World War II commander Field Marshal Erwin Rommel to a fox in the nickname "The Desert Fox."

All these comparisons are worth making in certain contexts. Yet there are limits to the value of any such comparisons. All analogies limp at some point or other; *so when we make a comparison that seems appropriate but is not, we end up with a false analogy.*

It will be helpful to set an example of successful reasoning by analogy alongside a false analogy for purposes of contrast. In arriving at his celebrated theory of evolution by natural selection, Charles Darwin made successful use of an analogy to solve his problem.

Darwin argues:

> c: Environment must act upon animal populations selectively, in a way that explains why only the best-adapted variants within any species are able to survive.
>
> G: Domestic breeders succeed in producing improved strains of domestic animals—for example, stronger or bigger ones—by controlling the breeding of their animals and selecting out preferred strains.

His assumption was

> w: Domestic animals change because farmers select out their breeding stock for desired characteristics, and presumably something similar accounts for the variation in natural species. Nature, or the environment, must "select" certain members of the species in preference to others, and this selection improves the adaptation of the species to the environment.

Here Darwin's argument is compressed to the point of caricature. Indeed all 500 pages of the *Origin of Species* were needed in order to spell out—that is, provide backing for—and defend his analogy between natural and domestic selection. The point is that Darwin succeeded in explaining vexing problems about the historical appearance of new species by drawing upon analogies that were part of the folk wisdom of his day. In this case, the appeal to analogy was successful; the points of significant similarity far outweighed the differences.

By contrast, the classic example of *false* analogy comes from political theory; that is, the likening of the state to an *organism*. This "organic" analogy has been widely relied on to support the claim that in a truly healthy state, the individual's interests must be completely subordinated to those of the state. (Naturally enough, the organic theory has been a favorite among totalitarian rulers.) It can be set out schematically as follows:

> c: Individual interests are subordinate to those of the state.

because

> G: Cells, organs, and limbs are subordinate to the entire organism; so, if a limb becomes gangrenous, we simply amputate it.

The presumption is that

> w: The individual's relationship to the state is *exactly* parallel to the relationship of limbs, organs, or cells to the whole organism.

Although the grounds are clearly true in this case, the warrant is only partly accurate. Certainly, the state resembles an organized living thing *in certain respects;* for example, both of them existed before and continue to exist after their constituent parts. However, the separate parts of an organism cannot survive for long independently of the entire organism (think of a human kidney existing apart from a human body) in the way that individual human beings can exist without a state (think of Robinson Crusoe). And it is those individuals themselves who conceive of, claim, and defend the "interests" of the state as much as they do their own.

So although state and organism are similar in *certain* respects, it remains to be shown that they are similar in *all significant and relevant* respects. For instance, my kidney cannot choose whether to obey or to disobey me in the way that I myself can choose whether to obey or disobey some official of the state. Although there may indeed be points of similarity between the state and an organized living body, these are not enough, by themselves, to clarify the most significant aspects of the state, and they are certainly not enough to justify subordinating human individuals to the state.

In short, just because two things are comparable in certain respects, it can by no means be assumed that they are comparable in any other respects. That further similarity must be established independently before argument from analogy can be secure.

This is not to say that *all* analogical reasoning is fallacious. On the contrary, such scientific phrases as "electric *current*" and "natural *selection*" have won acceptance just because of the successful analogies (with water flow and domestication) on which they rested. But although analogy can be an indispensable instrument of discovery in the understanding of the world around us, reasoning from analogy is nonetheless fraught with difficulties and pitfalls. It is an instrument that we must use with great care and circumspection—to *suggest* warrants whose adequacy, relevance, and backing we must take care to scrutinize later.

Poisoning the wells

In the course of practical argumentation, we are sometimes tempted to go overboard in our efforts to make a conclusion ironclad. At first glance, this may seem innocent enough; as always, it depends on how we set about achieving this result. For example; we may be tempted to put forward a claim against which *no evidence whatsoever* can be brought and use this argument to reinforce another, prior claim. This procedure commits the fallacy of poisoning the wells.

Nearly all social and psychological cure-alls—dianetics, orgonomy, EST, or whatever—rely on warrants that are accepted unquestioningly. Those who challenge their claims are dismissed as being in bad faith; they are not merely failing to "see the point" of the main claim, they are also failing to see that any evidence that appears to run contrary to the claim actually confirms the view when reinterpreted as the claim requires. All evidence is in this way reinterpreted so as to confirm the theory. Simpleminded believers in all kinds of faiths—psychotherapeutic, religious, and political alike—often fall into this trap.

For instance, the Fundamentalist may claim (*C*) that only the saved can act morally. What does he then do when confronted with an apparent counterinstance, for example, the local atheist who is also a pillar of the community? In reply, the Fundamentalist may insist that the atheist only *seems* to be a pillar of the community—only a sinner could fail to see that atheism renders actions that appear on the surface to be beneficial *evil*. Presumably, by giving the atheist a good standing in the community, such "good deeds" undermine the word of God and so "do more harm than good" in the Fundamentalist's eyes.

The point is not just that such a Fundamentalist questions the morality of anyone who disagrees with her views—she does so by committing the fallacy of arguing against the person. In addition, she reinterprets any factual evidence against her central contention in such a way as to turn it into further corroboration of her beliefs. This fallacy is, of course, the common property of all "true believers," including uncritical supporters of militant atheism, communism, Freud, and health food. They are committed to their positions in ways that require them to *explain away* absolutely everything that might justify exceptions or qualifications. When they cannot do this conveniently, they must fit the contrary evidence into their scheme of things by reinterpreting it. Their warrants are never restricted or qualified, so they can never admit the slightest exception or limitation on their views.

The fallacy of poisoning the wells is another one that involves misusing warrants. Effectively, *to commit this fallacy means refusing to qualify or restrict a warrant in the face of evidence that should oblige us to do so*. The arguer who perpetrates this fallacy simply refuses to consider data that do not conform to his general claims, and he turns counterexamples against his questioners by using them as evidence of bad faith or delusion on the questioner's part.

A NOTE ON COMMON SENSE

Fallacies of unwarranted assumption (and also fallacies of irrelevant grounds) often arise because people assume that a given warrant is part of common sense. However, common sense is an intricate concept that requires clarification. In the seventeenth century René Descartes, the founder of modern philosophy, asserted that of all things common sense was the most evenly distributed. He based this claim on the evidence that nobody wants more common sense than he or she already possesses. This view, however, presumes that people are normally right when they say things about themselves. It may well be true that no one wants more common sense than he or she possesses, but it is possible to be mistaken about such things, in that one may lack self-awareness. Unfortunately, those among us who are lacking in common sense are usually the last ones to recognize that fact.

In a similar vein, common sense is a *familiar* notion which nobody would think that they misunderstood even if they in fact did misunderstand it. Actually, the procedures and conventions that constitute common sense (i.e., the shared experiences of the members of a social group) are devilishly complex and elusive when we attempt to analyze them. In short, we often assume that a particular claim rests upon common sense when it does not. For example, what is obviously a matter of common sense for one person is utterly denied by the common sense of another person. An industrialist or financier will consider maximizing profits a matter of common sense and thus will want to eliminate social services such as welfare and day care which in his mind have the effect of 'eating up' his profits in taxes. On the other hand, a welfare mother would certainly see the elimination of such programs as obviously disastrous (i.e., as a matter of common sense). This simple example ought to clarify how what is obvious to one person is utterly unacceptable to another as a matter of common sense.

The society in which we live (unlike, for instance, Homeric Greece) is just as faction-ridden as it is coherent. We are apt to be misled by the fact that we use a single term, *society,* to designate a complicated system of cultures and sub-cultures, each with its own values (See the discussion of *reification* in Chapter 19). There are every bit as many contested beliefs as there are shared assumptions in our "society." This very fact ought to put us on guard against simply assuming that everyone shares the generalization that they find crystal clear and compellingly reasonable with other members of their society. Indeed, the individuals who get farthest in politics or business often are precisely those who recognize just how polarized and divided their constituency or market actually is.

19

Fallacies resulting from ambiguities

A cursory glance at the dictionary shows us how many words in common use have more than one meaning. The word *pen,* for instance, may refer to an instrument for writing, to an enclosure for animals, or to a prison. The word *pen* is not, of course, the sort of word that presents serious problems; it is normally clear from the context of any discussion which sense of the word is intended. (It all depends on whether the subject under discussion is writing, animal husbandry, or jails.) But if the discussion turns instead to, say, the role of "private interests" in politics, matters may not be so clear-cut. In this context, the term *interest* may refer to those things that a given group or individual *desires* or alternatively to their *needs*—which may not be the same as their desires or wants. Thus a political argument about "interests" that fails to distinguish between desires and needs at the outset can easily end in chaotic misunderstanding or unproductive digressions.

It is not just individual words but also statements and questions that can be ambiguous and so lead to confusion. One newspaper reporter was supposedly asked to do a feature on Cary Grant for the Sunday supplement. Rereading his draft article, the reporter discovered that he had not included Cary Grant's age. Anxious about his deadline, he hurriedly wired Grant's agent:

"How old Cary Grant?"

The agent responded with a telegram that read:

"Old Cary Grant fine. How you?"

More seriously, it can be important to recognize and be on our guard against the most bothersome types of ambiguity that commonly occur in writing and speech. In what follows, we shall glance at some of the pitfalls that await us if we disregard the subtleties and ambiguities of language.

Equivocation

The fallacy of equivocation occurs when a word or phrase is used inconsistently—that is, in more than one sense within a single argument—with the result that its various senses are confused. Under this general blanket heading are included five more specific kinds of fallacies of ambiguity. They are traditionally referred to as *amphiboly, accent, composition, division, and figure of speech.*

One historical example of the fallacy of equivocation occurs in an argument by which Lorenzo Valla, an Italian Renaissance humanist, attempted to justify free love. His argument was based on the dual meanings of the Latin word *vir*, which means both "man" and "husband." Exploiting the fact that this single word has both these meanings, he claimed that *Every man is a husband* and concluded that marriage is therefore a superfluous institution. His argument was, however, fallacious on grounds of inconsistency: although *vir* can legitimately mean either "man" or "husband" according to context, it cannot consistently mean both in a single passage. You cannot switch from one sense to another in midstream, as it were; that would be no better than perpetrating a pun on the two senses of the word *pitcher*:

> "This team needs a new pitcher. So go and get one from off the shelf in the kitchen!"

We can also commit fallacies of equivocation through failing to note the peculiarities of relative terms like big *and* small. Thus you cannot support the claim (*C*), "This is a small animal," by producing as grounds (*G*) the statement, "This is a small hippopotamus." Such terms refer to different specific qualities when used to modify different nouns. In a slightly more subtle case, just because a man is of ordinary and common appearance, you cannot conclude that he is a man of ordinary and common talent. This would be to equivocate upon the phrase "ordinary and common," which means quite different things when it refers to a person's abilities and when it refers, say, to his mode of dress.

Nor does the fact that Don Carlo Gesualdo wrote great madrigals imply that he was a great man. There are quite different criteria for judging someone to be a "great man" than there are for judging him to be a "great musician." For all his musical talent, Gesualdo was apparently responsible for the deaths of his wife and daughter, and he may actually have killed them in cold blood himself. So theories of aesthetics that make the quality of work of art depend on the character of the artist lay themselves open, among other things, to the fallacy of equivocation.

Amphiboly

One special kind of ambiguity gives rise to the fallacy of amphiboly. *This occurs as a result of faulty grammar: omission of a comma or other punctuation, careless positioning of qualifying phrases or words, and the like.* Instruction manuals, advertisements, and public notices often contain amphibolies.

The *New Yorker* magazine often prints humorous examples of such ambiguities to fill the space at the bottom of columns. The following announcement is one of these:

> Astronomy Club—meets Thursday after school with Mr. Nocella broken in two parts.

Presumably the club was to be broken into two parts, but the grammatical structure of the sentence left it unclear whether it was not Mr. Nocella who would suffer that fate.

On occasion, such ambiguities may be more than a joke. Consider the dilemma facing a lawyer, on discovering the following bequest in a will:

> "I hereby leave $5,000 to my friends John Smith and William Jones."

Supposing that the estate amounts to more than $10,000, the lawyer must decide whether the deceased intended to leave a separate $5,000 to each of the two friends or whether the lump sum of $5,000 was to be divided between them.

Another example of amphiboly may occur in mathematical arguments. Sometimes a problem is inadequately formulated, owing to some syntactical ambiguity. Thus the equation:

$$X = 2 \times 3 + 9$$

is ambiguous as it stands, for lack of parentheses. The calculation may yield "$X = 15$" or "$X = 24$," depending upon where we insert our parentheses, that is, on our syntax. For if we write

$$X = (2 \times 3) + 9, \text{ then } X = 15;$$

Or, alternatively, if we write

$$X = 2 \times (3 + 9), \text{ then } X = 24.$$

From this kind of example, we can see how much difference grammatical slips can make to the soundness of an argument. So although amphiboly is neither the most insidious nor the most frequently encountered kind of fallacy, practice in identifying grammatical ambiguities can help us to pay greater attention to the clarity of our own presentations. Once identified, such fallacies are easily enough eliminated through rewriting.

Accent

The fallacy of accent occurs as a result of misplaced emphasis. As a normal feature of everyday language, emphasis is not in general fallacious or distorting. Once again, it leads us into fallacy only in certain circumstances, when misplaced emphasis leads our understanding of an argument astray.

In spoken arguments, accent can lead to fallacy when our gestures or inflections serve to distort the meaning of what we are saying. Consider the statement:

"He should not have treated his wife that way in public."

Depending on whether we emphasize "he," "his wife," "that way," or "in public," we suggest slightly different meanings. So the written transcript of a public speech or of verbal evidence in court can be very misleading. From different accentuations, differences of meaning arise, and from these differences of meaning comes the possibility of ambiguity.

There are basically two ways in which emphasis may give rise to fallacy in written arguments. These are

1. Taking something out of context.
2. Using italics, boldface, or other techniques to lend a false significance to a statement that is literally true, or vice versa.

When we quote statements from others, for instance, there are all sorts of subtle ways in which the meaning can be altered; for example, by leaving out punctuation or italics or putting them in the wrong place, or alternatively, by omitting parts of the quotations, which can alter the whole sense of the quoted material.

Just as individual words are just about meaningless outside the contexts of the sentences in which they appear, individual sentences can be interpreted with any exactitude only in the larger contexts in which they figure. It may be of crucial importance to know, for example, whether a particular argument was intended for presentation to a group of labor union members or to college students or to a scientific congress. Without this information, we cannot hope to assess it properly, that is, as its author intended it to be taken. Similarly, it is crucial to know whether the author of a passage was being ironical, expository, or analytical and whether his aims were literary, scientific, or moral. Without this information, we shall again be unable to assess the claims he makes.

Consider, for instance, the publisher who issued and titled two books, *A World Without Jews,* by Karl Marx, and *German Existentialism,* by Martin Heidegger. The first of these books contains a number of extremely ironical essays, which Marx actually did write. The latter book consists of some public speeches by Heidegger, as well as a collection of newspaper clippings that associate Heidegger with the Nazi movement. No doubt, Marx's attitude to Jews and Heidegger's relationship to the Nazis are both problematic, but publishing their arguments under titles that they did not choose has the effect of wrenching them completely out of context and inviting a fallacious interpretation from the reader.

Hardly any book is more misquoted than the Bible. We can "prove" just about anything we please from the Bible's passages, which—taken overliterally—seem to state whatever it is we wish to establish. In this way, the most outrageous points can be given a scriptural basis. For example, in order to demonstrate that God does not exist, we need merely turn to Psalm 13. There we find the assertion, "There is no God." Unfortunately the context in which the assertion appears is once again important: the whole sentence reads, "The fool has said in his heart: 'There is no God.'"

A second type of fallacy of accent may be found in many advertisements and newspaper headlines. An ad for a supermarket chain in the food section of the newspaper reads:

FREE CHINA WITH EVERY PURCHASE*

This looks like a good deal until we discover the small print to which the asterisk refers. There the eye-catching phrase in bold print is severely qualified: it turns out that we can obtain one free saucer if we purchase $25.00 worth of food and that only one such bonus will be allowed per family. The rest of the set is then obtainable through the supermarket at $4.95 per item, plus tax.

Many tabloid magazines and newspapers exploit the same type of fallacy. They promise something salacious on the cover but disappoint the prurient reader's curiosity once he buys the periodical and looks inside. For example the cover may carry a picture of Jacqueline Kennedy Onassis, together with the words, "JACKIE'S TRUE LOVE REVEALED." Once we have paid and looked inside, a glance informs us that her "true love" is—her children. Another favorite is the "CANCER CURE" headline, covering a story about the remote possibility of finding a cure for *some* types of cancer *within our lifetimes*.

When such tactics are used in good faith and are not intended to deceive us, they are of course fairly easy to correct. When we reread a draft presentation from a reader's standpoint, we can often recognize for ourselves the necessity of scaling down the boldface, or making up a more modest headline, or adding missing italics, or whatever.

Composition and division

Two other related fallacies of ambiguity are the fallacies of composition and division. These are two sides of the same coin. *Composition occurs when we assert about an entire group something that is true of all its parts. Division occurs when we assert about all the parts of a thing something that is true of the whole.*

If we were to argue that because the constituent cells of the human body are microscopic, the entire body too must be microscopic, that would be to commit the fallacy of composition. Conversely, if we were to argue that because the entire human body can be seen with the naked eye, all the constituent cells that make up the human body must also be visible to the naked eye, that would be to commit the fallacy of division.

Those two arguments are no doubt transparently fallacious, and it is unlikely that anybody would be taken in by them. But consider the following example:

> c: Sodium chloride must be poisonous.
> g: Its two constituents, sodium and chlorine, are both of them deadly poisons.

This argument relies upon the warrant:

> w: What is true of the constituents of a chemical compound is true of the compound.

Plausible though it may seem, a cursory glance at the facts about chemical compounds and their constituents shows that such a warrant is without foundation. (In fact, sodium chloride is simply the chemical name for common salt.) This argument illustrates the fallacy of composition. Conversely, of course, claiming that sodium and chlorine must both be edible on the ground that sodium chloride is edible would commit the fallacy of division.

It is not hard to confuse the fallacies of composition and division (which are fallacies of ambiguity) with the parallel pair, hasty generalization and accident (which are fallacies of unwarranted assumption). A little attention to the subject over which confusion arises in each case can resolve this difficulty. In composition and division, we are discussing *things or groups of things* (the relationship between a whole and its parts or between a set and its members), whereas hasty generalization and accident are *mistaken ways of reasoning about general rules* or warrants and about qualifications and exceptions to such general rules or warrants. The fallacy of hasty generalization occurs when we try to justify a rule on the basis of too few instances. "One swallow does not make a summer." The fallacy of accident occurs when we fail to recognize that rules are liable to exceptions: "Circumstances alter cases." Both kinds of fallacies involved mistaking what is *usually or often true* for what *must always be true*.

The fallacies of composition and division involve no such mistakes. As our last example indicates, the grounds of a fallacious argument may be simply true: the two elementary components of sodium chloride are both of them highly poisonous. We go wrong if we fail to note that when they combine, a real change of chemical properties takes place. So in fallacies of division, we move from *true grounds* to a *false claim*. Figure 19–1 summarizes the difference between the two sets of fallacies.

Fallacies with Deficient Grounds Reasoning fallaciously about *generalizations* and exceptions. Failing to recognize that you cannot always generalize and that rules have exceptions.	Fallacies of Ambiguity Reasoning fallaciously about wholes and parts or vice versa.

Hasty Generalization
The claim must formulate a generalization which is fallacious because either:
  1. too few instances
    or
  2. exceptional rather than typical cases
have been cited in support of the generalization.
 	
Example
  G Students occasionally take open book exams
  C Students ought to be allowed to look at their book in *any* exam.
	Composition
	Inferring that something must be true of the whole of a given object because it is true of all of its parts.
	
	Example
	  G The pieces of this pie are (roughly speaking) triangular.
	  C So the pie itself must be triangular too.

Accident
The claim must infer something about a specific case on the basis of a general rule but it ignores some specific circumstances which make the rule inapplicable.
 	
Example
  G New cars run better than old ones.
  C So my Pinto ought to run better than your twenty-year-old Rolls Royce.
	Division
	Inferring that something *must* be the true of all of the parts simply because it is true of the whole.
	
	Example
	  G The pie is round.
	  C So its pieces must be round.

What is Wrong Here? Either: Insufficient evidence has been assembled to ground the rule you want to formulate Or: some exceptional circumstances prevent you from applying the rule.	*What is Wrong Here?* There is an ambiguity with regard to the way that things are said to be 'true' of parts and wholes and vice versa.
When you suspect either of these occurs, ask: Does the argument go wrong from lack of facts?	When you suspect either of these, ask the following: Is the argument about the relationship between wholes and parts?

FIGURE 19-1

Figure of speech

The fallacy of figure of speech results from taking grammatical or morphological similarities between words as indicative of similarities in meaning. The classic illustration of this fallacy occurs in John Stuart Mill's essay on "Utilitarianism." Mill was discussing what is "desirable": just as *visible* means that an object *can be* seen, and *audible* means that an object *can be* heard, so too (Mill argued) *desirable* means that an object *can be* desired. Actually the latter word normally means that the object in question *ought to be* desired, but Mill chooses to play on its surface similarity with *visible* and *audible*.

To give a more practical illustration of this kind of fallacy, consider the structure of the English word *inflammable*. It is natural enough to mistake the prefix *in* as indicating negation. Just as *ineligible means* "*not* eligible," *inedible* means "*not* edible," and *incontestable* means "*not* contestable," so *inflammable* looks as though it means "*not* flammable." (In French, this is correct: the word *inflammable* in French means the same as *noninflammable* in English. Unfortunately languages are not always consistent on such points.) There are in fact two prefixes in English spelled *in:* one of these is negative, but the second signifies "thoroughly." (The latter form is recognizable in words like *invaluable,* where the prefix serves to *intensify* the meaning of the adjective.) So the English word *inflammable* in fact means "*Highly* flammable."

Another variation on the fallacy of figure of speech occurs if we assume that every noun stands for *a thing or object*. Nouns can represent aggregates (e.g., *army* or *output*) or relationships (e.g., *marriage* and *equality*) and do not refer only to the traditional triad: persons, places, and things. Nouns can also be used metaphorically or to represent abstractions, so we may speak of "the ship of state" or discuss the nature of "legitimate authority." However, we cannot conclude that all these subjects of discourse are the same kinds of things just because they are denoted by the same sorts of words.

A humorous illustration is Gilbert Ryle's imaginary visitor to Oxford University, who visits all the colleges that make up Oxford and asks at the end, "But where is the university?" Other more serious examples involve what is called *reification;* for instance, the prolonged controversy in the history of physics over the concept *force*. For a long time, it remained unclear just what sort of "thing" *force* was, and scientists were at serious cross-purposes because they could not agree on what they should be "looking for" as the *thing* to which the word *force* referred.

Avoiding fallacies of ambiguity

The problem of avoiding ambiguities in argumentation is not one that can be dealt with by any mechanical procedure. Rather, it demands, above all, that we make ourselves aware of the complexities of language. The person with the greatest facility for detecting fallacies ambiguities will, most likely, also be the one who is most attuned to nuances of meaning and usage. This attuning comes largely from familiarity with the manifold means of deploying language which are developed through a careful study of language and literature.

In conclusion, we should once again underline one central point. There is nothing inherently fallacious about ambiguity as such. Not all ambiguities give rise to fallacies. Indeed ambiguity plays some important roles in literature and in life in general. Much that is beautiful, humorous, and even wise can best be expressed in usage that takes advantange of it—think of the poet's use of metaphor, the dramatist's use of puns, or the scientist's use of analogy. Rather than eliminating ambiguity entirely, and so impoverishing language, we need to develop our sensitivity to the ambiguities in language, and so train ourselves to avoid the pitfalls to which ambiguity can lead if its presence in argument goes unrecognized.

20

Summary and exercises on fallacies

Now we must bring together the various points that were made in the preceding discussions on the types of fallacies. It is important to emphasize that the fallacies we have discussed are merely those that have been traditionally discussed by students of reasoning. Indeed, we have not even exhausted that list. This is because our aim was not to present a comprehensive treatise on the subject but to examine the ways that arguments have typically been recognized as going wrong as it related to our model of argumentation. Presenting too many fallacies can have the effect of confusing rather than enlightening. The point of an introduction to the subject is to awaken you to the concept of fallaciousness so that you may develop a facility for recognizing and dealing with the virtually infinite number of ways that arguments can fail to hang together. In the end it is less important that people can classify different unsound arguments on the basis of some preconceived schema than that they develop a talent for detecting shakiness in arguments. This is best accomplished by becoming aware of the junctures at which arguments are likely to go wrong. We have oriented our discussion of fallacies to that end. Thus, mastering the concept of fallaciousness will carry with it the added benefit of enabling you to develop a firmer grasp of how the elements in our model are interdependent.

DETECTING FALLACIES

The business of detecting fallacies should not be conceived of as a "mechanical" process. You should not expect to commit a set of definitions or model fallacies to memory and then "apply" them to identify arguments as fallacious. This is because arguments do not exist in a vacuum. They are always set forth in a specific context, and this has a great deal of bearing upon whether or not they are sound or unsound. What may be a fallacy in one context may not be in another. For example, someone might argue as follows:

> Our nation is a democracy and dedicated to the proposition that all men are created equal. We believe in equality of opportunity for everyone, so our colleges and universities should admit every applicant, regardless of his economic or educational background.

Generally speaking, the argument contains a fallacy of equivocation. Equality as defined in the constitution signifies equality in a court of law; it does not mean equality of opportunity. However, the matter is not as cut and dried as it might first seem, for the meaning of the term *equality* is "essentially contested," that is, it is a legitimate subject of debate. Indeed, in some parts of the country equality has come to be construed as equality of opportunity. In some places this has led to open-admissions policies on precisely the grounds advanced in the argument. Thus there are contexts in which one and the same argument may be construed as sound and still other contexts in which it may be construed as legitimately unsound.

WHAT SHOULD YOU DO WHEN YOU DISCOVER A FALLACY?

Discovering that an argument contains a fallacy is not fatal to the discussion in question. It simply indicates that the perpetrator of the fallacy has to reformulate the fallacious argument in a manner that eliminates the fallacy. We are assuming here that the fallacy has not been committed intentionally to deceive us and that the person who commits it is willing to let go of the fallacious element in the argument. The point is that the perpetrator of a fallacy does not have to withdraw from the discussion in disgrace but simply must restate the argument with modifications that eliminate the fallacy. How are we to do this?

There is no formula for eliminating fallacies, but there are considerations which will help us to do so. First, we can *modify our claim* by making it weaker or more precise (possibly in some instances stronger). Second, we might eliminate a fallacy by *modifying the grounds* upon which the claim rests. We can do this by adding more grounds or more relevant grounds. This may involve additional research on our topic. To do either of these really is to change the scope of the warrant. To accomplish this it will be necessary to take the third step of *articulating the warrant*. It is important to bear in mind that in practice we cannot select grounds to establish our claim in the absence of an implicit warrant. Nor can we really press a claim rationally without some criteria upon which the claim is based (i.e., we cannot say that a Pontiac is a better car than a Gremlin unless we know precisely what we mean by "better"). In order to do any of these things, we must begin by asking ourselves just how much it is worth pressing the argument in its fallacious state. We must ask what hangs upon the argument as it stands which might not fit into a more acceptable argument. Usually the answer to that question will be "not much."

We can illustrate how we might go about reformulating a fallacious argument by referring to the example we used in Chapter 17 to exemplify the fallacy of hasty generalization. Our argument advanced the claim that Poles are unintelligent on the basis of a given individual's encounters with some thirty-odd Poles. When it is pointed out to the person who holds this view that this is an insufficient sample upon which to base so strong a claim, the arguer can alter the claim to fit his data or look for more evidence. Thus, the claim might be weakened to something like, "My experience with Poles *seems* to indicate that they are generally unintelligent." Note that this is a much weaker claim and one which could easily be ignored in a serious discussion of national characteristics (or the stereotyping they usually involve). Another tactic would be to look for more evidence. Of course, more evidence may not always be available, but in many instances research may allow us to "beef up" our grounds to the point of being able to maintain our original claim (though it is unlikely that the proponent of the argument in our example will be able to do so).

A CHECKLIST OF QUESTIONS TO ASK WHEN WE SUSPECT A FALLACY IS PRESENT

1. Are grounds really advanced in support of the claim?
2. Are the grounds advanced in support of the claim *directly* relevant to the substance of the claim?
3. Do the grounds advanced present *enough* evidence to justify the assertion in question or do you need more?
4. Are the presumptions upon which the argument rests justifiable?
5. Are there any ambiguous elements in the argument?

Exercises

I. Some of the following contain fallacies. Discuss the reasoning in each argument and identify the fallacy where one is present.

1. Republicans are traditionally the defenders of the interests of big business, so it makes little sense for a working man to vote for a Republican candidate.
2. The Equal Rights Amendment was endorsed by Senator Proxmire, Senator Kennedy, and former Representative Abzug. It is clearly worthy of universal support on these grounds.

3. All of the great discoveries of mankind were made during the occurrence of sunspots. Our mental powers wax and wane during their eleven-year cycle. The great discoveries of Einstein and Newton were made at the time of the greatest sunspot activity.

4. SMITH: Look, there is Professor Green. Say, Professor Green, I'd like to ask you a question. What do you say to the many cynics who put down your best-selling book?
   PROFESSOR: As Oscar Wilde so wisely remarked, a cynic is someone "who knows the price of everything, and the value of nothing."
   SMITH: Wow!   Heavy.

5. Adolf Hitler recognized the political advantages of a disarmed citizenry. He went around the country proclaiming that the gun had become the criminal's stock in trade and warned of the growing danger from subversives who were stockpiling arms. He claimed in order to restore law and order and make the country safe from subversives it would be necessary to confiscate privately owned firearms. We all know that Hitler had some opposition to this idea but when the program was completed and all the guns were confiscated the opposition seemed just to fade away.

   Argument against gun control in the "Letters to the Editor"
column of the Philadelphia Bulletin

6. ROY: I'm scared, Jill said the devil was under my bed!
   SALLY: How absurd!
   ROY: He's in the closet in my room?
   SALLY: Absolutely ridiculous.
   ROY: He's hiding behind my dresser?
   SALLY: Certainly not.
   ROY: Well then, if the devil isn't under my bed, in my closet or behind my dresser, he must be under my pillow! AAAAGHH!

7. Susie Smith of Springfield was brought up in a good Republican household. She has gone haywire over hippies and yippies and has become herself one of the dippies. The dailies carried a story about her entanglement with the law while on an assignment for an underground newspaper. That's what comes of sending a daughter to Berkeley.

8. Your somewhat fuzzy thinking on this subject [gun control] is shown by quoting N.Y. police commissioner Patrick Murphy as saying that the answer to our ever increasing criminality is the confiscation of all guns. You have not purged yourself of all your erroneous convictions when you quote him out of context.

   "Letters to the Editor," Philadelphia Bulletin

9. Tornadoes are caused by cars say four scientists at the Foundation for Ocean Research at San Diego, whose hypothesis has the backing of statistics, vortex calculations, and publication in the august scientific

journal *Nature*. Their paper shows that the effect of the 2 million cars and 600,000 trucks that are on the move at any time in the United States—keeping properly to the right—is to inject into the atmosphere an anticlockwise force that aids and abets natural tornado-creating forces. As the observant will have noted, those of us who drive on the left in the Northern Hemisphere will be doing the world a service by reducing the natural vorticity because most tornadoes north of the equator are cyclonic, and British traffic is stoutly producing anticyclonic forces.

Adapted from *The Guardian Weekly*

10. There are one hundred and ninety-three living species of monkeys and apes. One hundred and ninety-two of them are covered with hair. The exception is a naked ape self-named *Homo sapiens*. This unusual and highly successful species spends a great deal of time examining his higher motives and an equal amount of time studiously avoiding his fundamental ones. . . . He is an acutely exploratory, over-crowded ape, and it is high time we examined his basic behavior.

Desmond Morris, *The Naked Ape*

11. **CAPITAL CRIMES**

We've heard a lot of unpersuasive arguments for capital punishment, but none to top the one that New York State Senator James Donovan offered the other day. "Where would Christianity be," he asked, "if Jesus got 8 to 15 years with time off for good behavior?" Where indeed? And where would the civil rights movement be if black men had not been lynched in the South? And where would the Indian movement be today if Indians had not been massacred in the West? And if six million Jews had not been slaughtered by the Nazis, where would Israel be? Senator Donovan, evidently a historical revisionist as well as a proponent of the death penalty, is telling us that when Pilate asked the people of Jerusalem what evil Jesus had done that he should be killed and they cried out, "Let him be crucified," they knew what they were about. But does Senator Donovan understand what Jesus was about when He told His disciples to turn the other cheek?

The New York Times

12. All Americans have political rights, so the Hatch Act, which prevents civil servants from running for public office, is essentially undemocratic.

13. A woman dreamed that she went downtown and was followed by a monkey. The next day she actually went downtown and sure enough there was a monkey there, not paying much attention to anything. The woman screeched, "My dream! My dream!" Her cry caught the monkey's attention and it began to follow her. Thus, even though she was instrumental in causing it, her precognition actually occurred.

Psychic World magazine

14.   "You're putting me on the spot. I sell what comes in from the distributors.

"Sure, some people may consider them to be pornographic. I don't.

"In my mind, these are magazines that display female figures. I do not consider the female form to be pornographic. These are, simply, girlie magazines.

"To me, what is pornographic is the stuff often solicited through the mails.

"Even the girlie magazines I carry, I will not sell to anyone but an adult.

"They are on open display but on the other side of the store, away from the regular magazines. We do not allow any kids near there.

"In fact, I have closed circuit television watching that section to make sure there aren't any kids looking at the magazines.

"Of course, the television prevents thefts too.

"But, people buy them so they must serve a purpose."

Boston *Globe*

15.   Premature separation of the placenta from the uterus wall—called placental abruption—raises the risk that the baby will die or be born prematurely. Now a team headed by pathologist Richard L. Naeye of Pennsylvania State University College of Medicine has found that smoking during pregnancy is strongly related to one type of fatal abruption.

In a study of 45,470 pregnancies, the team found that the death rate from this type of abruption was 3.3 per thousand for babies of nonsmokers. The rate increased to 4.7 per thousand when the mothers had smoked one to ten cigarettes per day while pregnant, and rose to 5.2 per thousand when they had smoked 11 to 20 cigarettes a day. Dr. Naeye advises women who want to be safe not to smoke during pregnancy.

Jay Nelson Tuck in *Women's Day* (cited in *Reader's Digest*)

16.   Perhaps one of the most staggering of the new concepts is that which makes such operations as alchemy plausible. Accepting the premise that there can be interaction between the mind and the physical world, it becomes apparent that any experiment must include the experimenter as one of its elements. It has long been observed, for example, that the expectation of success has a great deal to do with one's scores in ESP card guessing. Those who have no faith in ESP seldom score better than what is predictable by chance alone.

From this it seems to follow that the alchemist himself must be considered as one of the critical ingredients of the process. With a dedicated and expectant operator, unconsciously establishing a link between the mental and physical aspects of the universe, the transmutation of a base metal into gold no longer seems quite so incredible.

Psychic World magazine

17. But what has happened to Smith? Those who have watched the tenacious Rhodesian Premier battle the Moscow–Washington Axis for all these years fear that their champion, greatly beloved in his country, is nearing physical and emotional exhaustion. Many close to the situation say that Smith has never been the same since his famous meetings with Henry Kissinger at Geneva, in which the Premier is said to have aged ten years in a week.

American Opinion magazine

18. Lovemaking is an art you can develop to any degree, according to *How to Be a Happily Married Mistress*. You can become a Rembrandt in your sexual art. Or, you can stay at the paint-by-numbers stage. One husband, by the way, felt his wife was more like Grandma Moses because she always wore a flannel granny nightgown. The benefits in your becoming a Rembrandt just cannot be overemphasized. You can begin now to be a budding artist.

Marabel Morgan, *The Total Woman*

19. Dr. James H. Sammons, the highest ranking staff physician of the American Medical Association, told a Congressional subcommittee last month that hysterectomy was justified when the uterus was healthy but the woman feared cancer or pregnancy. However, the Canadian group rejected these reasons, saying there were far less hazardous ways than hysterectomy to sterilize a woman or prevent uterine cancer.

"If you take out every uterus at age 13, you would prevent all uterine cancers," Dr. Frank Dyck, the director of the Canadian project observed. "It's not a very logical argument."

The New York Times

20. Each and all of those "what if's" could be a hard reality almost instantly by killing the importance of—the image of—the automobile, the automotive business and the people in it.

That won't happen overnight. But slowly and methodically the possibility is being set up.

The conspiracy against the automobile will create a transportation crisis, deep recession will follow, and perhaps economic chaos.

When transportation stops, progress stops. And when progress stops, America stops. Every American should be concerned to see that those things do not happen.

The New York Times

21. Were the great personages of the past victims of a stupendous hoax? Could such eminent men of the ancient world as Socrates, Pericles and

Alexander the Great have been deluded, and cast under the spell of witchcraft—or did the oracles whom they consulted actually possess *a mysterious faculty of foresight?* That *the human mind can truly exert an influence over things and conditions* was not a credulous belief of the ancients, but a known and demonstrable fact to them.

Advertisement for the Rosicrucians

22. The idea that Bergman could deliberately cheat on his taxes is absurd to anyone who has seen even a handful of his films. Why would a man incapable of telling a lie in his art succumb to telling one on his income tax return? The idea is inconsistent with the sense of integrity which permeates Bergman's work—work conspicuously non-commercial.

Editorial in the Boston *Globe*

23. A commission appointed by President Nixon to investigate the effect of pornographic literature on American society reported that there was no evidence that it has a "deleterious effect" upon people. President Nixon, obviously perturbed by a finding contrary to his expectation, argued as follows in rejecting the report, "If that's so, it is an argument in effect that great books, paintings and plays cannot have much beneficial effect."

24. A cloud is constituted of minute drops of water. These droplets are so tiny that 200 million would be necessary to fill a single teaspoon. This being the case, clouds themselves must also be very small. Perhaps our perception of them is merely the result of some optical illusion.

25. Quoted by SMITH, who is reading a newspaper, to Jones: "Political opponents have criticized the president for his involvement in foreign affairs."

    JONES: The *president* is having an *affair*, with a *foreigner* no less!

26. SMITH: The first thing you need to know if you want to become a musician is the scale.

    JONES: What is the scale?

    SMITH: It all depends upon the union. In this town it's about eight dollars an hour.

27. Feminists constitute only a small percentage of the total number of American women. Their ideas represent the radical fringe of current thinking. Their life-styles conflict significantly with traditional American values. In the light of these considerations, it hardly seems necessary to take their claims for equal rights seriously. Right-thinking Americans will ignore their demands.

28. The steamfitters contract expired on April 30, as did the electricians.

29. The life of nations merely repeats, on a larger scale, the lives of their cells; he who is incapable of understanding the mystery, the reactions, the laws that determine the movements of the individual can never hope to say anything worth listening to about the struggles of a nation.

30. "I never read a book by a woman because I never met a woman who had sense enough to write one."

   Billy Carter, quoted in *New Woman*

31. Homosexuals should not be allowed to live and work where they choose. Laws protecting them from discrimination are, in fact, tacit modes of promoting degenerate and sinful practices within society. We have Anita Bryant, the well-known singer and Miss America runner-up pointing this out to us. Her opinion ought to suffice to prove this point.

32. President Eisenhower must have been a good president, for he was a good general and a better-than-average golfer.

33. SUE: Once you've seen one of these X-rated movies, you've seen them all.

   BILL: You're absolutely right, Sue. After I saw one, I went to see them all.

34. Professor Smith must be fair in assigning grades to his students. All of his students have remarked upon his fairness.

35. Smith had better not criticize Republican energy policy. Mr. Jones, who manages the office in which Smith works, is a died-in-the-wool Republican and has seen to it that critics of Republican policies on issues of national importance have been quietly dismissed from the firm or, at the very least, relegated to menial jobs with little chance of promotion.

36. Child eating what seems to her a detestable dinner, "All I keep hearing from Mom and Dad is the importance of nutrition. Why do I have to eat carrots, spinach, and liver? Why don't they just give me some nutritions to eat?"

37. Baseball, football, and basketball are all team sports, so meatball and matzoh ball must be team sports as well.

38. "You couldn't have it if you *did* want it," the Queen said. "The rule is, jam to-morrow and jam yesterday—but never jam *to-day*."

   "It *must* come sometimes to 'jam to-day,'" Alice objected.

   "No, it can't," said the Queen, "it's jam every *other* day: to-day isn't any *other* day, you know."

   Lewis Carroll, *Through the Looking-glass*

39. ... using psychiatrists to negotiate with terrorists is simply a part of our contemporary craze of psychiatrizing all human situations that involve conflict. The other is that psychiatrists have a special expertise in terrorism because they are themselves terrorists. There is ample support for both views.

   Here is some of the evidence in support of the view that the psychiatrist is an expert in terrorism. The South Moluccan terrorist leader identified himself as Dr. Mulder's "colleague on train 747." Dr. Benjamin Rush—the father of American psychiatry, whose portrait adorns the seal of the American Psychiatric Association—endorsed terrorism as a method of psychiatric treatment. "Terror," he declared, "acts powerfully upon the body through the medium of the mind, and should be employed in the cure of madness." It is the conventional American wisdom that Russian psychiatrists are terrorists whose task is to torture "dissidents." Perhaps we are slowly approaching the realization that, unless proven otherwise, all psychiatrists who are not the paid agents of their own voluntary clients are terrorists.

Thomas Szasz, M.D., The New York Times

40. Resentment of homosexuality runs deep in this country. If one needs proof of that, one has only to read the letters to the editor in the current issue of Time magazine, responding to its cover story on Leonard Matlovich, the recently discharged homosexual Air Force sergeant. "From time immemorial we have recognized yellow fever, malaria, syphilis, leprosy, perversion, degeneracy, garbage and homosexuality in about that order. There need be no change," wrote a retired US Army colonel.

Boston Globe

II. Use the pattern of analysis explained in Chapters 2 through 7 to set out the arguments presented in some of the following examples. Indicate in which cases the fallacy arises from inadequacies in the *grounds* offered, in the *warrant* relied on, or in the *backing* supporting the warrant.

Ray's fingerprints were found on the rifle when it was recovered near the shooting scene.

"When we think about the fact that Raoul's fingerprints don't exist on that rifle at all, doesn't that indicate that Raoul doesn't exist at all?" Ray was asked.

"It doesn't to me," Ray replied.

International Herald Tribune

DEATH WISH

Steven Judy is a 24-year old construction worker from Indianapolis. In the spring of 1979 he stopped to help, or so she thought, a woman stranded with a flat tire. Instead, he further disabled the car and offered her and her three young children a lift. She was raped and strangled; the children were tossed in a creek where they drowned.

If Judy is electrocuted tomorrow, as scheduled, the State of Indiana runs no risk of executing the wrong man—which takes care of one argument against capital punishment. Nor does Judy think his punishment is cruel and unusual: he has taken to citing Bible passages that indicate his fate is appropriate. And to make sure that no one extends to him the humanity he denied his victims, he has refused to support an American Civil Liberties Union petition for clemency. His contempt for life, it seems, is absolute.

But though his death may be, so far as one can gauge such imponderables, no loss to society, the manner of his dying is a blow to civilization. To civilize is not only to nurture cultural and technological developments but to advance morality and justice out of a primitive state. By that definition, the United States is a civilized country. Mr. Judy is, for whatever reason, a barbarian. A civilized country can afford to deal with people like him in other wiser ways. What it cannot afford is the return to the club implicit in responding to his brutality with the like. To endorse execution, however understandable the impulse, is quite simply to come down to his level.

New York Times

An academic adviser to Republican presidential nominee Ronald Reagan argued before a Harvard audience Thursday night that a President should not be chosen on the basis of "intellectual sophistication." We had a man (as President) who never went to college—Harry Truman—and he did superbly well," said Richard Pipes, professor of history and Soviet specialist. If candidates were chosen for their intellectual ability, Pipes argued, "We would have to choose a university professor. They are by definition the smartest. In fact, we had a university professor as President in this century, and he did rather miserably. That's Woodrow Wilson."

The Boston *Globe*

Church and state, religion and politics should be kept separate as much as possible. But this requires that the state too remember its proper place. Many people criticized the churches for failing to speak out more forcefully when the German state was killing Jews. Why is it meddlesome for the churches to speak out against the killing of unborn children? Many applauded when clergymen supported civil rights and peace. Why act shocked when they support the family?

If religious people are refusing to leave politics alone, it's because they feel politics can't be trusted to leave them alone. Government has gotten ever more aggressive in its attempts to remake American society and morals. Men of faith didn't pick this fight. The separation of religion and politics ended when the state started trying to redefine right and wrong in pornography, abortion, race, economics and the relations of the sexes.

Joseph Sobran, the Boston *Globe*

WOMAN'S WORK

"You know what the problem is? There aren't any housewives anymore." The speaker was a Census official worried that not enough people have signed up to be enumerators for the 1980 Census that starts April 1. In 1920, or 1940, or even 1970, being a census-taker was ideal work for women who stayed home most of the time. The job lasts for only a few weeks. The pay is at least passable for a casual job; this year, $4 to $5 an hour is the bare minimum. The work is interesting. And it is imbued with an air of sensible good citizenship.

But as the Census Bureau's own figures show, the term "housewife" is under double challenge. Women are considerably less likely to be wives, or mothers, than even a decade ago. And they are much less likely to stay in the house. In the 1970's, the job rate for those aged 25 to 34 went from 45 percent to 67 percent. Many fewer want casual work, even if it is patriotic.

Census officials hope, consequently, that many college students and others will call to fill the jobs. We share the hope, but we're still preoccupied by all those former housewife-enumerators. They suggest something about the way our society organized itself in a time when few women worked, and many of those who did were apt to be nurses, say, or teachers.

Society got an immensely big intellectual bang for the buck. It probably should be no surprise that it used to be easy to find able census-takers, or that college freshmen 50 years ago did better on the same English test than their counterparts do now. Many women of exceptional intelligence used to take teaching jobs at public school salaries. Their counterparts today are partners in law firms or book publishers or advertising executives and are paid accordingly. But it has paid.

The New York Times

No matter how often it is repeated by the worldly-wise that people are much the same everywhere: and that national characteristics are mostly superficial and have more to do with local customs than with any real differences in thinking and behaviour, most people are not convinced. They do really believe that the average Chinaman is very different from the average Irishman; and I am inclined to agree that there is a certain folk wisdom here. The fundamental human impulses of survival, reproduction, love, hate egotism and death are indeed common to all; but what a fascinating world of light and shade exists between the culture of one country and another.

The Irish Times

Walking is also a dandy way to help shed weight (brisk walking burns 300 calories per hour) and reduce the hips (since the invention of the automobile, the adult hip width has been increasing at the rate of one inch every generation). Jennifer Pader, a young New York advertising copywriter, went from 187 to 125 pounds in a little over a year by following a diet–walking program prescribed by a nutritionist. "I found that the more you walk, the more you like it," she says.

Parade

Sir, it is well understood on Wall Street that the main reasons oil companies diversify into these other fields are a sense that their own business is getting to be completely politicized and a mounting apprehension about the viability of the business as one politician after another carries on about "obscene profits" or about a big "rip-off"—the latter being a term you have employed yourself in talking about oil-company profits. My question is whether you realize that, in continuing to emphasize and denounce the alleged immensity of their profits, you encourage the very tendency to diversify that you say you oppose?

Fortune

It is very difficult to describe the growing despair of the German masses because it is itself blind and uncomprehending. A working woman will receive her dole of paper marks that seem enough to keep her family for a week, but in a few days it will be almost worthless, and she will be destitute. How can she be expected to understand the complex financial machinery that has impoverished her without actually depriving her of a single one of her notes? It is an oppression far worse than any previous oppression directly exercised by master over slave, or by one class over another, for the oppressor is invisible and intangible, at least to most of the oppressed, who are filled with a growing rebelliousness, but do not know against whom to rebel.

Inflation has corroded every link in the chain that connects producer with consumer. The farmer refuses to part with his goods in exchange for a paper currency that shrinks to worthlessness overnight. The oscillations of the mark are so uncertain that the wholesale dealer does not know what price to fix.

Attempts to control prices are largely futile now that depreciation is so rapid and uncertain. . . .

The vicious circle is completed by the fact that depreciation has reduced the purchasing power of the masses. At the present moment the skilled workman of the highest category receives an average wage of five million marks a month—that is to say, about one pound at this morning's rate of exchange.

SOVIET MATH

As delegates to the International Congress of Mathematicians, we take issue with the article published in the Aug. 17 edition.

If your reporter had sought the feelings of the individual members instead of the "official" version of the Finnish organizers, he would have formed a more accurate picture with regard to the large number of invited Russian speakers who did not show up. It is common knowledge among mathematicians, supported by long experience, that their Russian colleagues are under severe scrutiny by their government, and that trips abroad are an envied favor which scientific merit alone does not achieve. Official pretense or not, the fact is that the recipient of the Fields Medal, and a majority of other invited Russian speakers, were denied permission to attend the congress.

Of course, this is a small matter compared to the harassment of refuseniks for being Jewish and wanting to emigrate, and compared to the long prison sentences for political dissent. But it is significant that this should happen in the very city where the Helsinki treaty was signed.

FRANK H. CLARKE
IVAR EKELAND
Helsinki *International Herald Tribune*

ADOLF HITLER is alive and well in Argentina—where he masterminded both the seizure of the Falkland Islands and the new outbreak of Middle East fighting as part of his insane drive for world domination.

From the day Hitler supposedly killed himself in 1945, top Allied officials have scoffed at reports of his death. Here are just a few examples.

In 1952, Dwight D. Eisenhower conceded, "We have been unable to unearth one bit of tangible evidence of Hitler's death. Many people believe that Hitler escaped from Berlin."

When President Truman asked Joseph Stalin at the Potsdam conference in 1945 whether Hitler was dead. Stalin bluntly replied, "No."

Stalin's top army officer, Marshall Gregory Zhukov, whose troops actually occupied Berlin, flatly concluded after weeks of thorough investigation in 1945: "We have found no corpse that could be Hitler's."

Tuwiah Friedman, the Israeli who helped track down mass murderer Adolph Eichmann, estimated that only 20 percent of the Nazi criminals who participated in the systematic butchery of millions have been caught and brought to trial.

"The others—numbering in the thousands—are free. Most of them have gone underground. They sit and wait for a new set of circumstances that will enable them to regain lost power."

At 93, Hitler could retain the physical and mental capacities needed to command armies, plot devishly clever strategy and rule with an iron hand, according to leading authorities.

Man could actually live to age 200, says top Argentine doctor Anthony Lulie, who bases his claims on research among the primitive tribes of South America.

Dr. Carol Dye, a psychologist at the Aging and Human Development Program at Washington University in St. Louis, said:

"At 93, you have a very select group of people," she explained. "The very fact that they have lived so long indicates they are in special mental and physical shape.

"It really is a question of mind over matter. If you think you're capable of doing something, you generally are."

Lark Allen, *The Examiner*

MOTHER NATURE IS LUCKY HER PRODUCTS DON'T NEED LABELS

All food, even natural ones, are made up of chemicals. But natural foods [the ad shows a picture of an orange] don't have to list their ingredients. So it's often assumed they're chemical-free. In fact, the ordinary orange is a miniature chemical factory. And the good old potato contains arsenic among its more than 150 ingredients. This doesn't mean natural foods are dangerous. If they were, they wouldn't be on the market. The same is true of man-made foods. All man-made foods are tested for safety. And they often provide more nutrition, at lower cost, than natural foods. They even use many of the same chemical ingredients. So there really isn't much difference between foods made by Mother Nature and those made by man. What's artificial is the line drawn between them.

Advertisement for Monsanto Chemicals

A PLANE WHICH FLIES FOR 450 YEARS

Our DC-10 has flown for a total of 4,000,000 hours, that's the equivalent of 450 years. As impressive as these figures are they are not as impressive as the number of passengers we have flown. More than 230 million persons have traveled on our DC-10. Every ten days we add a million more. The destinations to which we fly are more numerous than any other big carrier: 168 cities in 88 countries on five continents. . . . For your next trip be among our millions of satisfied customers.

Advertisement for McDonnell Douglas

Considerable efforts by the maintenance department to enhance the main entrance and corridor to the administration building over the past year were given a touch of class with the gift of a chandelier to the college by the head of the alumni association, H. O. Ray, now hanging in the center foyer.

STUDENT: Dad, can I borrow a couple of hundred for some sorely needed new clothes?

DAD: Why don't you go to work, if you need money?

STUDENT: But I can't find a job.

DAD: If you dressed better, you wouldn't be out of work.

STUDENT: I see, no matter how I do this, I lose.

III. Analyze the arguments that make up the following Art Buchwald column. Identify any fallacies it may contain. Be prepared to discuss Buchwald's strategy in arguing as he does. Do you find that he makes his point effectively? If so, how does he do it?

JUSTICE IS SERVED

Washington–The justice system in this country seems as loused up as everything else. One of the reasons for this is that the law provides that anyone who has a legal dispute involving more than $50 is entitled to a jury. Most jurors can deal with personal injury and liability cases. But you have to have an MBA from Harvard, a law degree from Stanford, and an accounting diploma from the Wharton School to be able to follow the complicated suits that ordinary citizens are required to adjudicate these days.

How can the average jury understand the issues in a multi-billion dollar corporation lawsuit?

A well-known trial lawyer told me they can't. Most juries involved with any business litigation make their decisions based on things other than the thousands of pieces of evidence and months of testimony that neither they nor the judge understand.

This is how it goes in the jury room, he told me.

"I think we should find for the plaintiffs."

"Why?"

"Their chief lawyer always looks so fresh and neat no matter how hot it is in the courtroom."

"I'm for throwing out all the charges. The defense has a woman lawyer on the staff, and I think if we voted for the defendants, it would encourage large corporations to hire more women lawyers."

"That's the stupidest reason I ever heard for judging a case. If we're going to play by those rules, we have to take into consideration that one of the plaintiff's executives has a bad limp. Why not give the billion dollars to them for hiring the handicapped?"

"Wait, we're getting away from the evidence. Let's go over it again."

"Are you crazy? No one in this room knows what anyone out there was talking about."

"Okay. Let's NOT go over the evidence. How do we arrive at a decision?"

"I'm for giving the nod to the plaintiffs. Their backup lawyer always came over to us when he wanted to make a point. The defendants' lawyer preferred to address his remarks to the judge. If he wanted to win, the defense counsel should have paid more attention to us."

"You're too sensitive. Only the fat defendant's lawyer ignored us. The cute one with the horn-rimmed glasses spent a lot of time leaning against the jury box. He had beautiful eyes."

"But he had a beard. I'd never trust a person who sports a beard."

"My son has a beard."

"I thought as much, and while we're on the subject—I don't trust you either."

"Hold it. We've been together five months. Let's get a decision so we can all go home. How do you vote?"

"How is she voting?"

"I'm voting for the plaintiffs."

"Then I'm voting for the defendants."

"We're never going to see our loved ones again. There has to be a compromise. I suggest we give the plaintiffs half of what they are asking."

"Why?"

"Do you remember when the president of the injured company testified? His entire family sat in the first row for five days. I thought that was very loyal of them. You don't see many families that close any more."

"Are you planning to give the plaintiffs half a billion dollars because their chief executive officer has a nice family? How do we know what goes on behind closed doors?"

"I agree. Besides, the defendant company's chairman of the board wore his Shriner's pin when he took the stand. I happen to be a Shriner, and I'll take a lodge brother's word against anyone who drags his kids out of school to sit at a trial."

"We appear to be split on a verdict. Shall I report to the judge that we can't come to a decision?"

"Don't do that. He'll make us read the court transcript again. I say we flip a coin. Heads we find for the plaintiffs—tails for the defendants."

"Okay, as long as she takes back what she said about men with beards."

"I take it back, but only because I believe justice should be served."

IV.   Identify the fallacy discussed in the following excerpt from the Boston *Globe's* Arts column. Discuss similar instances of this fallacy you have encountered. How would you go about eliminating this sort of fallacy?

HOW ACCURATE ARE REVIEW QUOTES IN MOVIE ADS?

By Leo W. Banks
Arizona Daily Star

If Hollywood is blessed with nothing else it is blessed with the gift of hype. The firmer the grip on unreality the better. Earth to Hollywood. Come in Hollywood. Has the town ever produced a bad movie?

Review ads are a fine breeding ground of movie hype. If a film critic says anything laudatory about a movie, a promoter will pull the remark and use it in his ads. So we find that "Urban Cowboy" is what Hollywood movies are all about; "The Electric Horseman" is the best American romantic comedy of 1979; and "The Island" is jolly good fun.

But is "Urban Cowboy" really that good? Did the reviewer say that? Could "The Electric Horseman" be that funny? What self-respecting critic would describe a movie as jolly good fun?

How accurate are review ads?

Richard Schickel, Time magazine's critic, said:

"It seems to me that after 60 or 70 years of Hollywood history, a buyer ought to know that Hollywood has a tendency to hype, and a reader ought not to believe anything in a movie ad."

A comparison of dozens of review ads with the actual reviews from which the quotes were taken support Schickel's point. Some are flights of brute imagination.

The most common example involves pulling one word, or a few words, from an ad to convey a thought. For instance:

An ad for "Yanks" said: "Lavish . . . overstuffed with talent."—Frank Rich, Time.

But in context, Rich wrote: "The film is so lavish, so long (2 hours, 20 minutes) and so overstuffed with talent that one at first expects an epic of Homeric proportions. As it gradually turns out, director John Schlesinger has a trifle up his sleeve, not a bombshell: 'Yanks' is nothing more and nothing less than an extravagant soap opera about star-crossed lovers on the British home front during World War II. The results are often entertaining, but only for audiences who are prepared to open their tear ducts and put their brains on hold."

An ad for "The Electric Horseman" said: "A delight!"—Richard Schickel, Time.

But Schickel actually used the word "delight" to refer to a specific scene, not the entire movie. Nor did he use an exclamation point.

He wrote: "The cowboy simply hops aboard the animal and clippetyclops him straight down the runway of the industrial show in which they're both appearing, past the dancing girls, past the hysterical director, through the audience, past the slot machines in the lobby and on down the Las Vegas strip. The scene is an outrageous assault on probability, but in its unexpectedness, it is a delight."

On occasion, a reviewer will praise a performance, but torpedo the film, and still wind up being quoted.

An ad for "Luna" quoted Vincent Canby of the New York Times: "Jill Clayburgh is extraordinary . . . a fine complex performance."

It should be pointed out that Canby did not write that in his review of the film, but in a Sunday feature. (Clever, huh?) But what is more significant is that Canby did not like the movie. He called it a "decided disappointment" and "ultimately ludicrous."

The phenomenon of review quotes not appearing in the review at all is not as unusual as one might expect. A promoter will sometimes call a critic and ask to change a few words or a few sentences, because they sound better or read better. If the change does not violate the spirit of the review, the critic might agree.

In addition, a promoter might screen a movie for a critic before it opens publicly and get comments at that time, which may or may not show up in the finished review.

One of which probably explains why an ad for "The Electric Horseman" quotes Richard Grenier of Cosmopolitan as saying, "Fabulous!" when the word does not appear anywhere in the review.

The closest Grenier's review comes to "Fabulous!" are the last two sentences: "The story that unfolds is touching and timely, gorgeously shot by director Sydney Pollack, written with truly exceptional wit and vividness by Robert Garland. You'll be uplifted."

There is no exclamation point, but then how can you have an exclamation point at the end of a word that isn't there?

V. Take a position for or against the disclosure of aptitude tests to unions. Point out the fallacies in the arguments of the position with which you disagree.

UNIONS VS. THE MULTIPLE-CHOICE TEST

Monroe, Mich.—Since 1970, Richard Burger has worked as a power-plant operator at Detroit Edison's generating plant here, often working the midnight shift, sometimes returning home covered with black dust from the mounds of coal piled up alongside Lake Erie.

For the entire time, Burger has been dreaming of becoming an instrument man. It is a cleaner job that would give him more money, more security and regular daytime hours. However, he has no hope of being promoted. Seven years ago, the company gave him a battery of aptitude tests. He failed—or, in the company's words, scored "not recommended."

Burger, 27, is a man capable of building and wiring his new house but he admits he is not so good at multiple-choice tests. "The arithmetic they gave us was easy, but some of the vocabulary was ridiculous," he recalls. "I can't seem to get over those tests but I know I'd be an excellent instrument man."

Now, Burger and his union, the Utility Workers of America, are bringing to life the fantasy of millions of test-takers across the United States. In a seven-year legal battle, they have been challenging—and so far, defeating—the people who make up multiple-choice tests.

Last year, the U.S. Court of Appeals for the Sixth Circuit ruled that under federal labor law, whenever a company gives tests to employees, a union has the right to examine the tests—the questions, the answers and the test scores. That was the first time any court had ever held that an employer's duty to provide a union with information relevant to collective bargaining extends to psychological aptitude tests.

The Supreme Court has agreed to hear Detroit Edison's appeal of the lower-court ruling during the term that begins in October. It is one of the most unusual labor cases the justices have reviewed in the past few years (Detroit Edison vs. National Labor Relations Board).

The case has produced an odd alliance between the American Psychological Association and the U.S. Chamber of Commerce. In separate friend-of-the-court briefs, the two groups have suggested that the entire future of psychological testing of employees hangs on the outcome of the case.

These groups reason that if a union has the right to obtain copies of a company's tests, then the usefulness of those tests will be destroyed. A company will have no way of knowing, they say, whether a union has turned over copies of the test to some employees—thus permitting them to score higher than they otherwise would have.

"Disclosure of tests to persons with no professional obligation to protect their security will destroy the tests' validity," the Psychological Association says in its brief.

"Publishing psychological tests is a big industry," says Dr. Joseph Sanders of the APA. "We're talking about millions and millions of dollars. This case could have such a chilling effect that most companies would say: 'It just isn't worth it'."

The cities of Los Angeles and San Diego have filed a joint brief at the Supreme Court, urging the justices to rule that psychological tests should remain confidential.

Richard Burger was one of 10 employees at the Monroe plant who applied for promotion to instrument man in 1971. Although there were six openings in that classification, none of these men got the jobs. Instead, Detroit Edison filled the vacancies with employees brought in from its other plants—employees with higher test scores but lower seniority than the 10 applicants from within the plant. The rejected employees, all members of Utility Workers Local 223, then filed a grievance, claiming that the company had violated its contract.

The standard multiple-choice tests that Detroit Edison used to rate prospective instrument men were called the Engineering and Physical

Sciences Aptitude Test and the Minnesota Paper Form Board Test. The questions were designed to measure an individual's ability to visualize in three-dimensional space and his aptitude in mathematics, arithmetic, verbal comprehension and the physical sciences.

Company officials say that, although the materials are commonly termed psychological tests, they are fundamentally tests of an individual's aptitude, not his personality. Employees are not asked about their sex lives or their family, officials emphasize.

A sample question on the vocabulary section of the test asks employees to decide which word means most nearly the same as "antipathy": A) animosity B) discomfiture C) sobriety D) deception E) negation. (The answer: A.)

Detroit Edison tests for many other jobs besides instrument man. There is one battery of tests for cable-splicers and another series for linemen; there are tests for customer-service representatives and tests for computer programmers. Would-be supervisors are required to take a "human relations battery," and clerical employees must take a "clerical battery." According to court testimony, Detroit Edison even has a battery of tests to decide who should be meter readers.

At the company's headquarters in downtown Detroit, William Roskind, director of psychological services, estimates that 6,000 to 7,000 of Detroit Edison's 10,000 employees have had tests given to them at one time or another.

The company does not use tests to hire lawyers, accountants or other professionals. "We assume that if someone comes from an accredited school, they've learned what they're going to learn," Roskind explains. "How can you develop a test to choose the president of the company?"

But, Roskind says, tests are extremely important in selecting people like instrument men—people in jobs where "a mistake can cause a blackout of the entire system."

"These tests are an objective demonstration that an applicant has the mental abilities we are looking for," Roskind says. "Take spatial perception. No one's ever been able to teach people that. You either have it or you don't."

Two years ago, the National Labor Relations Board voted 2 to 1 to order Detroit Edison to give the union copies of its tests and scores. It is the NLRB, represented by the Justice Department, that will defend Local 223 before the Supreme Court.

The NLRB contends in a legal brief that the union needs to see the tests "to determine the extent to which questions were asked that called for knowledge beyond the requirements of the instrument-man job." It points out that the NLRB ordered union officials not to release copies of the tests to past or future test-takers. It argues that the company should trust the union to obey this order.

Detroit Edison, the APA and the Chamber of Commerce all are arguing that, if company psychologists gave test scores and papers to a union, they could thereby violate what the APA calls "the confidential relationship between the psychologist and the client."

While the case is being reviewed by the Supreme Court, Burger will continue to fix equipment at the Monroe plant, rotating weekly from the 8 a.m.–4 p.m. shift to the 4 p.m.–midnight shift to the midnight–8 a.m. shift.

A few months ago, Burger—still seeking the same promotion he wanted seven years ago—once again took the tests for instrument man. "They told me I scored much higher, but still in the 'not-recommended' range," he says.

It was Roskind who told Burger that he had failed once again. "He told me chances are I'll never be able to do that job," Burger recalls. "He said the tests show I can handle the job I'm in now, and that's where I should stay."

Jim Mann, *Los Angeles Times*

VI. Classify the following ambiguous statements. What should have been done to correct them?

DRUNK GETS NINE MONTHS IN VIOLIN CASE

The Cambridge Herald 10/30/76

ONE WITNESS TOLD THE COMMISSIONERS THAT SHE HAD SEEN SEXUAL INTERCOURSE TAKING PLACE BETWEEN THE TWO PARKED CARS IN FRONT OF HER HOUSE.

The Press (Atlantic City, NJ) 6/14/79

CHILD'S STOOL GREAT FOR USE IN GARDEN

Buffalo Courier-Express 6/23/77

CONNIE TIED, NUDE POLICEMAN TESTIFIES

Atlanta Journal b 1/7/76

COLUMNIST GETS UROLOGIST IN TROUBLE WITH HIS PEERS

Lewiston (Idaho) Morning Tribune 3/17/75

THE THREE HIGHEST MOUNTAINS IN SCOTLAND ARE BEN NEVIS, BEN LOMOND AND BEN JONSON.

GEOMETRY TEACHES US HOW TO BISEX ANGELS.

QUEEN ELIZABETH WAS TALL AND THIN, BUT SHE WAS A STOUT PROTESTANT.

MONASTERY IS THE PLACE FOR MONSTERS.

THE WIFE OF A PRIME MINISTER IS CALLED A PRIMATE.

Part V

Critical
practice

21

Language and reasoning

In Part V we will discuss elements associated with critical practice. This chapter will address the interrelationship between language and reasoning. The following three chapters will present ways to classify arguments, explain the importance of fields of discussion, and end with an examination of the history and criticism of reasoning.

To begin with language: evidently reasoning could not exist in the absence of language. Both claims and all the considerations used to support them must be expressed by some kind of a linguistic symbol system. As a result, language, reasoning, and culture are deeply, even inextricably, intertwined.

Some people, indeed, even regard a culture as a "system of meanings." When people employ concepts—their fundamental ideas, their arts, institutions, skills, and instruments (whether they identify a flash of color seen in a tree with a particular kind of bird or two pieces of wood set up as a cross as a religious symbol or hear the unhappiness in a speaker's tone of voice)—their "conceptual" grasp puts them in a position to recognize "meaning" in what might otherwise appear to be an incoherent bundle of sounds or objects.

THE DEVELOPMENT OF LANGUAGE AND REASONING CAPACITIES

The possibility of communication between the members of any community rests on their sharing of concepts. Since concepts vary to some extent from place to place and people to people, so do language and communication. This is true not just of different countries but even of different subcultures within a single country. For example, some people would argue that, by now, black American English is a distinct language, differing significantly from standard American English.

During infancy, children often develop their own personal languages. Sometimes twins or siblings who are close in age may even generate a language that only they understand. In the case of one pair of twins, the parents spoke two different languages at home, but the two little girls spoke neither. Instead it was observed that they employed a third language of their own, which only they shared. This went on so long that their parents began to worry that they might be mentally retarded. But when they were examined, they could *understand* both English and French perfectly well, but they chose to *speak* in their own language. Presumably, these twins not only *communicated* with each other but also *reasoned* in their own private language—and reasoned in ways that only partly coincided with the ways in which their parents reasoned.

The story of the twins may be an unusual one, but similar points can be made about more normal cases as well. For example, it is not uncommon for a child to call all men, "Daddy." When the wrong man is addressed this way, adults often laugh because they think of the possibility of questionable paternity. But for the child, nothing of this sort is at issue. The word *Daddy* simply makes sense for them in a way that does not conform exactly to adult language. Similarly the child who said, "I can hit the ball back three out of four times," was actually trying to communicate that she succeeded in hitting it once in four tries. So children begin by developing for themselves language systems that may differ substantially from that used by "the grown-ups," but as time goes along, they modify that language so that it becomes increasingly consistent with the adult language to which they are exposed.

Ordinarily, then, children's use of adult language increases along with their need to interact and their ability to learn. As more concepts are learned, more elements of the culture are learned. In this way, the child does not merely "learn a language"; it also becomes socialized and enculturated—coming to understand what things are, how they are evaluated, what people think and do with them, and how people reason together.

One of the functions that children learn to accomplish through language, of course, is the systematic pursuit of "reasons," making use of the question, "Why?" So the seeking of reasons becomes an important part of linguistic behavior, as the people with whom the child interacts respect that question. At some stages of development, children demand reasons endlessly: Why? Why? Why? Patient adults consider it a duty to respond as much as possible, regarding these answers as an essential part of the child's learning process. But part of that learning, of course, consists in understanding how to reason and when the chain of "reasons" comes to an end.

> "Why is the snow cold?"
> "Because it's frozen."
> "Why is it frozen?"
> "Because it's winter."
> "Why is it winter?"

"Because it's February."
"Can I go play in the snow?"
"No."
"Why not?"
"Because I don't want you to."
"Why don't you want me to?"
"Because you have a cold."
"Why do I have a cold?"
"Go play with your train and stop asking questions!"

This dialogue might not turn out the same way in all parts of our society. Elsewhere the interaction between child and parent might sound more like this:

"I'm going out to play stick ball in the street."
"No. You can't."
"Why not?"
"Because I say you can't."
"Why?"
"You do and I'll have your daddy whip you."
"Daddy's not here and he can't whip me."
"I'm gonna call the cops and they'll get you!"

In the first case, the reasoning practices are designed to help the child generate its own internal foundations for supporting a claim. The parent tries to give reasons that the child can understand and use for itself in the future. In the second case, the force of reasoning lies simply in an appeal to external power figures. The mother, the daddy, and the police are all presented as "authorities" with the ability not so much to *explain* as to *enforce* the claim.

Later on, children learn to use language in a more *informative* manner, which allows them to give answers to other people's factual questions. This is a comparatively advanced development and is closely associated with the ability to engage in processes of reasoning. If the child in the first conversation had reached this more advanced stage, its final rejoinder might have been:

"My cold has gone away."
"How do you know?"
"My nose has stopped running and I haven't coughed today."

By this stage, the child has learned what will be recognized as "legitimate grounds" in support of a claim and can begin to advance more and more acceptable lines of reasoning. This advanced learning of reasoning through language, of course, never really reaches completion. Throughout their lives, individuals engage in novel interactions from which they can learn to use new ways of reasoning or to modify old ones. The resulting selection process can be seen at work most clearly in the ways that a child learns the language in the first place, for it commonly learns both the language and the acceptable modes of reasoning at the same time.

Consider the following conversation:

> "Can I go play in the snow?"
> "No, you have a cold."
> "Alan got to go out to play in the snow."
> "Alan doesn't have a cold."
> "Alan isn't fair. If I can't play in the snow, he should come in and play with me."
> "It wouldn't be fair to Alan to make him stay in just because you have a cold."
> "I don't care what's fair for Alan. I only care what's fair for me."
> "That doesn't make sense! Something can't be fair for one person and unfair for the other. It has to be fair for both of you."

Here the child learns something about the concept of "fairness"; in particular, it learns that an argument based on *unilateral* appeals to fairness will not work in this family.

There are difficult steps along the way, both in language learning and in the acquisition of reasoning abilities. Merely to grasp the functions of the question "Why?" and to learn its role in the relationship of claims to grounds, is far from easy. A child was heard to say:

> "Mr. Nielsen is going to the lake; you know why?"
> "No, why?"
> "I saw him hitching his boat to his truck."

The adult was surprised. The expected explanation of the neighbor's motives for taking a trip to the lake turned into a statement of the child's evidence about the neighbor's movements.

As the growing child learns to handle the different units of language and communication—whether engaging in conversation, telling a story, reporting what has happened, acting out a role, arguing with someone, saying a prayer, reciting poetry, developing elaborate support for a claim, talking to an animal or to itself—the child becomes more knowledgeable about who exactly it is, about its cultural and social "locus," and about the consequences of being so placed. A "unit of communication" is, indeed, a decidedly complex phenomenon. It involves a linguistic system whose meanings depend on our perceptions of reality and may vary from one social situation to another. Earlier theories about communication tended to depict the process as linear and sequential, the people being addressed as simple "receivers"—the objects toward which your preconceived thoughts and meanings were projected. Nowadays it is realized that what we mean and how we seek to communicate it will depend in part on whom we wish to communicate with and in what situation, on the linguistic systems available to those involved, and even on the larger social and cultural framework within which the communication will occur.

To sum up, language learning necessarily involves developing a competence in communication also, that is, the capacity to analyze—however crudely—the relevant features of the entire environment in which we have to communicate, to recognize the options and restraints present, and to proceed in the most effective manner. The choices that children make may be comparatively elementary and transparent, but they can also be surprisingly effective. For instance, they soon learn what forms of reasoning and interaction are acceptable at home but forbidden in school, or vice versa, and they easily make these transitions. In this way, they adapt their conduct to the requirements of their culture, and they reason accordingly.

In fact, studies of children's development of both language and reasoning skills suggest a more or less steady evolution during the first five years or so. By the time children reach the age of five, they have acquired most of the discourse and reasoning skills they will use during their lifetime of unplanned interaction. The term *unplanned* is important here: it suggests situations in which speakers and writers have not planned carefully before communicating. This term must be placed in contrast with the reasoning we will discuss in specialized fields where it can be assumed that both specific training in the preferred patterns of reasoning has been experienced and that extensive planning has preceded the preparation of the final product whether written or spoken.

The term *evolution* is also chosen consciously. It would seem as if the development of reasoning skills in children is shaped by their environment. They try out a variety of modes of reasoning, and quickly learn those that are reinforced by the people to whom they are presented. The evolution also selects situations in which some forms of reasoning are appropriate and others are not. For example, college debaters who had been extensively trained in the appropriate forms of reasoning in debate tournaments employed reasoning behaviors that were not significantly different from those used by children and people without debate training in an unplanned situation.

LINGUISTIC STRATEGIES

The development of communication competence includes the recognition of various *language strategies*. In becoming aware of the choices available to us in communication, we also come to understand better the basis on which such choices should be made. Even though people share a culture and a language, some language choices will be "better" than others. Word choice influences meaning, and in many cases there are important practical differences even among words that have essentially the same meaning.

For example, our own culture is particularly sensitive toward ways of speaking about sexual intercourse. (Notice that the choice of the phrase "sexual intercourse" at this point itself indicates a desire to distance ourselves from the topic and to engage in an objective, intellectual discussion of the process!) On one occasion we may say, "They made love." On another we may say, "They were copulating." Perhaps we might soften the issue a bit and ask, "Did they sleep together?" or "Are you two still seeing one another?" In a moment of enthusiasm, you might even shout, "Man, did we ball!" While each of these expressions refers to basically the same activity, there are significant differences in their meanings. Virtually everyone has learned the strategies associated with choosing among these references—just as everyone who hears the question, "How are you?" knows the various meanings it can have and is able to analyze the situation and respond as expected.

The language strategies have a number of general features. For instance, many uses of language involve *abstraction.* By *abstraction* we mean the distance separating the sense of a word or phrase from any specific empirical object or situation. For example, the phrase "the Washington Monument" is at once recognizable as indicating a particular tall, white marble obelisk located in the capital of the United States. This phrase is thus a *concrete* one, and we have a comparatively tight control over its meaning. Alternatively, however, people often speak of "monuments" in a much less specific way, leaving considerable leeway as to their precise reference. Thus one can speak in this more *abstract* sense of Beethoven's nine symphonies as a "monument" in the history of classical sonata form.

The varying need for *precision* in language involves us in another set of choices and strategies. Sometimes it is essential to control the meaning of our words with great exactness. When replacing a pane in a window, your order for glass must be quite precise: "Two feet five inches, by three feet one inch." If the glass does not fit when delivered, you can then legitimately complain to the seller. If you are ordering lumber, on the other hand, you may have no basis for objection when the "two by fours" you call for turn out to be slightly less than two inches wide; exactitude is not so necessary here.

Another matter of linguistic choice has to do with the *intensity* of our language. By *language intensity* we mean that some words and phrases are essentially neutral in the feeling or emotion they express, whereas others are far removed from this neutrality. The further from neutral a word is, the more intense it can be said to be. When describing the meal I had last night, I might give a fairly neutral description: "The abalone was tough and the crust soggy." Alternatively I could say, "For a restaurant that expensive, they served us slop!" Though no absolute generalizations are possible, the use of high-intensity language may easily reduce the credibility of a speaker and reduce the persuasive effectiveness of what he says or writes. Highly intense language is fully appropriate and effective only in certain carefully chosen situations.

The availability of *tropes,* or "figurative" language, provides a further range of choice in language. We use metaphors and similes so habitually that they often become unconscious:

"That test was a breeze!"
"Yeah, but studying for it was a living hell!"

We freely engage in personification: "My car is a sweetheart! I tell her she's great, and she purrs back to me." There are many other figurative choices in language—that is, opportunities to use words and phrases in unusual ways or in violation of their literal meaning—and the choice of suitable tropes has been found to increase the comprehensibility, emphasis, and credibility of speakers or writers and even to make their utterances more persuasive.

There are, of course, significant opportunities for choice in *sentence order* also. Simple sentences (e.g., "Reasoning requires language") are valuable when straightforward presentation and clarity are required. But other, more elaborate ones may often be the clear choice for their power to communicate what is desired (e.g., "Some books are to be tasted, others to be swallowed, and some few to be chewed and digested"—Francis Bacon, "Of Studies"). The precise placing of different phrases and clauses within a sentence can itself influence emphasis and comprehension; using such devices as the repetition of words or phrases, the omission of some elements that can be supplied by the reader or listener, or the inversion of the usual sentence structure may also increase the effectiveness of a sentence as an instrument of communication.

Consider, for instance, the difference between the active and passive forms of a statement: "The dog chased the cat" and "The cat was chased by the dog." Think of the difference between "Tom is a fine person" and "Tom is a fine, fine person," or between "We went riding, and we went swimming, and we went fishing" and, more simply, "We went riding, swimming, and fishing." (In black English, we often hear the construction, "She a nurse." Anyone who becomes familiar with this form of English will quickly learn to supply the missing *is*.).

Similarly the location of *clauses* within sentences can influence meaning. If I say to you "Let me introduce you to the sister of Mary whom I am going to marry," you may not be able to tell whether I am engaged to Mary's sister or to Mary herself. A change in the location of a semicolon—and thus the change of a clause—can even mean the difference between life and death. The condemned prisoner appealed to the governor for clemency, and the governor's reply arrived, reading: "Clemency impossible; to be executed." Actually the governor had intended to say: "Clemency; impossible to be executed." But by the time the correction arrived, it was too late.

REASONING STRATEGIES

In their first three years, children live in a world centered on themselves: they cry and someone comes to care for them. Accordingly, their selection of strategies of reasoning tends to be similarly ego-centered: they command, demand, or desire and expect satisfaction. They assert and expect to be taken seriously; they threaten—"I'm gonna sock you"—and see no reason to provide additional proof.

A simple *yes* or *no* is common without any backing, as in the example of the professor in Chapter 1.

By the time they are five years of age, children begin to have a repertoire of reasoning strategies available to them approximating those of an adult. Their demands and desires now tend to include a warrant: "Mommy says so." They may request evidence or proof from others. They have learned the power of social pressure through established mores: "Everybody will see you in your shorts." And, they begin to employ reference to established values as the basis of their claims: "You should let the bug go because his Mommy will be worried about him." A worried Mommy is a powerful value.

In unplanned reasoning, adults show a selection of reasoning strategies relevant to the situation. They may turn to heavy use of authority, as in the case of lawyers speaking to a jury in which most of their claims rest on the authority of the law. Or, it may be the authority of experts as in the resolution of a disagreement about the best team in the conference by reference to the national rankings by sportswriters.

Use of values as the warrants for arguments does not change fundamentally from children to adults. There is simply an increasing range of values to which to appeal. The reference to personal freedom by a child, "I have a right to go home," may simply be broadened by an adult to a reference to human rights: "People should not be held against their will." Or the adult may be able to choose from a wider range of values and so be able to apply them more appropriately.

In Chapter 22, we will look more specifically at the range of arguments available in reasoning. There, our attention will be upon the planned construction of arguments. We can summarize reasoning strategies at this point by saying that apparently most people develop an increasing set of reasoning strategies as they move through childhood, so that most adults freely and easily employ them appropriately. The systematic study of reasoning may increase critical awareness and understanding of reasoning strategies, and help in the development of those more or less indigenous to specialized fields or forums, but virtually all of us have been reasoning most of our lives.

REASONING AND INTERACTION

The interactive aspects of language learning also are relevant to the growth in reasoning ability. In the study of communication behavior, it is important to focus not just on single messages but also on exchanges of messages, including both initial utterances and the responses to them. The meaningful unit of analysis in communication may thus be called an "inter-act": what you say together with what is said in reply to you. (The same could be said about written communication—we have to consider also the response of the reader.) The study of reasoning accordingly rests on what has been called the *cooperative principle*. We expect successive utterances to be connected, and we expect to find relationships between them. We do not expect people to say things that are totally pointless or incoherent, so we set out to find some point or sense in what they say—even though it may be a struggle. Thus, if a friend says to you, "That product ought to be good because it has a name brand," you may reply, "You mean, that company has a reputation for high-quality products?" Your friend may not have meant this at all, but you have provided what many might consider a more reasonable claim, and you have given the friend credit for it.

Through the cooperation of all the people involved in a linguistic interaction, a reasonableness may be generated that has as its outcome a thoroughly sound line of reasoning. The person who first advanced the claim may then take credit for it and feel good about it, even though a perceptive observer will recognize that this outcome was really a social product. In this kind of way, children learn to perfect their reasoning, while learning language and communication. They may offer grounds for a claim and receive a response that asks whether they did not mean to say something else that would in fact be stronger or more appropriate support for the claim. The respondent may actually be trying to make sense out of the original statement and may not realize that he is in fact offering significant modifications or improvements. The child who originally advanced the claim, hearing what appears to be a better argument, adopts it and agrees that the modification was, in fact, what was originally intended:

> "We ought to have a dog."
> "Why?"
> "Well, a dog is worth lots of money."
> "Do you mean it would be valuable to us to have a dog?"
> "Yeah, that's what I meant."
> "How would a dog be valuable to us?"
> "He could do work around the house so we wouldn't have to pay other people to do it for us."
> "Do you mean, for example, that he could be a watchdog and we would not have to hire guards?"
> "Yeah, he could be a real good watchdog!"

(Sometimes the child may recognize the difference between adult and child interpretations and may merely refuse to adapt. For example, a child said, "My voice is horny." She immediately went on to explain that it sounded just like a fog horn and added, "I know what you think, but I didn't mean that.")

REASONING AS COMMUNICATION

Students of formal logic and reasoning have found some difficulty in arriving at a formal analysis of arguments originally expressed in ordinary language and located in a communicative environment, for the abstract symbolism of formal logic, like that of chemistry or theoretical physics, is adapted to certain specialized theoretical situations. So it is not always possible to start with a line of reasoning presented in a practical situation and expressed in ordinary language, translate it into the logician's abstract symbols for purposes of analysis, and then return to the practical situation with a final judgment about the validity or invalidity of the argument. The reasoning, the language, and the communication are too closely locked together, and all of them must commonly be analyzed together in their natural setting.

By the same token, procedures of reasoning are inherently embedded in particular cultures. To engage in reasoned discourse, individuals must share more than a language. If they have quite different backgrounds, they must make the effort required to discover how far their total cultures are alike, and if there are no relevant overlaps, reasoning may be difficult or impossible. Years ago the general secretary of the Communist party of the USSR, Nikita Khrushchev, declared to a group of Los Angeles businessmen, "We will bury you." Hours of discussion were invested in the effort to discover what he meant. Many Americans interpreted it as an open declaration of future war and used the statement to support arguments for more arms spending. Yet more careful observers argued that we could not understand the statement without also understanding the culture from which it sprang. Maybe he was just using an old Ukrainian idiom, like a widow who says, "I've buried two husbands," meaning only that she has survived them. Or he may have meant that his country would bury the West in economic competition or that communism would bury rival social/economic theories. Literalminded translation will not help to interpret such a statement, and as world communication, transportation, commerce, and diplomacy become more efficient, we shall have to be more sensitive to the limitations in our analysis of reasoning across the boundaries between cultures.

ARGUMENT AND DEFINITION

In practical reasoning, it is often difficult for the parties to agree on the definitions of their terms. If you allow either party to an argument the freedom to decide on all her own definitions, that individual will have the power to win virtually any argument. In one debate between Findlay College and Ohio State University, for instance, the question was "Can a better liberal education be obtained in a state or a private institution?" and a simple definition made all the difference to the outcome of the debate, for Findlay insisted that a good liberal education must be understood to include direct religious training, which by law could not be provided in a state university. Once that definition was accepted, Ohio State would inevitably have lost the debate. So the whole evening was spent talking about the definition of the phrase "a liberal education."

On a more serious level, one complaint put forward by black Americans and other minority groups is that those in power exploit their power to control the accepted definitions of current political terminology to the detriment of the minorities. During the era of slavery, for instance, white people claimed to be superior to blacks and supported their argument by manipulating the accepted definition of *superiority*—implying that such things as speaking standard American English, behaving in accepted white ways, and possessing light complexions, thin lips, and straight hair were essential to being "superior." At first, blacks made the mistake of arguing back within the limits of that definition, only to find it impossible to compete. They were able to argue successfully only when they challenged the definition. Women have found themselves in similar difficulties: as long as they allowed men to claim superiority on the basis of their own definition—including as necessary elements such things as physical size, strength, and conventional "masculinity"—they were in a no-win situation. (Interestingly, those with the power to control definitions may also become locked into embarrassing positions. Thus some whites have not found it easy to meet the demands that their own definition of superiority has placed on them, and plenty of men have complained about having to be "masculine" in the conventional, American white middle-class sense of being required to be a self-reliant breadwinner who does not openly express his feelings.)

Finding what people mean by their terms is thus not simply a matter of looking in the dictionary. At its simplest, meaning has to be discovered from the ways a term is used within the entire communication environment. In complex cases, elaborate lines of, say, legal or scientific reasoning may have to be explored and tested just to settle the adequacy of one single definition.

With the help of an example, let us finally study the differences between an analysis that concentrates on the literal and explicit "meaning" of the terms in an argument and one that looks rather to the implications of the argument in its communicative context. Thus consider the simple-looking exchange:

> "Do you favor the establishment of a Palestinian state?"
> "Yes."

The simple affirmative answer implies a claim of some kind, but because no argument is provided, the nature of that claim is at first unclear. However, if it is known that the response came from the president of the United States, the implications of our "cooperative principle" will by themselves do a lot to clarify what is at issue. A look at formal definitions alone will yield nothing, even if combined with an effort to supply the implied assumptions of the speaker's position. But a sufficiently detailed understanding of the practical context (i.e., of the relevant foreign policies of the United States, past, present, and prospective) will help us to understand much of the force of the simple "Yes."

Suppose, next, that the response had not been a straightforward "Yes." It might instead have been a more indirect, even an evasive reply, designed to provide both a response and an argument:

> "Do you favor the establishment of a Palestinian state?"
> "I will support whatever is necessary to find peace in the Middle East."

Strictly speaking, this response is neither plainly affirmative nor plainly negative. Neither is the implicit warrant clear. In fact, the response may be understood in various different ways. It could be taken as saying that the president does, indeed, support a Palestinian state, insofar as that step is necessary to finding peace. Or it could be taken as saying that he is opposed to a Palestinian state, insofar as it would be an obstacle to finding peace. Or again it could be intended as offering only a *conditional* statement of policy: the president might be signaling to the Israeli government that unless it becomes more cooperative in the pursuit of peace arrangements, the United States might become more receptive than hitherto to the Palestinian demands.

Evidently such an ambiguous response might well be used with a devious intent. The president may be quite happy to allow some people to believe that he really does support a Palestinian state, when in fact he does not, or vice versa. His immediate purpose may be to frighten the Israelis or else to maintain a politically ambiguous position so as to "keep the options open." Diplomats and politicians will thus have to analyze any such statement by a national leader—together with the relevant supporting considerations—with an eye to overall policy, the current situation, previous positions taken, their own guesses, and much more. Their interpretation of the president's reasoning will thus be arrived at in pragmatic terms.

Exercises

We have discussed the ways in which language and reasoning are essentially related both in their acquisition by children and in the ways they are employed by both children and adults. Our goal here has been to help relate the analytical discussion of reasoning in the first four parts of the book to the kinds of communications people use everyday. Doing the following exercises will assist that effort.

1. Tape-record two children playing together for at least ten minutes. Listen to the recording and make note of every time a child uses reasoning. Be prepared to justify your decision to label a comment as reasoning.
2. Locate a piece of writing that is essentially unplanned—a letter, note, journal entry—and identify and explain the reasoning in it.
3. In a group of three others, go over some written school work and analyze the reasoning used. Then take some time to talk about the reasoning the group used in talking about the reasoning in the papers.

22

Classification of arguments

In presenting the different elements of a practical argument in Part II—particularly the warrants that authorize the move from grounds to claims—we emphasized the *differences* between the considerations relevant to arguments in different fields of reasoning. Thus, in the natural sciences, it is "laws of nature" and the like that perform the warrant function; in legal contexts, it is statutes, precedents, and rules that provide warrants; and in medicine, it is diagnostic descriptions that often generate the warrants by which claims are justified. Specialized studies which qualify people to become scientists, physicians, lawyers, and the like heavily involve instruction on the ways to construct arguments appropriate to the special field under investigation. Presumably, those who have completed such graduate or professional study are prepared to construct arguments appropriate to their field. Those who do not, quickly learn this skill during early practice or they face difficulties.

However, in Chapter 21 we observed that people generally develop skills in reasoning during the first five years, and go on during adulthood to refine and enrich their repertoire of argumentative practices. We also noted that there is a wide variety of reasoning situations outside specialized fields, and even trained professionals do not necessarily resort to their specialized arguments when reasoning in these general situations. This may be explained in part by the fact that the criteria that obtain in individual fields may not apply in general argumentative situations.

In this chapter, we will call attention to the fact that all warrants share certain common functions, and over the years students of reasoning have discovered that regardless of the field in which these occur, many of our warrants tend to share certain other features also. So specific warrants may be alike in resting on certain deeper assumptions or rules. By identifying and discussing these relatively deep assumptions or rules of reasoning, we can expose the types of arguments likely to be found in the communication of people outside their special fields.

Before turning to a specific discussion of various common classes of arguments, it is useful to reiterate a point suggested throughout this book: given the same set of grounds, one can generate different claims depending upon the warrant chosen. This is important both to the critic and to the creator of arguments. There is no single "correct" warrant to be attached to any set of grounds. Choice of warrant is a matter of the process of argumentation and is governed by the type and strength of claim sought as well as the audience—readers or listeners—to whom the argument is addressed.

For example, on January 4, 1983 Bruce Kimmel, writing as a representative of the Communist Party of the U.S.A., said, " . . . the Communist Party has played and continues to play an active role in the U.S. peace movement." On March 2, 1983, the following was said on the floor of the United States Senate: " . . . the Soviet Union is very interested in developments in the nuclear freeze movement in the United States. . . . the Communist Party of the U.S.A. (CPUSA) is closely aligned with the Soviet Communist Party." [*Congressional Record*] Given this information as grounds, what claim can be justified?

Reasoning from a basic assumption of *cause and effect,* one might claim that "The Soviet Union is behind (the cause of) the U.S. peace movement." The warrant, operating on a premise of a string of causes, suggests the Soviets cause the CPUSA to take action, and the CPUSA has caused American opposition to the development of nuclear energy and weapons. The argument can be diagrammed as shown in Figure 22–1.

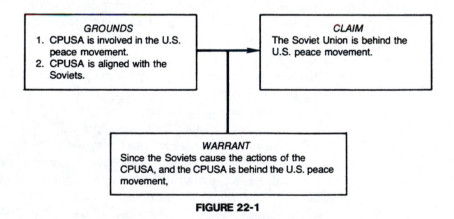

FIGURE 22-1

But, a claim suggesting that the Soviet Union is the prime cause of the U.S. peace movement is difficult to sustain against rebuttals showing many people with no connection to the CPUSA actively behind the movement. In such a case, the claim might be changed to one more viable by a change in the warrant employed.

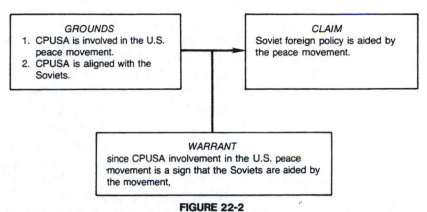

FIGURE 22-2

A claim based upon the warrant of *sign* might be more likely to survive critical scrutiny: Soviet foreign policy is aided by the U.S. peace movement. Note Figure 22–2.

This, however, is by no means the end of the claims that might be supported by this set of grounds. Opponents of the first two claims might find reasoned support for the opposite conclusion by arguing from *analogy* to the following conclusion: "The Soviets are intent upon discrediting the U.S. peace movement." Notice how this might be diagrammed (Figure 22–3).

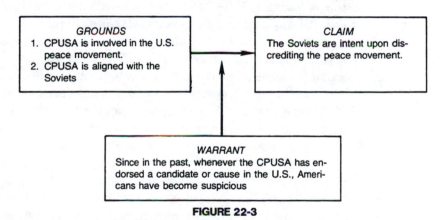

FIGURE 22-3

The fact that it is the critics of the U.S. peace movement who are intent upon calling attention to the CPUSA involvement might lend further support to this claim. On the other hand, it is most likely to be critics who would have the courage and motive to reveal a potentially disastrous situation.

To review, our point in this chapter is to identify and explain some common assumptions or rules on which warrants may be based. Warrants draw their strength from the fact that they have persisted over the years and across many cultures as rather basic ways of viewing relationships. In any particular case, there is no one proper warrant to be discovered. Rather, selection of warrants is a matter of reasoned choice informed by the perspective of the arguer and the audience. As with all arguments, strength or soundness will be a matter of critical judgment, as we shall discuss in Chapter 23, Fields of Discussion.

If we set up for ourselves, in this chapter, a classification of *general types* of argument, it must be used with caution. Nothing said here will undermine our earlier conclusion that arguments need to be examined with an eye to the context and field in which they occur. Nor shall we be suggesting that there are any *fixed rules* for determining the correctness of arguments of one type or another. Nor, finally, shall we be offering our classification of arguments as *exhaustive*. Still, over the two thousand years or so that people have been studying argumentation, it has been possible to identify a number of familiar general assumptions in terms of which claims can be justified, and the classes discussed here represent samples of these assumptions.

Reasoning from analogy

Theoretically every object or system in the world is in certain respects unique. Yet practically speaking, people and things tend to look and act very much alike. In "arguing from analogy," we assume that there are enough similarities between two things to support the claim that what is true of one is also true of the other. If the Teton Dam was earth-filled, was constructed on a fault line, and was more than thirty years old, it is reasonable to compare it with some other dam that shares these characteristics, even though in other respects they may not be identical. So, given that the Teton Dam burst, we may claim that the analogous dam is also liable to burst. On the basis of such an argument, engineers may find it necessary to modify the second dam, even though it has given no signs of weakness up to now. What happened with one dam may reasonably be expected with another one that *shares characteristics relevant to the claim being made* and does not have *differences that would destroy the analogy*.

Analogies appear frequently in ordinary conversation. Tell a friend about your personal problems, and the chances are good that you will get back the answer, "That's like what happened to me." Advice may then be presented based on the warrant that what happened to your friend formerly is analogous to what is happening to you now: "I solved my problem this way. It should work for you."

In the law, the principle of *stare decisis* effectively obliges the courts to reason from analogy. The principle directs judges to avoid unnecessary changes in legal practice by deciding similar cases in similar ways.

Suppose that a case before the Court has the following essential facts:

1. A 27-year-old woman was
2. arrested for possession of a controlled substance and

3. confessed, but
4. she was not informed of her right to counsel or to silence

Lawyers for both the state and the defendant will then look for previously decided cases that share the same essential facts.

For instance, counsel for the defense will search out previous cases in which the one critical fact was the failure to advise the accused of the right to counsel or to silence. Reasoning from analogy, the court may then conclude that if previous cases were dismissed on this ground, the present case should also be dismissed. Counsel for the state will similarly look either for critical differences between the facts of the present and previous cases capable of destroying the analogy or for other precedent cases similar to the present case that were decided differently.

These examples illustrate relatively straightforward analogies. Dams, legal cases, and personal experiences can be seen as alike comparatively easily. The more dissimilar the objects being compared, however, the more difficult it is to find credible analogies between them. Arguments based on comparisons between family finances and federal budgetary policy might not pass the critical scrutiny of economists, but they seem quite reasonable to many lay people. Comparisons between human thinking and computer processing meet with a more mixed reaction, and between objects of widely different kinds, the alleged similarities may be dismissed as being merely rhetorical or speculative and as lacking any power to carry conviction in argument.

Those comparisons that are generally perceived as rhetorical devices are sometimes called *figurative analogies* and are thought of as falling into a different, nonargumentative category. They may be helpful as ways of making some point clearer, but they cannot actually warrant any claim:

> If you have a well that receives 1,000 gallons of water a day from underground sources, and you remove 1,500 gallons of water a day from it, the well will run dry; similarly, if the government receives $500 million a day in social security payments and pays out $600 million a day in benefits, the social-security system will also "run dry."

The distinction between literal and figurative analogies is not, of course, an absolute one. No two phenomena are exactly alike, so the comparisons involved in all analogies are more-or-less imperfect. The key question is how *close* the analogy is, and an analogy will be judged as "closer" when the points of comparison between two objects are greater in number, are more directly relevant to the claim being supported, and are countered by fewer relevant points of difference.

Examine the following arguments in Figures 22–4 through 22–6 from analogy and discuss them critically. Among other things, consider particularly the extent to which the points of comparison seem strong enough to warrant the claim,

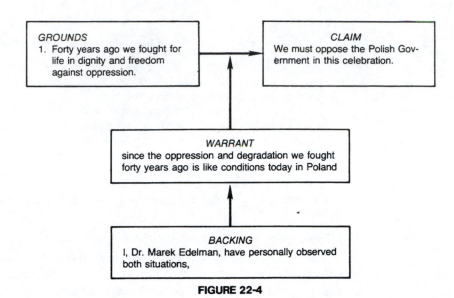

FIGURE 22-4

and consider whether or not analogy is the most appropriate way of warranting the claims.

On April 19, 1983, the Polish government announced an eight-day program of ceremonies to commemorate the fortieth anniversary of the Warsaw Ghetto uprising against the Nazi Army. Dr. Marek Edelman, who was a leader of the

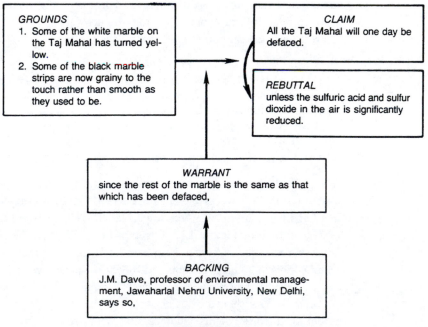

FIGURE 22-5

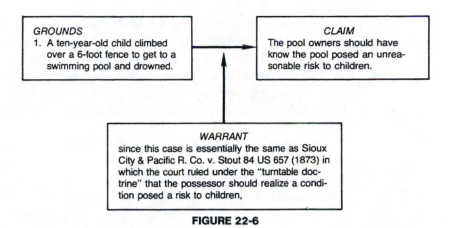

FIGURE 22-6

fight against the Germans and who is the only known survivor now living in Poland, called for a boycott of the celebration using the argument diagrammed in Figure 22–4.

Reasoning from generalization

Where people or objects are sufficiently alike, it becomes possible to group them into populations, or "kinds," and to make general claims about them. Whereas arguments from analogy typically involve claims based on a close comparison between a few specific instances, arguments from generalization involve examining a sufficiently large and representative sample of the "kind" in question. The operation of public opinion polls illustrates well the problems involved in reasoning from generalization. A sample of the population is selected, based on a carefully thought-out set of criteria, as representing all the people to be included in the generalization, or alternatively, the sample is picked at random, so that every member of the population has the same statistical chance of being selected. Either way, it must be possible to argue that what is true of the sample is very likely to be true of the group as a whole. From this sample, a generalization may be made. If 67 percent of the men sampled report extramarital adventures, it is claimed that the same is true of something close to 67 percent of all men in the relevant population.

Reasoning from generalization demands the use of sufficiently representative samples, samples large enough so that the addition of more items will not change the outcome, samples that have been objectively observed or selected, samples that have been accurately measured, and samples close enough in time to the generalization they are used to support so that historical changes have not invalidated the generalization. Biased questionnaires and sloppy research design can yield unreliable data; unreliable measuring instruments can yield untrustworthy results; and the continual changes in people's habits raise the possibility that the lapse of time between the observation of the sample and the assertion of the claim invalidates the claim itself. (Rapid developments in public opinion during the last weeks of an election campaign can make political prognostication a risky business.) So critics of reasoning from generalization will be greatly influenced by the nature of the sample on which it is based, particularly by the relationship between that sample and the larger population about which the subsequent claim is to be made.

In informal, unplanned reasoning, the specific *example* is often advanced as the grounds for a claim based on generalization. In the absence of any counter examples, it often is deemed sufficient. For example, a group planning to eat out might proceed this way: "Sally, I think we should go to La Paloma. They have the best Mexican food in town." "How do you know, Randy?" "I was there last Saturday, and it was great." Look at this argument in Figure 22–7.

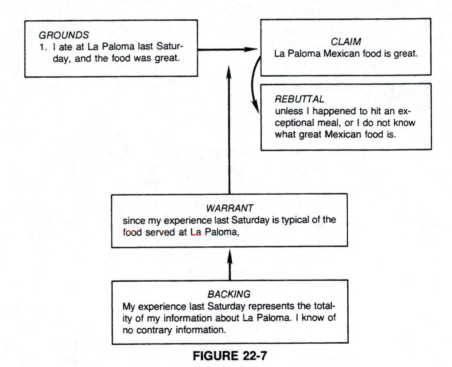

FIGURE 22-7

This simple everyday line of reasoning illustrates rather clearly argument from generalization. The warrant constitutes an expression that from a selection of experiences, in this case only one, a general claim can be made. Can one example or experience constitute sufficient basis for an argument from generalization? We do it all the time and survive critical scrutiny. If Sally and Randy go to La Paloma tonight and the food is terrible, the claim is quickly swept away. If they go and Randy continues to be pleased and Sally reports the food to be reheated, bland, tourist Mexican, they will need to engage in some talk about the definition of great Mexican. Sally may suggest Randy does not know good Mexican, and this is also a possibility in argument from generalization: the data base may be poorly or improperly measured. If they both agree the food is great, the claim holds with one additional experience added to the data base plus an additional analyst in Sally. Two months later, when they are joined by another couple, they can say, "La Paloma food is great. Randy has eaten there twice, and I was with him the second time. We loved it." Chances are, the claim will serve effectively in making the dining decision.

However, should the four people agree that this last visit found the food uniformly unacceptable, a new claim may be tried. A common one might be, "La Paloma has gone downhill. They are not as good as they used to be." With that one four-person experience, a new generalization is quite possible: "We are not going back there again." With both good and bad experiences at the same restaurant over time, the data support several potential claims:

1. The good food was atypical; La Paloma was never a good place.
2. The bad food was atypical; La Paloma is generally a good place.
3. Some change has turned the food from good to bad.

It would now be necessary to make several more trips to La Paloma to gather additional data before any of these claims could be given much credence. People, however, rarely have enough stake in restaurants to go back after even one bad experience.

Taken in such a limited situation, reasoning from generalization does not appear very different from analogy. More firm claims based on generalization are warranted by citation of a number of examples, each of them representing a sample of specific instances. Again, the examples must stand up to the questions of whether they are representative of the whole and if they were properly measured. Determining whether a large enough sample is presented is usually a function of the test of whether the addition of more instances requires modification of the claim: *are there contrary instances?* If so, how do they compare to the original sample? Figure 22–8 shows a more common example of generalization.

Here there are two generalizations: (1) two heavy thunderstorms in four years are claimed to support a generalization that thunderstorms can be expected regularly; (2) two-thirds of the community, 2,500 residences, five people drowned, and $60 million in damages constitute four different measures of specific instances leading to the claim that storms result in serious damage. Notice that the latter argument asserts a *causal* generalization, which we will discuss later.

Finally, let us examine in Figure 22–9, a claim based on a generalization using opinion survey techniques. Here, as we have said, methods of generalization have been carefully developed so that a relatively small number of specific instances can be used to warrant a claim about the population as a whole. Selec-

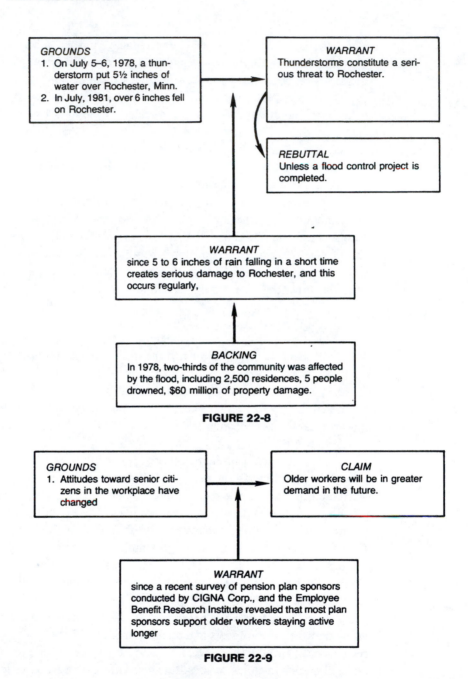

FIGURE 22-8

FIGURE 22-9

tion of sample groups is done within established guidelines to permit the claim that what is true of the sample is true of the entire population.

Reasoning from sign

There is nothing complicated about our use of "signs." In driving, we "reason from sign" repeatedly. We see a flashing light and conclude that some kind of hazard is present; we see a red, white, and blue shield with a number on it and know that we are driving on an interstate highway; and so on. These claims rely on arguments from sign. Whenever a sign and its referent can reliably be expected to occur together, the fact that the sign is observed can be used to support a claim about the presence of the object or situation the sign refers to.

In the law, circumstantial evidence often sets up an argument from sign. Lacking direct proof of the defendant's guilt, the state may present a series of signs of guilt. The day before the murder, the accused bought herself a one-way air ticket to Mexico; when stopped by the police, she tried to run away; when asked about her whereabouts at the time of the murder, she told a highly detailed story about what she was doing, which there was no way to corroborate. The state then claims that these facts are all signs of guilt, because in the past guilty people have regularly behaved in just this way.

Similarly many aspects of medical diagnosis rely on reasoning from sign. Certain observable characteristics—sudden changes in mood or behavior, a loss of appetite, the development of phobias—may not be connected with specific diseases directly and inevitably, but they may accompany them often enough to justify the physician in making certain additional tests when he observes enough of these symptoms.

If the rules for constructing reliable sign reasoning are straightforward, so are the guidelines to the critic. The central question is, simply, just how certainly any sign is associated with what it is supposed to signal. (Are we sure that a flashing light indicates a hazard rather than a roadside café? May not a person afraid of being accused of murder behave in the same way that a guilty person does?)

Reasoning from sign provides a sensible way of supporting claims in highly complex forums of deliberation where more precise arguments are difficult to advance. For example, national economics reveals such a myriad of interacting forces that "economic indicators" or *signs* are commonly used in support of broad claims. Notice this common example (Figure 22–10).

Diplomacy is another complicated area for constructing arguments that turn to reasoning from signs. Since the U.S. Department of State is not privy to beliefs and plans in the foreign offices of other countries, but is still required to understand their position and predict their behavior, sign-reasoning is a common tool. In fact, because of the delicacy of diplomatic relations and the resultant problems with direct communication, diplomats have formed a system of signs with which to communicate. Figure 22–11 shows a common example of diplomatic sign reasoning.

Another forum for use of reasoning from sign is in the area of "actions speak louder than words." When Ronald Reagan became President of the United States, he proclaimed his administration as being in favor of women's rights. Opponents were skeptical: they announced they would watch for signs; his actions would speak louder than his words. After the new administration was well in place, the claim shown in Figure 22–12 was advanced.

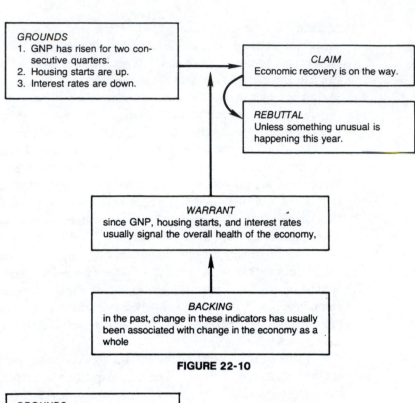

FIGURE 22-10

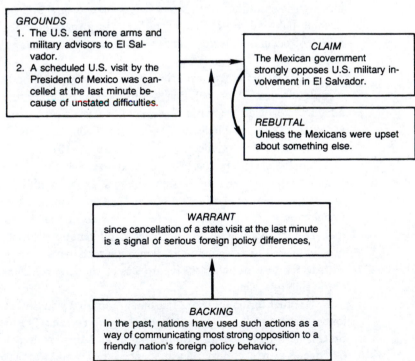

FIGURE 22-11

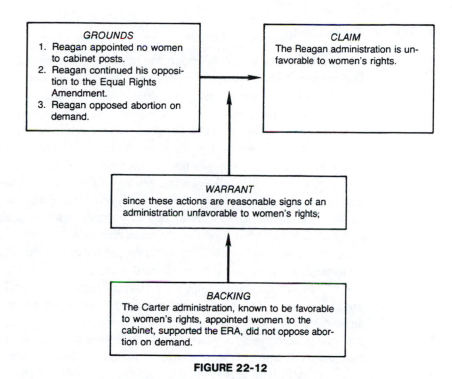

FIGURE 22-12

In time, supporters of Reagan could counter this argument with signs of their own (Figure 22–13).

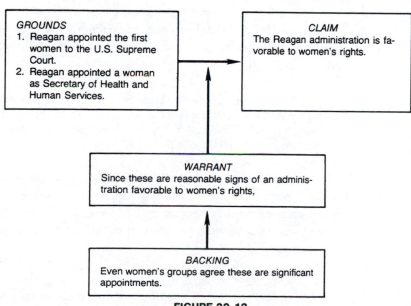

FIGURE 22-13

Reasoning from cause

In certain cases, we can assert the presence of a relationship stronger than that of sign and referent; that is, we may claim that an event or a condition of one kind is the *cause* of an event or a condition of another kind. These two kinds of event do not just regularly appear together: they are *causally connected.* Fingerprints and bloodstains may be not only signs of guilt, they may be caused by the presence of the accused at the scene of the crime. High temperature and a rash may not only be signs of a disease, they may be caused by it.

Arguments from cause require, first and foremost, a causal generalization asserting that if such-and-such a cause is observed, its effect can be expected to follow. Alternatively the generalization may sometimes be asserted in the other direction: if the effect is observed, the cause may be presumed. If the existence of either the cause or the effect can be demonstrated in a particular situation, the existence of the other can then be claimed to follow.

There are various different ways in which significant causal generalizations can be established or backed. Sometimes people have relied on traditional or commonsense beliefs about the universe to support their causal interpretations of experience. Sometimes they have relied on the multiplication of observations: they have observed case after case in which changes in the phases of the moon have been associated with changes in the tides and have inferred that the moon somehow or other causes the rise and fall of the tides. John Stuart Mill presented a series of methods for generating causal generalizations. These are called the methods of *agreement, difference, agreement and difference, concomitant variation* and *residues.*

The principle of *agreement* suggests that if two or more instances of the object of the claim have one and only one circumstance in common, that circumstance can be taken to be the cause (or the effect) of the phenomenon under investigation:

> For example, if we find high life expectancy and low infant mortality in certain nations and discover that the only way in which these nations are alike is that they have a national health program, it may be argued that the health plans are the cause of the good medical records.

According to the method of *difference,* if an instance in which the object of the claim occurs and one in which it does not occur share every feature except one, which is associated only with the first instance, that point of difference is the cause or effect (or an indispensable part of the cause) of the phenomenon under investigation:

> Studies designed to show the relevance of genetics and environment to human development and behavior use this form of reasoning when they work with identical twins. Genetically such twins are precisely alike. Where, for one reason

or another, they have been separated at birth and have grown up in different families and locations, subsequent differences in personality, behavior, or other respects can be attributed to environmental rather than genetic causes, for those are the only relevant points of difference.

Claims based on *agreement and difference* combine these two methods to add strength to the causal generalization. Mill stated his canon this way:

> If two or more instances in which the phenomenon occurs have only one circumstance in common, while two or more instances in which it does not occur have nothing in common save the absence of that circumstance; the circumstance in which alone the two sets of instances (always or invariably) differ, is the effect, or the cause or an indispensable part of the cause, of the phenomenon.

> The use of control groups in scientific experiments is designed to apply this method. By isolating and studying two separate groups of subjects (whether crop plants or human invalids) that are in most respects alike, and then treating them in different ways, we can look out *both* for the respects in which members of each group develop in similar ways *and also* for the respects in which members of the two different groups develop differently. Where some specific feature (e.g., crop yield from the plant or the cure of the invalids' disease) can be picked out as showing both agreement within the experimental group and difference between the experimental and the control group, we are in that much stronger a position to see this feature as *causally* associated with the special treatment given to the experimental group.

The method of *residues* argues that if you subtract from any phenomenon under investigation any parts for which the cause is already known, the residue of the phenomenon can be taken to be the effect of the remaining possible causes.

> If an industrial corporation is searching for the cause of a quarterly decline in earnings, it may analyze all its various operations, eliminating those causal relations already known. This much loss came from international exchange rates affecting cash holdings. Consumer demand for the product remained constant; still total sales were down. The only remaining cause unaccounted for is lower productivity, and it is here (according to the method of residues) that the company should look for the cause of the decline in earnings.

The idea of *concomitant variations* corresponds to what, in modern terms, is called *correlation*. If one phenomenon varies whenever another one varies, it is argued that one may be taken as the cause or the effect of the other or else that the two are causally related. That last phrase is important. Correlations often reveal two factors that vary together, because both of them are effects of a third cause or causes:

> Insurance companies have discovered that students who get good grades in school are better risks for automobile insurance and so offer them lower premium

rates. No one argues that getting an "A" in a logic class instantly makes you a better driver, deserving a premium reduction. Rather, it is argued that those same people who get good grades also tend to be good drivers. Both sets of phenomena are attributed to other, unstated and even unknown causes. Because grade averages are easy to measure, they provide an easy way of justifying causal associations with good driving without the company's having to delve into the other unstated causes.

The critic of causal generalization is sensitive to potential problems with all these methods. The apparent cause of any phenomenon may turn out to be only a sign of an as yet unobserved cause, and the question will always be how carefully the factors to be observed were selected. The critic will thus search for other potential causes that may have been overlooked. More important, critics of causal generalization have often charged that the world is not simple enough to permit the discovery of single causes for many (if any) important phenomena. Instead we should expect a complex of interrelated factors to be relevant to many of the things we need to understand. It is even argued that assuming a single directionality (from cause *to* effect) may be naive. Specialists in systems analysis talk about *mutual* causality—about situations in which different factors affect and are affected by each other simultaneously.

Criticize the following arguments from cause (Figures 22–14 through 22–16) and comment on at least three questions: (1) what is the causal rationale (agreement, difference, or other factors) for the claim; (2) does the argument satisfy the requirements for generalization, *per se;* (3) what possible rebuttals can you advance?

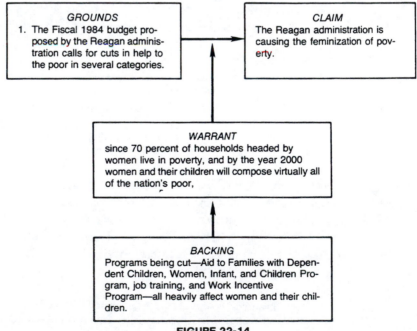

FIGURE 22-14

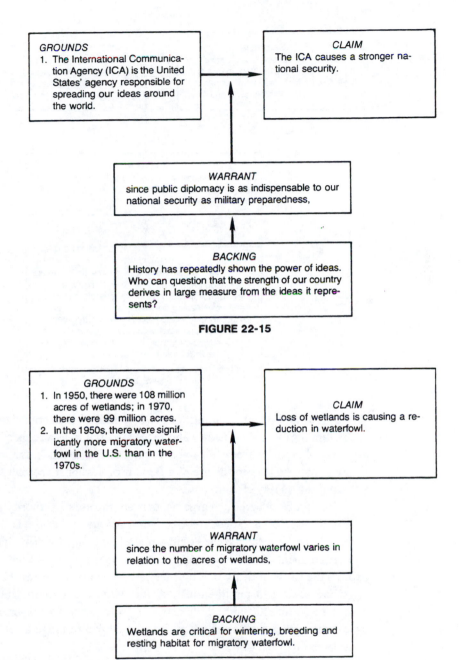

GROUNDS
1. The International Communication Agency (ICA) is the United States' agency responsible for spreading our ideas around the world.

CLAIM
The ICA causes a stronger national security.

WARRANT
since public diplomacy is as indispensable to our national security as military preparedness,

BACKING
History has repeatedly shown the power of ideas. Who can question that the strength of our country derives in large measure from the ideas it represents?

FIGURE 22-15

GROUNDS
1. In 1950, there were 108 million acres of wetlands; in 1970, there were 99 million acres.
2. In the 1950s, there were significantly more migratory waterfowl in the U.S. than in the 1970s.

CLAIM
Loss of wetlands is causing a reduction in waterfowl.

WARRANT
since the number of migratory waterfowl varies in relation to the acres of wetlands,

BACKING
Wetlands are critical for wintering, breeding and resting habitat for migratory waterfowl.

FIGURE 22-16

Reasoning from authority

Reasoning based upon the judgment of authorities is at once one of the most common forms of argument and one of the most commonly misused forms. We are bombarded in commercial advertising with instances of *Ipse dixit* or "He or

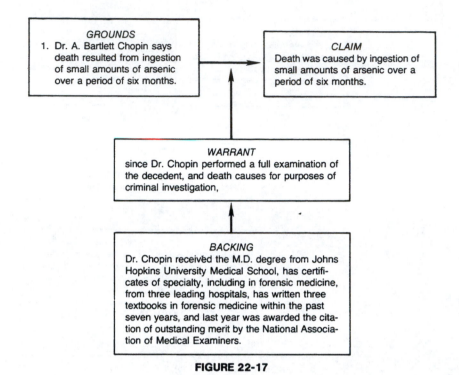

FIGURE 22-17

she says so" and therefore it must *be* so. Celebrities whose only claim to authority is the familiarity of their names and faces are used to assure us of the quality of a variety of products from bras to barbecues, cars to cabins in the mountains. The ultimate may have been the use of a famous professional football quarterback to tell us of the quality of pantyhose.

The problem with such arguments is not the use of authority *per se;* it is the failure to establish an adequate *foundation* for the authority. To justify a claim with any cogency, the authority cited must be qualified as capable of providing expert judgment on the subject of the claim. If the claim is used in the court to express the cause of death in a murder case, the authority must be qualified as a physician, specializing in forensic medicine, with experience in determining death causes under questionable circumstances, with extensive experience in recent times, and with a reputation among those qualified to judge as an expert in this area. (See Figure 22–17.)

In a world of such complexity as ours, it would make no sense not to recognize the need to call upon expert judgment from time to time. If causes of death were judged only by lawyers and jurors, much would be lost from our system of justice. If only politicians judged the qualities of space vehicles or economic analyses, our government would have even more trouble than it has. Accordingly, we do rest claims upon the judgment of authorities under the following circumstances:

1. The person testifying is demonstrated to have had recent and full access to the necessary data or objects about which a judgment is to be made.
2. The authority is identified explicitly, not vaguely as in a reference to a "national research lab" or "a well known commentator."
3. The individual is demonstrated to have the education, training, and experience to be considered an authority.
4. This authority is acknowledged by other specialists qualified to judge authority.
5. The authority is shown by past performance to be one worthy of respect.
6. The person's credentials or experience are current.
7. The authority is expressing a judgment that falls within his or her area of expertise.
8. The authority's judgment is weighed against the testimony of other qualified experts.

When, some years ago, Linus Pauling, a Nobel Laureate in Chemistry, published claims about the physical and psychological values of large doses of vitamin C, many were skeptical. While his authority in his field was unquestioned, many doubted his expertise in this particular area of inquiry. For the claim about vitamin C to be given serious consideration, Pauling needed to establish himself as an authority, or other researchers with clear expertise needed to provide confirmation.

Analyze the examples of reasoning from authority in Figures 22–18 through 22–20. Test them to see if sufficient foundation has been advanced, and if a clear consistency between claim and specialty is shown.

Other possible classifications

Some reasoning is based on the *argument from dilemma*. Here a claim rests upon the warrant that two and only two choices or explanations are possible, and both are bad. When a Congressman was arrested for soliciting a prostitute in the red-light district of Salt Lake City at 2:00 A.M., many people saw him as being in a dilemma. Either he was guilty as charged and thus should be condemned, or he was talking to the woman innocently, and this—under the circumstances—showed stupidity in a politician running for reelection, so that once again he should be condemned.

A dilemma must be established in relation to the specific claim at hand. If the Congressman can generate a third possible explanation consistent with the admitted facts in the case that does not leave him exposed to condemnation, the claim from dilemma will fall. Dilemmas based on linguistic appearance, rather than on substance, may not survive close criticism:

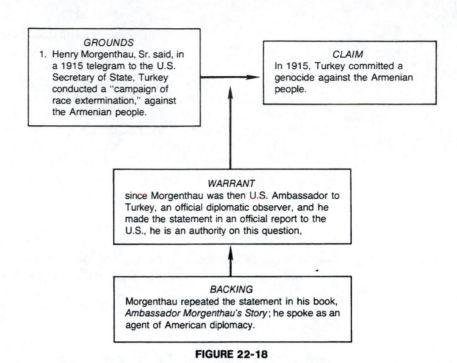

FIGURE 22-18

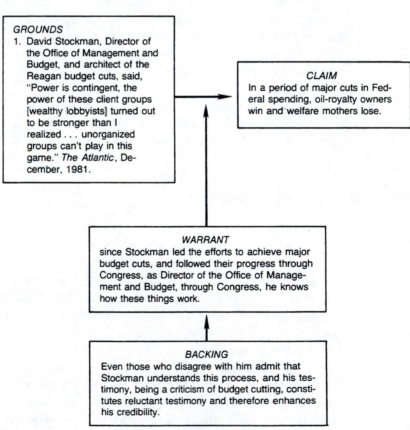

FIGURE 22-19

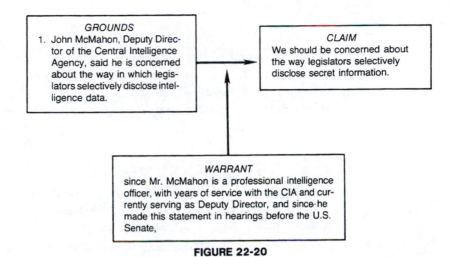

FIGURE 22-20

For instance, the United States has been charged with facing a dilemma in foreign policy. If we intervene in the problems of other countries, we are accused of imperialism; if we do not intervene, we are accused of insensitivity. This situation seems clearly to result in a dilemma. Even if we allow that these are the only alternatives and that either conclusion is undesirable, it still is possible to rebut the dilemma by challenging the terms in which it is framed. For *intervention* need not always be taken as objectionable or "imperialistic"; if it is undertaken at the urgent request of the United Nations, for example, it may be wholly positive and so escape the charge of being imperialistic.

Other types of arguments frequently encountered in practical reasoning include:

— Arguments from *classification*, in which the typical properties of plants, prize cattle, or whatever are used as the basis for claims about them.
— Arguments from *opposites*, in which things that are known to be radically different in some given respect are presumed to be equally different in some other respect.
— Arguments from *degree*, in which the different properties of a given thing are presumed to vary in step with one another.

Here as elsewhere, it turns out not to be possible to give an exhaustive or formal account of all the possible types of argument. On the contrary, it is practicable only to characterize the general kinds of acceptable reasoning most frequently to be met with in practical situations. Even so, many of the types listed here merge into one another and are hard to distinguish sharply from one another.

Exercises

Below are several narrative statements, including various kinds of information and claims. Take each statement and try to develop as many different kinds of arguments as possible. If you find some element lacking in order to complete an argument, indicate the type of material you would need to discover in order to sustain your claim.

1. According to *The New York Times* (April 17, 1983), Richard N. Perle, an Assistant Secretary of Defense, recommended that the Army consider buying weapons from an Israeli company a year after he accepted a $50,000 consulting fee from the company's owners.

2. Ambassador Jeane J. Kirkpatrick, U.S. Permanent Representative to the United Nations, testified to the U.S. Senate, "From the very earliest days of the UN, we . . . have had a fundamentally flawed mental picture of how issues are decided at the United Nations. We have imagined that the General Assembly . . . is made up of individual voting members who listen carefully to the arguments pro and con, decide what is right and just and in their country's interest, and vote accordingly. . . . You may be surprised to learn that voting behavior . . . is rather like [that] in any legislature. That is, voting alliances, temporary or of longer duration are formed on the basis of shared interests. Favors are extended, obligations accumulated and discharged, arms are twisted . . . a vote may be bought—or least rented."

3. A plane, flying from Syria to Nicaragua with medical supplies, was forced by engine trouble to land in Brazil. There it was discovered that the plane actually contained arms and ammunition. The U.S. Department of State observed that we can now be sure that troubles in Latin America are being supported by outside parties.

4. Dr. Robert M. Bowman, President of the Institute for Space and Security Studies and retired Air Force colonel, said, "Proponents claim that space-based defensive systems can be deployed: (1) using existing off-the-shelf-technology, (2) at a reasonable (about $15 billion) cost, (3) within five to six years. . . . None of these claims are true. The facts are as follows:

    1. Most Pentagon experts I have talked to agree that the technology requirements have been grossly underestimated. There is no off-the-shelf technology for this mission—except on paper. . . .
    2. Responsible Pentagon analysts estimate the true cost at anywhere from $100 billion to over a trillion! . . . .
    3. Even with an Apollo-like commitment, it would take eight or nine years to start deployment of the first layer."

5. Should parents of minor female children be informed when their daughters

are given a prescription for birth-control devices? Some say that if this is required, there will be more teenage pregnancies. But Paul Howie, writing in the *Atlanta Journal* of January 17, 1983 says, "Yes, kids will be kids and nothing will ever stop that. But many a grappling session in the back seat of a jalopy has been cut short by the thought of what Mama would say." To deny parents such information will amount to a sanction for sexual activity among youngsters. It will lead to more sexual promiscuity.

23

Fields
of
discussion

In Part V we have turned our attention toward specific reasoning practices as they actually occur from day to day. Our objective has been to make our discussion more practically meaningful. We demonstrated, in Chapter 21, the fact that reasoning typically does not occur in the simple examples that must be used in a textbook. It appears in discourse of ordinary communication. In Chapter 22, we examined more closely the specific types of arguments people tend to use in their reasoned communication. Here we explored the relationship between the analytical pattern of analysis set out in Parts II and III and the process of practical reasoning.

In Chapter 23, we will take still another step toward understanding and evaluating reasoning within its natural settings such as law, business, science, art, and politics. Looking at actual arguments people have advanced, we will notice that it rarely happens that some are altogether sound and others fully unsound. Within any subject on which people reason, there will be a variety of arguments of varying character and soundness, and it will fall upon us to evaluate them and make reasonable choices among them. This discussion will focus on the process of reasoned appraisal among competing arguments.

THE RATIONAL MERITS OF ARGUMENTS

First we must ask:

— What makes one practical argument better than another?
— What features of any argument do we have to investigate in order to arrive at a clear view of its merits or defects *as an argument?*
— In particular, how are we to tell when an argument is truly convincing

(i.e., when it *deserves to* carry conviction) as distinct from being simply attractive (i.e., when it is able to win applause regardless of its merits)?

Evidently an eloquent speaker or writer can dress up arguments in all kinds of ways so as to conceal their defects and make them attractive to the audience. To the extent that he understands the tastes and prejudices of the audience, he will be able to slant his arguments to take advantage of those inclinations. But in most cases, it is possible to separate the features that give our arguments genuine "rational merit" from those other rhetorical devices that have the effect of making them more attractive and persuasive than they deserve to be. So let us begin here by setting aside all considerations of charm and eloquence and by concentrating on those rational merits alone.

Some of the essential merits of our arguments are already clear from what has been said earlier. For instance:

— It must be clear just what *kind* of issues the argument is intended to raise (aesthetic rather than scientific, say, or legal rather than psychiatric) and what its underlying *purpose* is.
— The *grounds* on which it rests must be relevant to the *claim* made in the argument and must be sufficient to support it.
— The *warrant* relied on to guarantee this support must be applicable to the case under discussion and must be based on solid *backing*.
— The *modality*, or strength, of the resulting claim must be made explicit, and the possible *rebuttals*, or exceptions, must be well understood.

Clarifying the purpose and standpoint of an argument

Before a practical argument even gets started, there are certain ambiguities that may have to be resolved. There are a lot of claims (e.g. "Jack's crazy," "Mary really ought not to have done that") whose status may not initially be clear. Are the issues being raised legal or ethical, say? (Is the objection to Mary's conduct that it involved a breach of the law or a lack of human consideration?) In such cases, the parties to the argument may simply start off at cross-purposes, lacking a clarification of the basic issues. One of them may start off looking at Mary's conduct from the legal standpoint and see no harm in it ("She broke no law"), while the other party is taking up the other, moral standpoint ("Law or no law, it was a shoddy thing to do") and so disapprove.

Until these initial differences have been clarified, there may be no basis for a fruitful argument at all. The parties may simply be unable to agree about what procedures, considerations, criteria of judgment, and so on are *to the point* for the purposes of the argument. For they *have* no shared point or purposes.

Often enough, it is true, one can find enough clues in the situation within which an argument arises to ensure a sufficient degree of mutual understanding in practice. For instance:

Within the context of a psychiatric consultation, questions about sanity and insanity will naturally be given a medical rather than a legal interpretation, so any ambiguities that might otherwise have arisen about those questions can be avoided.

Conversely, within the context of a law court hearing, questions about sanity and insanity will naturally be given a judicial rather than a psychiatric interpretation, so once again the risks of ambiguity will be avoided.

Law court proceedings, medical consultation, professional scientific meetings, and the like are deliberately structured and conducted—in their role as "forums of argumentation"—in such a way as to eliminate doubts and confusions about the "rational standpoint" of the arguments presented within them.

Once we leave the professional sphere, however, difficulties of this sort arise much more easily and frequently. In political discussions particularly, it may often be unclear at the outset whether a given speaker is concerned with the issues in debate from the standpoint of ethics, finance, diplomatic propriety, national defense, social welfare, or whatever. So when two people enter such a debate from very different directions and points of view, the result may be complete *cross-purposes:*

> Going into lunch at a private club, an insurance executive recognizes a famous country/western singing star and invites her to join him. During conversation, the singer mentions the fact that the holding company which owns the Grand Ole Opry in Nashville has offered it for sale. The executive acknowledges this fact and presents some financial information about the debt situation of the holding company. The singer tells something of the history and significance of the Opry. They part each thinking the other has demonstrated a lamentable ignorance of the situation.
>
> How does this happen? The insurance executive approached the topic with full attention upon the ways in which businesses sometimes must sell off valuable properties in order to manage cash flow problems and keep investments within a relatively focused thrust. The singer, on the other hand, perceived the Grand Ole Opry as a significant cultural phenomenon that should be treasured and not exploited for profit.

In such a case, the danger is that the two parties will not even reach an understanding about the *starting point* of their argument, to say nothing about its conclusion. Instead of their paying proper attention to each other's arguments, the executive is liable to see the singer as naive and uninformed, while the singer sees the executive as unfeeling and lacking in cultural appreciation rather than as just businesslike.

> "Our company needs to generate between $400 and $700 million to offset debts which rose to $950 million with the purchase of the Opryland complex and other properties. Besides, the Opry is not central to the thrust of our investment package."
>
> "You're just bottom-line people with no appreciation of the historical and cultural significance of the Grand Ole Opry. Can't you see that an outside owner might destroy the Opry in a search for increased profits?"

Evidently the two parties involved have a lot of ground clearing to do before they will be in a position to understand and judge each other's actual arguments. Either they must establish some shared standpoint from which they can address the current problem in agreed terms, or else they must at least come to acknowledge the differences between their respective standpoints clearly enough for them to be able to "agree to differ." Neither of those tasks may be easy.

This kind of situation is particularly apt to happen in discussions about ethically and politically touchy topics. For there—as we shall be seeing later in more detail—one of the central tasks in any debate is to decide from just what standpoint any given problem should be addressed. (Is this a situation, say, in which ethical considerations ought to outweigh merely financial calculations, or one in which arguments of national defense require us to set aside moral scruples?) But similar kinds of cross-purposes can arise in other, less heated areas as well. A painter and a physicist, for instance, may start talking about "color" and fall into a misunderstanding on account of their different starting points and preoccupations. Someone professionally familiar with the electromagnetic theory of light may, perhaps, come to questions about color with very different initial considerations in mind from someone whose professional concern is with techniques for applying oil-based pigments to canvas. (Is it wholly obvious that these two standpoints have nothing to do with one another? Not necessarily: the impressionist painters of the late nineteenth and early twentieth centuries were fascinated by scientific discoveries about the light spectrum and used them to justify their own adoption of a new palette confined to "spectral" colors.)

Criticizing the elements of an argument

Once the standpoint of an argument is clarified, we can attend to the different elements that make it up. Give the claim in support of which the argument is being presented. This means looking at the grounds, the warrant, the backing, and so on to make sure that they are as satisfactory and detailed as the nature of the case requires. For example:

> An argument that presents fully relevant and sufficient grounds in support of its claim is better than one in which the relevance or sufficiency of the grounds is open to doubt.
> An argument that relies on a clearly applicable and solidly backed warrant is better than one in which the applicability of the warrant or the solidity of its backing is uncertain.
> An argument that claims on behalf of its conclusion no more certainty or universality than can be rationally justified is better than one in which the true strength of the conclusion is left unstated or in which the possible exceptions and rebuttals are concealed.

How are we to ensure that our "grounds" and other elements are all that they should be? That question has two distinct aspects. On the one hand, it is a *substantive* question about the specific technical or circumstantial considerations relevant to the particular matter under discussion. On the other hand, it is a *procedural* question about the general manner in which an argument in the field concerned needs to be presented. For example, notice the following arguments that appeared in the same presentation before the United States Senate Committee on the Judiciary:

1. "It is completely false that the [San Francisco] *Chronicle* participated in any 'under the table deals', as Mr. Clinton has charged. Such a statement is completely irresponsible, and I wonder at the temerity which prompted it."
2. "Mr. Clinton ... would have you believe that there is something improper about a newspaper becoming interested in community antenna television. However, this impropriety apparently does not apply to his San Mateo *Times*. The Amphlett Printing Company, owner of the San Mateo *Times,* of which Mr. Clinton is the editor and publisher, in joint ventures with Community Television, Inc., is at this very time applicant for a CATV franchise in the City of San Carlos. . . . The application was formally presented to the City of San Carlos under date of August 23, less than a month after Mr. Clinton's appearance before this Committee and his denunciation of newspapers becoming involved in CATV franchising."

Clearly, the speaker believes firmly in both claims and would have the members of the Committee join in that belief. But, consider the grounds provided for the two arguments.

ARGUMENT #1 GROUNDS: "It is completely false." "It is irresponsible."

ARGUMENT #2 GROUNDS: "The Amphlett Printing Company is at this very time applicant for a CATV franchise. . . ."

To join in the claim advanced in argument #1, the committee members have first-hand knowledge that the arguer *says* the charge is false, but they must go further to accept the warrant that "whatever this arguer says is true," before accepting the claim. It is easy to see that in developing this line of reasoning, the speaker should have provided some evidence of falsity going beyond his own bare assertion of it. The committee members have a right to demand grounds on which they can reasonably satisfy themselves. They should not be asked to judge on their faith in the speaker alone. Even if they are inclined to accept the claim, they would be hard-put to justify it to still other critics without additional evidence.

Now, turn to the second argument. Here again, the committee knows that it has been *asserted* that the Amphlett company has applied for a CATV franchise, which if accepted would damage or destroy Mr. Clinton's posture as an opponent of such ventures. But beyond the assertion, the committee has been given enough information—dates, places, times, parties involved—to verify for themselves the accuracy of the grounds. They need not accept them on faith alone.

In a rational sense, the assertion, "It is false" is sufficient relevant information to support the claim, "It is false," given a relationship of complete trust between the parties. For example, it is possible for one person, a parent for example, to say to a child, "Tell me if the charge is true or false. I will take your word for it." On the other hand, we are all familiar with persons accused of crimes coming before the television cameras to claim, "The charge is completely false," only later to be convicted in court on the charge. We still do not know, in any absolute sense of truth, whether the charge is false or not. But we *do* know that the accused was unable to provide grounds in such a way that their relevance and sufficiency were apparent to the members of the jury.

Quite frequently, we reach conclusions about matters of everyday experience for which we *in fact have* sufficient grounds and so can trust those conclusions—as "personal opinions"—as a basis for our own actions. At the same time, we may be unable to *state convincingly* what those grounds are and so convince others.

In technical and nontechnical areas of discussion alike, the art of *seeing* what grounds are needed to justify any opinion is a substantive art. The technique of *stating* those grounds in a way that can stand up to public criticism is a procedural technique. But whatever the field of reasoning involved, our arguments will carry weight only if we can both *see* and also *state* the grounds for our opinions. Otherwise, our personal opinions will remain *personal* opinions, however well-founded they may be. Only when we both possess relevant and sufficient grounds for those opinions and can also explain those grounds to others can they be promoted to the status of "well-supported claims" and be open to rational acceptance by others.

Having established a common starting point for argument (which requires some careful communication), acceptance by others of an argument necessitates still more precise common grounds: all those involved in the reasoning must share acceptance of a common perception of that which the argument is being built upon. They must be satisfied that the foundation is firmly in place and not floating on a cloud of fancy.

When the argument claims that Mr. Clinton's attack on newspapers owning cable systems is discredited because he, a publisher of a newspaper, is himself seeking to establish a cable system, the critic has a right to ask, "Is that true?" To survive criticism, the argument must supply the material necessary to answer that question confidently. Merely to reassert "Yes, it is true," provides no additional confidence beyond that originally given on the basis of the interpersonal relationship among those arguing.

The critic needs information going beyond mere assertion. The critic will look for information that goes beyond the credibility of the one making the assertion. To be shown an application, with official signatures of officers of the Amphlett Printing Company, seeking a CATV franchise in the City of San Carlos submitted on August 23, provides a more confident, more public, basis for acceptance of the grounds. Public records in San Carlos can be checked, independent of any individual's assertion.

In criticizing grounds as vital elements of arguments, some guiding questions must be asked:

— Is enough information provided?
— Is the information clear?
— Can the information be verified beyond one person's assertion?
— Is the information consistent with other verified grounds?
— Is the information internally consistent?
— Is the source of the information competent?
— Is there any reason to suspect bias in the information?
— If statistical, is the information soundly prepared?
— Is the information the most current and best available?

Look back at the argument claiming Mr. Clinton's conflict of interest in newspapers and CATV. Is enough information provided? The Amphlett Printing Company is identified in the application, but Mr. Clinton's role in the company is not established with certainty. Is the information clear? The application seeks a franchise, but it is not clear what they intend to do with the franchise. Can the information be verified? The public records of San Carlos can be examined. Is the information consistent with other verified grounds? It is certainly inconsistent with Mr. Clinton's testimony before the committee, but that is the point of the argument. Still further investigation may be appropriate. Is the information internally consistent? It seems so, but reading of official records may be helpful. Is the source of the information competent? Only the officials of San Carlos are in a position to know fully the facts of the situation. Is there any reason to suspect bias in the information? When our only source is the person making the attack on Mr. Clinton, we must suspect bias. Public officials and documents would be less suspect. Is the statistical information soundly prepared? There is no statistical information in this argument. Is the information the most current and best available? We do not know what has happened since August 23. It would be important to know whether the application has subsequently been withdrawn.

What we have said about grounds can be extended to the other elements of any argument. It is one thing to possess a warrant and so a reliable way of arguing from symptoms to diagnosis. It is quite another thing to be able to *explain* that warrant and convince others that it is applicable in a particular case.

Again it is one thing to *know* that a warrant is supported by solid backing of the appropriate kind; it is quite another thing to have that backing at your fingertips, when it comes to convincing others that the warrant is a truly *reliable* one:

> The physician who diagnoses pneumonia rather than some less serious respiratory infection will very likely do so on the basis of minor signs and symptoms—perhaps an extreme lethargy on the patient's part or the rapid onset of the fever—that rightly attract his attention. Yet, at the same time, he may be unable to *say* precisely what those indications are, by stating the general warrant on which he is implicitly relying, with anything like the cogency and conviction that he himself has on the basis of *seeing* them.
>
> The student who reacts to the schoolteacher's sarcasm may in fact have spotted some genuine indication—the schoolteacher always blinks rapidly twice just before saying something sarcastic—but be unable to convince his fellow students that this double blink "means" what he thinks it does. They may acknowledge the ground, that is, but be unconvinced by the supposed warrant: "When he blinks rapidly twice, his next remark *may be taken* as being sarcastic."

Once again, the art of recognizing what warrants are applicable and reliable is a *substantive* matter. The technique of presenting an argument in such a way that the warrant clearly authorizes the required step from grounds to claim is a *procedural* matter. The case is similar for modalities and rebuttals: the art of recognizing just how strong a claim one is entitled to make in any given case—whether the conclusion may be presented as "necessary" or "certain," as "highly probable," as "very possible," or as "presumably the case"—is part of the corresponding *substantive* art, and so too for the exceptions and exemptions that might conceivably undercut the conclusion in question:

> Thus a physician will come to know, from experience, just how confident he can afford to be about the outcome of any particular course of treatment when the patient displays such and such symptoms.
>
> Similarly a person with wide experience of human oddities and frailties will come to know, from experience, just how likely it is that a personal mannerism like blinking can be relied on as a "sure sign" of, say, sarcasm.

On the other hand, the technique of presenting your argument in a way that makes explicit just what strength the conclusion is entitled to and just what exceptional circumstances would undercut that conclusion is a *procedural* matter.

The techniques of practical argumentation and criticism thus come into play at the point where the arts in question—science or medicine, law or technology, character judgment or finance—have assembled the material needed for the purposes of an argument and the time has come to present it in a form open to public criticism. Whatever the field of inquiry and discussion, the art of recognizing what features of any situation are significant for the purposes of the current argument and the technique of presenting the results in a convincing manner complement each other.

COMPARING THE MERITS OF DIFFERENT ARGUMENTS

It is not enough, however, just to know what makes a practical argument a "good argument." In addition, we need to consider in what cases and in what conditions one argument can be judged *better than* another argument. Can we compare the "rational merits" of *all* arguments? Given any two arguments, does it *always* make sense to ask which of them is the stronger? Or can we divide up arguments into different classes or types that differ from one another in ways that make them incomparable—like chalk and cheese? And if arguments can be divided up into different types in this way, how is such a classification arrived at? What is it based on?

Let us begin by looking again at some examples so as to see what kinds of considerations are involved in such comparisons. We may take as samples three pairs of arguments from rather different fields.

Public policy decisions

Consider the following two arguments Policy (P) 1 and 2, made by members of the U.S. House of Representatives in March of 1983, both concerning a bill to save the Social Security System:

(P_1): "I observed the work of the National Commission on Social Security . . . and . . . I assigned two parameters that I personally will use to decide whether or not to support this program: First, is the program fair. . . . ?

Mr. Chairman, just a few days after the Commission's report was ready, I went back to Florida and held a series of public hearings. Several thousands of my constituents came to those hearings, and I found that there was not anyone who really liked the recommendations. There was some to object to about all of it. Because of that, I made up mind that I thought it was pretty fair because if nobody liked it, it had to be fairly fair."

(P_2): "Rather than rush to approve a proposal which may not cure the system's chronic ills, I suggest that we refrain from hasty judgment on this package.

The burden of this reform package falls unfairly on the shoulders of senior citizens, Federal employees, small business men and women, and farmers.

Delaying the cost-of-living adjustments will harm senior citizens and low-income recipients. . . . Federal employees are burdened because the inclusion of new hires under social security will undermine the financially sound civil service system . . . raising the self-employment tax damages our commitment to small business. . . . "

If we say that P_2 is a better argument than P_1, what does this assertion mean, and how can we justify it? For a start, the question in this case is *not* whether the bill *is in fact* fair or unfair. Rather, it is whether the arguments offered give us *good reasons* to decide on the fairness of the measure. More exactly, it is the question:

Suppose we compare what each person has said, does either one give us good reasons for deciding the fairness of the social security bill? Specifically, does the reasoning in P_1 or P_2 do *more to support* the claim that the bill is fair or unfair?

First, examine each argument separately to form a critical judgment. In P_1 the claim is made that the bill is fair, but attached are the modal qualifiers, "pretty" and "fairly." An initial question is this:

> Does an argument that claims a bill is "pretty" fair or "fairly" fair justify enacting it into law?

Consider the grounds for P_1: a series of meetings in Florida found no one who "really liked the recommendations." A second question is this:

> Are the people who attend public hearings representative of all citizens in Florida, much less the United States?

Is it reasonable to suspect that mostly those who opposed the bill would attend and be outspoken in their feelings.

Is it possible that the level of not really liking the bill varied from person to person, with some seriously concerned and others just not totally satisfied? The grounds do not tell much about what the people at the hearings said or the strength with which they said it. Still another critical question should be asked:

> Do we have enough clear information about the people in Florida to understand their feelings?

Can we be satisfied that the people who attended the hearings were competent to judge the fairness of the bill? The argument does not give us information on the level of understanding held by those testifying. Thus, we must ask

> Can we place much confidence in the testimony of the people attending the hearings?

Finally, look at the warrants in P_1. The first is this: citizens affected by legislation are the proper ones to judge its fairness. The second is this: if no one likes a bill, it must be fair. Neither of these warrants is given any backing by the speaker. The critic is left to imagine possible rebuttals such as the fact if no one likes a bill it may be uniformly unfair, or the possibility that those who unfairly benefit from the bill did not bother to come to the meeting.

Now turn to P_2 and do the same critical examination. Here the claim is that the bill "falls unfairly on the shoulders of senior citizens, Federal employees, small businessmen and women, and farmers." The claim is not directly qualified, but it is prefaced by an appeal to refrain from hasty judgment. The critic must ask

Does an appeal to avoid hasty judgment constitute a sufficient challenge to put off approval of the bill at least for now?

Specifically, those advocating a new law carry the burden of proof and are expected to sustain confidence, say, in the fairness of the bill. An opposing argument may be adequate if it only raises doubts as to fairness.

The grounds of P_2 include representation that the social security package contains delayed cost-of-living adjustments, inclusion of new Federal employees under social security, and an increase in the self-employment tax. There is little problem with these grounds because anyone can read the bill and varify this information apart from the assertion. It is also asserted in the grounds that these provisions would affect—"harm"—the individuals (senior citizens, Federal employees, and so on) named. Here the critic must divide the question. It can be learned from reading the bill that the package will reduce payments or increase taxes for those mentioned. However, the argument says it will "harm" the people. Now the critic must ask the question

Does reduced payments or increased taxes constitute harm?

The argument does not provide grounds to support harm, unless the critic is willing to grant the implied warrant that any loss of money is harmful.

The warrant in P_2 creates problems for the critic in that it is not clearly stated. Suppose we accept that the bill costs these people money and that this is harmful. How do we get from there to the claim that the burden of the bill "falls unfairly on the shoulders" of those groups named? The critic must therefore inquire

By what warrant do we get from grounds to claim here?

Conceivably this argument supports, rather than opposes, P_1: since apparently everyone will share the cost of social security (which no one likes), it is fair. On the other hand, a critic can imagine alternative warrants: the people in the groups mentioned cannot afford to share this cost, so it is unfair; there are groups of people who should share the cost of social security who are not given their full share, and that is unfair.

Because the argument fails to present warrants, and because there are several alternatives, some of which lack grounds, it is difficult to reach clear conclusions on P_2.

To return to the point of origin, we are not trying to learn the truth of the fairness of the social security bill. That will never be known with certainty and it would take several years of experience in living with the law to gain even modest evidence of its actual fairness. We are trying to judge the *rational merits* of P_1 and P_2 to see whether either one gives us *better reasons* for deciding on the fairness of the social security bill. Specifically, upon reading the two arguments, can we place confidence in the fairness of the bill? If so, we can proceed to support it at least on that criterion. If not (and if we have serious doubts about the fairness of the bill after reading the two arguments), we may decide to withhold support on the warrant that no matter what other qualities a law may possess, if it is unfair, or if we doubt its fairness, we should refuse to support it until those *doubts* can be satisfied.

Legal claims

Consider a contrasted pair of examples:

(L_1): He signed a contract with me, knowingly and with his eyes open, undertaking to deliver the coal to my factory by March 31. So presumably he is liable for damages in lieu of performance in case he fails to deliver.

(L_2): He assured me, face to face, that he would pay me back the money he owes me by the end of the summer. So surely there must be some way of making him repay.

Suppose that we ask whether L_1 or L_2 is the "better" argument. The question is once again *not* which of the two speakers is the more deserving. It is, rather, which of the two speakers has the better case:

Supposing the facts (about the signed contract or the personal promise) are as asserted, which of them can then provide *the stronger support* for the associated claim? Does the signed contract *do more to* justify a claim for damages in lieu of performances than the face-to-face promise does to justify the claim for repayment, or the other way around?

Here too, we can consider the merits of the two arguments on three different levels:

1. There is a certain initial ambiguity about the issue in dispute in the two cases. It is clear enough that L_1 is offered as a "hard" legal argument, but there is something slightly ambiguous—even "soft"—about L_2. Does the speaker mean this to be taken as a real legal claim, or is it offered rather as an ethical appeal—"Oughtn't he to be shamed into keeping his promise?"
2. Suppose, however, that L_2 is indeed meant to be understood as a legal argument. We can then go on to compare the grounds, warrants, and backing involved in the two cases. The differences between the two arguments can be put in such statements as:

A signed document is worth a thousand verbal promises.
The law of contract in most states will not normally enforce verbal undertakings of which no written confirmation is available.

The state legislature and the authors of the Uniform Commercial Code alike decided not to include mere verbal undertakings, about which no reliable testimony can be produced, among the "commercial transactions" of which the law of contract takes cognizance within U.S. jurisdictions.

In these three statements, the central respects in which L_1 is a *better argument* than L_2 are indicated by reference, first, to the grounds (a signed contract is *better evidence* than oral testimony about an alleged verbal promise), then to the warrant (the current law of contract provides *better authority* for the enforcement of written contracts than of verbal promises), and finally to the backing (both the acts of the state legislature and the content of the currently accepted code provide *better backing* in the one case than in the other).

3. The two arguments are offered with different qualifications and implied exceptions. In L_1, the claim is explicitly presented as "presumably so," and this presumption is implicitly subject to any exclusions or other conditions in the small print of the actual contract—"unless performance is prevented by War, or Act of God, or other occurrences beyond the Contractor's control," or whatever it may be. In L_2, the modal qualifier is, once again, overemphatic ("surely"!?), and there is no hint of the exclusions or exceptions that might serve as rebuttals of the conclusion.

In the legal situation, therefore, the question is *not* whether the *conclusion* of L_1 or L_2 is in fact the more reliable. That is a legal matter, and it might yet turn out that in some jurisdictions (for example, Scotland) verbal promises may be as enforceable as written contracts. The question is only whether, as they stand, the *rational merits* of L_1 and L_2 are open to comparison. And in this regard, it is once again clear that there is no problem in *making sense* of questions about the relative merits of different legal arguments.

Critical analysis of arguments becomes more difficult when they are expressed in ordinary language—the way people talk to one another. Even in law, when attorneys make their closing argument to a jury, they do not speak in crisp, clearly stated arguments. The critic—the member of the jury—has a difficult job. Observe two lawyers actually speaking to a jury. The case [Pasillas *vs.* Frederick Engineering] concerns an employee who lost fingers in a punch press manufactured by one company and installed in the firm where the employee worked. The employee is suing the manufacturer of the press, and the question we will examine is this: Did the manufacturer issue a warning about the danger of using the press?

(L_3): "There was a total failure to warn. It has been suggested to you that there was the warning in the form of a brochure . . . and that this warning went to somebody at Borg-Warner.

It may well have. And you know, I as a reasonable human would believe that, instead, this did go to somebody. . . . It has no warning in it that is even close to being adequate. . . .

And most importantly, the law requires this person to be involved, the user; whether this was shown to anybody up in the ivory tower is not significant. . . . We are talking about warnings that were communicated to people that would use the machine, so the warning . . . has no validity."

(L₄): "Let's talk about another form of a warning here, let's talk about the O.S.H.A. [Occupational Safety and Health Administration] requirements which is in evidence. . . . this, ladies and gentlemen, is from the Federal Register and it says . . .

'Safeguarding the point of operation. General requirements. It shall be the responsibility of the employer'—Borg-Warner—'to provide and insure the usage of point of operation guards or properly applied and adjusted point of operation devices on every operation performed on a mechanical power press.'

Now, ladies and gentlemen, is this a warning? Of course it's a warning. . . ."

Try doing this critical evaluation for yourself. The following questions will guide your work.

1. The grounds for L₃ seem to be that no warning was given to the person who operated the press. Can you be satisfied that this is so?
2. The warrant of L₃ calls upon acceptance that "the law requires this person, the user" to be given the warning. Are you clear as to what law is being invoked? Do you feel confident in your understanding of that law?
3. The rebuttal mentioned in L₃ is that some brochure was sent to Borg-Warner which seems to have gone to the management—the ivory tower—but may or may not have reached the user of the press. Do you have a clear basis for accepting the claim that the user did not learn of the brochure?
4. The grounds for L₄ are presented in a quotation from the Federal Register indicating that the company using the press, and not the manufacturer, has the responsibility to warn employees of any danger, or otherwise to protect them from the dangers. Do you feel as if you have enough information about this O.S.H.A. requirement? Are you satisfied that this paragraph sufficiently covers the situation?
5. Is there a warrant stated in L₄? If so, can you state it? If not, can you suggest which warrant or warrants might be implied?
6. Reviewing the two arguments, do you have a clear understanding of what is meant by "warning"? Do you believe the two lawyers were talking about the same thing? Do you have enough data in the two arguments to satisfy yourself as to the kind of warning under discussion?
7. Now, can you write a full analysis of the reasoning of the two lawyers discussing the rational merits of both? Can you *make sense* of the relative merits of these two legal arguments?

Film criticisms

Finally, consider a pair of arguments from a very different field:

(F_1): In *A Special Day*, Loren and Mastroianni give restrained performances of unusual delicacy, and the director gives them all the space they need. So all in all, this is an unpretentious movie with the ring of truth.

(F_2): Seventeen million Americans all across the country have stood in line to see *The Gutted Skyscraper*. So evidently we once again have here a triumph of Hollywood filmmaking.

Leave aside for present purposes the question whether this or that (or any) "disaster" movie is in fact *better or worse as a movie* than one or another (or any) "character" piece. That is not our present question. What we are concerned with is whether F_1 is *better or worse as an argument* than F_2, or the other way around:

Let the facts be as stated, whether about Loren and Mastroianni or about the lines at the box offices. Which set of facts then provides *better support* for the critical claim in question? Do the remarks about the two stars *do more to* back up the claim about the Loren film than the box office figures do to prove the "artistic triumph" of *Skyscraper?*

The same steps as before are open to us:

1. The standpoint of F_2 is not wholly clear. Is this really offered as a genuine critical assessment? Or is it only a commercial "puff" for purposes of public relations? In the latter case, maybe we cannot really compare it with F_1 as we could compare two real pieces of movie criticism.

2. Suppose that we do take both F_1 and F_2 as critical arguments. We can then compare the respective grounds, warrants, and backing implicit in the two arguments:

Quality of acting is better evidence of a well-made film than box office figures alone.

You cannot conclude anything about the artistic merits of a movie from its financial success or failure alone.

Plenty of trashy, ill-acted movies have been wild successes at the box office before now.

The comparative merits of F_1 and F_2, as arguments, are indicated here by a focus on questions about the *relevance* of the considerations put forward in the two cases. Like the behavior of birds and animals in meteorology and the existence of verbal promises in the law of contract, the box office figures are here dismissed as *less relevant* than the acting performances of the stars to the critical claim.

Whatever one may think about disaster movies in general, or even about whether disaster movies and character movies are strictly comparable from an aesthetic point of view, there is thus no problem at all in *making sense* of the question whether F_1 or F_2 is *the better piece of critical argumentation.*

Cross-type comparisons

In each of these pairs of examples, one of the arguments may be judged better than the other, not merely as an argument but as an argument *of a given type*. In expressing a critical preference, we take for granted a particular standpoint—the standpoint of public policy decisions, or law, or film criticism. If the standpoint is changed or we seek to compare the merits of arguments offered from quite different standpoints, our judgments may be undercut.

In each of these three pairs of examples, one of the arguments is finally adjudged better than the other, not merely as an argument but as an argument *of a given type*. In preferring P_2 to P_1, L_1 to L_2, or F_1 to F_2, we take for granted a particular standpoint—the standpoint of meteorology, or contract law, or film criticism. If the standpoint is changed or we seek to compare the merits of arguments offered from quite different standpoints, our judgments may be undercut:

Suppose that we reconsider some of the same arguments from quite other points of view. Suppose, for instance, that we reconsider L_1 and L_2 from the standpoint of ethics. Looking from this new angle, we may well decide that there is less to choose between the two arguments, that is, that from the standpoint of "deserts," the claimant in L_2 is just as deserving as the claimant in L_1:

Ethically speaking, a verbal promise given in all seriousness carries just as much weight as a formal contract.

Similarly, if F_1 and F_2 are looked at not as critical assessments but in the context of financial statements from the production studios or distribution companies, it is no longer so obvious that box office figures are "beside the point," since the *point* has now been changed:

Financially speaking, *Skyscraper* was indeed a "triumph" in a way that few foreign "art" films are.

By this change of standpoint, the *context dependence* of our rational judgments is made apparent. The standpoint from which any particular argument should be considered is commonly "written in invisible ink"—the phrases making the standpoint explicit ("ethically speaking" and the like) are commonly omitted—because all parties to the discussion recognize the standpoint from clues in the situation or from the forum in which the discussion is going on. Only when there is an ambiguity about the standpoint do we have to take note of it.

Suppose we take pairs of arguments from different forums or situations and ask which of the two is the better argument. Suppose that we try to compare P_1 or P_2 either with L_1 or L_2 or with F_1 or F_2. What sense is to be made of such comparisons?

This much can be said at once: P_2, L_1, and F_1 are all good arguments from the standpoints of their respective enterprises, whereas P_1, L_2 and F_2 are all pretty shaky. So we may be tempted to say that P_2 is, presumably, a *better* argument than L_2 or F_2—at any rate, it is solid enough in its own terms, so far as it goes. But what are we to say, if we now try to compare all the others? Between arguments of such different types, there is scarcely any room for comparison.

Does the existence of a signed contract establish the presumption of liability for nonperformance *better or worse* than the uniform disapproval of a proposed Federal law by citizens establishes the law's fairness?

Is the wording of an O.S.H.A. regulation more or less irrelevant to the warning of employees than box office statistics are to the artistic qualities of a movie? Faced with questions like these, we see that good and bad arguments in politics, in contract law, and in film criticism are no more like one another than good and bad chalk, good and bad cheese, and good and bad poetry. We can make sense of rational comparisons between different arguments only when they are arguments *of the same type*. The practical consequences or implications of claims will clearly be of different kinds, according as they raise technical issues of science or law as everyday matters of personal life and practical prudence. Correspondingly the considerations relevant to all those claims will also be different. (The "evidence" relevant to a scientific hypothesis is of a different sort from that which is relevant to a lawsuit or a movie criticism.)

The differences between arguments of different types can be of serious importance. By demanding that arguments of one type have strengths or merits appropriate only to arguments of quite other types, we generate only confusion. To return to a familiar example, difficulties of this kind frequently arise in discussions of *madness* at the boundaries between psychiatry and law. Being unclear in our minds about the relations between these two enterprises, we may move too quickly from one to the other, appealing, for example, to medical diagnoses of normality and pathology to support legal claims about mental incompetence, or vice versa. Thus, in different contexts, the claim "James is mad" may call for quite different responses. If it is intended as a medical diagnosis, it may mean, "James's personal difficulties and confusions have psychotic origins, and these cry out for psychiatric treatment." If the statement is intended as a claim about his proper legal status, it may mean, "James can no longer handle his own personal finances and must be subjected to judicial restraints." Given the profoundly different basic purposes of psychiatric medicine and the law of insanity—between the practical consequences of a medical diagnosis of schizophrenia, on the one hand, and a legal ruling of incompetence, on the other—there are (at best) a very rough correspondence between the two fields and a very unreliable connection between the arguments appropriate to the two fields. Failing a careful scrutiny of what precisely is at issue in the individual case, it remains anything but clear just what is the relevance of psychiatric diagnoses to legal decisions, or vice versa.

THE VARYING FORCE OF CLAIMS

As we move from one field of argument to another, the claims put forward differ substantially in force, depending on the exact character of the argument in question.

If a sports enthusiast makes a bold claim for his favorite team, he risks a public prediction of a kind that invites collective scrutiny and criticism: "Are the Raiders really such a certainty?"

If a movie buff comments on a new film, by contrast, he may expect intelligent understanding rather than universal agreement: "I see what you mean about the new version of *King Kong* having a greater psychological subtlety, but wasn't something also lost in the remake?"

If two parties are involved in a legal dispute, they may not be interested in persuading one another. It is the judge or the jury they have to convince: "The judge seemed to buy my story, but the jury found against me all the same, worst luck!"

Notice that both the *force* of these assertions and the *implications* of assenting to them depend on the "type" of argument involved. A sporting prediction, an aesthetic comment, a medical diagnosis, a legal plea, a business proposal—all of these call for rather different kinds of responses, and carry with them rather different consequences. For example:

In the sporting case the question will be "What are we to expect?"

In the film criticism case, it is, rather, "What critical attitude can one reasonably adopt?"

In a judicial context, it will be "Who is to be upheld, who overruled?"

In a business discussion, "What prices are we to decide on?"

Success or failure in defending a claim will likewise have consequences that can range from simple intellectual tolerance at one extreme to the imposition of a heavy prison term at the other.

ADVERSARY AND CONSENSUS PROCEDURES

Just whose agreement is required for the success of any argument, and on what terms, also varies from field to field and from one type of argument to another. In particular, some enterprises rely on achieving *consensus* between the parties to an argument; others involve *adversary* procedures, by which general agreement is not required.

Both natural sciences and art criticism, in different ways, aim at *consensus:*

> In our hospital example, for instance, it was claimed that an infection had been carried by food-service equipment. The goal of the supporting argument was to provide the basis for a shared acceptance of this claim—bringing any knowledgeable questioner to the point of adopting the same opinion on his own account.
>
> In our movie criticism examples, a totally shared judgment may not be necessary, but partial consensus is still the aim. Discussions about works of art never reach completion. There is always "more that could be said" about *Othello,* or the *Choral Symphony,* or Picasso's *Guernica,* or both versions of *King Kong.* In this respect, aesthetic arguments are never self-terminating. An aesthetic claim need demand agreement to only a partial truth: "Yes, I see what you mean—that's fine, as far as it goes."

By contrast, much judicial argumentation operates according to *adversary* procedures:

> At the outset of a case, two parties are usually opposed: a plaintiff or a prosecutor on the one hand, a defendant or defendants on the other. In the American system of law the party whose claim initiates the action must produce an argument that reaches the standard of proof for a case of the kind involved and persuade the court to "rule" or "find" in his favor. In a criminal case, he must establish the guilt of the accused; in a civil case, he must demonstrate the plaintiff's right to some kind of redress. If this is successfully done, the argument has achieved its purpose. It is of no relevance whether the defendant is also convinced by the argument and now concedes that the initial claim was after all "true." Consensus is not required. On the contrary, once there is a formal ruling of the court, the aims of the judicial proceeding are entirely fulfilled, whether or not the defendant himself assents to or agrees with it at all.

In matters of business and public policy, the situation is different yet again. The required outcome of argumentation is not a simple consensus or a ruling between adversaries but a practical *decision.* Rather than expecting to arrive at unanimity about the superior wisdom of any one course of action, it is necessary to balance off rival uncertainties: to weigh prospective gains against possible losses according to general maxims of political wisdom or financial strategy. And the resulting compromises will commonly involve a mixture of adversary and consensus procedures.

In short, when we consider what kinds of rational criticism are called for in any particular discussion, we must take care to note how the force and the implications of any claim vary with the type of argument involved. There are significant differences between the modes of argument, standards of criticism, and degrees of certainty in scientific meetings, courts of law, company board meetings, and other forums of argumentation.

Chatting idly among friends or talking with a group of physicians, for instance, we can reasonably say things about James's state of mind that we would never say before a judge in open court, to a political audience, or from a church pulpit. That is so not because we are free to think and speak "less strictly" in one case than in the other. These differences have to do not with the *strictness* of our arguments but with their *relevance*. By their own standards, for instance, psychiatric diagnoses need to be justified quite as carefully as judicial decisions by their own standards. In either case, so much is at stake, either in terms of medical treatment or in terms of civil rights, that only a strong argument of the appropriate kind can be accepted as satisfactory.

The crucial point is simply stated:

Context determines criteria.

The terms we use to criticize and judge the merits of particular arguments and claims depend on their "type," and so on their "field." Whether it be politics or ethics, science or aesthetics, psychiatry or law, the underlying goals of the human enterprise concerned determine the fundamental context for the arguments and claims in question, and so give them their power to "carry conviction," by establishing the claims on a secure basis.

Exercises

Read the following examples of arguments that have actually been used in the fields indicated. Prepare an analysis of them.

PUBLIC POLICY

1. "Mr. Speaker, today His Holiness, Pope John Paul II, begins an historical mission of peace to Central America, one of the most troubled regions in the world. Even as he begins his mission, our government is preparing to seek another $60 million or more in military assistance to a repressive government and to broaden involvement of U.S. personnel as advisers to the Salvadoran military.

When I visited El Salvador a year ago, the Salvadoran military even said they did not want a broader involvement of U.S. personnel. The Bishop of El Salvador, Rivera y Damas, said that the most important thing to his country was to end the killing on both sides, and that increasing arms to the Salvadoran military will increase the resistance on the other side and innocent people will suffer.

Mr. Speaker, the enemies in El Salvador are ignorance, poverty, deprivation, and hunger. . . . What we need is humanitarian assistance."

2. "Mr. President, I . . . often wonder whether Congress has forgotten the Monroe Doctrine. [I] applaud Secretary of State, George Schultz, for standing firm against negotiations with the guerrillas, and for reaffirming our commitment to the democratic process in El Salvador. Secretary Schultz said 'no dice' to the idea of letting the guerrillas shoot their way into government.

. . . The United States could pull out of El Salvador if the two sides were to engage in dialogue, but we could not long ignore the consequences of such an action. Sooner or later, Congress will have to realize that what is at stake in Central America is, its security—and our security."

Congressional Record

LEGAL CLAIMS

1. "The ultimate foundation of a free society is the binding tie of cohesive sentiment. Such a sentiment is fostered by all those agencies of the mind and spirit which may serve to gather up the traditions of a people. . . . The flag is the symbol of our national unity, transcending all internal differences. . . . A society which is dedicated to the preservation of these ultimate values of civilization may utilize the educational process for inculcating those almost unconscious feelings which bind men together in a comprehending loyalty."

2. "The Constitution may well elicit expressions of loyalty to it and to the government which it created, but it does not command such expressions or otherwise give any indication that compulsory expressions of loyalty play any part in our scheme of government as to override the constitutional protection of freedom of speech and religion.

U.S. Supreme Court

24

History and criticism

The account of practical reasoning that we have given here has increasingly focused on the *procedures* of reasoning and of rational criticism. Different fields of activity (different *rational enterprises*) employ different procedures of reasoning. Similarly, the forums and standards for the criticism of reasoning, vary from field to field. It is helpful at this point to sum up a series of points made in earlier chapters:

— Our childhood upbringing introduces us to a whole range of reasoning procedures and modes of criticism.
— Apprenticeship into a profession involves learning the technical procedures relevant to its activities.
— The collective goals of the professions vary from case to case; in one, victory may be an appropriate aim, in another, consensus is the goal.
— The methods and aims of the professions vary, to some extent, from country to country and age to age.
— In any given field, different special occasions and issues may demand different reasoning procedures.

The scope for variation in reasoning procedures gives rise to some general questions about history and ethics.

THE HISTORY OF PRACTICAL REASONING

If the course of practical argumentation depends on where you start from (i.e., on the occasion that gives rise to an issue and on the initial presumptions that direct the subsequent discussion), a further important set of problems at once suggest themselves:

— Does everybody have to start from the same point?
— May not people in different cultures or at different times in history begin from different initial presumptions?
— So, may not the actual course of practical reasoning go quite differently in different cultures and epochs?
— Does this not mean that different ways of arguing are going to be "rational" or "irrational" for you, depending on who and where you are?

And if these suggestions are followed up, what is going to become of our notion that "rationality" provides an impartial, universal arbiter in deciding disputes and disagreements? At this point, we seem to be on the verge of an alarming kind of skepticism about our procedures of argumentation.

Certainly the *procedures* relied on by different peoples to arrive at "reasonably acceptable" answers to questions in law and science and politics have varied considerably at different stages of history. That much is surely common knowledge. For example:

1. In many medieval jurisdictions, the familiar twentieth-century criminal court procedures—of producing physical evidence and subjecting personal testimony to both direct and cross-examination—were by no means common form. In their place, the customary procedure was to put the matters at issue "beyond reasonble doubt" by subjecting both the accused and his witnesses to penalties, or ordeals, that should guarantee "truth telling." (Anyone who testified on oath in support of a man who was eventually found guilty was liable, for example, to have his right hand cut off. So he had to be pretty sure of what he said!)

   Trial by ordeal was thus certainly very *different* from our own modes of trial by examination of testimony and physical evidence. But—however barbaric it may appear to us—was it necessarily, on that account alone, an "unreasonable" or "irrational" way of putting criminal charges to the test?

2. In earlier generations, people's likely characters and conduct were often estimated not from seeing how they themselves behaved or what they themselves said but by considering their lineage or ancestry. Quite different things were expected of "well-bred" and "ill-bred" people. As a result, when their characters and conduct came up for discussion, people of different "origins" came under the scope of different warrants:

   That's not the kind of conduct *to be expected of* a gentleman.

   (The idea is far from dead even today, especially in organizations like the Daughters of the American Revolution. Are not some modes of behavior still thought of, and spoken of, as "gentlemanly" and others as "boorish," that is, "peasantlike"?)

If we ourselves are much more inclined to judge people as individuals—on the basis of their personal performances rather than their family trees—this fact has a real interest from the standpoints of social change and the history of manners. But does it follow, for sure, that we are right and our predecessors were wrong, or the other way around? May not their estimates have been more "reasonable," at an earlier stage in the development of society and manners, than they would be today? And may not their ways of arguing have been more appropriate during some earlier phases of social history than they would be today?

3. Attitudes toward children have varied in some fundamental ways over the centuries. Nowadays children are expected to be objects of parental care and concern. Failure to show such care and concern is viewed as "unfatherly" or "unmaternal." At other times and in other places, children have been seen very differently. For instance, they have been regarded as desirable sources of cheap farm labor.

If we consider how the same "fact" would have been viewed at different times and places, therefore, the information

John has three sons—George, James, and Willy—

would have been accepted in different social and historical milieux as grounds for quite different kinds of conclusions, for example, about John's worldly good fortune rather than about his emotional and financial commitments. (A large family of children used to be—and still is, in many countries—the only real form of old-age insurance.) In other words, arguments that were reasonable enough formerly, in a subsistence economy, may no longer be equally reasonable today, in an overpopulated industrial society with well-developed social services.

4. Ways of arguing that fall out of use may even in some cases come back into currency again. During the heyday of scientific medicine (i.e., during the first fifty or sixty years of the twentieth century), all the ideas and practices of traditional folk medicine were under a cloud, as old wives' tales. As a result, the fact that a treatment was "natural" rather than "scientific" came to count against it. Now, in the final third of the twentieth century, the pendulum has swung back again. Even apart from such exotic traditional treatments as acupuncture, it nowadays does a medicine or other kind of treatment no harm to be labeled as "natural." (The television commercials are full of "natural" remedies—"natural" tonics, laxatives, skin treatments, and the rest.)

In 1935, giving somebody a natural remedy for headache or constipation, say, might have been understood as a desperate resort to unorthodox traditional treatments for lack of a scientific alternative. Nowadays, we hear the appeal to naturalness quite differently. It means "going the body's way" and "helping it put itself right," rather than "filling it full of artificial pharmaceuticals." Who, then, is to say that either of these two attitudes is wholly "rational" or "reasonable" in opposition to the other? Is not the task of striking a reasonable balance between traditional and scientific medicine a delicate, long-term business within which some differences of standpoint can be accepted as quite legitimate?

5. Even in science, the fundamental presumptions around which our arguments are organized change as time goes on. One of the most significant novelties in the modern scientific movement, as it has grown up since the seventeenth century, has been its capacity to frame laws and principles (i.e., warrants) that apparently hold good for bodies and systems anywhere in the universe and at any time in history. For example, if astronomers study the production of light in a distant galaxy, they begin today with the initial presumption that whatever happens here and now on the Earth in a physics laboratory will also be found to be happening when similar processes go on in astronomical bodies a million light years away from the Earth. The burden of proof is thus on anyone who refuses to accept arguments about physical processes in distant galaxies framed in the same terms as for those on the Earth.

Yet as little as five hundred years ago, it was still quite unclear that such analogies could be developed at all—still less, relied on. Physics was split down the middle, into two quite separate systems of thought. One of these applied to things on the Earth and in its immediate vicinity, the other to things beyond the moon. The track of the moon was the dividing line between distinct regions that fell within the scope of two distinct sets of laws and principles: *sublunary* for things "below the moon," *superlunary* for things "above the moon." Yet was there anything "irrational," on this account, about the physics of the Middle Ages? Surely it was a major intellectual achievement of seventeenth-century science to find a way of reformulating physics in new terms capable of transcending the superlunary/sublunary division. But until that reformulation had been carried through, there was surely nothing unreasonable about continuing to accept that division. After all, the best available theories of physics were all framed in ways that took it for granted.

In short, the actual content and procedures of practical argumentation have not been, and presumably never will be, historically immutable. The ways in which situations provide occasions for issues to arise, the ways in which the burden of proof is allocated in those situations, the initial presumptions with which arguments of different kinds begin, and the sorts of considerations that carry weight on account of those initial presumptions—all of these things *have a history*. There is no guarantee—and there can be no guarantee—that the same general kinds of reasoning, and the same initial presumptions, must be accepted as authoritative and compulsory in all cultures and in all historical epochs.

At one extreme, discussions about political issues have varied, in rather obvious ways, from one nation to another and from one epoch to another. In the seventeenth century, for instance, even so "modern-seeming" a book as Thomas Hobbe's *Leviathan* put forward a case for giving the monarch unrestricted sovereignty in terms that are—in part—quite foreign to us nowadays. The arguments that Hobbes presented about the overriding imperatives of "national defense" are still quite familiar to us today. But his extensive appeals to Holy Scripture come as a surprise to us from a man who otherwise seems to think so much in the same way we do.

At the opposite extreme, arguments in natural science may seem at first sight to have been conducted in permanent and unchanging ways, according to the canons of some universally applicable "logical schema" or "scientific method." Yet there too, closer historical examination brings to light significant changes in the actual methods of thought and argument employed in those fields of inquiry. The abandonment of the division between sublunary and superlunary worlds is only one illustration of this point; we shall look at some other illustrations shortly.

Across the intervening spectrum—between the seeming parochialism of political debate and the seeming permanence of scientific argumentation—other fields of thought and inquiry display a greater or lesser variability in their occasions of argument, procedures of reasoning, initial presumptions, and the rest. Freud's discoveries and arguments have substantially affected some of the ways in which we "read" or "interpret" each others' states of mind, motives, and so on, at any rate, in certain limited areas of conduct. Yet in many other ways we still view and talk about each others' conduct in ways that go back to antiquity and may even in some respects be shared by all cultures. The personal situations depicted in the tragedies of Sophocles present nothing like the same difficulties to us as, for example, the astronomical ideas of Aristotle. (We can at once see Oedipus at Colonus as a man with whose emotions and difficulties we are largely able to sympathize.)

Complete immutability in our rational procedures and standards of judgment is not to be found even in Plato's exemplar of "rational immutability," that is, pure mathematics. The standards of rigor relied on in the judging of mathematical arguments have had their own history, just as much as the standards relied on in natural science, medicine, law, politics, and psychology. Proofs that were rigorously valid for Theaetetus and Euclid were not up to the standards demanded by Diophantus and Apollonius of Perga in later antiquity. Nor were those accepted by Wallis, Newton, and Gauss in the seventeenth and eighteenth centuries up to the standards imposed by Dedekind and Weierstrass in the nineteenth century.

The entire history of human life and thought could, indeed, be mapped in an illuminating way if one studied how the initial presumptions and standards of rational adequacy employed in different fields of practical argumentation have changed in the course of their history. Our largest and most comprehensive ideas about the world—our general guiding assumptions about nature and humanity and about the relations between them—can in practice be seen most clearly in the things that we *take for granted*. We find out what someone regards as "natural" by seeing what arguments he or she lets pass as not worth challenging and what considerations he or she challenges as "unnatural" or "contrary to nature," quite as much as in downright assertions and declarations of belief.

HISTORICAL VARIABILITY AND SKEPTICISM

This historical variability in our ways of thinking and arguing gives rise, however, to some controversy. We are tempted to demand that the standards for judging the "reasonableness" of arguments should be immutable before we allow them any real authority. So how can an argument be solid by the standards of the here-and-now, yet come to be seen as shaky in China two hundred years hence? To allow for this possibility would—surely—be to imply that many of our own current ways of arguing are simply *wrong!* And as there is no way in which we can absolutely guarantee, in advance, that any particular procedure of argumentation currently accepted as sound will not eventually suffer that undignified fate, it may seem as though *all* our reasoning procedures alike were, on that account, open to skeptical doubts. If at some future time other people elsewhere are going to *put us right,* how can we avoid concluding that we are already *in the wrong?* In this way, the pursuit of timeless, immutable standards of judgment is apt to drive us, once again, into skepticism.

In response to these skeptical temptations, we have to recognize that the very changes to which our rational procedures are subject are themselves capable of being made in a rational manner. These changes, too, can be made for good reasons, in the light of solid, well-founded considerations. That is to say, changes of this kind need not involve the sheer *abandonment* of our current standpoints and beliefs in favor of other, quite different standpoints and beliefs. Rather, the further pursuit of the same general goals that have animated our rational enterprises from the beginning leads to the further *refinement* of our own positions and procedures.

Indeed what makes it possible to speak of such enterprises as science and law and management as "rational" enterprises at all has as much to do with the ways in which they transform themselves in the course of their history as it does with the particular "rational standards" employed within them at any one time. It is not the truth or the solidity of the positions adopted by scientists at any particular moment that makes the natural sciences "rational." It is, rather, the "adaptability" of scientific procedures and principles in the face of new experience and new conceptions. In this respect, stereotyped *beliefs* are no more rational than stereotyped feelings or behavior. It is the *openness of scientists to argument*—their readiness, if need be, to revise even their most fundamental procedures of argument—that marks their activity off as an enterprise with some genuine claim to rationality.

Novel procedures of reasoning and methods of argumentation thus have to be not merely *invented* but also *justified*. The things that appear natural to the generations since Darwin or Freud, for example, may greatly differ from those that appeared natural to Newton or Saint Augustine. But those differences have not come about through any arbitrary or whimsical choice of the people concerned. On the contrary, they were arrived at by a *progressive refinement* of earlier views. And even now, they are themselves still apt to be further refined, and even displaced, as a result of innovations and discoveries yet to be made.

The steps by which new procedures prove their worth and come to be accepted vary, of course, between different rational enterprises. But they all tend to do so in a piecemeal way by the accumulation of smaller changes. As an outcome of all these changes, people's overall view of an entire field of discussion and inquiry is gradually transformed, until it no longer bears any resemblance to the original. Between Copernicus and Newton, for instance, astronomers and physicists made dozens of minor readjustments in the ways they reasoned about the structure and workings of the solar system. And the pre-Copernican view of the planets (organized around a stationary Earth) was finally displaced by the post-Copernican, or Newtonian view (organized around a central Sun) as a total outcome of all these changes.

At any given moment, however, some established repertoire of argumentative procedures—scientific, legal, or whatever—possesses rational authority for the time being and so carries weight within the corresponding enterprise.

THE ETHICS OF ARGUMENT

The procedures involved in rational debate and the critical assessment of arguments evidently require the *participants* in any such debate to enter into well-defined roles, and perform in well-understood ways, within the activities of a profession or the conduct of everyday life.

In actual practice, a law case can be resolved only if the parties to the case are prepared to enter into the trial in an orderly manner. (Deliberately disrupting the proceeding of the court implicitly challenges not only the authority of the state, but also the *reasonableness* of the proceedings in question.) In actual practice, similarly, a scientific disagreement can be resolved only if the parties to it are prepared to present their arguments in a form, and in a forum, that allows the arguments on both sides to be judged impartially by other well-informed professional scientists. (Hence, scientists object to their colleagues "going public," by—for example—leaking reports of their work to the press before the professional debate is completed.) Even in everyday family life, once tempers have been raised and differences become bitter, it is necessary to establish some accepted "forum" and "procedure" before these differences can be resolved: for instance,

Mother has to move in and persuade all those involved to accept her arbitration. ("Come on, now: let's all sit down and work this thing out. . . . ")

The Greek philosopher Socrates called tyrants, bullies, and other intractable people—who will not agree to sit down, and talk out their differences—"misologists," or *haters of reason.* As he saw, a rational discussion or reasonable debate can go on only between people who are ready to behave in ways that show that they are "open to argument." Practical argumentation, in short, involves its own special modes of *human conduct,* and so its own *code of ethics.*

What kinds of rules and considerations enter, then, into the *ethics of argument?* This is a topic that students will do well to think about carefully for themselves. Here are some first hints.

— A first, inescapable obligation for any "rational" arguer is the obligation to *listen* to the other party, so that someone who is "deaf" to all arguments is not playing according to the rules;

— Anyone who is committed to the *spirit* of rational debate will try to understand how his adversary sees the issue dividing them, and so will "put himself in the adversary's shoes";

— Having entered into a rational forum, each party is obliged to abide by the outcome and to accept the verdict of the established arbiters, subject to the possibility of appealing or reviving the issue afresh in another equally authoritative forum; and so on.

You do not win a chess match by tipping over the board, or a football game by rejecting the decisions of the referee: all you succeed in doing by adopting these tactics is to reveal something about your own character and personality. ("She is entirely unsporting.") Similarly, you cannot win a law suit by kidnapping the judge, or establish a scientific discovery by insulting those colleagues who disagree with you: once again, you merely reveal your own personal defects. ("He is completely unreasonable.") The whole *point* of developing procedures and forums of practical argumentation has been to establish methods by which people who are prepared to collaborate in a debate can collectively arrive at resolutions of their disputes which best meet their common needs and interests. (Of course, it may not always be possible to do this in a way that will please all parties: no one can pretend that the defendant in a murder case must be *happy* at hearing his death sentence! But these cases are the exception rather than the general rule.)

Behind all the activities of practical argumentation, there is thus an implicit commitment to *the ethics of cooperation.* People who are prepared to "be reasonable" are people who are ready to collaborate in creating the opportunities for arriving at mutual understanding: that is, who will listen to arguments, try to see the other side of any case, accept the decisions of impartial arbiters, and otherwise enter into the procedures of dispute-resolution within which "practical arguments" find their place and their use.

Exercises

1. Study these facts:

   a. Late in the nineteenth century medical science accepted the ovaries as the location of a woman's center of personality. The procedure of choice for the correction of various personality disorders in women was the surgical removal of the ovaries. By the start of the twentieth century, thousands of women had undergone such surgery and the results reported were positive. This surgery is no longer performed.

   b. In the mid- to late-twentieth century, medical science believed that periodic adverse mood changes, menstrual pain, and the growth of a tumor—even of the common fibroid type—called for the removal of the uterus. The procedure of choice for a wide variety of "female" complaints was the hysterectomy, and by the last third of the twentieth century, millions of woman had undergone this surgery. Today, unless a clear diagnosis of malignancy is possible, hysterectomies are not recommended.

   Discuss the reasoning that led to these popular medical procedures. Try to say why these arguments which once were considered sound would not survive critical scrutiny today. Is the answer simply that medicine has *learned* more, and if so, what do you believe it has learned?

2. Study these facts:

   a. In 1896, in the case of Plessy v. Feguson (163 U.S. 537) the Supreme Court of the United States decided that the Jim Crow Act requirement that Homer Adolph Plessy sit in railroad cars reserved for blacks separate from whites did not deny his constitutional rights. The reasoning was that this was not discriminatory since whites were separated just as much from blacks as the blacks were separated from whites. It was admitted that the Fourteenth Amendment was designed to enforce the absolute equality of the two races before the law but it could not have been intended in the nature of things to abolish distinction based upon color or to enforce social, as distinct from political, equality. The decision stated as follows: "If one race be inferior to another socially, the Constitution of the United States cannot put them upon the same plane."

   b. In 1954, in the case of Brown v. Board of Education of Topeka, et al. (347 U.S. 483), the Supreme Court of the U.S. decided that separate but equal facilities for the two races *did* deny constitutuonal rights. They reasoned as follows: "In approaching this problem, we cannot turn the clock back to 1868 when the [Fourteenth] Amendment was adopted, or even to 1896 when Plessy v. Ferguson was written. We must consider public education in the light of its full development and its present place in American life throughout the Nation. Only in this way can it be determined if segregation in public schools deprives these [blacks] of the equal protection of the laws.

Today, education is perhaps the most important function of state and local government. . . . [Education] is the very foundation of good citizenship. Today it is the principal instrument in awakening the child to cultural values, in preparing him for later professional training, and in helping him to adjust normally to his environment. . . .

We come then to the question presented: Does segregation of children in public schools solely on the basis of race, even through the physical facilities and other "tangible" factors be equal, deprive the children of the minority group of equal educational opportunity? We believe that it does."

Discuss these two cases and the reasoning that led to opposite decisions. Do you believe the 1954 decision "corrected" an erróneous one in 1896? Try to say why reasoning that made sense in 1896 did not stand up to criticism in 1954. Did it make sense in 1896. Why?

3.   Study these facts:

a.   In 1977, the Food and Drug Administration announced a ban on the use of saccharin in foods and beverages because of evidence that its use caused malignant bladder tumors in test animals. Immediately an outraged opposition emerged claiming that the tests were conducted in Canada, not the U.S.; the tests were on rats, not humans; and that the dosages used on the test animals were higher than is usually ingested by humans. They further argued that saccharin had a long record of safety and that dieters and diabetics would suffer from this denial of choice. Ultimately, Congress made saccharin an exception to the law requiring the F.D.A. ban and allowed its continued use, at least for a time.

b.   Also in 1977, the Consumer Product Safety Commission (C.P.S.C.) voted to ban production and sale of sleepwear that had been treated with Tris (a chemical designed to make some fabrics flame-retardant). The evidence for the ban was a Canadian study which indicated that Tris had carcinogenic effects in test animals. There was no great public outcry and the ban held.

Discuss these two cases and consider why the first ban generated great opposition leading to elimination of the ban while the second, based on essentially the same grounds, led to no great opposition and was allowed to stand. Was one situation irrational and the other not? If so, which was irrational? Why? If you judge both to be sound arguments, then explain the success of one and the failure of the other. For further discussion of these two cases, see Charles R. Bantz, "Public Arguing in the Regulation of Health and Safety," *Western Journal of Speech Communication,* 45 (Winter 1981), pp. 71–87.

Part VI

Special
fields
of
reasoning

25

Introduction

Up to this point, we have concentrated on aspects of argumentation and reasoning that can be found equally in all kinds of rational discussions. With only minor exceptions, all features of our basic pattern of argumentation can be illustrated from any field of practical reasoning. Whether we concern ourselves with law or ethics, medicine or business, scientific explanation or aesthetic appreciation, we can identify and consider separately:

1. The *claims* put forward and criticized in any particular context.
2. The *grounds* by which these claims are supported and the *warrants* by which grounds and claims are connected.
3. The *backing* available to establish the soundness and acceptability of these warrants.
4. The *modal qualifiers* that indicate the strength and/or conditions of rebuttal of the initial claim.

In all these respects, practical argumentation involves similar elements and follows similar procedures, whatever the different human activities that provide forums for reasoning and so defines "fields of argument."

In Part VI, we shall be approaching the same general subject matter from a different angle. We will consider how reasoning proceeds in particular fields. Law and medicine, science and aesthetics, sports writing and politics—each of these enterprises has its own basic goals, and the procedures of argumentation developed to further those goals vary correspondingly from one enterprise to another.

THE VARIED PROCEDURES OF DIFFERENT ENTERPRISES

Degree of formality

To begin with, there are differences in the degrees of formality characteristic of reasoning procedures in different fields. The methods of argumentation typically employed within some rational enterprises are more formalized and stylized than in others.

Suppose that we have just seen a new movie and that we sit down over a cup of coffee to discuss its merits. In such a situation, there is no set or fixed form, or sequence of steps, to which our exchange of views must adhere. Certainly it will help matters if we take care to make it clear just what we are and are not claiming or disputing, because that will help us to arrive at a mutual understanding. But if we do eventually come to any agreement, this will commonly happen not through strict adherence to any formal procedure but rather through a roundabout and discursive exchange of perceptions and opinions.

The proceedings in a court of law, by contrast, are required to follow a standard sequence of steps, if they are to satisfy the necessary conditions of orderly procedure, or "due process." Failure to follow the proper sequence can, in fact, be an effective ground of appeal: a "formally defective" legal proceeding can often be declared void. Too much is at stake in legal proceedings for us to tolerate sloppy, casual procedures. Ensuring the ritual "formality" of our proceedings is a precaution adopted to protect the interests of the different parties fairly and equitably.

Between these two extremes—film criticism and law court proceedings—we shall find all sorts of intermediate examples. In the natural sciences, for instance, formalized journals and learned meetings serve as standard channels of debate and publication. But the actual "validity" of argumentation in scientific contexts does not depend, as closely or immediately as it does in courts of justice, on its conforming to any set procedural forms. Meanwhile, in some other areas—for example, ethical discussions and business decisions, where personal preferences may count for more than formal procedures—the procedures of argumentation are frequently even less elaborate and ritualized than they are in science.

Degrees of precision

There is more scope for *precision and exactitude of argument* in some fields of practical reasoning than in others. In theoretical physics, for instance, many of our arguments can be formulated with mathematical exactitude. Although such precision is not common in most fields, the kind of abstract exactitude typical of physical theories shows up in many rational enterprises. In business and politics, for instance, many claims are made that turn, in part or in whole, on a delicate balancing of economic advantage and disadvantage, and where this is the case, the mathematical machinery for performing economic calculations of "profit and loss" can be brought into play. In many enterprises likewise, formal problem-solving procedures have been developed suitable for handling by computer. Such programs must be spelled out in exact detail, but their use greatly simplifies the corresponding modes of argumentation, at any rate in routine cases.

In many fields of experience, by contrast, our ability to present and argue for our opinions depends rather on our capacity to recognize complex patterns or "constellations" of features, and to bring these to the attention of others. This is largely the case in everyday psychology, when people's "states of mind" are at issue; it is true also in aesthetics and literary criticism, where the critic may have to master and explain the subtleties of a richly organized canvas or a complex plot; and also in clinical medicine, when it comes to putting together a whole collection of small signs and symptoms and arriving at a defensible diagnosis. In cases of this kind, it is an overall, qualitative appreciation of the relationships in which all the relevant features stand to one another that carries most weight rather than the precise, quantitative measurement of any single feature by itself. Precision, in the sense of "quantitative exactitude," thus has a genuine importance in many situations, but only so long as its claims are properly balanced against those of "the larger picture."

It was the classical Greek philosophers, around 400 B.C., who first explicitly recognized the intellectual power of such "mathematical" exactitude. It seemed to them to mark off certain entire enterprises or fields of argumentation as lending themselves preeminently to "rational" treatment. (Geometry was Plato's favorite example.) By now, however, it is clear that at one stage or another, this kind of exactitude may find a place in any field or enterprise. Even in a seemingly "informal" activity, such as literary criticism, certain procedures may conveniently be computerized. On the other hand, no enterprise can rely on this kind of strict or exact argumentation *alone*. Even the exact sciences, such as physics, involve phases of unformalizable interpretation that depend in part on the exercise of personal judgment. So it is a mistake to assume that argumentation is always "formal" in some fields (e.g., natural science) and always "informal" in others (e.g., aesthetics). On the contrary, whatever our field of reasoning, the question can always be raised how far arguments and procedures of great exactitude are relevant to our purposes in dealing with different kinds of problems.

Modes of resolution

Because different human enterprises have different objectives, their procedures of argumentation lead up to different kinds of *completion or resolution*. Although the arguments employed in all fields of practical reasoning are somewhat alike in their beginnings—for instance, they all start with the making of claims—there is nothing like the same uniformity about the ways in which they are brought to a close.

In forums such as courts of law, the proceedings are conducted on an *adversary* basis. That is to say, the action before the court involves two opposing parties, or "adversaries," who present the strongest cases they can assemble for their opposed claims. In such a forum, the proceedings terminate when, after going through the due process, the court presents a "verdict" in favor of one or the other party. For this end, or resolution, to be arrived at, all that is required is for *the court itself* to reach a conclusion. It is by no means necessary for *the losing party* to be convinced that his initial case and argument were unsound. As often as not, of course, he will continue to protest his grievance, or his innocence, despite the verdict of the court. Indeed, the very fact that a particular dispute is actually brought before the court commonly indicates that the two adversary parties were unable to reach an agreement without resort to the judicial process. The essential function of the court proceedings will be, as a result, to choose (or "rule") between two adversary positions, rather than to work out an intermediate position (or "settlement") agreeable to both parties. If that could have been done, the issue would presumably have been dealt with earlier ("out of court") without the need for a judicial hearing.

In rational enterprises such as labor/management negotiation, the goal is just the opposite. The goal is to arrive at a practical *compromise or consensus* that will be acceptable to parties who had initially occupied sharply contrasted positions. The outcome of a successful negotiation is, accordingly, not a decision in favor of one of the parties rather than the other. Instead it aims to find some middle position that all the involved parties can consent to, or at least something they can live with.

These two contrasted modes of procedure and determination—adversary and consensus—are not the only ones. In other fields of argumentation, such as aesthetics, neither complete agreement nor an outside ruling is essential to the resolution of a discussion. We do not need, in such cases, to insist either that the parties should come to a shared position for themselves, as in a negotiation, or that a definite decision between them should be pronounced, as in a court proceeding, by a third party acting as "judge." Instead, the central function of argumentation may be confined to *clarification*. If we are asked to support (and so "justify") our initial claims about a novel or movie, for instance, this request need only require us to spell out more precisely the relevance of our claims to the content of the work in question. We would explain the *significance* of our claims, rather than prove that they are *correct*. Others will be at liberty to dispute our interpretation of the work by questioning whether our comments are really to the point. But once these preliminary doubts have been dealt with, we do not always have to go on and make an outright choice between the alternative readings. Insisting that one or another reading is exclusively correct need not serve any practical purpose. In aesthetic discussions, it is often an acceptable termination if others can recognize the initial reading as relevant and well-founded—if they can finally reply, "Yes, I see now how one might say that." In such contexts, we can conclude our discussions rationally, as well as gracefully, without pretending to have settled any final and absolute "rights" or "wrongs" in the process.

Goals of argumentation

The kind of procedure appropriate in any particular field of argumentation depends on *what is at stake* within the forum involved. To recall our earlier example, within the context of different human enterprises one and the same set of words ("Jack is insane") may well express quite different claims. These alternative claims will have to be judged in quite different ways because of the different kinds of things that are at stake in the two contexts.

On the one hand, the assertor presenting the claim may be Jack's attendant physician, and the critical hearer may be a psychiatrist whom the physician is consulting about the exact diagnosis and proper treatment of Jack's afflictions.

On the other hand, the assertor presenting the claim may be an attorney acting on behalf of Jack's wife, and the critical hearer may be a judge to whom the attorney is applying for powers of administration over Jack's financial affairs.

In the first case, the very point of the consultation is to arrive at some agreed psychiatric diagnosis that can serve as a medical basis for dealing clinically with Jack's condition. Thus the functions of the medical or psychiatric context call for the parties to employ *consensus rather than adversary* procedures. By contrast, in the second case, *adversary rather than consensus* procedures may be unavoidable. The fact that the issue has been brought into open court at all may indicate that Jack himself (or perhaps some close relative) wishes to prevent this transfer of his financial affairs to the wife. Where such an opposition exists, a judicial ruling cannot be dispensed with, and the court's task has an adversary character built into it.

It is worth nothing, incidentally, how the professional training of psychiatrists creates difficulties for them when it comes to dealing with the legal aspects of insanity. This training prepares them to operate primarily within the consensus procedures of science and medicine, and as a result, they often find it frustrating to be involved in law court proceeding, when they feel that their "expert testimony" is being chopped about and distorted to suit the legal cut and thrust of the adversary process. What needs to be understood more clearly is the underlying aim of that "cut and thrust," that is, the practical importance of getting judicial issues settled clearly, one way or the other, not left hanging in ambiguity. As most psychiatrists know very well, few of their diagnoses are concerned with translucently clear, yes-or-no, black-and-white issues; all too often, mental troubles and diagnoses involve more-or-less differing shades of gray and resist clear or dogmatic assertions. A case might, accordingly, be made out for treating judicial issues about insanity, personal status, and the like—wherever possible—as matters for arbitration, aimed at a consensus about what is *equitable,* rather than as matters for judicial decision, leading to a ruling about what is *right*. Yet the goals of the law being what they are, it would be unrealistic to insist on following this course in all cases, regardless of the interests of all the parties involved. Here as elsewhere, the attempt to achieve an equitable arbitration may simply fail. It may be impossible to reach any consensus, and the final resort to litigation—that is, to adversary procedures—may be impossible to avoid.

The central point is well illustrated by this example. The characteristic differences between the kinds of argumentation conducted in adjacent fields (psychiatry and law being only one case) are best understood in terms of the respective purposes of the enterprises concerned. Medical diagnosis and psychiatric treatment, for instance, allow scope for flexibility—particularly for variations in "degree" of a kind that would be impracticable, and even infuriating, in dealing with questions of law and administration. A clinical psychiatrist may prescribe either one drug or several drugs, either alone or in conjunction with other modes of therapy, and she may prescribe them in many different dosages and proportions. But the practical issues coming before the law courts can rarely be handled in this flexible manner. Commonly they demand clear and definite rulings—decisions that will be truly "determinative." Can Jack go on writing valid checks on his own bank account, or will his wife be given powers of administration over his monetary affairs instead? Given such a question, there is no room for vagueness or degree. Either his checks will remain valid, or they will lose all value entirely.

Similarly, in other enterprises and fields of argumentation, the modes of practical reasoning we expect to find in any particular field—in natural science or art criticism, in ethical discussion or elsewhere—will once again reflect the general purpose and practical demands of the enterprise under consideration. In the chapters that follow, we shall look in succession at five enterprises that provide forums for practical reasoning, and we shall inquire into what kinds of argumentation typically find a place within these forums. These five fields of reasoning—law, art, science, business, and ethics—have been chosen as being broadly representative of the situations that serve as occasions for argumentation. By studying them, we shall identify most of the characteristic modes of reasoning to be found in different fields and enterprises, and we shall recognize how they reflect the underlying aims of those enterprises.

REGULAR ARGUMENTS AND CRITICAL ARGUMENTS

In all fields of argument and rational enterprises, we have occasion to argue in two rather different ways. On the one hand, the very purpose of developing rules of thumb, laws of nature, procedures, recipes, statutes, and similar ways of reasoning, is to establish patterns of argument that can generally be relied on to yield the kinds of results required in the enterprise concerned. Scientific laws must generally lead to successful explanations; medical procedures must yield generally successful diagnoses and therapies: judicial procedures must determine at least rough justice; and so on. For the most part, therefore, we can safely rely on the accepted body of *warrants* without having to call them into serious question on every occasion. The general run of arguments, in which we rely on the accepted rules or warrants, may thus be called *regular* arguments.

On the other hand, it would be dogmatic or unthinking of us, if we never asked ourselves about the continuing adequacy or relevance of the rules of argument which we were taught in childhood and picked up during our education. If we are at all critical, we must surely, from time to time, have second thoughts about those warrants, and ask ourselves whether the ways of thinking we learned hitherto may not need to be made more subtle and discriminating, if not actually abandoned. Maybe the accepted laws of electromagnetic theory need some refinement or emendation; maybe the current treatment for arthritis only works well with certain classes of patients; maybe the defense of criminal insanity is not working out in a just and acceptable way. In all fields of argument, we sometimes have to *rethink* currently accepted procedures and, if necessary, modify them. The arguments by which this is done will here be called *critical* arguments.

Notice that in regular arguments the warrants are simply *used;* in critical arguments they are *evaluated*. Hence, regular arguments are *rule-applying* arguments, while critical arguments are *rule-justifying* arguments.

Once again, the deeper sources of the rational power which our arguments possess can be fully recognized only if we go behind the arguments themselves and look at the human enterprises that provide the larger contexts of those arguments. For example, the critical arguments of one field may be closely related to the regular arguments of another. Considerations of scientific physiology, for example, may have a direct bearing on the criticism of current procedures in medicine: in this way, biological science creates the instruments used in medical criticism. In the chapters that follow, we shall begin to see something of the complex relationships in which our different enterprises are linked.

INTERFIELD AND INTRAFIELD COMPARISONS

Notice one thing at the outset: our present method of analysis will be strictly *comparative*. Moving from field to field, we shall note resemblances and differences between the modes and styles of argumentation typical of the different fields. We shall not present arguments in any one field of practical reasoning as being *better* or *more rational* than others. The only judgements that we shall pass will, as a result, be "intrafield" judgments, having to do with the features that make some scientific arguments weightier than other scientific arguments, some legal considerations more forceful than other legal considerations, and so on. We shall not be concerned with "interfield" comparisons. It is not our aim to argue, for example, that all scientific arguments are—simply because they are "scientific"—weightier than any legal or ethical argument.

The character of our present analysis must be emphasized, if only because so many people are tempted to make interfield (rather than intrafield) comparisons. They are often tempted, for instance, to contrast the nature of ethical arguments with that of scientific arguments. In this way, they set out to develop a kind of "rational" order of merit for grading entire fields of reasoning as more or less adequate, more or less excellent.

Many people are inclined to assume that "hard" intellectual enterprises like mathematics and natural science are more "logical" or "rational" than such emotional areas of discussion as ethics or aesthetics. A similar assumption occurs with the question of whether *all* historical understanding is less or more "rational" or "well-founded" than *all* knowledge in physics. Once again, for our present purposes, such interfield comparisons are beside the point. Some historical arguments are sounder than others, some arguments in physics more rigorous than others.

But to compare the merits of *all* historical arguments with *all* arguments in physics has no practical purpose.

Similarly, when it comes to deciding, say, about Jack's sanity or insanity, we do not have to choose psychiatry *as a whole* over the law *as a whole;* or the other way around. Rather, we have to choose between alternative psychiatric diagnoses and/or between alternative judicial rulings. The judge who approves the application for Jack's wife for powers to manage his financial affairs is in no way setting up his judgment (i.e., ruling) in competition with the judgment (i.e., prescription) of the consultant psychiatrist who recommends treatment with lithium, or the other way around. Regarded as *problems,* the task of arranging for the prudent administration of Jack's affairs and the task of finding a suitable therapy for his mental troubles involve basically independent problems. As a result, the trains of argumentation involved in *solving* these problems are no more than partially relevant to one another.

The first step toward understanding what gives legal arguments their force is, therefore, to recognize the character and the goal of the judicial enterprise. The first step toward understanding what gives scientific arguments their force is to recognize what is at stake in doing science, and so on. If we can keep in mind the respective aims and purposes of the different "rational enterprises," we shall then be in a position to see for ourselves *how and why* making scientific issues a topic for adversary disputes, instead of consensus procedures, would distort the basic character of the natural sciences; or conversely, *how and why* replacing the adversary processes of the existing judicial system by consensus procedures would undermine the current enterprise of the law.

In each of the following chapters, therefore, we shall explore the questions about argumentation that arise *within* one or another of our five chosen enterprises. This will mean considering

1. The general character of each of the enterprises, as providing a forum for practical argumentation.
2. The various kinds of forums that exist within each enterprise, and the issues and outcomes characteristic of each kind.

On this basis, we shall go on to examine

3. The types of claims and grounds, warrants and backing, that find a place within the corresponding modes of practical argumentation.
4. The way in which the kinds of judgment and criticism appropriate to natural science (or aesthetics or the law) reflect the basic goals and requirements of the enterprise in question.

Given these intrafield considerations, we shall see how it is that legal arguments are sound or shaky, *as* arguments taking place within a larger judicial frame; how it is that scientific arguments are weighty or negligible, *as* arguments that succeed or fail in their aim of forwarding the larger scientific enterprise; and so on. For these purposes, it is clearly irrelevant to criticize scientific or legal arguments *in general,* simply because they lack the absolute "certainty" of geometrical arguments; but it is entirely relevant to criticize *particular* scientific or legal arguments for failing to serve the purpose of their own proper enterprises. Good natural science is good *as* science, not because it succeeds in putting on the appearance of pure mathematics. Bad law is bad *as* law, not because it fails to promote the goals of psychiatry or social science. And likewise in other cases.

What parts, then, do reasoning and argumentation play in such human enterprises as natural science, law, and the rest? What kinds of forum for argumentation do these enterprises provide? How do we recognize the force of the arguments that are advanced within those situations? And what is involved in recognizing that some scientific argument is a *good* argument, from the standpoint of natural science, or, alternatively, in detecting that some legal argument is an *unsound* argument, from the standpoint of *law?* These are the kinds of questions to which we shall now turn our attention, in each of the five fields of practical reasoning and argumentation that we have chosen for examination.

26

Legal reasoning

Whether we are aware of the fact or not, almost all of us have some familiarity with the general rules and patterns of legal reasoning. It is not necessary for us to sue someone or to be arrested in order to be influenced by the arguments that lawyers and judges have carefully constructed. For the law itself is a system of procedures and principles intended to provide systematic decisions that will help to secure the life and liberty of individuals, protect property, ensure the performance of valid contracts, resolve conflicts between different individuals, maintain public order, and provide other ends agreed on as desirable for social purposes. Even though you never come near a courtroom, therefore, you may be influenced by legal arguments or use them yourself in the courts of everyday affairs.

While still quite young, children can already be heard using legal rationales:

> One small boy is accused of taking another's money. He denies it and shouts, "I'm innocent until you can prove me guilty!" When asked how he knows he is innocent until proved guilty, he may reply, "Everybody knows that."

In truth, everybody does not *know* that, because this basic ground rule of legal reasoning is not operative in all jurisdictions. In some parts of the world, an accused person is treated as guilty until innocence is demonstrated. But the small boy is essentially correct: were the friend's charge of theft to be considered by a U.S. criminal court, he would be presumed innocent. So without formal legal training or prior experience of the legal system, the youngster still has a rough understanding of one important aspect of legal decision making.

Throughout society, we use the general principles of legal reasoning to resolve our everyday conflicts, short of actually going to trial:

> College students protest that school officials seeking evidence for some disciplinary action have no right to search dorm rooms uninvited. Evidence gained

from such an unlawful search cannot be used to convict someone: "Everybody knows a man's home is his castle."

In fact, everybody cannot *know* this, for it is certainly not clear that college dormitory rooms are to be treated in exactly the same way as a citizen's private home when it comes to applying the rules against unlawful search and seizure. Yet, once again, the students have a crude understanding of the need to exclude "tainted evidence" from legal reasoning.

> You are stopped by a patrol car while driving home one night, under suspicion of being under the influence of alcohol. The police ask you to perform a number of tests: breathing into an alcohol analysis machine, walking along a straight line, touching your nose with your finger. Before agreeing to perform such actions, you ask to call a lawyer and have her present during the tests. When asked what makes you think you have this right, you respond that everyone knows an accused person has a right to counsel.

Again, it is hard to say everyone *knows* this because this right, too, varies from place to place, time to time, and situation to situation. Yet, you do grasp one fundamental feature of our procedures of legal reasoning, that trained advocates present the arguments on behalf of clients and that we are not obliged to defend ourselves. This is so basic a notion that lawyers always have a saying: "Anyone who conducts his own defense (even the most skilled lawyer) has a fool for a client."

Thus traces of legal reasoning pervade much of our social life and practice. Of all our social institutions, the legal system has provided the most intense forum for the practice and analysis of reasoning, and it has been doing so for hundreds of years. So it should be no surprise that many of the techniques of legal reasoning have been adapted to other purposes by other elements in society, and it will therefore be fruitful to begin our studies of practical argumentation by looking at legal reasoning first.

LAW AS A FORUM FOR ARGUMENT

Fortunately, minor everyday conflicts between individuals can mostly be resolved without recourse to the legal system. When you break up with your lover, there may be a dispute over who gets the original Beatles records and who keeps the gold watch, but you can normally work that out for yourselves. If you accept a job understanding that you have been promised a high salary, only to find on arrival that the actual pay is less than you thought, you may complain to the boss and possibly reject the position if no correction is made, but you probably will not go to the length of suing.

Even when people cannot work out their own conflicts, other counseling and mediating services are available to help resolve these conflicts, short of going to court. Psychologists, psychiatrists, and counselors earn a living in this way. Religious organizations provide trained help to people with differences and problems. Labor-management disputes are handled by experienced mediators.

Still there are times when none of these methods of counseling and mediation is powerful enough to satisfy the parties in conflict:

> The roof of your apartment building leaks, allowing water to seep through your ceiling and leaving spots on your carpet. What courses of action are open to you? First, you talk to the landlord, hoping that he will agree to fix the roof. But if water still comes in even after the repairs and the landlord refuses to pay for cleaning your carpet, you may go to a local dispute-resolution center. But if the landlord also refuses to cooperate with the dispute center, you may feel forced to go to a lawyer.

Going to a lawyer does not automatically turn this dispute into a legal argument. On the contrary, many disputes are resolved at this point and never formally enter the legal system. Your lawyer hears about your problem and makes an appointment with the landlord. The landlord is informed of your complaints and is told that a suit will very likely be filed if no satisfaction is forthcoming. At this point, he may agree to fix the roof again and even offer some payment toward cleaning the carpet. If the leaks are truly stopped this time, if your carpet once again looks all right, and if you have not had to pay all the costs, you may well be content and the dispute will be ended. Up to this point, there has been no genuine legal reasoning, although the threat of a lawsuit has clearly played a role in this outcome.

Before we forget your apartment, consider an alternative scenario. When your lawyer talks with the landlord, your story may be challenged:

> In fact, you are the person at fault, claims the landlord. You have wild parties every Saturday night, which cause both the stains on the carpet and the water marks on the ceiling. He produces a bill marked "paid" from the roofing company (showing that a new roof was put on the building one month before you moved in) and also written complaints from your neighbors, one of which reports that you spilled so much liquid on your floor that it leaked through to the apartment below.

At this point, your lawyer may well advise you to forget the whole thing and to be more careful with future parties, for fear of facing a lawsuit yourself. Once again, strictly legal reasoning has not yet been employed. Still your lawyer has clearly evaluated the situation from a legal perspective. If this dispute went to court, you would stand little or no chance of winning. Your arguments are too weak in comparison with those of your landlord—so weak, in fact, that there is no chance even of a negotiated compromise.

As the stakes involved become greater, and as the underlying disagreements—about what was really promised, what actually happened, or what the law in fact permits—become more severe, it becomes that much more likely that a dispute will result in formal legal proceedings. When the parties involved can reach no mutually acceptable settlement (even with the help of mediators, counselors, and lawyers) and they stand to win or lose too much as a result of the conflict to forget about it, the only remaining way to resolve it may be to turn to the socially organized decision-making system, which is backed by powers of enforcement. This is what the law provides.

But the legal system provides much more than powers of enforcement. In addition, it undertakes to give "reasoned" decisions, so that in case of future conflicts lawyers can make sound estimates about what would probably be decided if the differences were to go to court. As a result, few conflicts will actually have to be decided by formal legal procedures. Many will be resolved in the lawyer's office, where the client is advised what the court's decision would probably be and recognizes that it would be much less costly and risky to end the conflict by negotiating and settling in advance.

Overriding all this is the further promise that legal decisions will be made in ways consistent with those broader principles we refer to as the *demands of justice*. If individuals in conflict turn to social mechanisms to help resolve their problems, they will not be content with a flip of a coin or an arbitrary choice. They will demand an equitable judgment. Whether the conflict is between an individual and society (involving a criminal charge) or between individuals or corporations (as in a civil proceeding), the parties will want something more than a *decision*. They will insist that this decision be shown to reflect fair and impartial consideration of the opposing stories, to see how both can be reconciled with established statutes, codes, or common-law precedents.

Fundamentally, the legal forum exists to provide this consideration and evaluation of opposing stories. Each side in a dispute presents its own version of what happened to give rise to the present dispute. Opposing lawyers present witnesses, documents, exhibits, or anything they can legitimately present, in order to convince the decision maker—whether judge or jury—that their client's version of the story is correct. The judge or jury meet then to determine what are the "facts," that is, which version of the story will be deemed "correct" for the purposes of the law. In the absence of any procedural error—failing any violation of legal standards or any outrage to what society deems just and fair, such as a disproportionately large award of damages—the decision so made will be final and enforceable, and the parties must live with it.

All the same, one side or the other will often feel that it had not been treated justly and will charge that some violation occurred in the course of the proceedings warranting a reversal of judgment or at least a new trial. So they appeal the decision. Thus a second forum for legal reasoning (appellate courts) is needed in order to review the trial decisions of the lower courts. The arrangement of appellate courts varies from jurisdiction to jurisdiction. Typically there are two more layers of courts—a network of regional appeal courts, supervised by a single supreme court—each charged with the responsibility of examining the reasoning and decisions of the courts immediately below it. For the most part, appellate courts do not reevaluate the competing stories about the facts of the case. They accept the determination of "facts" from the original court and work from this record. Thus appellate courts do not normally hear witnesses, receive documents and exhibits, or even read the transcripts of witnesses' testimony; they would argue that one needs to hear and see witnesses in person in order to judge their credibility, so that an appellate body is in no position to second-guess the trial court about oral testimony.

Appellate courts, accordingly, hear arguments from attorneys and read detailed briefs containing the reasoning of each side. They consider opposing interpretations of the relevant statutes, codes, and precedents, and they accept arguments from authorities competent to suggest what the meaning of these arguments should be. Ultimately it is the task of an appellate court to show the reasons that one or the other party's position is more consistent with the overall demands of justice; either in review of the broad values and prescriptions set down in the Constitution of the United States, or else in terms of values and prescriptions apparent in the evolution of our society. For the decision of a court of appeals does not affect only the individual parties involved in this particular controversy. It will be read by lawyers throughout the society, including judges on other appellate courts, and on the basis of the present court's reasoning, others will decide what is fair or just in subsequent controversies of similar kinds. Through the force of its supporting arguments, each appellate decision thus has the potential of contributing to the evolution of law itself.

To summarize, first and most commonly the law provides a forum for arguing about competing versions of the facts involved in a conflict irresoluble by mediation or conciliation. So legal reasoning focuses primarily on what these "facts" are—that is, what will be accepted as "facts" for the purposes of legal decision making. As a secondary forum, an appellate court then focuses on opposing lines of argument about the "law"—that is, about what the precise state of the law is, or should be, in relation to the "facts" found below. And through the written reasons for their decisions, they stand a chance to influence the future development of the law.

THE NATURE OF LEGAL ISSUES

This first rough description of the major forums for legal argument has referred to two general types of legal issues: "questions of fact" and "questions of law." But there are, of course, also other subordinate issues having to do with questions of proper jurisdiction, the standing of the various parties in relation to a suit, and whether or not a proper cause of action has been presented to the court.

From the standpoint of the parties directly involved, there is only one real issue: who is right, the plaintiff or the defendant, the prosecution or the defense? That may well be true for the jury, too. Although the judge instructs the jury on the law prior to their deliberations, the jury makes its decision, whether they believe one side or the other and what they are to determine on this basis about the law, after retiring from public view. What exactly goes on in jury rooms is unknown beyond what former jurors tell us and what has been learned from experiments with simulated juries, but from these sources, there is much evidence to suggest that jurors do in fact make their decision in this manner.

For legal purposes, however, the distinction between questions of fact and of law has real importance. It determines how advocates will prepare their cases and when judges can make rulings for the dismissal of suits and for directed verdicts. And it remarks on the issues that are central to the decisions in trial courts and appeal courts. Therefore, we must look a little more closely at this distinction.

Questions of fact

The first step toward a lawsuit is taken when a prospective client sits down with a lawyer to tell a story. "Listen to what has happened," says the businessman who finds himself in trouble with a large competitor, "and tell me if I can secure relief through the law." The lawyer hears the story and thinks of the possible remedies available from the law. "Perhaps," he responds, "you could charge your opponent with an antitrust violation." But as past decisions indicate, that will mean proving five kinds of things for a judge or jury to take as indispensable "facts":

1. That there was a combination or agreement among the business competitors with whom you are in dispute not to sell to or buy from you.
2. That this action resulted in damages to you.
3. That you have incurred attorney's fees to correct the problem.
4. That this action has involved trade across state lines.
5. That the issues therefore come within the jurisdiction of the federal courts.

"Now," says the lawyer, "let us look at your story in the light of this potential remedy. Your story is as follows":

"You own a small manufacturing plant, and a representative of a large conglomerate offered to buy you out. When you refused, a firm supplying essential parts for your manufacturing process—which turned out to be a subsidiary of the conglomerate—informed you that it could no longer meet your orders. Furthermore you heard that the conglomerate was putting pressure on your customers not to buy your product and had offered them a competing product at a sharply reduced price. As a result, you have suffered a loss of $250,000 in gross sales to date, and these losses are continuing at about the same rate. You have retained counsel to help you, but negotiations with the conglomerate have led to no change. They deny that they have done what you allege. Your plant is located in Illinois, the supplier of essential parts is in Utah, and your customers who have cancelled orders are located in three other states."

Questions of fact become "issues of fact" once you have prepared your claims and presented them to the court and so made them known to your future opponents in the case. They will now prepare their response, and where they deny your statements of fact, specific "issues"—or points of disagreement—will emerge for determination by the court:

> The conglomerate, the subsidiary, and your customers respond that it was you, not they, who made the first approaches about selling your plant. When the conglomerate expressed no interest, you claimed that the supplier was failing to honor your orders. In fact, the supplier has continued to sell you the same quantity as it has done over the past two years. Your customers respond that they were not pressured; instead they found your competitor's product and prices more desirable than yours. You are charged with covering up poor business practice by seeking to place blame on the actions of others. There is no denial that this trade crosses state lines, so that the dispute falls within federal jurisdiction. Your claim of damages is denied; instead it is alleged that you yourself are operating a failing business.

Thus the issues emerge: (1) Did the defendants combine to deny trade with you? (2) Is your current loss of $250,000 caused by this alleged combination against you? If the trial court is to agree that you have a proper case, all five questions of fact must be addressed; your opponents will do their best to refute your assertions at the two points indicated by the factual issues in dispute.

In the actual course of legal reasoning, each issue of fact will be further broken down into subordinate issues. For example, as to whether there was a combination to deny you trade, you need to prove that the conglomerate did indeed approach you first, seeking to buy your business. (They say *you* came to *them*.) You may reason as follows:

Grounds

1. *You testify to a meeting in your office with Mr. Jones of Conglomerate Associates.*
2. *You offer your appointment book indicating that such a meeting was scheduled.*
3. *Your secretary testifies that he recalls Mr. Jones talking about buying your plant before you brought up the subject.*

Warrant

As the meeting was held in your office and Mr. Jones first raised the question of the purchase, it is reasonable to infer that

Claim

The conglomerate approached you seeking to buy your plant.

The defendants contest this question. They say it was this way:

Grounds

1. *Mr. Jones testifies that the meeting was held in your office at your request.*
2. *He submits a letter from you to him asking for such a meeting.*
3. *He testifies that you first mentioned the question of selling your plant.*

The business of judge or jury is to arrive at a choice between these two stories, or rather, as you are making the complaint, they have, more precisely, to decide whether or not your version of the story carries conviction. Unless it does so, your suit against the conglomerate fails at this point.

Questions of law

Questions of law surround the determination of questions of fact. It is not enough to make a bare choice between two different stories. This choice must be made with an eye to the demands of the law and of justice. Throughout the proceedings, the trial judge will be making many decisions on questions of law. In order of increasing generality, she will be having to ask herself such questions as these:

— Is that a proper question for the law to consider at all?
— Is this particular court the proper court to consider the question?
— Is that a proper question to argue, given the nature of the present charge?
— Is this a proper procedure for taking the matter to trial, and conducting the trial?
— Is that a proper question to ask of this witness?
— Is this a proper document or exhibit to receive in evidence?
— How can I properly instruct the jury about the law prior to their deliberations?
— Did the jury behave properly, or were they prejudiced?
— Is the jury's decision acceptable within the boundaries of justice?
— Is the law under which the decision was made consistent with the Constitution of this state or of the United States?
— Is the action taken today consistent with the overall demands of justice?

Such questions of law become "issues of law," once the judge's decision has been contested by a party in the suit. Trial lawyers speak of "building and preserving a record"; this means constructing a transcript of all that happens in a trial, which provides the basis for any appeal to a higher court. Even before a trial begins, of course, opposing counsel may enter objections that will require a decision by the judge, and if this ruling is successfully appealed, the trial may not take place at all. For example:

> Some people picketed a women's clinic carrying signs reading "Baby Killers for Hire—$200 and Up," and a supporter of the clinic asked the court for an injunction against the picketing. But the individual who filed this suit against the picketers was deemed not to have "standing"; that is, she was ruled to have an insufficiently direct personal involvement in the matter, and the judge dismissed the suit.
>
> This ruling could be appealed, and the judge's decision could be overturned by a higher court. If so, the trial would proceed, with the possibility of still other objections on the law, and so on.

In this case, the defendant claimed that the plaintiff did not have standing to sue, and the plaintiff claimed that she did. The issue of law was thus created, and the judge made a ruling. In this case, the ruling went against the plaintiff, and the suit was therefore dismissed. If there had been an appeal, the plaintiff would have become the appellant (the one challenging the ruling), and the defendant would have become the appellee. The issue of law, however, would have remained the same as before: Does the law permit an individual of this kind to sue the picketers on account of the action described?

In a strictly hypothetical illustration—as the case was not in fact appealed—the arguments might be developed this way:

Appellant:
Grounds

1. *The plaintiff, Ms. Brown, is a volunteer worker at the women's clinic.*
2. *In* Figbee v. Alloys, *the U.S. Supreme Court ruled that a volunteer worker had standing to sue those charged with "imputing criminal activity."*
3. *This suit claims that the defendant-appellee imputed criminal activity on the part of the women's clinic.*

Warrant

Because the U.S. Supreme Court is the highest court in the land, and it has ruled that a volunteer has standing to sue in such a case as this, we may infer that

Claim

Ms. Brown should be allowed to proceed with her suit.

Appellee:
Grounds

1. *The plaintiff-appellant, Ms. Brown, has in fact no regular role at the women's clinic. She has not been seen there for over a year and is a volunteer only in that her name appears on a list of potential volunteers.*
2. *The U.S. Supreme Court in* Snodgrass v. Shagnasty *ruled that in order to have standing to sue, a volunteer worker must be actively involved in day-to-day operations.*

Warrant

Because *Snodgrass v. Shagnasty* is more applicable to this case than *Figbee v. Alloys,* and because the U.S. Supreme Court is admitted to rule here, it may be concluded that

Claim

Ms. Brown should not be allowed to proceed with her suit.

The court of appeals would then make a decision, and in so doing, it would accomplish two things. First, it would determine the fate of the present case, and second, it would contribute to the common law for the benefit of future cases.

Interplay of law and fact

Now that the basic reasoning associated with answering questions of fact and law has been set out, we can examine the interplay between the two types of reasoning in applied situations. First, we need to review three basic concepts that have importance in legal reasoning: (1) presumption; (2) burden of proof; (3) prima facie case.

Presumption must be understood in two contexts: as a question of law to be determined by judges, and as a perspective held by jurors. In law, presumption describes the occupation of argumentative ground, a point of departure, and a guide to decision. It is a point of departure in that the law expresses presumptions such as innocence or absence of negligence as indicators of the way argument should proceed. If a person is presumed innocent, then he or she will remain innocent until someone undertakes the responsibility to argue him or her off that ground. Presumption is a guide to decision in that it determines the decision in the absence of a clear preponderance of the evidence (or the presence of reasonable doubt in criminal matters). What if we cannot decide which side made the better case at the end of the trial? Suppose the arguments tend to cancel each other. Then, presumption guides the decision: in the absence of a clear preponderance of the evidence, the decision goes to the side holding presumption.

As a perspective held by jurors, presumption describes their point of departure as well, but *that may conflict with the presumption of the law.* In criminal matters, the accused is presumed innocent until proved guilty in the eyes of the law. However, the jury may enter the trial presuming the accused guilty. For example, two black joggers were killed by gunshot wounds while running in Liberty Park in Salt Lake City, Utah. Joseph Paul Franklin was tried in Federal Court on a charge of violating the civil rights of the joggers, and was convicted. Shortly thereafter, a state court accused Franklin of murder. Considering the extensive publicity associated with the first trial, it is possible that jurors in the second trial started from a presumption of guilt rather than innocence.

In sum, lawyers must take note of presumption from both legal and jury perspectives. The law will demand a procedure based upon its concept of presumption, but the lawyer will be well-advised to consider the state of mind of the jury in planning the trial.

Burden of proof coordinates with presumption. The side seeking to overcome presumption carries the burden to prove its claims. That is, if we claim someone should pay us money for a negligent action, it is our responsibility to prove negligence by a *clear preponderance of the evidence.* We must, in the eyes of the law, do more than match arguments with the defense. We must overcome their presumption by advancing stronger claims than they.

Similarly, in terms of jury perspectives, burden of proof can be rephrased as the burden of persuasion. If the jury starts with the notion that the accused is guilty, the defense will bear the burden of persuading them away from that idea in spite of the legal presumption of innocence. Of course, if it can be shown that the jury was prejudiced, new jurors can be requested, new locations for the trial can be sought, and new trials can be obtained. But jurors rarely admit their prejudice, and proving it is difficult.

A *prima facie case* must also be considered in terms of law and jury. In law, a prima facie case is one that *on first face* justifies a decision in behalf of the side advancing it. To have a prima facie case is not necessarily to be judged a winner. A prima facie case is one that offers claims in affirmation of all the essential elements or issues associated with the cause of the trial. For example, a prima facie case for a cause of action for negligence requires claims affirming the following essential elements:

1. Is the area in which you were damaged protected against unintentional invasion?
2. Was the action of the other person negligent?

3.   Did the other person's action legally cause your damage?
4.   Did you behave so as to be free of contributory negligence?

As the other person about whom you are complaining is presumed to be free of negligence, you will need to advance a series of claims asserting, with some evidence, an affirmative answer to each of these questions *before the defendant needs to make any claims at all.*

Before the defense presents any arguments, it will typically ask the judge whether a prima facie case has been presented. For example, suppose your case discussed only the first three questions listed, and failed to make any statement about your own potential contributory negligence. In this instance, your case would not, *on its face,* warrant a decision in your favor. That is, even if you established *all* your claims by a clear preponderance of evidence, you would still not deserve a judgment. In that event, the judge would dismiss the case without requiring any argument at all from the defense: if there is no prima facie case, there is no need for the presumed side to argue.

Let us pause here to identify the interplay of questions of fact and law. Where did the judge come up with the essential elements of a case of negligence? How did she know what was required of a prima facie case? These essential elements stem from legal reasoning. Based upon past decisions of appellate courts, codes and statutes relevant to the jurisdiction, and authoritative judgment, it *seems reasonable* that if an appellate court should review this case it would demand these essential elements to satisfy prima facie demands. The question of law can be diagrammed as shown in Figure 26–1.

The reference used for backing is an authoritative discussion of legal precedents and interpretations published by the American Law Institute. Mention of specific precedent cases would probably also be made.

Having satisfied, for the purposes of our example, the question of law concerning a prima facie case on negligence, we must turn attention to the demands of the jury. Since the judge has accepted the legal claim of a prima facie case, the questions of fact can be given to a jury. Now, however, what it takes to satisfy a jury that negligence has been shown may be different from that required by the judge. The argumentative demands they might hold for the plaintiff could be stronger or weaker than those required by the judge. Once the judge gives them the right to answer questions of fact, they are free to proceed as they see fit. What they do in their deliberations, to render a decision perhaps in favor of plaintiff, will remain a matter for them alone.

For the judge to say a prima facie case has been presented is not to decide the questions of fact. What might they be in this case?

We can see the interplay of fact and law if we return to the lawyer's office where a new client has just come for advice. Libby Scott tells the lawyer that she was a guest in the Savabuck Motel on June 13. During the night, plaster fell from the ceiling and struck her head, causing shock, concussion, and persistent head-

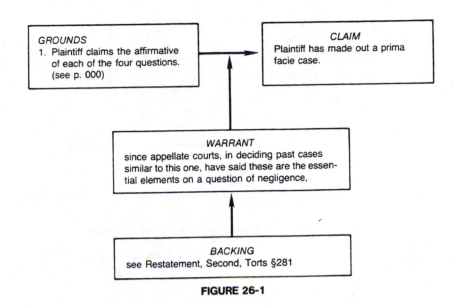

FIGURE 26-1

aches. She has medical bills of $2,000 and they continue to rise. Can she sue the hotel?

Considering the essential elements of such a case, drawn from claims on the law, the lawyer will consider whether a guest in a hotel can expect to spend the night without being hit by plaster. Knowing legal precedent, the lawyer will be inclined to think such a matter speaks for itself (*res ipsa loquitur*) and that no further proof of fact is needed. However, to be on the safe side, the lawyer will ask, "Was there a disturbance on the floor above yours which might have caused the plaster to fall?" "Was there a sonic boom or explosion or an earthquake?" Knowing the law, the attorney will understand that such an obvious accident can be ascribed to negligence of the hotel owner unless the owner can show some intervening fact to mitigate the suggestion of negligence. If the case were to go to trial, the lawyer will need to be prepared for such arguments on fact. Look at the possible argument from the hotel owner/defendant (Figure 26–2).

Now, Libby Scott's lawyer must consider whether it is possible to argue in favor of the *fact* that the hotel was negligent in the face of the owner's ability to argue the *fact* of the earthquake. The matter is not over, but the prospect of convincing a jury of negligence now seems less likely. The presumption that might have been gained by plaintiff through *res ipsa loquitur* (falling plaster speaks for itself as negligence), is lost, but the argument is not over.

With further investigation, Libby's lawyer may find the basis of another argument on fact (See Figure 26–3).

These competing claims on the question of fact will be presented in trial, and because the law has determined it to be a legitimate question for the jury to decide, the answer will come from jury deliberations. In this, the interplay of questions of fact and law can be seen clearly.

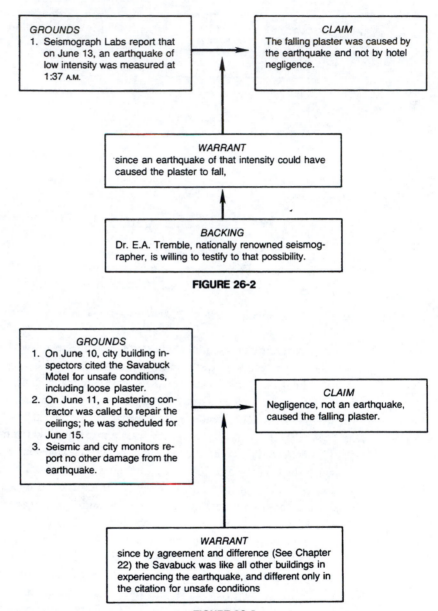

GROUNDS
1. Seismograph Labs report that on June 13, an earthquake of low intensity was measured at 1:37 A.M.

CLAIM
The falling plaster was caused by the earthquake and not by hotel negligence.

WARRANT
since an earthquake of that intensity could have caused the plaster to fall,

BACKING
Dr. E.A. Tremble, nationally renowned seismographer, is willing to testify to that possibility.

FIGURE 26-2

GROUNDS
1. On June 10, city building inspectors cited the Savabuck Motel for unsafe conditions, including loose plaster.
2. On June 11, a plastering contractor was called to repair the ceilings; he was scheduled for June 15.
3. Seismic and city monitors report no other damage from the earthquake.

CLAIM
Negligence, not an earthquake, caused the falling plaster.

WARRANT
since by agreement and difference (See Chapter 22) the Savabuck was like all other buildings in experiencing the earthquake, and different only in the citation for unsafe conditions

FIGURE 26-3

ESSENTIALLY CONTESTED ISSUES

The examples we have considered thus far reflect the routine case at law: ordinary people with ordinary problems that are solved in relative short order by the straightforward application of fairly clear rules of law. In fact, of all the cases that even reach the point of being filed through official channels, most are resolved by agreement of the parties before any trial occurs. And of the cases that go to trial, most are settled by the decision of the jury or the judge and are not appealed. The dramatic shout so familiar from books, movies, and TV—"We'll take this all the way to the Supreme Court!"—does not by any means represent the norm. Out of the cases actually taken to appeal, most end with the decision of an appellate court well below the level of the U.S. Supreme Court.

However, some few cases do raise issues of such fundamental importance—issues about which there is ongoing debate—that they require the attention of our highest court. Here the focus of attention ceases to be the particular individuals involved or what has happened to their lives as a result of the case. In fact, these individuals tend to be forgotten amidst all the fuss over the critical issues of general concern raised by their case. Few people recall who "Miranda" was or what happened to him, but many people will recognize the statement of the rights of those accused of crimes that emerged from his case and is associated with his name.

One can learn about these essentially contested issues by reading any complete text on constitutional law, and it is not our purpose here to survey this whole range of issues fully. Our aim is simply to indicate how the kind of argumentation typical of Supreme Court cases plays a part in the whole legal enterprise. For this purpose, two examples will suffice.

Executive power of the President

Throughout U.S. history, there have been challenges over the exact powers of the president. In recent years, the circumstances surrounding the Nixon resignation have raised such questions about the limits of presidential power. For example, several presidents have sent troops to fight in foreign conflicts without a declaration of war by Congress, claiming exercise of the president's role as commander-in-chief. This power has recently been challenged.

Again, the Congress asked to be allowed to hear tape recordings of conferences in the president's private office in order to investigate possible wrongdoing. Invoking the constitutional separation of powers, Richard Nixon, under a claim of executive privilege, refused permission. He said that the ability of the executive to conduct its proper business required an ability to keep some conferences and other materials in confidence. This claim too was challenged.

Again, Nixon claimed the right to do as so many of his predecessors had done and take his vast collection of presidential papers away with him upon leaving office. This right also was challenged.

Probably the most compelling question raised during the Nixon years, however, was the question of whether the president, as chief executive, is above the law. May the president, or members of the FBI, the CIA, or other agencies operating under executive orders, violate laws in the course of performing their jobs? Nixon claimed that the answer is yes. Others have challenged this answer to the point of having several members of the executive branch convicted of federal crimes. Briefly the arguments involved might follow this line:

Grounds

1. *The president is elected by the country to lead us as chief executive and commander-in-chief.*
2. *Sometimes the pursuit of the general national interest, as perceived by the executive, can be enhanced by the ignoring of such narrower laws as those forbidding wiretapping, unlawful entry, and even in extreme instances murder.*

Warrant

Because pursuit of the general national interest takes precedence over conformity to narrower and more specific laws, it follows that where these claims conflict,

Claim

The executive can act in ways above the law.

The other side might argue this way:

Grounds

1. *The laws are passed by the representatives of the people in the Congress and other legislative bodies.*
2. *The laws are interpreted by the courts, which have the task of interpreting and acting in accordance with the Constitution of the United States.*
3. *The United States system establishes the legislative, executive, and judicial branches of government as coequal and does not place the executive branch above the other two.*

Warrant

Because the laws are enacted and interpreted by branches of government coequal with the executive, it follows that

Claim

The executive cannot be above the law.

Freedom of speech, press, and religion

Of all the essentially contested issues in law, the most pervasive and topical are probably those associated with the First Amendment to our Constitution.

Many people believe that freedom of expression is the fundamental element in a free democratic state. With it, all other issues can be resolved, but without it, all other rights can easily be lost. Many people also believe, however, that totally unfettered and irresponsible expression can do great harm. How can a society keep expression free and yet place reasonable restrictions on it?

The First Amendment states simply:

> Congress shall make no law respecting an establishment of religion or prohibiting the free exercise thereof; or abridging the freedom of speech; or of the press; or the right of the people peaceably to assemble, and to petition the Government for a redress of grievances.

But how are these simple words to be applied to the many specific problems surrounding them?

— Do they imply that schoolchildren cannot be allowed to study religion in the public schools or to pray in school?

— Ought the amendment to require us to take the words "In God We Trust" off our coins?

— Does it mean that you cannot be sued if you state during a public debate that your opponent's manager is a former bagman for the Mafia?

— What if you have an article printed in the newspaper claiming that the governor of your state is crooked, communistic, and incompetent? Can he not take action against you?

— Does the statement that "Congress shall make no law . . ." apply to state and local governing bodies by virtue of the Fourteenth Amendment?

— Should we understand that the rule is that no one can abridge these freedoms? If so, what is meant by the terms *abridge, speech, press,* and *assembly?*

If the Congress has the right to pass laws protecting national security or maintaining internal order, may they "abridge expression" in the course of doing so? No one challenges the government's right to protect the United States from violent revolution. So if you speak out in favor of violent revolution, must the government wait until the shooting starts before they arrest you, or may they shut you up in advance and thereby ensure that the shooting never starts? If you are the publisher of a newspaper, and you receive some classified documents stolen from the U.S. government, may you choose to publish them, or can you be prevented from doing so?

Some explosive aspects of the free-expression issue spring from efforts to prevent the distribution of books, movies, and pictures that are felt to be obscene. Almost no one defends obscenity per se, but there is great disagreement about what exactly is obscene. This is an issue that almost defies reasoned analysis. One frustrated Supreme Court Justice is reported to have said, "I can't define obscenity, but I know it when I see it." There have been continued attempts to set criteria for judging something obscene, but these seem never to carry conviction in the courts for long enough to provide the citizens with clear guidelines. For example, should the obscenity of a book or a movie be judged by consideration of it as a whole, or is it sufficient objection that it contains a small number of obscene passages? Is this obscenity to be judged by its impact on children, on adults, on those who are easily aroused sexually, or (as one person unkindly put it) on nine very old men? Is something regarded as obscene by most people in rural areas to be outlawed also in cities where most people find it quite acceptable? If a book or a movie has some social value, even though small, is this enough to protect it against charges of obscenity, or may this "social value" in some cases be too trivial to outweigh the obscenity? How do we judge if something "appeals to prurient interests" or "is patently offensive"? Can any routinely empaneled jury of six or twelve people be taken as expressing "local community standards," or must the courts conduct larger-scale opinion polls to determine these standards?

Here, with the obscenity issue, we reach the effective boundaries of current legal reasoning. Given the flux of criteria determining the grounds and warrants on which such reasoning can be based, the resulting arguments rest on no clearly agreed-on or secure backing, and the operation of the law remains in continued doubt.

THE NATURE OF LEGAL DECISIONS

No matter how compelling the issues or how sweeping their ultimate significance for society, any legal decision is aimed specifically at a single dispute. The case of *Marbury v. Madison* established the general principle that acts of Congress are subject to judicial review, but it was specifically aimed at solving the problems of William Marbury, who was promised an appointment to a judgeship by President John Adams at the end of his presidential term, which the new incoming secretary of state, James Madison, did not deliver. In this case, Marbury did not get his judgeship but the chief justice, John Marshall, protected the independent status of the Supreme Court by successfully asserting the right of judicial review.

Thus the heart of the law lies in those specific disputes for which no other kind of settlement exists. The Supreme Court does not have the freedom to send our general pronouncements on broad aspects of the law whenever it wishes to do so. For example, if the court wanted to make some new statement on the meaning of the term *obscenity* under the First Amendment, they would have to wait until an appropriate dispute came to them on appeal. This might begin several years earlier, in some small town in the Great Plains, perhaps, with a police officer purchasing a book and then arresting the seller because the book was locally regarded as obscene. Tried and found guilty in a local court, the owner of the bookstore appeals the conviction, arguing that the meaning of the word *obscenity* relied on by the trial court was inconsistent with the First and Fourteenth Amendments of the Constitution. After considerable delay, much legal expense, and possibly several appearances in different appeal courts, the case eventually comes to the U.S. Supreme Court. Then, if the court chooses to do so, the case will be considered and a new general pronouncement about the meaning of *obscenity* may be set forth in the course of the opinion written for the purposes of this particular decision.

Although the resolution of specific disputes may be the heart of the legal process, "rule-setting" decisions become the focus of most subsequent attention and ultimately come to play the more important role in society. If all disputes had to be decided in the courts, the legal system would break under the pressure. Legal counsel must settle most problems in the office, and their advice comes from their estimations about possible judicial decision making. Thus many legal decisions are not made in court at all! They are made by professional lawyers or even by legally informed citizens who can reason from the facts of their present dispute or problem following the rules set forth by courts in earlier cases.

In the past, many philosophers of law taught that a strict application of formal logic would serve judges and others in making their decisions. Let a statement of the law serve as one "premise," and a statement of the facts in the present case serve as the other "premise," and the rules of logic will dictate the proper decision as a valid and necessary inference from those premises. Although the arguments used to present legal decisions are still often cast in forms and terms drawn from traditional logic, few people seriously believe any longer that the rules of logic can adequately account for the actual procedures involved in legal decision making. Instead, most commentators now more often describe the law as a system of rules designed to achieve "reckonability." According to some authorities, such rules function not to dictate decisions but rather to guide inferences. Rules steer or modulate, rather than determine absolutely the ratiocination leading to any decision. As a result, some critics have charged the law with "irrationality"; yet others claim to find a mid-point between the unobtainable certainty of formal logic and the apparent unpredictability underlying this charge of irrationality.

Given our approach to practical reasoning, the "rule-oriented" character of legal reasoning is easy to understand. If legal decisions were to rest on formally valid, or "logical" arguments only, then for each set of particular facts in any dispute there would have to be a single rule of law to determine the resulting decision. The task of the court would then be, quite simply, to find this "correct" rule and put it into the logic as a "premise." Yet at least in some respects, each dispute is unique, and each sets a number of different principles against one another. So this is an impractical model of legal decision. On the other hand, those critics who charge the law with irrationality suggest that courts are free to decide as they please, according to the immediate pressures of political, personal, group, ideological, and other forces. But this explanation cannot account for the remarkable regularity and predictability actually to be found in judicial decisions. From the practical reasoning standpoint, the facts of any dispute can be seen as unique, the principles raised may be conflicting, and the court can be seen as exercising clear choice, yet the *orderliness* of legal decisions can be recognized nonetheless. For the task of the court is to work from the unique facts of the case at hand and to reason through to a decision by weighing against one another all the relevant warrants available in the field of law, bearing in mind the legislative history and other backing on which the applicability of those warrants rests.

There is indeed *choice* in the selection of the warrants used to justify the court's ultimate decision, but that choice is made within the confines of what is called the *common law tradition.* That tradition has been built up by centuries of legal decisions evolving in an orderly and reasonable manner. When the specific facts of any case are clearly and unquestionably covered by a previously enunciated rule, that rule will control the deciding. Where there is room for doubt, broader considerations of legal doctrine guide their reasoning. And when the doubt is substantial, their decision must strive to be consonant with the overall spirit of the entire body of legal doctrine and tradition.

Any legal decision involves a complex line of reasoning. It does more than just decide the fate of the particular parties in conflict. It has to work within an established legal tradition of long standing, so as to construe and apply legal rules in ways that will make the work of the courts, "reckonable," that is, sufficiently intelligible so that lawyers can in most situations make reliable predictions of what a court would do if their client were to bring a particular problem before them. It is in this sense that one can truly describe the legal enterprise as embodied in a *legal system,* for, in any specific case, the decision is by no means the ultimate end: it is merely one further step in the continuing process of deciding social disputes in the forums of the law.

THE CHARACTERISTICS OF LEGAL ARGUMENTS

It is worthwhile to look at some of the special characteristics of the arguments used to support claims about "questions of fact" and "questions of law." In courts of original jurisdiction, the dispute up for trial usually turns on the differences between rival accounts of the same episode. Each side tells its story, and the task of the judge or the jury is to determine what the "facts" are. Because dispute resolution is here the primary goal, such a "reasoned" appraisal of the facts has not always been the preferred mechanism for reaching a decision. In Anglo-Saxon times, in fact, "trial by combat" was an accepted method. The complaining person challenged the accused to an individual combat, and the winner of the fight won the dispute. (Guilty parties—it was reasoned—would lack the courage to stand up to such a contest.) Later, "trial by inquisition" was employed. The neighbors of those in dispute were called together as a tribunal to decide the dispute on the basis of their personal knowledge of the parties and their situation. Later this tribunal of neighbors was formalized into a group of twelve persons who, still later, were empowered to call in yet other persons to give additional testimony on the situations. Finally, the basis for selecting the initial group of twelve, which we nowadays call a jury, was changed. Now they were chosen because they did *not* have personal knowledge of the dispute and could thus be relied upon to act as *impartial* judges of the facts.

In a trial involving an impartial jury that can make a binding and legally enforceable decision in favor of one side or another, reasoned examination of evidence is indispensable. Evidence, in law, is the means of satisfying the court about the truth or untruth of various aspects of the stories being told by the disputants. Early in a trial, both sides tell what they believe to be true. In the opening statement of the trial, opposing counsel tell the jury what they intend to prove. So far, none of this is "evidence." The heart of the trial is the presentation of the evidence on the basis of which (as "grounds") the lawyers will present their arguments in support of the opposing claims. But these arguments do not appear at the outset. They come at the end of the trial, after all the evidence has been presented.

Over the years, elaborate rules of evidence have grown up to control what a jury is permitted to hear. In clear contrast to political reasoning, where the First Amendment commitment to free speech permits all kinds of reasoning (even what most sane people would consider absurd), in the law a jury is carefully protected from being exposed to evidence deemed unfit for their attention. Aristotle explained this distinction between political and legal reasoning as follows: in a political or legislative context, he said, the judges—either the voters or their chosen representatives—have a stake in the outcome and use this self-interest to sift out irrelevant or improper evidence. In law, by contrast, the judges—either impartial and uninformed jurors or designated judges—have no stake in the dispute. Indeed, if they have one connected with the dispute, they are to be disqualified. Lacking the filter provided by enlightened self-interest, reasoned Aristotle, the jurors need a law of evidence to do their sifting for them.

Legal reasoning is accordingly centered around the examination of evidence. This evidence is carefully filtered, so that the jury receives only that which promises a certain amount of authenticity. Furthermore, evidence is also sifted so that information that is apt to distract the jurors from the questions immediately at issue is avoided. In most jurisdictions, for example, the jury is not supposed to know whether a defendant is insured against the kind of judgment (e.g., for medical malpractice) that they might make against him. This rule is intended to make sure that the jury does not tend to decide in favor of the plaintiff simply on the theory that an insurance company, rather than the defendant, will have to pay. Further, the rules protect certain classes of people from being forced to tell what they know on the grounds that certain kinds of confidences are more sacred than the mere resolution of disputes. Thus doctor-patient, lawyer-client, priest-penitent, and husband-wife confidences cannot typically be required as evidence.

Claims

The claims put forward in trials cover as broad a range as the disputes that can arise in a society. They range from claiming that X is guilty of spitting on the sidewalk or being drunk and disorderly, to the claim that he has committed murder or treason. They include claims that X breached the terms of a contract, sold a defective product, damaged a car, damaged a reputation, is entitled to an award by way of workmen's compensation, occupied another's land, failed to pay debts owed, violated another's civil rights, engaged in fraud, should be prevented from building an interstate highway, did not pay minimum wages, or violated a zoning ordinance. These claims arise out of the opposing stories told by plaintiff and defendant, prosecutor or defense, and it is the task of the jury or the judge to decide between them.

Grounds

The most frequent source of grounds is the testimony of witnesses. Those who have firsthand knowledge of some matter in dispute are questioned by lawyers on both sides of the case. Their testimony is subjected to cross-examination as a test of its credibility and its consistency. It is tested again by the rules of evidence so that it may be determined that what is said is *relevant* to the issues in the case, is *material* (or significant enough to warrant attention), and is *competent* (or has the appearance of authenticity and is consistent with policy on admissibility). The rival attorneys can then argue on the basis only of the testimony that survives this scrutiny.

Other testimony may come from those who have no firsthand knowledge of the current dispute but who have used their expertise to come to an authoritative *opinion*. Medical experts, psychiatrists, handwriting experts, and actuarial, scientific, and other specialists are often called to give their expert opinion about some matter in dispute. Their opinions, too, are subjected to the same close testing, by examination, cross-examination, and the rules of evidence.

More rarely, witnesses are permitted to testify about things that have not come to them firsthand. Such *hearsay* evidence is admitted reluctantly because it does not have the stamp of firsthand experience, but sometimes—as with statements of one co-conspirator to another, confessions that were not coerced, statements that tend to go against the interests of the person reporting them, and dying declarations—other considerations make the hearsay evidence worthy of attention.

Circumstantial evidence is also used as providing grounds for determining questions of fact. Here the witness does not testify to firsthand knowledge of the facts *included in* the claim. Instead he testifies to firsthand knowledge of other facts that support an *inference to* the claim. Again the process of gaining the testimony is the same, and the basic line of reasoning is the same, but with an added step from the suggestive circumstances to the facts claimed.

Not all grounds, of course, come from oral testimony. Additionally the court can accept physical objects to serve the same purpose. Objects cannot be cross-examined, but people can be questioned about them to show their authenticity and to lay the foundation for their admission as evidence. These objects, too, can be further tested for relevancy, materiality, and competency. *Documents,* such as contracts, letters, memoranda, and other official instruments, may serve as grounds for claims that they in fact exist and that the agreements mentioned in them were in fact made. Under the concept of *best evidence,* indeed, the law demands the production of an actual document in preference to oral testimony about it from a witness. Other physical objects are called *real evidence.* This phrase refers to the physical materials so familiar from thrillers: bloodstains, weapons, fingerprints, photographs, tape recordings, materials picked up at the scene of an accident, and other objects that might contribute to supporting a claim.

Warrants

Evidently reliance on witnesses depends on a general underlying warrant that those directly involved in a past event can be trusted to report about it with sufficient accuracy to provide an element of support for one of the competing stories. The reasoning looks like that which is diagrammed in Figure 26–4.

At the same time, recent research on the psychology of perception tells us

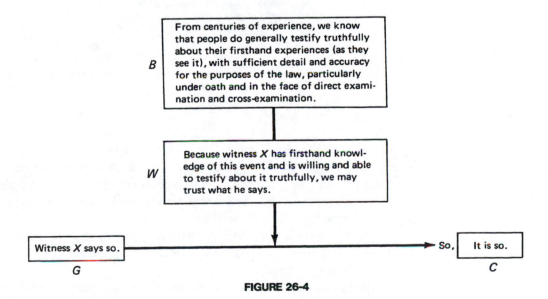

B From centuries of experience, we know that people do generally testify truthfully about their firsthand experiences (as they see it), with sufficient detail and accuracy for the purposes of the law, particularly under oath and in the face of direct examination and cross-examination.

W Because witness *X* has firsthand knowledge of this event and is willing and able to testify about it truthfully, we may trust what he says.

Witness *X* says so. So, It is so.

G *C*

FIGURE 26-4

that "detail and accuracy" are not unlimited. People are not very good at perceiving and at reporting in detail what they have experienced with any great accuracy and consistency. Studies in communication cast some doubt, furthermore, on the ability of the legal process to yield accurate reports of past experience through severe direct examination and cross-examination. On the contrary, a forceful counsel is quite often able to confuse or lead the witness and so distort his account. The crucial elements of the warrant are therefore the phrases "as they see it" and "for the purposes of the law." When witnesses supporting each side of the case have had their testimony severely tested, sufficient material will commonly have been generated for the jury and/or the judge to make up their minds—as the goal of the trial requires—about a set of "facts" that will resolve the dispute.

The use of *expert opinion* as testimony requires a more elaborate warrant. Whereas we assume that ordinary witnesses can report firsthand experiences with ordinary accuracy and truthfulness, we assume further that witnesses having special expertise can be relied on to form reliable judgments as well. (Figure 26–5).

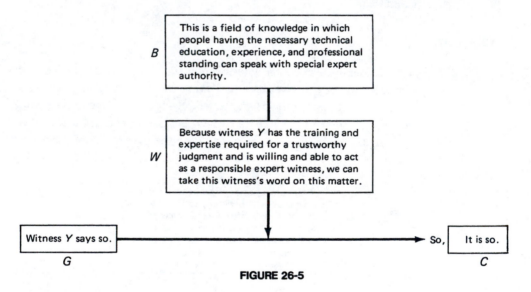

FIGURE 26-5

Circumstantial evidence employs more specific warrants. For example, if the police notice a person running down a street in the dark, they may become suspicious and stop him for questioning. When other witnesses later establish that a robbery had taken place shortly before, one block from the same point, the police can provide circumstantial evidence. (Figure 26–6).

Physical evidence employs similar warrants. Sometimes, as with a document, its mere admission as evidence will directly support a claim of its existence (see Figure 26–7).

At other times, physical evidence may be only circumstantial. Evidence that Person *B*'s fingerprints were found on a table in the room where a murder took

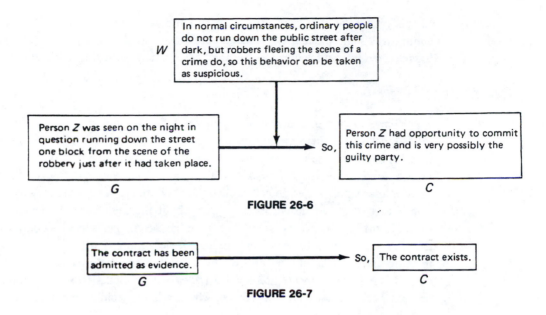

FIGURE 26-6

FIGURE 26-7

place directly supports only the claim that Person *B* had been in that room at some time or other, not necessarily at the time of the murder. The warrant, of course, is that where a person's fingerprints are found, there he must have been.

Modalities

The different parties to a trial will vary in their reservations about the claims involved. Advocates for each side will advance their own claims as strongly as they can, with few reservations. It is their professional duty to present a point of view with conviction. Juries, on the other hand, do not present their reasoning publicly. Their reservations must be inferred from their actual decisions. In a case for money damages, for example, a jury may indicate its reservations by awarding more or less money, even though the law may not in theory permit this. In criminal cases likewise, the jury's modalities will be apparent from its findings, that is, from its declaring the accused either innocent or guilty of the most severe charge, either guilty of a lesser charge, or guilty on selected counts.

Judges have an opportunity to state their qualifications and reservations in open court. They may enter into the official record that they feel more or less reservation about the strength of the argument on which final ruling of the court was based. Sometimes judges may speak quite strongly:

> This has been a great trial to the judge to have to put up with the kind of performance that has been demonstrated on both sides as a matter of fact. For this city to have its position so poorly represented here is surprising to me. The taxpayers deserve better.

In this case, as always, however, judges are subject to appeal. Given the risk of committing some judicial error that would cause the decision to be overturned, judges often refrain from expressing their reservations with full frankness.

Rebuttals

The structure of a trial at law provides for systematic expression of rebuttals. Opposing attorneys are always prepared to engage in refutation. Their proposed rebuttals to each claim made by the other side become part of the official record, so that appellate courts as well as the immediate judge and jury can take them into account. Juries do not publish their rebuttals. Once a unanimous decision is arrived at, we do not usually learn about the unsuccessful counterarguments in the jury room. We know that there has been a genuine clash only when the jury cannot achieve consensus. Judges deciding alone, without a jury, may indicate the strengths and weaknesses of each party's case before rendering a decision. It is in fact not uncommon for the judge to enter such a two-sided summary or "balanced account" into the record, whether he is deciding alone or whether he is instructing a jury.

APPELLATE DECISION MAKING

The modes of reasoning and argumentation characteristic of appeal courts are different from those characteristic of courts of original jurisdiction, chiefly because the focus now shifts from "questions of fact" to "questions of law."

In reasoning about questions of law, the *claims* may once again cover a wide range, from efforts to have a case dismissed because it does not present a proper cause of action or because it is presented in an improper jurisdiction or because the party bringing it does not have legal standing to pursue the case, to efforts to have certain evidence excluded as violating the rules of evidence or to have a judgment quashed because of some procedural error in the trial or even because the law under which the decision was made is repugnant to the Constitution.

The *grounds* relied on in appellate decision making come from the records of the original trial, together with the content of past decisions by other appellate courts, the text of appropriate statutes, the testimony of legal authorities, and so forth. In a highly simplified example, reasoning from *precedent* looks like that illustrated in Figure 26–8.

The facts of this case include items 1, 2, and 3. The facts of a precedent (i.e., already decided and authoritative) case also included items 1, 2, and 3.

G

So, The present case should be decided in the same way as that particular precedent case.

C

FIGURE 26-8

When the *warrants* are examined, the many rules of law relied on to decide the previous cases are combined with the general principle of consistency known as *stare decisis*. See in Figure 26–9 how the reasoning works when warrants and backing are added.

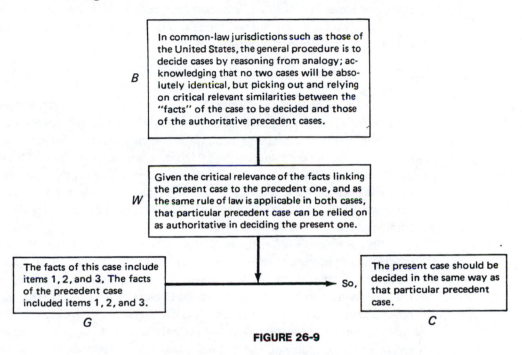

B   In common-law jurisdictions such as those of the United States, the general procedure is to decide cases by reasoning from analogy; acknowledging that no two cases will be absolutely identical, but picking out and relying on critical relevant similarities between the "facts" of the case to be decided and those of the authoritative precedent cases.

W   Given the critical relevance of the facts linking the present case to the precedent one, and as the same rule of law is applicable in both cases, that particular precedent case can be relied on as authoritative in deciding the present one.

The facts of this case include items 1, 2, and 3. The facts of the precedent case included items 1, 2, and 3.

So, The present case should be decided in the same way as that particular precedent case.

G

C

FIGURE 26-9

In appellate reasoning, one important part of the grounds will often consist in a statement of the rule of law inherent in one or more of the precedent cases quoted. This rule of law is entered into the reasoning in the form of quotations taken from the written opinions of the courts that decided the precedent cases. Given this evidence, a further rule of law is then derived that can serve as the warrant in deciding the case presently before the court.

Modalities in appellate reasoning will be clearly expressed in the court's written opinion. Frequently appellate courts state clearly the scope and force of application they intend for the rule of law implied in their decision, for they know that future courts will use their opinions in deciding still other cases. In opinions from the U.S. Supreme Court, it is not uncommon to see the scope of any decision spelled out explicitly. If a given rule is not intended to apply generally but only on certain conditions or with certain reservations, the court will normally take care to say so.

In appellate decision making, rebuttals commonly take the form of *dissents*. Those members of the court who cannot subscribe to the majority opinion have a responsibility to publish the reasons for their dissent. Because the majority opinion reflects a compromise between the personal viewpoints of several justices, and has to stand as an expression of current law, it is typically written in careful style, showing close reasoning and severe restraint. Dissents, on the other hand, often reflect the personal opinion of a single justice, and it is not their function to express the law. Instead it is their business to impute faults to the majority reasoning. As a result, dissents tend to be worded more strongly, written in more flamboyant style, and aimed not merely at expressing concern over the present case but also at swaying future courts in the hope that one day the dissent may become the *majority*—and therefore *operative*—opinion.

AN EXAMPLE

As an instance of legal argument, we shall examine the reasoning of the United States Supreme Court. The opinions of the Court reflect the arguments presented in briefs, in oral argument, the arguments exchanged among members of the court during the conferences and deliberations, and the claims of the majority of the Court. For opinions are, indeed, arguments. The justices must show the reasonableness of their decisions so that they make sense to the immediate litigants who initiated the case and to the legal community at large who will use the opinion as the basis of future decisions.

In this example, we shall also illustrate the evolution of the law through the sequence of opinions on similar cases. Over the years, what we call the law—the prediction of what courts will do—evolves as courts refine and modify the reasoning used. A decision yesterday may contain potential lines of reasoning that did not capture a majority but which suggest how lawyers in future cases of like kind might argue and ultimately move the majority further along. At the same time, social, economic, political, and cultural changes take place alongside changes in the personnel of the courts. All these factors generate warrants that may become stronger and ultimately may contribute to the evolution of the law.

The subject of this example is the right to counsel in criminal cases. The question is whether having a lawyer to advocate a cause is a Constitutionally guaranteed right such that instances in which a criminal conviction is secured and the accused has no lawyer, because of the inability to retain one, is a denial of the accused's rights. This right is made explicit in the Sixth Amendment of the U.S. Constitution: "In all criminal prosecutions, the accused shall enjoy the right . . . to have the assistance of counsel for his defense." The key question in our example is whether this federal right applies as well to the states through the Fourteenth Amendment which says

> All persons born or naturalized in the United States, and subject to the jurisdiction thereof, are citizens of the United States and of the State wherein they reside. No State shall make or enforce any law which shall abridge the privileges or immunities of citizens of the United States; nor shall any State deprive any person of life, liberty, or property, without due process of law; nor deny to any person within its jurisdiction the equal protection of the laws.

On its face, the Fourteenth Amendment seems to supply all Constitutional guarantees of the federal government to the states, but the courts have not chosen to interpret it that way. They have made selective application. For example, the recent battle over the Equal Rights Amendment essentially sought to apply to the states Constitutional guarantees against discrimination on the basis of sex. Again, on its face, the Fourteenth Amendment seems to do that, but the courts have not seen fit to accept such claims.

Specifically, until 1963 the Supreme Court allowed state laws to set the rights of their citizens, and if a state such as Maryland did not grant right to counsel, the U.S. Supreme Court would not overturn a Maryland conviction in which counsel was denied. This was asserted in Betts v. Brady (316 US 455) in which Betts was denied counsel in Maryland, convicted and sentenced to prison. He appealed his case to the U.S. Supreme Court, claiming that the denial of counsel was a violation of his rights under the U.S. Constitution through the Sixth and Fourteenth Amendments. The Court disagreed.

The opinion clearly stated that since the judgment was consistent with Maryland law, it was proper. The application of the Fourteenth Amendment was rejected in this *specific instance* on the warrant that Betts' denial of counsel was not "shocking to the universal sense of justice."

> The due process clause of the Fourteenth Amendment does not incorporate, as such, the specific guarantees found in the Sixth Amendment, although a denial by a State of rights or privileges specifically embodied in that and others of the first eight amendments may, in certain circumstances, or in connection with other elements, operate, in a given case, to deprive a litigant of due process of law in violation of the Fourteenth. . . . Its application is less a matter of rule. Asserted denial is to be tested by an appraisal of the totality of facts in a given case. That which may, in one setting, constitute a denial of fundamental fairness, shocking to the universal sense of justice, may, in other circumstances, and in the light of other considerations, fall short of such denial."

The argument can be examined by diagram (Figure 26–10).

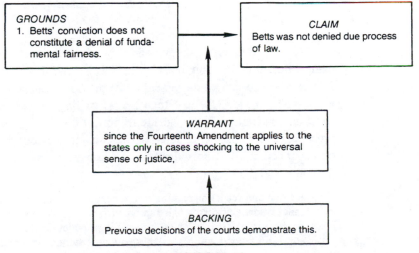

FIGURE 26-10

The argument supporting the claim that Betts' conviction does not constitute a denial of fundamental fairness, which became the grounds in the argument just diagrammed, was stated in this way:

> Originally, in England, a prisoner was not permitted to be heard by counsel upon the general issue of not guilty on any indictment for treason or felony. . . . In 1695 the rule was relaxed . . . to the extent of permitting one accused of treason the privilege of being heard by counsel . . . until 1836, when a statute accorded the right to defend by counsel against summary convictions and charges of felony. . . .

But in a dissent against this majority decision, a minority claimed that any denial of counsel is shocking to our sense of justice. They argued in part this way:

> What . . . does a hearing include? Historically and in practice, in our own country at least, it has always included the right to the aid of counsel when desired and provided by the person asserting the right. . . . Even the intelligent and educated layman . . . lacks both the skill and knowledge adequately to prepare his defense, even though he has a perfect one. He requires the guiding hand of counsel in every step in the proceedings against him. Without it, though he be not guilty, he faces the danger of conviction because he does not know how to establish his innocence. (See Figure 26–11.)

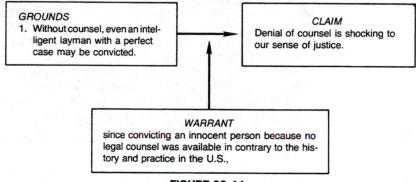

FIGURE 26-11

Only a relatively few years following this decision, another with similar facts came before the U.S. Supreme Court: Gideon v. Wainwright (372 US 335). The Justice who had written the dissent in the previous case now generated a majority to his point of view. Justice Hugo Black, writing for the majority, claimed the court had, in Betts v. Brady, "made an abrupt break with its own well-considered precedents." Essentially, he rejected the backing previously advanced to the warrant that denial to counsel did not shock a universal sense of justice. Black claimed the following:

> Reason and reflection require us to recognize that in our adversary system of criminal justice, any person haled into court, who is too poor to hire a lawyer, cannot be assured a fair trial unless counsel is provided for him. . . . Governments, both state and federal, quite properly spend vast sums of money to establish machinery

to try defendants accused of crime. Lawyers to prosecute are everywhere deemed essential to protect the public's interest in an orderly society. . . . That government hires lawyers to prosecute and defendants who have the money hire lawyers to defend are the strongest indications of the widespread belief that lawyers in criminal courts are necessities, not luxuries.

Figure 26–12 is a diagram of the argument.

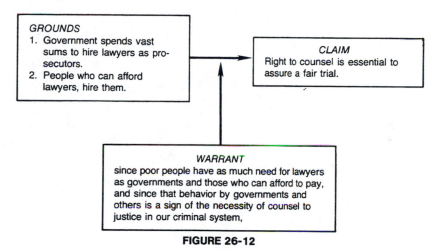

FIGURE 26-12

Exercises

Read the following argument presented as a dissent in the case of Time, Inc., v. James J. Hill (385 US 374) in which Hill charged that an article in *Life* magazine invaded his privacy. The case placed defense of the First Amendment guarantees of free press against the individual's right to privacy:

But I do not believe that whatever is in words, however much of an aggression it may be upon individual rights, is beyond the reach of the law, no matter how heedless of others' rights—how remote from public purpose, how reckless, irresponsible, and untrue it may be. I do not believe that the First Amendment precludes effective protection of the right of privacy—or, for that matter, an effective law of libel. I do not believe that we must or should, in deference to those whose views are absolute as to the scope of the First Amendment, be ingenious to strike down all state action, however circumspect, which penalizes the use of words as instruments of aggression and personal assault. There are great and important values in our society, none of which is greater than those reflected in the First Amendment, but which are also fundamental and entitled to this Court's careful respect and protection. Among these is the right to privacy, which has been eloquently extolled by scholars and members of this Court.

1. Diagram this argument.
2. Discuss it critically. Point out strengths and weaknesses and provide reasoning to support your judgments.

27

Argumentation in science

In every age and culture, human beings have shared certain ideas about the natural world. Many aspects of nature have initially provoked awe and wonder, fear and curiosity, and these reactions have given rise to both reflection and action. They have encouraged, on the one hand, intellectual discussion and criticism and, on the other hand, the development of practical techniques and religious rituals. In this way, patterns of life and institutions have been created that are more or less well adapted to different visions of the world.

In early times, the features of nature central to human thought and action usually reflected the local conditions of human life. In dry desert cultures, people were preoccupied with water in all its forms; in arctic cultures, with fire and warmth; and so on. So understandably enough, those things that had most power to influence communal life were the starting point for different peoples' collective arguments about "the nature of nature." Practical and theoretical needs alike required that the resulting conceptions about the natural world were adequately *realistic*. A farmer lacking reliable expectations about the succession of seasons in his region—warm and cold, rainy and dry—must fail in the tasks of a farmer. Anybody who has the sense of being at odds with the deeper powers of nature would likewise be at a handicap in fashioning a confident and orderly life.

Every human culture, as a result, has had at its disposal some body of collective ideas that are generally accepted as providing the most accurate and complete account of the workings of nature. Every human culture has developed institutions that embody those ways of thinking. And every culture has made some institutional provision for the critical transmission of those ideas. Within those broad limits, there are great variations:

1. In some cultures, these shared ideas are transmitted quite explicitly and articulately from generation to generation in a literary form that

can be learned and repeated, comprising either traditional mythological poetry or actual scientific theories. In others, they are passed on implicitly in a nonverbal form, through the traditional practices and rituals of the culture.

2.   In some cultures, these ideas are the general property of the entire community, being taught to the whole of each new generation of children. In others, they are confined to certain limited groups, such as the priesthood or the members of craft guilds.

3.   In some cultures, accepted ideas are exposed to conscious, critical reappraisal and refinement. In others, they are handled conservatively and form a static orthodoxy protected by custom against criticism and change.

Despite all these variations, it is usually easy to identify the ways in which any particular culture handles and passes on its own collective understanding of nature and to recognize what opportunities exist within the culture for critical discussion of those ideas. Where those ideas and conceptions are articulately expressed and open to public criticism, they can appropriately be classed as *scientific,* and the collective understanding about nature current in that culture approximates the condition of our own natural science. However, although every culture may possess *some* collective ideas about the natural world, not every culture possesses anything we could call natural science. Each human community has to discover for itself the virtues of an explicit and articulate body of "scientific" ideas and the independent institutions for criticizing and refining them.

For our present purposes, we shall be taking the basic values of the scientific enterprise—including the necessity of scientific criticism—for granted and considering:

1.   What forums for argumentation the resulting "scientific" debate requires.

2.   What types of practical reasoning are characteristic of those different forms.

3.   More specifically, what kinds of arguments (claims, grounds, warrants, and so on) are typically at home within these scientific discussions.

THE NATURE OF THE SCIENTIFIC ENTERPRISE

Whatever its specific content, the science of any period will display three very general features, which will largely determine the scope available for rational criticism or argumentation.

1.   It must deal with certain broad and familiar issues about the natural world, of which any scientific view of nature can be expected to give some account.

2. It must provide some systematic body of ideas for use in accounting for the observed course of natural events, together with recognized procedures for criticizing and refining those accounts.
3. There must be some group, or groups, of people in the society who have the responsibility for preserving and transmitting this critical tradition.

Broad and familiar issues

Four general kinds of issues have arisen for natural science, wherever and whenever it has been done:

— What kinds of things are there in the world of nature?
— How are these things composed, and how does this makeup affect their behavior or operation?
— How did all these things come to be composed as they are?
— What are the characteristic functions of each such natural thing and/or its parts?

Scientists have dealt with these issues more or less comprehensively, using different terminologies and theories, but all "scientific" accounts of the world have included some account of all these topics. Indeed, when the Greek philosopher-scientist Aristotle analyzed the tasks of science in the fourth century B.C., he described these basic problems in comparable terms. Everything in nature, he said, must be accounted for by considerations of four different kinds, which he described as the "what-sort-it-is," the "out-of-what," the "what-did-it," and the "for-the-sake-of-what." Here we can see the first explicit recognition of our own four basic scientific tasks: that of classifying the objects of nature, that of bringing to light their composition and mode of operation, that of reconstructing their origins, and that of understanding their inherent modes of functioning.

A systematic body of ideas

Whether or not they organize their theories around mathematical structures and mechanistic principles, scientists in all cultures develop *systematic procedures for representing* the natural world and its makeup, functions, and origins. (These may include "laws of nature" or computer programs, taxonomies or graphs, methods of inference or calculation, historical narratives or timeless theories.) For any given place or time, indeed, we can regard the currently accepted system of representation as defining the content of its scientific tradition: it is that culture's best attempt to date at generating realistic conceptions about the natural world.

Some cultures are, of course, unscientific or even antiscientific in their ways of thinking about nature. In certain highly stable societies, such as classical China, the general attitude toward nature was highly conservative, and there was little scope for subjecting ideas to rational criticism. In such contexts, intellectual change was perceived as subversion or corruption, and our own central question—namely, "What makes a scientific argument good or sound?"—had little or no application to their intellectual activities.

Scientific organizations

We can recognize how the character and force of scientific argumentation are related to the goals of the larger scientific enterprise, only by concentrating on those cultures that truly have "science" and expose their ideas about nature to rational criticism and modification. This means looking at the professional scientific world of university departments and scientific societies, learned journals, Nobel prizes, referees, and the rest, for it is these professional institutions that determine the character of the *forums* within which scientific argumentation proceeds and is judged.

We do not need to go into detail about the differences between forums of argumentation in one culture or another. What matters here is the common, general core of characteristics shared by all these different forums. The business of them all is to provide conditions within which received ideas about nature can be openly and effectively improved upon, conditions within which novel concepts and hypotheses can safely be developed at such length that their implications become apparent, and these novel ideas can subsequently be evaluated and sifted, so that worthwhile innovations can be accepted and incorporated into the current tradition of scientific ideas. Those ideas that survive this critical evaluation will be "good" *as scientific ideas*. If sufficient grounds and solid enough arguments are produced to demonstrate their merits clearly, that will mean that their *scientific basis* is also "sound." Where critical evaluation shows both requirements fulfilled, we can be satisfied that practical argumentation has demonstrated the "rational" basis of those novel ideas.

So when analyzing and criticizing the *arguments* of scientists, we shall have to bear in mind three things: (1) the general purposes of science, (2) the particular kinds of ideas and theories current at any time in any given field, and (3) the institutions in which scientific work is done.

THE FORUMS OF SCIENTIFIC ARGUMENTATION

Against this general background, we should now look:

1. At the procedures that scientists employ in dealing with their problems.
2. At the institutional arrangements within which those issues are tackled.
3. At the consequences of these features for the character of scientific argumentation.

Just as the general purposes of law impose an adversary character on much legal argumentation, so too the general purpose of Science ensure that reasoning and argumentation in the natural sciences aim at a consensus.

On a superficial level, the problems of science may seem to have an adversarial aspect, but on a deeper level they are directed toward a consensus, or rational agreement, between the parties concerned. Suppose that a scientist proposes some radically new hypothesis in biochemistry or geophysics or brain physiology. At the outset, there will usually be serious differences of opinion among the scientists directly concerned. Both as individuals and as collective groups (or "schools"), they may argue fiercely about the new suggestion, about whether it should be accepted or rejected, and even about whether it should be taken seriously at all or simply ignored. When this happens, much may be at stake for the individual participants—their personal reputations, career prospects, and professional following—so that the scientific question at hand may at first be fought out with as much passion, intensity, and even bitterness as any lawsuit.

All the same, it would be a mistake to think that *as natural scientists* either party has any direct interest in having one side win such an argument and the other lose. In the law courts, losing a case may have grave personal consequences. It may mean paying a million dollars in damages, or spending twenty years in jail. In a scientific dispute, by contrast, neither side wins a case "at the expense of" the other. Properly speaking, rather, both parties are "beneficiaries" of the outcome. If we prove unable to justify our scientific claims in the face of criticism or if we have to concede that a scientific opponent has made good a claim that we at first resisted, we may feel personal chagrin or disappointment. But we have not, in our capacity as scientists, *lost* anything—except our earlier unfounded beliefs. However contentious, disputatious, and even adversarial the style of scientific argumentation may appear, the successful resolution of scientific issues is, therefore, of *professional benefit to all scientists alike.* Accordingly, whereas deep and genuine conflicts of interest make it inevitable that law court proceedings tend to take on a basically adversarial character, the professional institutions of science are organized to promote *communal, collective goals and interests,* and the conflicts of interest occurring within them are transient and incidental.

The actual procedures of scientific debate and evaluation do include certain stylized elements of adversary procedure. In theory, every individual scientist is capable of being his own most severe critic, and his writings are expected to discuss with real care and seriousness the objections against his own novel ideas. So, in principle, there is no need for head-on confrontations in natural science of the kind that are inescapable in the law. Yet it is frequently more convenient for *different* scientists to act as "advocates" *for and against* any novel suggestion. An article submitted for publication in a scientific journal, for example, is commonly sent off to an anonymous "referee," who scrutinizes the arguments presented and draws attention to any obvious weaknesses. The seriousness with which other scientists regard any journal, in fact, reflects their confidence in its refereeing procedures. Similarly, at scientific meetings, individual scientists do not normally present their novel ideas baldly and without criticism, on a take-it-or-leave-it basis. Rather, a commentator or "respondent" who has seen the novel paper in advance puts forward his own evaluation and criticisms on the same occasion that the ideas are presented, so that the audience hears more than one view about the issue concerned.

In these and other ways, the intellectual enterprise of natural science is structured so as to serve the *critical* functions on which the reliability and "rationality" of scientific ideas depend. In the long run, the collective pursuit of "truth"—or, at least, of *better science*—may be to the shared benefit of all scientists alike; but the shorter-term improvement of scientific ideas is most efficiently promoted if individual scientists temporarily "take sides," act as "advocates" or "attorneys" for and against novel ideas or hypotheses, and argue out their merits and defects in a personally committed manner. Hence comes the odd mixture of short-term adversary *procedures* and longer-term consensus *goals* characteristic of scientific argumentation. The basic interests of all scientists alike depend on reasoned agreement about which novel ideas about the natural world are to be accepted as realistic, which are to be rejected as inadequate. In that respect, the consensus element in scientific reasoning is dominant. But if we are to have the guarantees we need that this eventual agreement is genuinely "reasoned," there must be critical methods for publicly testing those ideas in the face of severe criticism, and the necessary procedures of critical appraisal will inevitably comprise an adversarial element.

THE NATURE OF SCIENTIFIC ISSUES

What is the general nature of the intellectual tasks that scientists undertake? And how does reasoning or argumentation enter into the fulfillment of those tasks? Scientists engage in many different kinds of tasks. They design and build experimental apparatus, do mathematical calculations, program computers, and make field studies; they write papers, take part in public discussions, comment on each other's ideas; they propose and discuss novel hypotheses, theories, explanations, classifications, and so on. Yet all these varied activities are concerned with giving an improved scientific account, or "representation," of aspects of nature not adequately dealt with in our current scientific picture of the world.

This observation gives rise to two questions:

1. What are the signs that something needs to be accounted for scientifically?
2. What are the indications that scientists have succeeded in accounting for it acceptably?

What things need explaining?

First, how do we know when any feature of nature *needs* to be accounted for? When do we recognize something as raising a genuine *issue* for scientific investigation? Certainly not *everything* that happens poses problems for science. Many happenings take place in ways that call for no special scientific comment or questioning. This may be because they are so entirely "to be expected":

> I drop a glass on a concrete floor and it breaks. So what? That is so unsurprising an event that it raises no issue for science. If it had *not* broken, that might have prompted a scientific inquiry: "Why not?" Had there been some substance in the glass just before it was dropped that protected it from breaking? Was there something about the exact angle at which it fell? Or how else are we to account for its failure to break as expected?

Scientific questions arise most immediately, that is to say, about *anomalies*, about events that run counter to our reasonable expectations, not to say our scientific "presumptions."

Alternatively, some events take place in largely unpredictable ways simply because the natural conditions on which they depend are too complex to record and keep track of. But this does not make them mysterious from the scientific point of view. Weather forecasting, for instance, presents some serious challenges to science, to find ways of squaring the observed course of meteorological events with the accepted principles of physical science. But that does not mean that scientists feel any responsibility for explaining every last day-to-day or minute-to-minute change in the weather. Presumably such changes are brought about in a perfectly intelligible way by some minor local fluctuation in the atmospheric conditions, but normally no real scientific interest will be served by tracking down exactly what that fluctuation was. Only if a *significant* anomaly can be demonstrated—for instance, a storm that blew up "out of nowhere" under atmospheric conditions that apparently ruled out such a possibility—will there be a genuine *scientific issue* to face.

Another way of putting the same point is to say the following "Not everything that happens is a *phenomenon*." That term is used in science to mark off occurrences—especially general *types* of occurrences—that challenge existing ideas and so call for scientific investigation and explanation. Routine arguments and calculations about occurrences that pose no problem may be important for other purposes, in medicine, technology, or whatever, but they make only a marginal contribution to science itself. These routine applications of the results of scientific investigation as means to the practical ends of others (physicians, industrial designers, and so on) leave *the match between our ideas and the world* just where it was before and so do nothing to "advance" the scientific enterprise or promote the ends of science proper.

How do we know when something has been explained?

Once we have an anomaly or a phenomenon recognized, how then do we decide when it has been satisfactorily accounted for? That is a more complex question, to which there is no very brief answer. Here we shall take the question in two stages. To begin with, we shall give some particular examples as illustrations of the *specific kinds* of accounts that are commonly found acceptable in the natural sciences. For this purpose, we shall use familiar everyday examples rather than sophisticated technical ones. Then we shall go on to give a more comprehensive statement about the *general ways* in which such accounts contribute to the successful prosecution of the scientific enterprise.

We can divide up our specific kinds of explanation into four groups. We can account for events, objects, or phenomena by relating them to other things we already know, either about the *type* of thing we are dealing with, or about its *material make up or composition,* or about its *history or development,* or about its *goal or effect.*

Explanation by type.

PROBLEM: Your pet mouse will not eat or run around and just lies curled up in a corner of its box; yet it does not actually seem to have died, nor does it show any other signs of serious illness. What are you to make of this puzzling fact?

SOLUTION: It is now December, and your pet is a dormouse. Dormice are a hibernating species that pass the winter in a torpid condition, but they become active again in the spring.

This kind of example is particularly easy to fit into our standard pattern, and some logicians have taken it as the general example for *all* kinds of scientific explanation ("Your pet mouse is torpid because it's a dormouse"; "your pet bird is black because it's a raven"; and so on). In this case, the warrant is evidently the general statement about the species *dormouse,* that is, "Dormice pass the winter in a torpid condition." By citing this general item of zoological information, and pointing out the additional fact about the present situation (i.e., that winter is currently beginning), your respondent provides a perfectly reasonable solution to your problem, shown in Figure 27–1.

On a somewhat more technical level, similar issues may arise about the relationship between more-or-less comprehensive *types* of things, not just between particular *individuals* (like your pet dormouse) and the species to which they belong. For instance:

PROBLEM: To what larger botanical order does asparagus belong?

SOLUTION: Asparagus lacks the striking trumpetlike blossoms we tend to associate with lilies, but it has many of the less obvious features

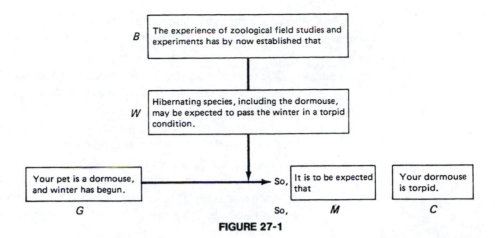

FIGURE 27-1

$(F_1, F_2, F_3 \ldots)$—number of stamens, type of base leaves, and so on—that are characteristic of the order Liliaceae; and besides, its spikes closely resemble, even though in miniature, the flowering spikes of the aloe, which is a member of that order.

Here we may again cast the argument in our standard form (Figure 27–2), but the grounds themselves will now all be general statements, rather than particular ones.

This kind of explanation is not confined to living things. Physical phenomena, too, sometimes display similar *regularities,* as we noted in Chapter 13, when we used a meteorological understanding of cold fronts and the like to illustrate

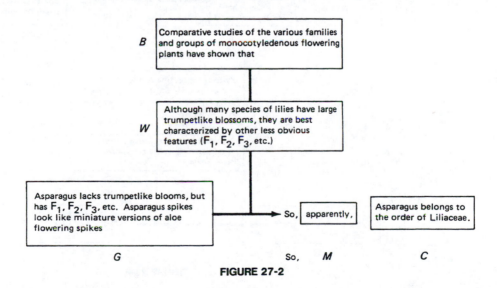

FIGURE 27-2

the relations between grounds and claims, warrants and backing. Instead of dorm-ice and asparagus, we might perfectly well have used tornados or waterspouts:

PROBLEM: The tornado took out the roof of the school across the road and the grocery store behind our house. How come we were not touched?

SOLUTION: The funnel clouds from which tornados are generated at ground level descend from overhead clouds, in suitable meteo-rological conditions, and move along generally linear tracks. But they frequently extend and retract as they go, so that they touch down only at certain points along the track and skip trees and buildings in between.

In order to underline our point about anomalies as the source of scientific issues, it is worth analyzing this case as a *two-stage* argument. Initially the inquirer has to show his reasons for regarding his problem as involving a genuine anomaly. Only subsequently does the respondent offer an account in reply, and this account deals precisely with the points the inquirer sees as anomalous (see Figure 27–3).

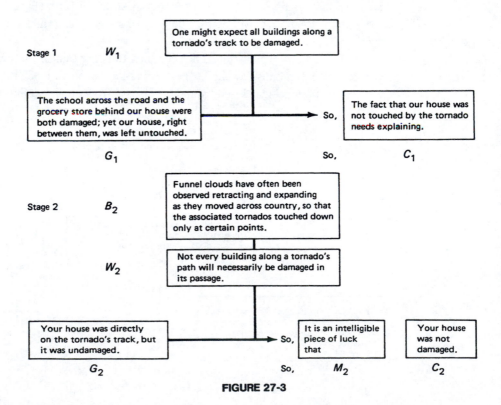

FIGURE 27-3

Similarly in the other two cases, a pet mouse that neither eats nor runs around may well be presumed sick or dead, while asparagus looks at first glance an unlikely member of the order Liliaceae. In either case, the "anomaly" must first be established—the reader can set out Stage 1 for himself—and the final account offered in Stage 2 shows how this anomaly is to be accommodated to current scientific ideas.

Explanation by material composition. This group embraces a variety of different kinds of cases. To begin with a familiar variety, let us consider the idea of *conservation*. Back in the scientific discussions that started up in classical Greece around 500 B.C., the conviction was expressed by some philosophers that "Nothing is ever, strictly speaking, created out of nothing or totally annihilated; in reality, there is only mixture and separation of the things that permanently exist." Some such general notion governs our understanding of natural phenomena in everyday life, too, in our recognition of the manner in which material substances are redistributed rather than destroyed.

A commonsense example:

PROBLEM: Billy is always drinking beer, yet he never seems to have to use the bathroom. How come?

SOLUTION: Certainly what goes in must come out or end up somewhere. But think how much Billy loses by the evaporation of his perspiration, and look at the amount of fat there is in his beer belly! If you could measure the quantity of liquid in his sweat and his stored fat, you might be surprised to find how much those contributed to his input-output account.

This example has one interesting feature that allows us to show how the pattern of presumptions and rebuttals operates in the scientific field. For the account given by the respondent in effect concedes that the inquirer's Stage 1 argument is valid, but it goes on to turn back its conclusion by showing that there are relevant exceptions available to rebut it (see Figure 27–4).

When we turn from everyday life to more professional science, of course, the idea of conservation has to be applied to something more technical, generalizable, and narrowly defined than simple "liquid bulk." A substantial part of physics has been concerned precisely with the question, "Just what is it that is *conserved* in the course of physical and chemical changes?" But the overall notion of conservation remains, within the natural sciences, a direct descendant of the everyday commonsense notion, and the forms of reasoning that apply to the one can in general be extended to the other also.

Explanation by history. A somewhat different type of scientific explanation sets out to make an occurrence or a phenomenon intelligible by placing it in a temporal

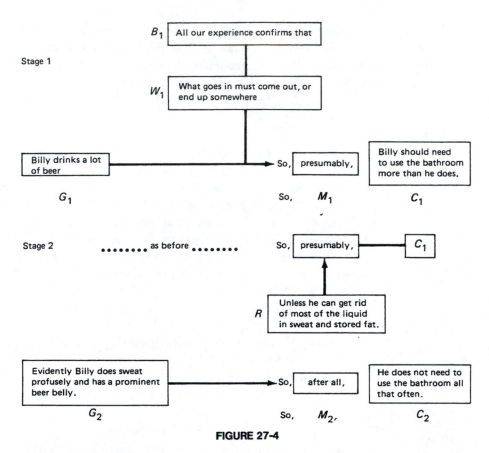

FIGURE 27-4

or historical sequence. This may, once again, be done on a simple descriptive level. On keeping careful records of some particular type of event, we may find that there is a certain pattern of recurrences. This may involve a pure repetition, as with Halley's comet, which has been shown to reappear at intervals close to seventy-six or seventy-seven years. Having plotted its path in A.D. 1682, Edmund Halley correctly foretold its reappearance in 1758—as well as retrospectively explaining the appearance of the same comet in the Bayeux Tapestry, associated with the Norman Conquest of Britain in 1066.

Alternatively we may find a number of separate cyclical processes going on together in ways that "add up" to produce the particular temporal sequence that interests us. This is the kind of calculation by which hydrographers produce tide tables, showing the expected times and heights of the tides at a given point on the coastline on any given day of the coming year. The same kind of *times series* is often used as the basis for economic predictions and explanations:

> PROBLEM: Industrial production has been rising slowly but steadily for
> months now, yet you are forecasting a business slowdown and
> even a recession. Are you trying to talk us into losing confi-

dence in the national economy, or have you some real basis for
the prediction?

SOLUTION: It is a well-established fact that the first sector of the economy
to reflect the onset of a recession is building construction. Over
the last three months, there has been a sharp and continuous
drop in building starts, showing that people's actions are
already giving evidence of their lack of confidence. The continuing rise in current output to which you point is the last ripple
from the previous wave of business investment. The building
slump is the first evidence of the trough following behind that
wave.

Here the complex phenomenon of business activity is shown to be made up of a
number of simpler time series, some of which lead, others of which lag behind the
general fluctuations in employment, investment, and industrial output.

Alternatively a temporal or historical explanation may account for an event
or phenomenon by drawing attention to its *origins*. Thus we may explain an epidemic of plague by tracing it back to the arrival of certain infected rats in a particular ship's cargo, the destruction of a building by fire to the dropping of a
lighted match into a wastepaper basket, or whatever it may be.

Finally, "explanations by history" can refer to sequences of events characteristic of the life cycle of a particular individual or species. We may explain how
early childhood events helped to shape someone's personality and abilities, or how
inadequate childhood diet left a person with a chronic bone weakness, or why it
is that certain shoots on an immature plant turn into flower heads, others into
leaves. This particular variety of historical explanation is commonly referred to
as explanation in terms of *development*. We come to understand why the feature
to be explained takes the form it does when it is demonstrated to us how the
processes of development typical in this kind of creature lead to that result. A
proper understanding of development will then allow us to explain either how
things will turn out if they go aright or else what specific oddities or pathologies
will result in case one or another particular factor in the situation is either missing
or deficient:

PROBLEM: Jack's a farm kid from Kansas, yet he apparently talks and
understands Turkish. Isn't that rather odd?

SOLUTION: Yes—but then he didn't have a normal Kansas farm upbringing. When he was a youngster, his dad was in the service and
was attached to the U.S. Army station in Izmir on the Aegean
Sea. Jack had a local nursemaid and became quite fluent in
Turkish at a very impressionable age. They came back to the
farm only when he was nine, and he's never really forgotten the
language.

This is simply an everyday, commonsense counterpart of a great many scientific explanations based on our general knowledge of what may be expected, or would not normally be expected, as a result of the typical development of an individual of a given kind. Not surprisingly, explanation by development shares some features with explanation by type, from which we began. For instance, as in the tornado case earlier, so in the present case, where something does not turn out as one would expect on the basis of "normal development," the problem that arises can be presented as the failure of a presumption (see Figure 27–5.) And similar patterns could be found in other, more technical examples, where the matters at issue might be physiological or medical or botanical.

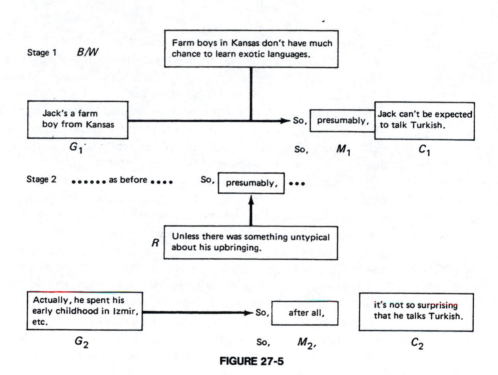

FIGURE 27-5

Explanation by goal. This final group embraces several varieties of explanations. What these have in common is that they look less to the past—like explanations by history—than they do to the future, specifically to the outcome or effect of the process or phenomenon under consideration. In some situations, that is to say, we understand a process or phenomenon better when we come to recognize "what good comes of it." This good, or goal, or effect, or outcome—we use different terms in different kinds of cases—was known to Aristotle and his fellow Greeks as the *telos,* or "end." Here are some explanations falling under this general heading.

In one kind of case, the goal of some processes or phenomenon is to preserve a necessary equilibrium:

PROBLEM: When we take violent exercise, we begin to perspire, and the warmer the weather is, the more profuse this perspiration is. What good does that do?

SOLUTION: Sweating—the opening of the pores, and the evaporation of the perspiration that comes from them—is one part of a larger bodily mechanism that plays a part in keeping the human body's temperature at a steady ninety-eight and a half degrees Fahrenheit. (Dogs are so furry that this mechanism doesn't operate for them, and they have to get rid of surplus heat by panting and evaporating fluid from their mouths.) Thus exercise—particularly in hot weather—generates surplus heat, which our bodies get rid of by releasing physiologically controlled amounts of sweat.

Underlying this kind of explanation is, of course, the very general presupposition that physiological processes and the like *do* lead to some "good" or "end." Where the specific kind of good produced in this way takes the form of an *equilibrium*—as with the constant body temperature of warm-blooded animals—the mechanisms responsible are called *homeostatic mechanisms,* and the overall process of maintaining the equilibrium is known as *homeostasis,* from the Greek words for "staying the same."

Speaking generally, physiological processes are often accounted for by their *functions.* (The explanation of homeostatic processes and phenomena is merely one special case of "functional" explanation.) For instance: Why do the eyes of cats have such different pupils from those of humans? The explanation is that cats are by nature nocturnal hunters, and their special eye structure enables them to see their prey even at night. Here we account for the presence of the features in question by pointing out that they make possible something (hunting at night) that would not be possible in their absence.

A goal may, of course, be either physiological or psychological in nature or both. (The release of adrenaline into the bloodstream when we are threatened has effects of both kinds on us.) And a third variety of explanation by goal has to do, more specifically, with *psychological* goals. Where we are discussing modes of behavior that strikes us as puzzling or bizarre, for instance, we may be presented with an account that shows what goal this behavior has. Such an account shows us less the function than the *purpose* of the behavior:

PROBLEM: Why did Jim clear his throat so loudly and start talking about the Super Bowl halfway through the conversation?

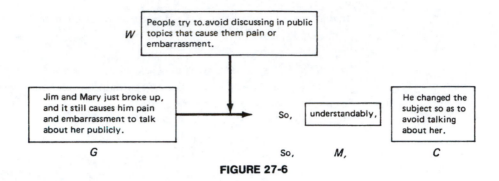

FIGURE 27-6

SOLUTION: Someone had mentioned Mary's name and that embarrassed him. They had been going together for a year now, and it all came apart ten days ago. He naturally finds it painful to risk being asked about her. Changing the subject so abruptly was simply defensive. (See Figure 27–6.)

THE BUILDING OF THE SCIENTIFIC WORLD PICTURE

Up to this point, we have been considering the different kinds of explanations that play a part in science (as they do in everyday life) in four different groups, but we have done nothing to show what those various kinds of explanations have to do with science as a whole. Explaining why things happen as they do in terms of their type, their composition, their history, or their goal does not distinguish science as a professional field of study. All of these are things we commonly do in everyday situations.

The goal of the scientific enterprise is not merely to account for all the different kinds of events, phenomena, and processes that come to the attention of scientists but to do so in terms of a coherent, comprehensive set of ideas, theories, and methods of representation—that is, a single coherent world picture. Alongside all the *particular* issues of these four kinds that arise for science, accordingly, there are some other crucial issues to be faced of a more *general* sort. These have to do not with questions about this phenomenon or that but with the way in which any particular account contributes to the building up of the larger world picture of science.

To go further, working out the answers to particular questions of the kinds that we have considered up to this point would in many cases not be regarded as a serious scientific task—or as raising scientific issues—at all. Particular examples and problems are of real scientific interest and raise genuine scientific issues only to the extent that they have larger, more general implications. Alongside the four groups of particular issues we have been looking at so far, therefore, there are other more basic issues to be attended to. For, in each case, it may be asked: "And what does the solving of this particular problem do *for science?*"

To turn to these more general questions, particular scientific studies can contribute to the advancement of science in several different ways. Looking briefly at four of these, we may find scientists saying:

1. "Here is something that we had no way of accounting for previously but that, as a result of this particular investigation, can now be fitted into the larger fabric of the science concerned."
2. "Here is something that we thought we had a satisfactory account of but that, as a result of this particular investigation, turns out not to fit into our larger scientific theories in the way we thought."
3. "Here are two general bodies of theory and explanation that have hitherto been separate and independent but that, as a result of this particular investigation, can now be integrated into a single theory."
4. "Here are two general bodies of theory and explanation that have hitherto been integrated but that, as a result of this particular investigation, must now be separated and distinguished."

For example: (1) At any given time, the ideas and theories available in any particular branch of science will explain the phenomena concerned in detail only *up to a point*. Beyond that point, there are still unexplained types of phenomena. Thus when Snell and Descartes first explained the refraction of light rays passing, say, from air into glass in the seventeenth century, their account covered only those "normal" cases in which the light rays simply change direction on entering the new substance. But there are also other "anomalous" cases, in which a light ray divides into two separate rays on passing from air into, say, a crystalline substance, such as Iceland spar. These anomalous cases were accounted for only by the extension and modification of Snell and Descartes's original theory. This was done shortly after their time by Christian Huygens, who recognized the phenomenon of polarization, that is, the fact that rays of ordinary light comprise two components, which are refracted in different ways and which can also be separated and handled independently. (These correspond to what we now call *polarized light*.)

(2) At other times, it turns out that an explanation hitherto accepted as generally satisfactory must be *restricted* rather than extended. Thus, by the mid-nineteenth century, physicists seemed to have a comprehensive theory of specific heats. But this theory had been established almost entirely as a result of experimental studies with solid and liquid substances. Once systematic experiments were carried out with gases, however, the previous theory turned out to have shortcomings and led to ambiguous results. As a result, it was necessary to place limitations on the scope of the existing theory, at least until the deeper reasons for these ambiguous results could be discovered.

(3) The classic example in this case is James Clerk Maxwell's work in the theory of electromagnetism. Up to the middle of the nineteenth century, electricity and magnetism had been studied—and theorized about—separately. There

had long been clues hinting at a connection between them. It had been observed, for instance, that pieces of metal became magnetized when struck by lightning, and lightning was recognized to be an electrical discharge. There were also certain striking similarities in the mathematical forms of the theories developed to deal with electrical and magnetic phenomena, and Michael Faraday had even taken advantage of these connections in his studies of electromagnetic induction, which made possible the invention of the dynamo. Until Maxwell worked out his integrated theory of electromagnetism, however, there was no way of accounting for all these analogies and connections.

(4) During the early nineteenth century, many leading biologists and chemists, especially in Germany, believed that the theory of life processes could be brought under the general heading of *energy*, like the phenomena of heat and the rest. They supposed that a special, variant form of "vital energy" was characteristic of living things in the same kind of way that magnetic, electrical, chemical, and other forms of energy were associated with the corresponding phenomena. (This idea was put forward very seriously, for instance, in Justus von Liebig's first great textbook on the chemical nature of organic processes, the *Animal Chemistry* of 1841.) After hanging around the scientific scene for quite a while, however, this hypothesis turned out to lead nowhere. In particular, there turned out to be no way of establishing any kind of constant rate of exchange for the conversion of this supposed vital energy into other forms of energy in the way that, say, chemical and mechanical energy can be converted into one another with a constant equivalency. So eventually the concept of *vital energy* led scientists to a dead end.

THE CONSTITUENT ELEMENTS OF SCIENTIFIC ARGUMENT

It is clear, by now, that scientific arguments and explanations are of many kinds. So it may seem a difficult task to indicate the general character of the *claims, grounds, warrants,* and other elements involved in scientific argumentation. Without denying the complexity of this topic, however, we can introduce order into our discussion by recalling certain points made about the nature of the scientific enterprise and the issues with which science is consequently concerned.

Suppose we accept that the general aim of all scientific work is to improve the match between our ideas (theories, concepts, explanatory procedures, and so on) and our actual experience of the natural world. In that case, genuine issues will arise for scientific investigation and argumentation wherever we can identify *shortcomings* in current ideas about the natural world of kinds that might be eliminated by investigations that are practicable at the present time. Starting from this position, we earlier identified five general types of scientific issues associated with the questions:

1. Can we extend such and such a general theory (T) so as to account for some specific phenomenon (P) that has not hitherto been scientifically explained?

2. Ought we not to recognize that some specific phenomenon (P) is, after all, not properly accounted for on the basis of the currently accepted theory (T)?
3. Can we find a way of integrating two or more hitherto independent theories (T_1 and T_2) to form a single, more comprehensive system of ideas and explanations (T_3)?
4. Ought we not recognize that two theories (T_1 and T_2) that have hitherto been equated and handled together need to be distinguished and handled separately?
5. Can we find a way of restructuring our whole body of scientific theories so as to yield a tidier and better-organized overall account of the natural world?

Each type of issue provides material for a corresponding class of scientific *claims*. Anyone who offers a way of dealing with such issues can do so by advancing his solution in the form of a claim. He can say, for instance, "Here is a way of bringing phenomenon P within the scope of theory T"—and likewise for the other types of issue.

Furthermore each type of issue can arise in connection with any branch of science or mode of scientific explanation. Whether we are concerned with explanations by type or composition, by historical origins or goal, the task of improving and refining the match between our ideas and our experience gives rise to problems of these same five general kinds. Suppose the particular task is to bring some novel and puzzling instance within the general scope of our current ideas: the topic in question may be some new astronomical object (e.g., a possible new planet), a new species of animal having a paradoxical combination of features (e.g., a mammal that lays eggs), some novel type of radiation (e.g., Roentgen's novel X-rays), or some hitherto unrecognized physiological system (e.g., the lymphatic system). In one case, the ideas needing to be refined and extended are those connected with a system of zoological classification; in another, they are involved in the astronomical description of the solar system, the general theory of electromagnetic radiation, or the physiological functions of the body.

Likewise with the other types of issues, we may have occasion to compare (or distinguish) different classes of phenomena, to integrate (or differentiate between) different systems of scientific ideas, and/or to reorder our overall theoretical categories, whether the specific topics in question involve systems of classification, causal or mechanistic explanations, historical or developmental analyses, functional and/or purposive interpretations. In the long run, all four kinds of scientific accounts (or Aristotelian *aitia*) have to be extended and refined in accordance with the same basic procedures and agenda.

Before we look specifically at the constituent elements of scientific arguments, however, one further important distinction must be made:

— On the one hand, there are those arguments that scientists put forward *within*, or *as applications of*, theories whose credentials they are not challenging.

— On the other hand, there are those arguments by which scientists seek to challenge the credentials of current ideas and put forward *alternatives* or *refinements* in their place.

Claims and arguments of the first kind *presuppose* that current ideas are sound, relevant, and applicable to the phenomena under consideration and use them as a source of reliable warrants. (Think of how the "laws of mechanics" are used in elementary physics to calculate, for example, the length of time it will take a smooth cylindrical log to roll ten feet down an inclined plane of 45° starting from rest.) The resulting arguments *conform to* the theoretical implications of current scientific ideas and follow the rules implicit in those ideas, without calling them into question. We may refer to them, accordingly, as *regular* scientific arguments.

When scientists challenge the credentials of current ideas, on the other hand, the soundness, relevance, and applicability of the corresponding warrants can no longer be taken for granted, and there is no question of relying on them as trustworthy support for our scientific claims. Let us refer to the arguments that arise in this second kind of context as *critical arguments*. They are arguments in which the merits of a theory are no longer presupposed but are themselves up for criticism and reappraisal. As we shall see, there are systematic differences between the kinds of claims, grounds, warrants, and so on that figure in *regular* arguments on the one hand and those that figure in *critical* arguments on the other.

To clarify these differences, think how differently we would have to deal with the following two questions:

"If a spherical cast-iron cannonball rolls off a battlement forty feet high, how long will it take to reach the ground, supposing that air resistance can be neglected?"

"Supposing that we now wish to make our estimate of this time more accurate, by allowing for the effect of air resistance, how should we set about making the necessary allowances?"

In the first case, we possess a simple, straightforward procedure for figuring out the time it will take for *any* heavy body to fall through a given distance, at or near the earth's surface, in the absence of significant air resistance. The necessary formula was established by Galileo in the early seventeenth century. So we can simply use Galileo's formula for free fall as a well-established *warrant* and calculate the desired result in an exact, mathematical way. In this way, we shall arrive at a regular scientific argument that conforms to Galileo's analysis of free fall and that permits us to infer the required time of fall from the stated conditions of the problem. In fact, the only condition we need know is the height of the battlement; we can calculate the time of fall without needing to know anything more about the shape and materials of the heavy object under consideration.

In the second case, by contrast, we are in a less satisfactory situation and must deal with the question in a more roundabout way. Instead of being able straight away to construct a regular scientific argument, in which we deduce the time of fall from the height of the battlement in accordance with a simple formula, we now must embark on a more elaborate investigation. Evidently Galileo's formula gives us a first approximation to the desired result; but in facing the further, more difficult problem "Just what difference will air resistance make to the time of fall of heavy bodies of different shapes and materials? And just how much will the air slow down the fall of our particular cannonball?" we have no simple, straightforward procedure to resort to. Consequently, our answer to the second question will be less strictly mathematical, more empirical, and more discursive than our answer to the first question. Instead of taking the relevance and applicability of Galileo's formula for granted, we will have to consider the precise degree of accuracy with which that formula can be applied—and, conversely, what precise degree of inaccuracy is involved in it, once we regard air resistance as a significant factor.

What is true in this example will be found more generally also. We may expect *all* critical arguments in the natural sciences to be less mathematical and more discursive than the "regular" arguments whose adequacy they are intended to reappraise. For *regular* scientific arguments conform to and follow the rules laid down in the standard theories and warrants on which they depend, but *critical* arguments seek to stand back from—or, to go behind—the existing warrants and take their validity, scope, or accuracy as an object of scrutiny and rational criticism.

Regular scientific arguments

In regular arguments, the goal of reasoning is to establish a factual conclusion by appealing to currently accepted scientific ideas. Such arguments commonly support more-or-less straightforward factual conclusions by backing them up with correspondingly straightforward factual grounds. Let us work here with four sample claims:

— This cannonball will strike the ground nearly 1.6 seconds after rolling off the battlement.
— The foliage and berries of the potato plant are very possibly poisonous.
— The earliest known anthropoid apes lived in the Rift Valley of central Africa.
— Goiter is caused by a lack of iodine in the diet.

Each of these claims puts forward a factual statement. To the extent that the facts in question are currently understood, they can be "established" from appropriate grounds, warrants, and so on.

Grounds.   As to the necessary *grounds,* these too will normally comprise straight-forwardly factual reports. The reports may be simple or complex. In the cannon-ball case, for instance, all we need point to by way of supporting evidence is the height of the battlement in question. In the case of the anthropoid apes, by contrast, we shall need to assemble a much larger body of geological and paleontological data, referring to many parts of the world, before we can justify our conclusion. The other two cases are intermediate in this respect. The medical and epidemiological data about the occurrence of goiter are rather simple and conclusive, and the claim about potato plants is rather weak ("very possibly") and calls only for suggestive, not for conclusive evidence. We may begin building up diagrammatic representations of these arguments as shown in Figure 27–7.

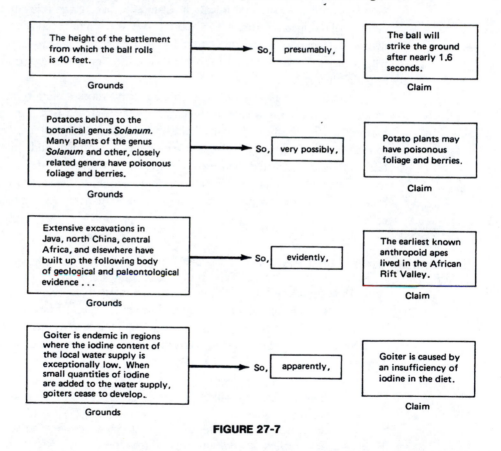

FIGURE 27-7

Warrants.   How will a scientist set about justifying the intellectual step *from* her data, evidence, or other grounds (*G*) *to* the original claim or conclusion (*C*)? As always, this question asks about the *warrant* for such a step. How can we assure ourselves that, with a battlement of this height, the time of fall of the cannonball will be 1.6 rather than 5.4 seconds, or that the botanical affinities of the potato raise well-warranted suspicions about the edibility of its foliage?

In the first instance, we can employ for this purpose a mathematical formula originally found by Galileo in the seventeenth century, relating the distance through which any freely falling body will move in a given time, starting from rest:

Distance = ½ (gravitational acceleration) × (time)^2

Or:

$$S = \tfrac{1}{2} gt^2$$

for short. We then require only one additional piece of information: that the constant in this equation—gravitational acceleration, or g—has been found by repeated measurement to have the value 32.2, measured in feet and seconds (i.e., that the speed of a freely falling body increases by 32.2 feet per second during every second that it falls), and we can set out the argument supporting the original

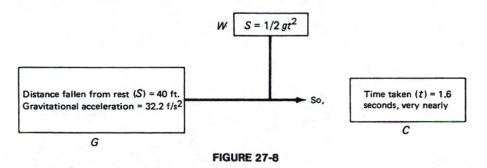

FIGURE 27-8

claim as shown in Figure 27–8. Correspondingly the other cases are diagrammed in Figure 27–9.

Even these four different examples, however, give only a small taste of the variety to be found in the warrants. The warranting procedures employed in the natural sciences may include mathematical formulas, computer programs, diagrams, graphs, physical models, "laws of nature," historical regularities, and so on. These warrants will authorize us to give "rational support" to our scientific claims, provided only that we have the additional data (grounds or facts) that characterize the actual state of affairs in any particular case.

Backing. All of these warrants, however, will be trustworthy and usable in practice only to the extent that they in turn rest on appropriate *backing*. In particular cases, scientists argue with assurance either from data about botanical relationships to conclusions about manner or growth and edibility; or from geological and paleontological observations to conclusions about the earliest primates; or from medical and epidemiological observations on rare diseases to conclusions about

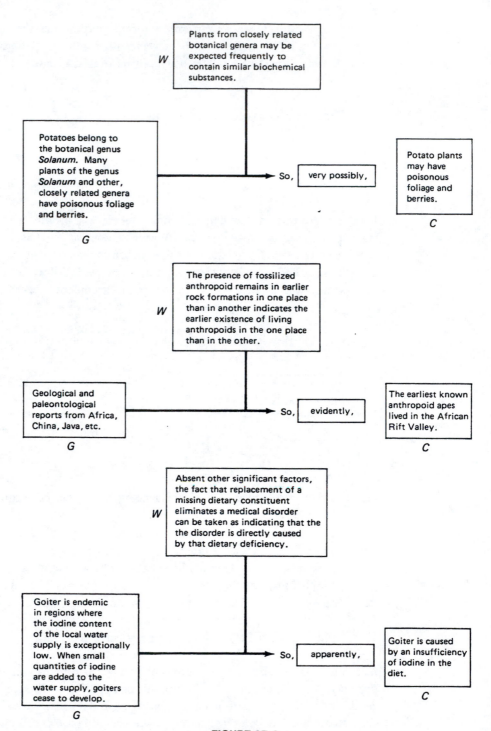

FIGURE 27-9

their causes; and so on. But they are able to argue with such confidence only because the reliability of the warrant used in each case has been securely established through the accumulation of past experience.

In the natural sciences, that is to say, there is as much variety and complexity in the *backing* on which our warrants rest as there is in the warrants and the warranting procedures themselves. Scientists decide what kinds of arguments they are prepared to employ and to trust partly on the basis of direct demonstration that those warrants have proved trustworthy in closely similar situations in the past. But they rely on them also because the concepts used in the corresponding explanations are ones that "make sense" in terms of the rest of their overall scientific picture of the natural world.

The task of showing just how particular scientific warrants find adequate *backing* in the currently accepted theories and observations of the natural sciences is, of course, a task for science rather than for logic. All we can usually do here is to set out in brief the forms of arguments that are relevant in our four sample cases, with the nature of the relevant backing (*B*) indicated, rather than fully explained (see Figure 27–10). Such diagrammatic representations of scientific arguments as these evidently do not guarantee the relevance of *B* to *W*. But they do put us in a position to see what standards our scientific theories need to meet in order to assure us that the corresponding warrants (*W*) are well founded and solidly based.

Modals and rebuttals.   To complete our present topic, we should look briefly at the *modalities* and *rebuttals* relevant to regular scientific arguments. To begin, once again, with the Galileo example of the falling cannonball, this relies on a strictly mathematical warrant. As a result, the initial claim is linked to its supporting grounds by a rigorously formal connection that admits of no exceptions. The natural "modal" adverb to use in presenting such an argument will be either one that emphasizes this formal character, for example:

G ($S = 40$ ft.);   so, *necessarily*, C ($t = 1.6$ secs.)

or, alternatively, one that emphasizes the lack of ambiguity of the corresponding physical situation:

G ($S = 40$ ft.);   so, *evidently*, C ($t = 1.6$ secs.)

Either way, a mathematical inference such as this leaves no room for "exceptions" or "rebuttals"; and, indeed, to raise the question of possible rebuttals would be to challenge the status of the entire argument. It would, that is, involve rejecting this regular scientific argument, and reopening the whole issue of freely falling bodies from a new, critical standpoint.

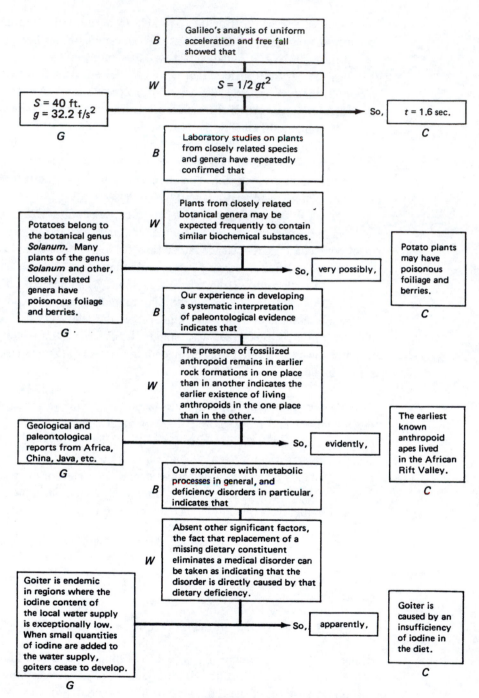

FIGURE 27-10

In the potato plant case, by contrast, there is plenty of room for exceptions and possible rebuttals. Even as it stands, the claim that the foliage and berries of potato plants are "very possibly" poisonous already has a modal qualifier built into it. All that this claim asserts is that the botanical affiliations of the potato plant make it a "real possibility" that these parts are toxic. Still, as we also know, there are some other closely related species that have perfectly edible fruits and berries (e.g., tomatoes, eggplants, and peppers). The question "Are potatoes more like nightshade (which is poisonous) or like eggplants (which are not) in their foliage and berries?" is therefore a legitimate botanical question and it turns out that the green upper parts of potato plants are in fact inedible. So far as it goes, then, our present argument can be set out as shown in Figure 27–11.

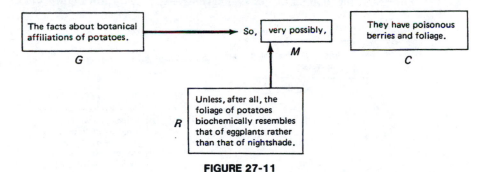

FIGURE 27-11

In the early-primates case, the difficulty of the argument lies in all the complexity and detail of the geological and paleontological evidence that serves as the final foundation for the claim. The strength of the argument depends more on the interpretation of all these detailed data than on any mathematical formulas or explanatory mechanisms. Indeed arguments between paleontologists about the chronology and genealogy of the early anthropoid apes often turn on the respective plausibilities of rival—and sometimes contrary—interpretations. Given the available observations, any claim in this field can afford to be presented with some modesty and appropriate modal qualifiers, as in Figure 27–12. Correspondingly the unavoidable inconclusiveness of arguments in this field shows up also in the variety of possible rebuttals that might be advanced against any particular interpretation.

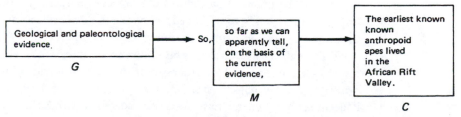

FIGURE 27-12

In our fourth, medical example, the points of interpretation involved are neither as complex nor as difficult as they are in the paleontological case. Taken together, the established epidemiological fact (that goiter appears most frequently in areas where the water supply has a low iodine content) and the associated medical fact (that the addition of minute quantities of iodine to the water supply largely eliminates the disease) provide the basis for a strongly suggestive argument. True, in the absence of a solidly based account of iodine's role in the body's physiological metabolism, this argument will be a purely "empirical" one, that is, one based solely on the observed correlation between the presence or absence of the disease and the presence or absence of iodine in the diet. But given the strength of this correlation, few alternative explanations remain to be considered, and the claim is correspondingly strong, as shown in Figure 27–13.

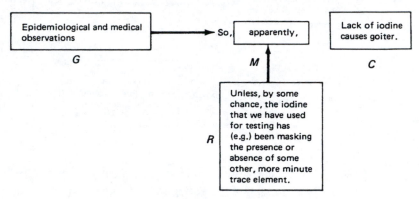

FIGURE 27-13

Critical scientific arguments

As well as simply *using* these regular modes of arguing, it is the business of scientists also to *criticize and improve* them. Hence the need for critical arguments in science: these represent *ways of arguing about our regular scientific ways of arguing.* When we move to the critical level, the rational procedures of explanation, classification, and so on used in our regular scientific arguments themselves come under scrutiny. Just as the topic of argumentation in medicine or engineering is how our practical procedures of diagnosis or therapy, television design or bridge building might be improved, so too the topic of critical scientific arguments is how our regular scientific procedures might be improved.

The subject matter of critical scientific arguments, therefore, is not simply the objects, systems, and/or processes of the natural world, so much as *our theories about* those objects, systems, and processes. The immediate questions at issue in such arguments have to do not so much with nature itself as with the adequacy of our current ideas about nature. To recall, Huygens's studies of polarization and double refraction demonstrated that the earlier theories of Snell and Descartes had been framed in overly simple terms. In order to make sense of the optical phenomena apparent in crystalline substances, Snell's simpler set of concepts had to be replaced by a more complex and sophisticated set built around Huygens's concept of *polarization,* with all its implications.

Looked at from our point of view, the *issue* Huygens raised belongs to the first class of general scientific issues listed earlier in this chapter, that is, a set of phenomena that had not been accounted for previously but that could be fitted into the larger fabric of the science concerned as a result of the conceptual changes now proposed by Huygens. Correspondingly the *claim* Huygens made had the form, "Theory T_1 (Snell's) should be superseded by theory T_2 (mine)."

What kinds of *grounds* are needed in order to support such a claim? If we are going to invite scientists to change their regular ways of arguing, they will of course ask us why they should do so—*what good it will do* to make the proposed changes, and so on. The kinds of grounds most directly relevant to this kind of critical scientific claim thus comprise demonstrations that the alternative or amended theory can be used to handle phenomena and problems that cannot (or cannot so easily and elegantly) be accounted for by use of the established theories and concepts alone. The best evidence that Huygens could produce to show the virtues of his new concepts of *double refraction* and *polarization,* for instance, was to show how the use of these concepts took care of phenomena that were left mysterious by Snell's earlier and simpler account:

> We can separate out the two differently polarized light rays and trace them independently through the crystal, taking account of the respective orientation of the two rays to the different faces of the crystal and so on.

Such critical scientific arguments therefore have a *pragmatic* character. Science has a job to do—a mission to fulfill—and proposed changes in scientific procedures are to be justified by demonstrations of how they contribute to that mission. Accordingly, critical scientific arguments involve *warrants* having such forms as:

> A theory (T_2) that can make sense of phenomena (P_1, P_2, . . .) that there is no way of accounting for by use of the currently accepted theories in this field (T_1) deserves, on the face of things, to supersede T_1.
> A theory (T_3) that succeeds in integrating two hitherto separate and independent theories (T_1 and T_2), while preserving all their explanatory power, has a good claim to be accepted as a replacement for those two separate theories.

Putting together claim, grounds, and warrant in the case of Huygens's work on polarization, we can then represent his argument as shown in Figure 27–14. Similarly, we can represent the minimum case for accepting James Clerk Max-

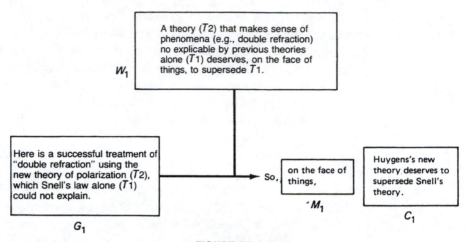

FIGURE 27-14

well's theory of electromagnetism—which illustrates our second class of general scientific issues—in the form shown in Figure 27–15.

With suitable substitutions, of course, we could equally well have illustrated the application of these two general warrants—W_1 and W_2—as they apply to botanical classifications, physiological functions, or hypotheses about organic evolution; in short, to ways of improving scientific accounts of all our four kinds. In each case, the best grounds for modifying our ideas about taxonomy, function, paleontology, or whatever are to demonstrate the actual *fruit* of the proposed changes, that is, to demonstrate how much more can be "accounted for"—or accounted for more elegantly or comprehensively—in terms of these modified ideas.

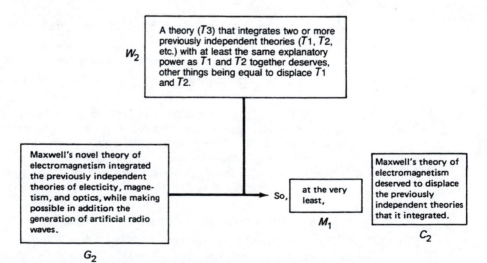

FIGURE 27-15

If we now go on to inquire about the *backing* for these warrants, a curious situation develops. For if such warrants as W_1 and W_2 are as suggested, it is not clear that their reliability or soundness needs any further backing. To produce the grounds required by these critical arguments is already to have shown that the suggested theoretical changes would make a genuine contribution to science. This is not to say that warrants such as W_1 and W_2 *lack* any backing that can rightfully be demanded. Rather, it seems to be a misunderstanding to call for backing at all in this case. If the basic mission of science carries conviction with us at all, then the warrants on which the Huygens and Maxwell arguments depend (W_1 and W_2) will also carry conviction. Beyond that, there is not much more to be said about the backing of critical scientific arguments.

The topic of *modalities,* on the other hand, raises more serious and substantive considerations. In setting out the Huygens and Maxwell arguments, we took care to include modal qualifiers such as "on the face of things" and "other things being equal." As they stand, of course, such phrases are simply colloquialisms, having the effect of weakening the conclusions in question by indicating the possibility of exceptions or rebuttals. But these exceptions or rebuttals must be made explicit if we are to take them seriously. In actual scientific practice, a whole range of modal qualifiers puts in an appearance. These vary in strength from *necessarily* and *certainly* at one extreme, by way of *presumably,* to *seemingly* and even *oddly enough*.

What modal qualifiers are appropriate and just how seriously we must scrutinize the implicit exceptions and rebuttals will vary from situation to situation. In some cases, where some proposed change in our ideas is quite out of line with our current ideas more generally, we may incline to the weaker (*seemingly* or *oddly enough*) end of the modal spectrum. In other cases, where the proposed change can easily be accommodated to our more general ideas, we shall choose modals (such as *presumably* or *very probably*) which imply fewer reservations. And occasionally, where some novel theory is strikingly successful, in the way that Maxwell's theory was, we may well accept its merits as *certainly* acceptable.

In presenting a full analysis of our two chosen examples (Huygens and Maxwell), we must allow for possible or conceivable rebuttals. Only in this way shall we arrive at a pattern of argumentation as complete as the requirements of scientific practice require (see Figures 27–16 and 27–17).

INTERESTS AND PROCEDURES IN PRACTICAL REASONING

We have contrasted two different modes of practical reasoning—argumentation in law and argumentation in science—thus underlining the connection between our typical procedures of argumentation and the deeper purposes of the rational enterprises within which they figure. Given the distinct functions of reasoning within law and science, for instance, it will be apparent by now (1) why the balance of emphasis, between *procedures* of argumentation and the *content* of

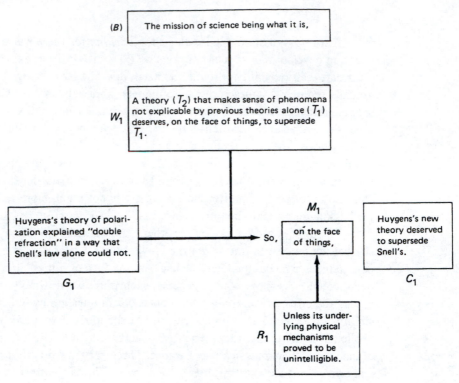

FIGURE 27-16

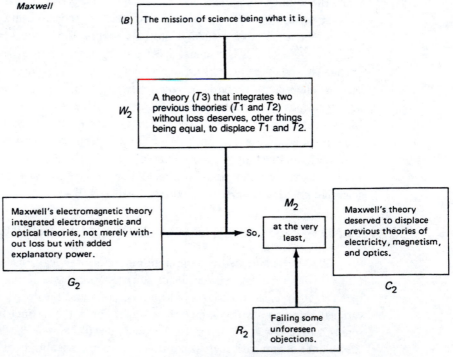

FIGURE 27-17

arguments, is so different in law and in science; and also (2) what different part the *personal interests* of the disputing parties play in the two kinds of argumentation.

(1) Legal issues will normally reach a judicial forum only when it is clear that the principal parties to the dispute are in genuine conflict and their claims are not amenable to compromise or arbitration. The formal resolution of the dispute by a court thus leaves one party the winner and the other the loser, and the practical consequences for the losing party may be grave. It is a matter of general public importance that the consequent penalties should be enforced only when their justice is quite apparent—that is to say, only when all appropriate care has been taken in settling the case and fixing those penalties. As a result, there has to be as much emphasis in the courts on procedures of argumentation as there is on content.

In the natural sciences, the relative significance of content and procedure is quite different. On a basic intellectual level, scientific disputes involve no real conflicts of interest, nor are there any permanent winners or losers as a result of their resolution. On the contrary, it is presumably to the good of everyone concerned that all scientific claims be strictly criticized to see whether the supporting arguments are strong enough to carry conviction. Provided that the *content* of a scientific argument is made explicit and exposed to critical scrutiny, the actual *procedures* of argumentation in scientific discussions do not need to be as formal or cut and dried as they do in a court of law. And if any participating scientist subsequently challenges the resulting professional consensus, he will need to produce fresh evidence about the strengths and weaknesses in the actual *content* of the scientific argument. It will never be enough—as it may be in the law—to challenge the forum within which the argument was criticized or to argue that the procedural steps followed in the argumentation were unfair or out of order.

(2) Participants to legal and scientific disputes also bring with them very different kinds of commitment and interest. The form of the proceedings in courts of law reflects genuine conflicts of interest, commitment, and motivation between the parties involved, and the readiness of both parties to accept the outcome of the current judicial system may do nothing to blunt the current opposition between them. In the natural sciences, by contrast, all parties share a strong common interest in the development of sound, well-founded theories. The fact that different scientists initially hold contrary or contradictory positions in no way means that they have any long-term interest—as scientists—in seeing their particular opinions victorious.

As human individuals, of course, scientists will have an initial commitment to their opinions, and they are at liberty to feel downcast or even humiliated if their arguments do not carry weight with their fellow professionals. But these feelings are a private matter that the individual scientist must deal with in a personal way. They do not represent a publicly acknowledgeable interest having any standing in the collective scientific debate. From the larger, collective point of view, all natural scientists must be ready to collaborate in the resolving of scientific disputes through the recognized procedures of scientific argumentation, and they are presumed also—going beyond the situation in legal argumentation—to share a common interest in the establishment of sound, well-founded scientific results.

AN EXAMPLE

We shall end this chapter by quoting a classic example of scientific argumentation, from Charles Darwin's *The Origin of Species,* on a contentious and much debated subject:

> If under changing conditions of life organic beings present individual differences in almost every part of their structure, and this cannot be disputed; if there be, owing to their geometrical rate of increase, a severe struggle for life at some age, season, or year, and this certainly cannot be disputed; then, considering the infinite complexity of the relations of all organic beings to each other and to their conditions of life, causing an infinite diversity in structure, constitution, and habits, to be advantageous to them, it would be a most extraordinary fact if no variations had ever occurred useful to each being's own welfare, in the same manner as so many variations have occurred useful to man. But if variations useful to any organic being ever do occur, assuredly individuals thus characterised will have the best chance of being preserved in the struggle for life; and from the strong principle of inheritance, these will tend to produce offspring similarly characterised. This principle of preservation, or the survival of the fittest, I have called Natural Selection. It leads to the improvement of each creature in relation to its organic and inorganic conditions of life; and consequently, in most cases, to what must be regarded as an advance in organisation. Nevertheless, low and simple forms will long endure if well fitted for their simple conditions of life.
>
> Natural selection, on the principle of qualities being inherited at corresponding ages, can modify the egg, seed, or young, as easily as the adult. Amongst many animals, sexual selection will have given its aid to ordinary selection, by assuring to the most vigorous and best adapted males the greatest number of offspring. Sexual selection will also give characters useful to the males alone, in their struggles or rivalry with other males; and these characters will be transmitted to one sex or to both sexes, according to the form of inheritance which prevails.
>
> Whether natural selection has really thus acted in adapting the various forms of life to their several conditions and stations, must be judged by the general tenor and balance of evidence given in the following chapters. But we have already seen how it entails extinction; and how largely extinction has acted in the world's history, geology plainly declares. Natural selection, also, leads to divergence of character; for the more organic beings diverge in structure, habits, and constitution, by so much the more can a large number be supported on the area,—of which we see proof by looking to the inhabitants of any small spot, and to the productions naturalised in foreign lands. Therefore, during the modification of the descendants of any one species, and during the incessant struggle of all species to increase in numbers, the more diversified the descendants become, the better will be their chance of success in the battle for life. Thus the small differences distinguishing

varieties of the same species, steadily tend to increase, till they equal the greater differences between species of the same genus, or even of distinct genera.

We have seen that it is the common, the widely-diffused and widely-ranging species, belonging to the larger genera within each class, which vary most; and these tend to transmit to their modified offspring that superiority which now makes them dominant in their own countries. Natural selection, as has just been remarked, leads to divergence of character and to much extinction of the less improved and intermediate forms of life. On these principles, the nature of the affinities, and the generally well-defined distinctions between the innumerable organic beings in each class throughout the world, may be explained. It is a truly wonderful fact—the wonder of which we are apt to overlook from familiarity—that all animals and all plants throughout all time and space should be related to each other in groups, subordinate to groups, in the manner which we everywhere behold—namely, varieties of the same species most closely related, species of the same genus less closely and unequally related, forming sections and sub-genera, species of distinct genera much less closely related, and genera related in different degrees, forming sub-families, families, orders, sub-classes and classes. The several subordinate groups in any class cannot be ranked in a single file, but seem clustered round points, and these round other points, and so on in almost endless cycles. If species had been independently created, no explanation would have been possible of this kind of classification; but it is explained through inheritance and the complex action of natural selection, entailing extinction and divergence of character, as we have seen illustrated in the diagram.

The affinities of all the beings of the same class have sometimes been represented by a great tree. I believe this simile largely speaks the truth. The green and budding twigs may represent existing species; and those produced during former years may represent the long succession of extinct species. At each period of growth all the growing twigs have tried to branch out on all sides, and to overtop and kill the surrounding twigs and branches, in the same manner as species and groups of species have at all times overmastered other species in the great battle for life. The limbs divided into great branches, and these into lesser and lesser branches, were themselves once, when the tree was young, budding twigs; and this connection of the former and present buds by ramifying branches may well represent the classification of all extinct and living species in groups subordinate to groups. Of the many twigs which flourished when the tree was a mere bush, only two or three, now grown into great branches, yet survive and bear the other branches; so with the species which lived during long-past geological periods, very few have left living and modified descendants. From the first growth of the tree, many a limb and branch has decayed and dropped off; and these fallen branches of various sizes may represent those whole orders, families, and genera which have now no living representatives, and which are known to us only in a fossil state. As we here and there see a thin straggling branch springing from a fork low down in a tree, and which by some chance has been favoured and is still alive on its summit, so we occasionally see an animal like the Ornithorhynchus or Lepidosiren, which in some small degree connects by its affinities two large branches of life, and which has apparently been saved from fatal competition by having inhabited a protected station. As buds give rise by growth to fresh buds, and these, if vigorous, branch out and overtop on all sides many a feebler branch, so by generation I believe it has been with the great Tree of Life, which fills with its dead and broken branches the crust of the earth, and covers the surface with its ever-branching and beautiful ramifications.

Exercises

Discuss our example from *The Origin of Species*. In your discussion answer the following questions.

1. What does Darwin's theory imply about classification in the biological sciences?
2. What systems of representation and "laws of nature" are discussed?
3. Does Darwin anticipate criticisms of his arguments? If so, what criticisms does he anticipate?
4. Does Darwin discuss anomalies in the argument? If so, identify them.
5. What is maintained about:
   a. The type of things that biological science studies?
   b. The composition of species?
   c. Their history or development?
   d. The effects of the process or phenomenon under consideration?
6. What is the basis for the claims that are made about the topics listed in the last question?
7. What aspects of the order and disorder that we find among living things are seen to require explanation?
8. Discuss the distinction between *regular* and *critical* arguments in science. What aspects of our example would lead you to put it into one rather than the other category?
9. How do modal qualifiers figure in the passage?
10. What is rejected in the passage?
11. Analyze the argument in the first paragraph of the example according to our standard pattern of analysis. That is, identify the claims that are made, the grounds upon which they are alleged to rest, the warrant that is appealed to, and so on.

National newspapers and news magazines often carry articles about recent developments in the sciences. Some magazines, like *Science, Scientific American,* and *Psychology Today,* exist for the purpose of informing the public at large about the latest work being done in the sciences. Students will find articles suitable for class analysis and discussion in these magazines. Each student should read through some of these sources and be prepared to discuss in class the reasoning encountered therein.

28

Arguing about the arts

As a preface to our next topic, let us begin by contrasting the fine arts with law and science (which were our concern in Chapters 26 and 27) and with management (to which we shall be turning in Chapter 29). In all three of those other enterprises, reasoning and argumentation have significant and even central roles to play. In both law and science, indeed, *arguments* are among the enterprise's chief products. It is part of any lawyer's business to construct arguments capable of winning cases on her clients' behalf; and it is part of a scientist's business to construct arguments capable of accounting for phenomena that were hitherto mysterious. So in both those fields, reasoning has a central part to play. In management, on the other hand, argumentation is a means to other kinds of ends: still, as this enterprise is essentially collective—in which the energies, activities, and interests of many people must be effectively coordinated—managers must have at their disposal arguments capable of carrying conviction with colleagues and shareholders. So though reasoning may play a somewhat less crucial role in business management than it does in the law courts and at scientific meetings, one can scarcely imagine twentieth-century managers carrying on their tasks without appealing to "reasons" and "arguments" to explain and justify their decisions.

The fine arts differ significantly from all three of these enterprises. Unlike the convincing arguments that are the attorney's and the scientist's products, the working artist's products comprise symphonies or statues, poems or photographs, novels or necklaces. Unlike the collective, collaborative activities of managers, the work of the artist is generally solitary and individual in character. Shut away in a study, studio, or workshop, the artist tackles creative tasks singlehandedly, in ways for which he is usually answerable to nobody but himself.

The fine arts are not all alike, of course, in these respects. For instance, movie making, theater, and the other performing arts are only rarely solitary, singlehanded enterprises, so the film maker's or stage director's craft demands managerial—or dictatorial—skills as well as artistic imagination. The same is true of architecture. To that extent, the arguments that follow need some qualification, as applied to those more complex media. But, to keep the issues clear at the outset, we shall concentrate here on individual artistic activities, such as painting and musical composition.

As a result, the regular course of the individual artist's life and work generally provides few of the occasions on which "arguments" are embarked upon in those other spheres of human activity. A story is told about the nineteenth-century English painter J. W. M. Turner. He found himself spending an evening among some students of Sir Joshua Reynolds who were engaged in a heated discussion about the relations between the sublime and the beautiful and other high-flown aesthetic topics. Instead of joining in the debate, Turner passed the whole evening in uneasy silence. The only remark he was heard to make was when he put on his overcoat and left the house toward midnight: "Rummy thing, painting!" There may thus be plenty of room for thinking, reasoning, and arguing about the fine arts, but as we shall see, the resulting argumentation is more peripheral to the central concerns of the artist than it is to the scientist's or the lawyer's professional mission.

CREATION AND CRITICISM IN THE ARTS

If the role of argumentation in the fine arts is peripheral to the artistic enterprise, the opportunities for argumentation in the arts are also fragmented. Speculations about aesthetic theory, for example, have little connection with the day-to-day criticism of particular artworks, still less with technical problems in the actual crafts of painting, composition, playwriting, and the rest. (Speaking more harshly than Turner, Pablo Picasso is reported to have declared, "The only aesthetic question that working artists discuss is where to buy decent turpentine.") Given the current, late-twentieth-century relations between working artists and their patrons, clients, audience, and critics, these different groups have somewhat different occasions for arguing about artistic matters, and their discussions go on in different circles and forums that are largely independent and almost entirely nonintercommunicating.

In the law, all sorts of rational considerations finally come together in the courts, the only place where disputed issues can be definitively decided. In science, too, the soundness and significance of novel arguments is finally decided in a collective debate, carried on among those who have a professional grasp of the relevant scientific problems. But in the fine arts, there exists no single collective forum within which the "rational adequacy" of new products and procedures—whether those of the working artist or the critic, the historian or the theorist—must finally be weighed.

One further point is also worth making, by way of introduction, to help differentiate further between the professional work of attorneys and scientists and that of artists. The *goals* of the lawyer's work are largely set for him from the outside, by the collective character of the judicial enterprise. In addition, the *procedures* he must go through to achieve that goal are also largely determined for him by the formal requirements of legal due process. In legal work, accordingly, both goals and methods are very largely matters for collective decisions and understandings. The individual lawyer's task is to find the best way of serving the interest of a particular client within the limits laid down by those collective demands. The proper *goals* of a scientist's professional work, too, are once again determined collectively, so that an organic chemist will demonstrate competence only if he turns his attention to one of the recognized current problems in that field of science. But what *procedures* he then adopts to solve his chosen problem are, by contrast, his own affair. He is free to use his imagination and his best judgment to devise whatever investigations seem to him most promising. Others may disagree in advance about the likely value of his investigations, but if he gets results, that is all that matters. In scientific work, that is to say, only the goals, or ends, are determined collectively. The procedures, or means, each scientist adopts in attacking his chosen problem are something in which he has great freedom of action.

Those who work in the fine arts find themselves in the reverse position from scientists. Most typically, they are confronted by a range of collectively understood procedures and techniques that form the established repertory of the medium and genre in which they propose to work. Within the limits set by the technical demands of those procedures, however, they are—as artists—free to do whatever they think fit. For an artist, what is laid down in advance is not the goal or ends of the work so much as the techniques, procedures, or means available. He may initially choose to go in for the writing of sonnets or drypoint engraving, making 16-millimeter movies or composing string trios; but whatever medium or genre he takes up, he will do well to begin by mastering its collective techniques and problems to the best of his ability. That done, he can go on and put them to work in producing works that express his own individual projects and personal imagination.

So as we move from science to art, the relations between the collective and the individual are reversed. Where the scientist uses whatever procedures he thinks fit to solve collective, defined problems, the artist uses technical procedures developed and refined collectively to serve his own freely chosen projects. Recognizing this reversal can help us to understand why, in the fine arts, the current forums of argumentation are so fragmented. "Arguing about the arts" goes on, in practice, in three separate independent forums. In one of these, working artists talk with one another, largely about matters of technique. In a second, members of the creative artist's audience compare their perceptions and interpretations of his work. And in the third, historians and theorists of art analyze the formal structures, historical connections, and aesthetic significance of those works.

The types of issues typically discussed in each of these three forums are equally different from one another. No doubt there is in practice some overlap. In comparing their views about particular films, moviegoers may be helped if they have some technical understanding of shooting and editing, directing and producing. (Academic historians of art who have little feeling for the paintings they discuss are like humorless psychologists discussing what makes jokes funny.) But the connections between these three fields of discussion are tenuous and indirect, so we shall discuss here the patterns of argumentation characteristic of each forum separately.

ISSUES OF ARTISTIC DEBATE

Technical issues

Whatever their medium or genre, working artists talking among themselves chiefly have to discuss questions of technique. Picasso's deliberately sardonic remark about "finding decent turpentine" caricatures the essential point. Though the working artist's day-to-day concerns are not all conceived with such down-to-earth housekeeping matters, they are more often than not concerned with the *means* of achieving some desired effect—with "how to do it." Onlookers and critics may focus on "what the artist was trying to do," but that is something the artist himself rarely has occasion to *talk about*. After all, it is precisely what he is attempting to *show*. Instead of explaining what he is attempting to do, he would rather get on with the business of *doing* it. If he stops work to talk with other artists, that will normally be because—as fellow craftsmen—they have practical experience on which he can draw and from which he can learn.

So the draftsman may lay down his pencil and turn to his teacher or colleague, saying, "I've got a problem with this hand—something's gone wrong with the way it joins up with the forearm. Can you help me?" Alternatively the film director may sit down over a drink with a collaborator and say, "I haven't yet figured out exactly how to handle the alternations between this cop car chase and the interview going on in the DA's office. Do you have any suggestions?" Or again, the poet may say to a friend, "I'm unhappy with the middle quatrain of this sonnet—there's something about the internal rhymes and rhythms that produces a disagreeable jangling. Can you spot what the trouble is?" And it would be easy enough to multiply examples involving artists of other kinds—sculptors, composers, landscape gardeners.

The issues that arise in such cases have, of course, little to do with "matters of taste" and a lot to do with the collective tradition of practical experience in the medium concerned. Beginning as an apprentice, the would-be painter or composer finds himself drawn into this tradition and makes it his business to master whatever he needs and whatever he can of the techniques developed and tested by his predecessors. Thereafter, in his working career, he is free to choose from these technical resources and refine them in creating his own chosen products. However imaginative and freely designed his eventual creation may be, however, the actual technical problems surmounted in the course of that work will be down-to-earth, collective problems:

— How can one best thin down oil paints so as to produce a "lightening" of the texture?
— Just what tonal qualities are characteristic of the lower-to-middle range of the clarient register?
— What kind of unsettling effect is produced on a movie viewer by the intercutting of two different scenes repeatedly and quickly?

These are things the artist simply has to know and understand if he is to bring off the effects at which he is aiming. Such technical issues are, accordingly not merely collective ones but also (in an important sense) *objective* issues, to which there is commonly a "right or wrong" answer.

Interpretive issues

The issues arising for the artist's audience are of a very different kind. Critics and onlookers are commonly presented with the outcome of the artist's work in isolation—in a gallery, a movie house, or a concert hall—and in its complete form. They are neither involved in nor parties to all the problems and experiments, brain-wracking, and labor that went into the actual work of producing it. In the long run, understanding about those things may give them a better appreciation of the finished work, but initially, the task of the audience is simply to figure out among themselves what sort of work it is, what is going on in it, and how we should look at it, read it, or listen to it, if we are to "respond to it" or "get a hold of it" at all. Hence the issues that arise for the artist's audience first are primarily interpretive rather than technical, for example:

— In this movie, what was the point of that unusually long and static opening sequence? Was it just self-indulgence on the director's part, or what mood was he trying to establish?
— In this painting, how are we supposed to see the relations between these two tightly organized areas? And how do they fit in with those other flatter quadrants?
— In this novel, is the comparative shallowness of the characterization deliberate? And, if so, what are we supposed to make of it?

Once we move to this level, the points at issue in debate do begin to include some genuine matters of taste as well as more straightforward matters of technique. Yet once again, matters of taste should not be thought of automatically as being personal or subjective. A person of taste—particularly a person of educated and experienced taste—in one or another branch of the fine arts does not merely speak about his private responses to works of art in a specially articulate manner. Rather, his education and experience mean that he can help us to attend to those works of art, so that we find out for ourselves many things about them that we might not otherwise have noticed.

> "See how the painter carries this line up from the bottom left-hand corner to the top right-hand corner and organizes all the more saturated blocks of color symmetrically around that diagonal."
>
> "Listen for that repeated rhythmical figure, made up of drumbeats and trombone chords; this whole movement is a sort of passacaglia with that figure serving as a thorough bass."
>
> "There is a deliberate gruffness about these particular poems; paradoxically, the writer is a kind of Jewish version of Gerard Manley Hopkins."

Where the working artist is confronted by technical problems in the *creation* of an artwork, the audience is confronted by perceptual and interpretive problems in its *reception* of them. Few moviegoers being themselves film makers, and so few listeners themselves composers, these two kinds of problems arise for groups of people with very different basic experience, and as a result, the "issues" so created are inevitably distinct from one another.

Theoretical issues

If we now turn and consider a third forum of debate—involving those academic historians, philosophers, and others who take the fine arts as their focus of study—the same will be true once again. In order to write sense about the historical, aesthetic, and other problems relating to perspective in Renaissance painting, the poetic reforms of Wordsworth and Coleridge, the role of Wagnerian opera in late-nineteenth-century German culture, or the social significance of the Theater of the Absurd, we must presumably be able to "understand" what is going on in these different artworks. But the academic theorist goes on to concern himself with issues that arise on a new level: either with the structure and makeup internal to the work itself, as this relates to some more general theory of, say, musical or poetic or cinematic "form," or alternatively with the interrelations between a particular artwork and other external features of the contemporary culture and society, so that the works of art themselves are now regarded simply as elements within a broader pattern of events.

Accordingly the academic theorist's perspective on the fine arts differs both from that of the creative artist and from that of the immediate audience. The artist is actively engaged in bringing the work of art into existence. The audience is seeking to interpret and understand it for its own sake and on its own terms. But for the theorist, the artwork is one object among many others; it is of direct concern to him only insofar as it exemplifies more general relationships—either internal, formal relationships, or external, social and historical ones:

> "Might one perhaps view the earliest eighteenth-century experiments in sonata form as instrumental adaptations of earlier vocal forms, such as the Handelian aria?"
>
> "How were the expressive resources of early-twentieth-century English poetry extended by the substitution of internal rhymes and stress patterns for older rhyming schemes?"
>
> "In what respects was the special character of theatrical production in mid-nineteenth-century Germany and Austria influenced by the unusual persistence of aristocratic patronage in those countries?"
>
> "How far did the alliance between popular music and political protest movements encourage the revival of the older ballad tradition by the pop musicians of the 1960s?"

Though fascinating in themselves, the issues that arise on this level will neither help the working artist solve practical problems nor help the audience to grasp just what it is that has been created. Instead they serve to provide links between our ways of thinking about the fine arts and our understanding of other subjects, for example, history and sociology, the psychology of perception and the theory of cultural change.

ESSENTIALLY CONTESTED ISSUES IN ART

In law and science, the presence of essentially contested issues is not at first obvious and takes some demonstrating. In the fine arts, such disputes are much more familiar. Arguments about what is or is not "really" music or painting (or art in general) have been endemic, particularly in the twentieth century. For many people in the early 1900s, Cubism was "just not art"; for some people today, the noises assembled by John Cage are "just not music"; and within living memory, the status of film as a legitimate medium of artistic creation was still open to challenge. Anybody who has taken the trouble to become informed about the historical development of artistic genres and styles and their public reception will know that these twentieth-century challenges can perfectly well be paralleled with those of earlier centuries. (Blake's paintings at first looked like childish bungling, Beethoven's music sounded "unmusical," and as for the infantile versifying of Emily Dickinson, . . .) Indeed it seems to be in the very nature of the shared artistic enterprise that creative artists in every medium are forever engaged in redrawing its boundaries.

One can go further. The issues that are open to permanent contention in the fine arts do not have to do with the legitimate boundaries of the currently available media alone. Looking at the fine arts in a longer historical perspective, we shall find that the very status of the artist as an independent creative agent, which we take for granted today, has itself been only one of several alternatives. Other epochs have viewed the relations between art and other human enterprises very differently. What, for instance, are the proper relations between art and industrial technology? How do the fine arts differ from the strictly technical crafts? Can a creative artist always, and without exception, claim complete freedom to choose how he may express himself and what use he may make of the techniques he learned as an apprentice?

If we pursue these questions far enough, we shall discover that the creative liberty we are familiar with in the artwork of twentieth-century North America and Europe has been far from universal. At other times and in other places, artists have been perceived—and have perceived themselves—in quite other ways. Until the late eighteenth century, for example, there was hardly any distinction between those groups of workers we would now call *artists* and *artisans*. At that stage, the fine arts remained merely one species of "the arts," alongside the industrial arts, the medical arts, and so on. For people in the eighteenth century, in short, the term *art* overlapped extensively into the areas that we would now label as technology, and there was for them nothing like the distinction there is for us today between a training in engineering and an apprenticeship in the fine arts. So in eighteenth-century England, it was quite natural that the newly founded official society to encouarge innovation in industrial technology should be called the Royal Society of Arts.

To go back still further, if we contemplate those masterpieces of medieval creation, the great soaring cathedrals that dominate the major cities of Western Europe, we may be tempted to ask, "What brilliant artists conceived and directed the execution of those sublime works of art?" If we ask this question, we shall find it difficult to get an answer. The procedures by which the medieval cathedrals came into existence do not lend themselves to description in terms either of the theory or of the practice of late-twentieth-century fine arts. Certainly there were "master masons" who had a large part to play in drawing up the plans for the cathedrals and who apparently supervised the construction work that put those plans into effect. But in addition, half a dozen other people, at least, seem to have been closely involved in the final decisions about those plans. So in the last analysis, it may be as hard to credit these architectural masterpieces to any single artist as it would be to credit a baseball pennant to any single player. It is not just that the building of the great medieval cathedrals was a team effort. It is that the whole enterprise of creating them was never perceived as involving artistic self-expression on the part of any single individual.

To go back even earlier, many of the icons and frescoes painted for use in Eastern Orthodox churches during the latter part of the first millennium A.D. strike us retrospectively as fine works of art. Yet discovering anything about the individuals from whose hands these paintings came is almost as difficult as finding out who designed the medieval cathedrals of Western Europe. At the time of their creation, the production of these sacred paintings was not seen as a matter of individual self-expression, and as a result, few of the ways of thinking and arguing relevant to art today would have seemed relevant to the people involved. We may be interested nowadays—adopting the standpoint of twentieth-century aesthetics—in investigating the styles, affiliations, and personal idiosyncrasies of the different icon painters and in developing a system of typology and criticism applicable to their paintings. But it is a highly problematic question whether the issues we raise as a result really have any relevance either to the intentions or to the performances of the icon painters themselves. Different epochs and cultures have sharply differing conceptions of art and so operate with very different perceptions of the artist's role. To that extent, when considered outside their original contexts, the fine arts are *always* apt to be a source of "essentially contested issues."

ALTERNATIVE PATTERNS OF REASONING

We have indicated that questions about the fine arts are debated in three distinct and independent *forums*. In short:

1. Working artists talk among themselves about the *technical problems* of their crafts.
2. Viewers, hearers, and practical critics of the arts discuss *interpretive questions* about the structure and significance of particular works.
3. Historians, sociologists, and academic critics debate *theoretical issues* about the relation of the fine arts to their larger contexts.

Because this is so, we may expect the *forms and patterns* of argument employed in handling these varied issues to be correspondingly different.

To say this is not to imply that the questions that arise in each case—technical, interpretive, and theoretical—are entirely independent and unrelated to one another. On the contrary, we can hardly hope to address issues of interpretation in literature, music, or the arts with any sense or relevance unless we have a sufficient grasp of the basic technical problems involved in the medium concerned; nor can we hope to talk coherently about the larger, theoretical issues unless we can handle both technical and interpretive questions with reasonable confidence. Let us look at some sample instances of the issues that naturally arise within each kind of forum.

Technical discussions

As we remarked earlier, the problems that working artists discuss among themselves very largely have to do with straightforward means of achieving certain artistic ends. For example, suppose that a painter is at work on a group of figures and is at first puzzled about how to handle the resulting problems of perspective—in particular, how to focus attention on the central figure in her group. She needs to find some way of creating a special sense of depth in the area immediately surrounding this particular figure and so capturing the viewer's eye. How can she do this? She talks to a colleague, who reminds her how problems of this kind were handled by the seventeenth-century Dutch painters. One of Rembrandt's most striking innovations, for instance, was to seize our attention by surrounding the focal point in a painting with a bright ring of illumination—almost like a searchlight beam. So perhaps we too could afford to experiment with the same technique today.

In this way, an argument may be built up that can be displayed in the form shown in Figure 28–1.

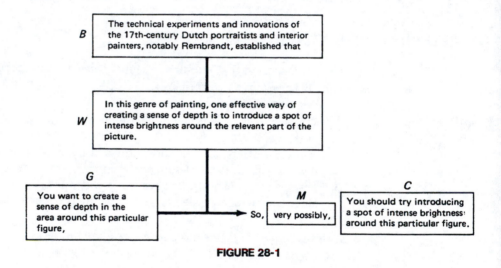

FIGURE 28-1

If we speak of this argument as concerned with a "technical" issue, we do so advisedly. For the point in question here—"How can I create a special sense of depth in this part of the picture?"—is a question of a perfectly straightforward instrumental kind, on a par with, say, "How can I cure the respiratory infection afflicting this patient?" The art of painting and the art of medicine alike rest on inherited bodies of technical experience, and these bodies of experience (or expertise) provide the natural first place to turn when we are faced with similar problems in the corresponding arts today.

Once the general character of this kind of means–ends reasoning is grasped, not much more needs to be said about it. The discussion of technical issues in the fine arts is like the discussion of technical issues in any other field of practical life. Provided that we know what we want to do, the only remaining question is what the inherited tradition of technical experience in the art concerned can teach us about possible solutions of our practical problems.

Interpretive exchanges

The issues that arise for viewers, listeners, and critics in dealing with completed works of art are very different from those that arise for working artists in the course of creating artworks. Normally the creative artist knows perfectly well what he wants to do, and his problem will simply be how to carry that intention into effect. But the onlooker will very often have real problems in figuring out what is "going on" in some particular work of art. So different onlookers and critics may come to exchange their views, opinions, and interpretations in the hope of seeing their way past those initial mysteries and difficulties.

What is the prime topic of such exchanges? Some people argue that they are essentially concerned with the "intentions" of the artist himself. In this view, what can be perceived in any particular work is what the artist intended us to perceive. Others regard references to the artist's intentions as fallacious. In their view, the artwork must stand on its own feet and be subjected to critical analysis and attention directly, without regard to "what the artist meant." But this disagreement seems to rest, in part at least, on cross-purposes. Certainly the anti-intentionalists have a point: if an artist fails to bring off the effect he was aiming at, we may comment critically on his actual achievement—for good or for ill—without being distracted by his unfulfilled intentions. But the intentionalists also have a point: the difference between understanding a novel correctly and misunderstanding it certainly involves "what the novelist meant"—in the sense, not *what he was attempting* but *what his message or meaning was.*

Suppose, for instance, that some question arises about Tolstoy's novel *Anna Karenina*. Readers of *Anna* often find it hard to know what the attitude of Tolstoy himself was toward his heroine. In view of the catastrophic effect that Anna's passionate affair with Vronsky has on her life, many readers have reacted against her: presumably the novel is a moral tract in which Tolstoy deliberately contrasted the exemplary modesty and unselfishness of Levin and Kitty with the impulsive selfishness and pride of Anna and Vronsky. Yet is this reading correct? Other critics and commentators point to many passages in which Tolstoy portrays quite unsympathetically the social attitudes and conduct of Anna's associates and contemporaries, contrasting Anna's warm and generous spontaneity with the stiff, conventional pieties of her husband's friends and the cynical worldliness of drawing-room society. No doubt, Anna's career is a total failure by comparison with Kitty's, but on this alternative view, Tolstoy presented it to his readers sympathetically—as a pardonable, understandable failure rather than a merely disgraceful one.

The interpretive arguments characteristic of such a discussion can be set out in the form shown in Figure 28–2.

In such a case, the connection between *G* and *C* is far from strict. In literature and real life alike, questions of character and motivation have to be judged with a sense of proportion and carefully chosen emphasis. As a result, we are

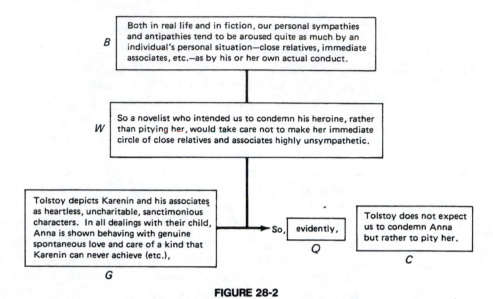

B — Both in real life and in fiction, our personal sympathies and antipathies tend to be aroused quite as much by an individual's personal situation—close relatives, immediate associates, etc.—as by his or her own actual conduct.

W — So a novelist who intended us to condemn his heroine, rather than pitying her, would take care not to make her immediate circle of close relatives and associates highly unsympathetic.

G — Tolstoy depicts Karenin and his associates as heartless, uncharitable, sanctimonious characters. In all dealings with their child, Anna is shown behaving with genuine spontaneous love and care of a kind that Karenin can never achieve (etc.),

So, *Q* evidently,

C — Tolstoy does not expect us to condemn Anna but rather to pity her.

FIGURE 28-2

rarely in a position to present arguments of "geometrical" rigor. Nonetheless, a critic can sometimes build up such a body of circumstantial evidence in favor of his "reading"—basing it on a full, elaborate, and detailed analysis of the work—that he ends by establishing his conclusion to the complete satisfaction of other readers. As with all circumstantial arguments, however, a case built up in this way is never capable of telling the whole story. Whatever may be possible when, say a scientist calculates the time of fall of a cannonball, critical discussions of literature, music, and the fine arts have more modest aims. However convincingly it is supported, every critical claim or judgment will be open to further comments and qualifications as we approach the work concerned from fresh angles and bring novel perceptions to bear.

Correspondingly the vocabulary of literary and artistic criticism is particularly rich in modal terms and phrases. We are almost never in a position to present our arguments in the form

"*G*, so necessarily *C*."

Rather, we normally have to qualify our claims and conclusions by indicating the particular standpoint or angle of view from which they are put forward:

"*G*, so (as a matter of psychological characterization) *C*."
"*G*, so (as a matter of plot construction) *C*."
"*G*, so (as seen from America a hundred years later) *C*."

In criticism, arguments carry conviction less because they are formally rigorous, surgically simple, or mathematically elegant than because they are rich, complex, and "true to life."

Critical theories

Those who participate in the debates that go on within the third forum of argumentation about the arts take up another, distinct stance toward the work under consideration and discussion. In the first forum, the artist is concerned with a half-finished work—a portrait, a novel, a string quartet, or whatever it may be—and the problems that arise bear on the steps that must be taken to complete the work. In the second forum, the critic, viewer, or listener is concerned with a completed work—a painting, a novel, or a musical composition—in itself. His problems bear on his understanding and interpretation of that particular work. In the third, academic forum of debate, the discussions are more theoretical. One is invited to stand back and to take a broader view of the whole artistic enterprise. The problems that arise from this new perspective normally require one to think about some *entire class of works* of music, art, or literature, either with an eye to the internal, formal characteristics of these works (sonnets, sonatas, or whatever), or with an eye to their relations with the larger social and cultural context of their production. For example:

> "Can we develop some general theory of sonata form with the help of which we can hear and understand better the instrumental and symphonic music composed during the period between C. P. E. Bach and Franz Schubert?"
>
> "What difference have changes of social structure in Western Europe and North America made in the artist's self-perception in the course of the last three hundred years?"
>
> "How did the invention of photography affect the art of portrait painting in the late nineteenth century?"
>
> "In what respects have the changing rhythms and vowel sounds of colloquial British and American speech left their mark on the style and structure of English lyric poetry?"

Critical theorists working in this academic forum are expected, as a result, both to look at works of art in themselves and for their own sake and to bring their understanding of other academic disciplines—history, sociology, psychology, or whatever it may be—to bear on their critical speculations.

Consider one particular example. Music lovers familiar with the development of classical forms and styles are rightly impressed by an extraordinary "loosening up" that took place in the treatment of these styles and forms between 1780 and 1820. Witness, for instance, the extraordinary contrast between the early music of Mozart and the later compositions of Beethoven. If we ask in what terms the rapidity of those changes can best be accounted for, we shall raise real problems of critical theory, for such a question might be approached from several different directions by a concentration of attention on:

1. Changes in the technical problems being tackled within the art of musical composition itself.

2. The personal idiosyncrasies of the individual composers involved.
3. The changing social situations within which musical composition and concert giving were going on at the time in question.

And at first glance, it is far from clear which of these three approaches is appropriate to the present problem.

We might be tempted to eliminate the second alternative early. Some of the most marked discontinuities took place not as a result of the transition from Haydn to Mozart or from Mozart to Beethoven but rather *within* the work of a single composer, for example, between Mozart's *Idomeneo* and his *Marriage of Figaro* or between Beethoven's Second and Third Symphonies. Yet neither of the other two approaches appears capable of answering our questions by itself. Certainly some of the striking differences between *Idomeneo* and *Figaro* resulted from Mozart's decision to set aside the older *opera seria* tradition in a favor of a new kind of satirical social comedy, and this decision confronted the composer with some serious technical difficulties. But how are we to account for that decision? Why did Mozart choose not to remain within the limits of the older operatic style? Evidently this change cannot be explained in technical terms because the technical problems arise only after, and as consequences of, the crucial decision itself.

In dealing with problems in critical theory, accordingly, we may have to cast our net more widely and turn our attention to broader connections between music and other things. Looking more closely at Mozart's work in the light of his life, for instance, one fact may strike us as relevant. *Idomeneo* is the last opera that Mozart composed while working as court musician to the Archbishop of Salzburg, with whom his relation had become strained. Shortly after it was completed, he and his patron had a final, irreparable quarrel, and from that time on Mozart worked as a free-lancer in Vienna. His three next operas (*Figaro, Don Giovanni,* and *Cosi Fan Tutte*) were all written for the Viennese commercial theater—so to say, as "musicals"—and were adapted to a more popular and less courtly taste. More than that, as a result of Mozart's changed situation, he was free to choose themes and plots whose ideas would scarcely have pleased the archbishop. After this time, Mozart returned to *opera seria* only once, in his late and comparatively unsuccessful work, *La Clemenza di Tito,* and, significantly, this was the only occasion on which he once again wrote an opera under aristocratic patronage.

Meanwhile the new freedom apparent in Mozart's composition of the later operas extended to his compositions in other genres and forms. Although the discontinuities in the development of his style are not as abrupt or obvious in his symphonies or string quartets as in his operas, we find the same movement away from older, stylized, and courtly forms and mannerisms toward an original, more fluent, and personal style. As for Beethoven, he was a free-lancer from the beginning of his career and did not suffer the kinds of constraints that had afflicted his eighteenth-century predecessors.

Using this example, we can now indicate the general pattern of argument characteristic of critical theory. Whereas the warrants to be found in discussions between artists (our first forum) are normally concerned with technical issues, and those characteristic of critical discussions between members of the artist's audience (our second forum) relate directly to the interpretation of particular artworks, the warrants appealed to in academic discussions about art are correspondingly more theoretical and general. In our present example, for instance, one of the implicit warrants can be stated as follows:

> The reigning genres and styles of musical or artistic creation in any particular situation may be expected to reflect, in part, the internal problems of the medium or genre involved and, in part, the external demands of the current system of patronage and the "market" for the art concerned.

The biographical facts about Mozart's life to which we have called attention will then support a claim that the rapid changes in the handling of classical forms around 1800 need not be explained entirely by appeal to "internal" or "technical" changes within the art of musical composition.

Setting the argument out in our standard pattern, we arrive at the form in Figure 28–3. In this case, as in the earlier Tolstoy case, we shall of course be far from having told "the whole story." Nor is it likely, given the richness and complexity of the associated issues, that there is any whole story to be told. By adopting new perspectives and enlarging the range of relevant external considerations, we could justify all sorts of other, further claims and so make our understanding of the stylistic transitions between early Haydn and late Beethoven richer and more detailed. Every claim of this kind may thus be judged sound or unsound *so far as it goes,* even though still further interpretations and refinements can always be added later.

THE RATIONALITY OF AESTHETIC INTERPRETATIONS

In looking at the procedures of argumentation employed in legal and scientific contexts, we have had to pay particular attention to the contrast between the adversarial and consensus modes of argumentation. Although the adversarial mode is almost easily illustrated from the law and the consensus mode from science, in actual practice (as we saw) both modes have a place in each of the two enterprises. In the public process of litigation, the judicial enterprise may appear unreservedly adversarial, but in labor management arbitration and in the settlement of cases that never come to court, lawyers as much as scientists aim at consensus goals. Conversely the need to expose novel ideas to thorough criticism in the conduct of scientific debate may make it advantageous for scientists, too, to employ adversarial procedures of advocacy and response, even though their longer-term goals may be to establish a critical consensus about the scientific ideas under discussion.

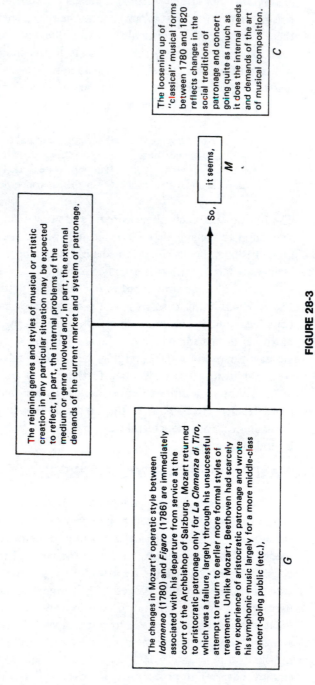

C

The loosening up of "classical" musical forms between 1780 and 1820 reflects changes in the social traditions of patronage and concert going quite as much as it does the internal needs and demands of the art of musical composition.

So, it seems, M

The reigning genres and styles of musical or artistic creation in any particular situation may be expected to reflect, in part, the internal problems of the medium or genre involved and, in part, the external demands of the current market and system of patronage.

G

The changes in Mozart's operatic style between *Idomeneo* (1780) and *Figaro* (1786) are immediately associated with his departure from service at the court of the Archbishop of Salzburg. Mozart returned to aristocratic patronage only for *La Clemenza di Tito*, which was a failure, largely through his unsuccessful attempt to return to earlier more formal styles of treatment. Unlike Mozart, Beethoven had scarcely any experience of aristocratic patronage and wrote his symphonic music largely for a more middle-class concert-going public (etc.),

FIGURE 28-3

Our present discussion of reasoning about the fine arts indicates, however, that adversarial and consensus argumentation are not the only possible modes. In the field of the fine arts, both the manner in which our reasoning is conducted and the judgments at which we eventually arrive have features that mark them off from judicial proceedings and verdicts, as well as from scientific discussions and conclusions. When we talk about paintings or symphonies or movies, we are not typically concerned about "getting a judgment in our favor" at somebody else's expense or even about "proving our own theories" at the price of refuting other people's ideas. Rather, we are commonly interested in "talking sense" about the work in question or in "presenting a legitimate and interesting point of view" about them. In our aesthetic discussions, that is to say, there need be no direct competition or rivalry between the positions we ourselves argue for and those put forward by other people in the same situation. In a law court, either the prosecution or the defendant will usually win the case. In a scientific discussion, either the advocate of some new theory will prove a point or will fail to do so. But in discussions about the fine arts—whether critical or academic—a freedom and a multiplicity of interpretations are available that exist in neither the legal nor the scientific forums. It was for this reason that we remarked earlier that a discussion about the arts may quite reasonably end by both parties' saying, "Now I see what you mean—now I understand your point of view and can recognize what you perceive in this work as a result of adopting that point of view."

This *multiplicity* of interpretations is one of the things that prompts people to speak about aesthetic matters as "subjective"—implying that everyone is free to adopt whatever standpoint and mode of interpretation he chooses. And some people have gone even further, concluding that there can therefore be no question of "right and wrong"—no sort of "rationality"—in the clash between rival interpretations and critical theories. Views about works of art are all (they suggest) a matter of feelings or emotions. The same work of art may have very different effects on different people, so there need be no surprise about the lack of any aesthetic consensus.

This last view is too extreme. The work of critical analysis and interpretation involves a kind of sifting that sorts out readings and points of view that make sense of any work of art from those that are misleading, misguided, or merely perverse. On the one hand, although few interpretations can ever claim to be uniquely correct, one particular reading or analysis may be so perceptive and well documented that it is regarded as "definitive." Yet even in this case, it is always open to later critics to put forward other equally perceptive and well-supported accounts from different points of view. Accordingly when critical questions arise about the fine arts, it is usually a mistake to insist on getting "the right answer" to these questions.

On the other hand, it is not hard for answers to critical questions to be plainly *wrong*. If, for instance, you do not understand that many of Rubens's large group paintings have allegorical or symbolic themes, the interpretations you offer of those paintings may end up by being merely silly. Instead of recognizing the implicit allusions to Greek mythology and the like, you may see these works, say, as pictures of orgies. In talking about the fine arts, that is to say, one can all too easily get hold of the wrong end of the stick. Even when all technical questions are left aside, therefore, literary, musical, and other kinds of criticism—without ever being uniquely right—may often go badly wrong.

What, then, are the proper demands of "rationality" in aesthetics? These demands have more to do with richness, candor, and "truth to life" than they do with, say, the formal simplicity and mathematical rigor of arguments in geometry. A critical account of some new movie that carries conviction succeeds in persuading us not by formal deductions but by assembling a rich, detailed, and well-chosen set of facts about the film in question. None of these individual factual statements may "prove" anything by itself, any more than the individual pencil strokes compose an entire picture; taken all together, however, they have the power to present a vivid, convincing, and well-supported view of the work.

The rationality of the resulting aesthetic arguments may not be the rationality of law or science. But it may nonetheless be the product of experience, reflective thought, careful deliberation, and well-chosen language—and so, in short, be a characteristic work of reason. However individual the point of view it expresses, it will be open to objection and criticism, qualification and refinement, in the same public manner as the claims made in any other rational enterprise. As a result, the freedom to choose our own standpoint and perspective does not place us outside the sphere of rational discussion and criticism. In art criticism, though the temptation to search for uniquely "right" interpretations or "correct" procedures may rest on a delusion, the weeding out of worthless, defective, misguided treatments and points of view continues in a rational manner.

Exercises

In the early seventies, when he recorded such songs as "Me and Bobby McGee," "Sunday Mornin' Coming Down," "Help Me Make It Through the Night," "Breakdown (A Long Way From Home)" and "Loving Her Was Easier (Than Anything I'll Ever Do Again)," Kris Kristofferson looked like he might be the next great American singer/songwriter. He had it all: the casualness of Hank Williams, much of the charisma of Bob Dylan and that particular, indefinable power that every straightforward and sentimental artist needs to elevate naive clichés into native myths.

Then, with *The Silver Tongued Devil and I* (1971), the initial cache of songs was spent, and everything that followed was embarrassing. Now, after long years of musical drought (during which the singer thankfully forged a second career as a solid and successful actor), Kristofferson is back with a new album he seems eager to endorse: "I'm proud of this one" he writes in the liner notes.

Apart from the fact that he's clearly trying again (just listen to his singing), the good news is that *Easter Island* isn't a disaster. The bad news is that it's a barely mediocre record, one short step up from the bottom. "Eight ounce gloves now, it's title time/ . . . I'm afraid we've gone and laid it on the line," Kristofferson sings on the LP's first song, "Risky Bizness," and you get interested. Nine songs later you wonder what he was talking about.

Both the title song and "Living Legend" are given the treatment of anthems and sound important enough to be about something, but if they are, it's a well-kept secret. "The Sabre and the Rose" mimics Leonard Cohen without much luck, "Spooky Lady's Revenge" is pointlessly passable, and "How Do You Feel (About Foolin' Around)" falls apart at the halfway point. Only "Forever in Your Love" really stays in the mind, and that's because of the familiar melody on the chorus.

If *Easter Island* isn't very good, it's better than nothing. And nothing's what Kris Kristofferson's been giving us lately.

Rolling Stone

1. Rewrite this argument in terms of our standard model. That is, distinguish claims from the grounds upon which they rest, as well as the warrants that are appealed to to justify the connection between claims and grounds. Are these warrants explicitly made? Are they qualified? How would they be rebutted?

2. Which of the forums for discussing aesthetic issues does this argument fit into?

3. Which features of the argument are characteristic of discussions of popular music (as opposed to some other field of argument)? How do modalities figure in this argument?

4. Are there rebuttals in the argument? If so, identify them.

5. Does the notion of consensus play a role in the argument?

6. We have suggested that the following are characteristics of rational discussions of the arts: experience, reflective thought, careful deliberation, and well-chosen language. Can you find indications of each in the article?

7. *Rolling Stone, The Village Voice,* and similar papers, as well as the national newsmagazines, run criticism and discussions of the arts every week. Be prepared to analyze a similar article on, say, film that you have read in one of these publications.

29
Reasoning about management

Over the last hundred years there has been an unprecedented growth in the scope of business, industry, government, and other social institutions, and this has aroused interest in the operation of such complex human organizations. In particular, a new class of "professional managers" has grown up. Where previously industries were run by craftsmen or tradesmen, such as mechanics, tailors, and accountants, the modern manager is a new kind of specialist whose primary skill lies in directing the workings of organizations. As such, the manager acts both as a decision maker and as an executive: the tasks are to determine what is to be done in a business and then to see that the different members of the organization act in the desired ways.

Serious analysis of management is new in comparison with the analysis of politics or science, law or aesthetics, so its characteristic forms of reasoning have not attracted as much attention or generated as rich a body of literature as argumentation in other fields. Still, management is a field of great importance in modern society. Many people find themselves required to engage in management reasoning, so this is a field that merits our attention here.

Developments in managerial behavior tend to focus on activities in business and industry, but management and organizational practices in government, education, research, and philanthropic institutions have also become important. In our discussion, we will use the business world as our primary focus, but our observations about reasoning practices will typically apply as well to other complex organizations outside business.

MANAGEMENT AS A FORUM FOR ARGUMENT

Not so many years ago, the typical business organization involved only one or two bosses and a fairly small group of employees. Often the boss had created the business personally, had done most of the work for the first few years, and had begun to take on other employees only when the scale of operations grew too big for him to deal with single-handedly. In such a situation, the "reasoning" behind any business decision was rarely explicit and was difficult to locate. The boss thought matters out and then announced what was to be done. Employees were usually not encouraged to disagree. They did as they were told. Thus there was no internal "forum of argument" within which the employer's decisions were open to collective discussion and criticism. Furthermore, in the early part of this century, business enterprises were often local in scope and limited in their range of activities: each of them manufactured its own few products and left the responsibility for other products to other companies. In addition, government involvement in business was minimal, and many companies were still private, family affairs without any body of outside shareholders. So there was no occasion for business decisions to be explained and justified to outsiders—or to government agencies either.

During the mid-twentieth century, the typical organization has increased in size and complexity to the point of possessing multiple departments, each run by its own manager, who is still several levels removed from any ultimate boss. And even the boss can no longer be the autocrat—the single-handed decision maker—he used to be. Now he or she will probably work with an executive committee and a board of directors to whom he will have to present reasons for the decisions made. The company may also contain diverse elements or subsidiaries in different locations around the nation or around the world, each of them consisting of a group of managers; and more likely than not, the company will be publicly owned, so that business performance and decisions will have to be explained and justified to shareholders in a "reasonable" way. (Public companies are, by law, "accountable to their shareholders.")

Government, too, has become much more involved in the day-to-day activities of businesses. The people, through their elected representatives, have now decided to keep a closer watch on the impact that business and industry have on the rest of society and the natural environment. The public wants to avoid the kinds of stock manipulation that may disrupt the markets. They object to wide fluctuations in prices if these result from collusion among what should be competitors. They worry about products that may do harm or that are presented under false advertising, and they dislike the damage that the smoke and waste products from the factories are doing to their environment. For these and other reasons, governments have increasingly required business managers to present reasoned justifications for many of their activities.

These modern developments have led to a variety of forums for management argumentation. In spite of the fact that arguments vary from situation to situation, with presentations to boards of directors being somewhat different from negotiations with governmental bodies or reports to groups of shareholders, two focal points can be identified as characteristic of management arguments. On the one hand, managers are required to take well-founded and rationally defensible decisions. On the other hand, much of the reasoning they engage in has to do with justifying their policies and performances to consumers, shareholders, governments, and the like. So we shall here concentrate on these two central types of management reasoning: decision making and policy justification.

Decision making

Old-style managers used to make their decisions in a way that may be described as intuitive. Businessmen use the expression "gut feeling" to indicate how such an old-style boss follows his hunches. However much reasoned argument may be possible concerning some business problem, there are always certain truly outstanding bosses or entrepreneurs whose talents, insights, shrewdness, and business sense give them a feeling for good decisions even in cases where they cannot fully articulate their "reasons" for that decision. And in plenty of cases, those who have followed these intuitive feelings, even in the face of contrary expert advice, have proved more farsighted than their expert consultants.

As organizations have become more complex, this mode of decision making has taken on a new dimension: the reasoned justification of intuition. Today, there are still those in authority who can act on their intuition, but increasingly they must ultimately provide reasons to back them. With governing boards and regulatory agencies more prominent, managers must be prepared to share with them a rational basis for decisions. There is an institutional and societal demand for reasons that can be critically tested. Trust and confidence in an individual manager may constitute one line of reasoning behind a decision, but probably other reasons will be expected.

But why do we call this kind of reasoning *decision making?* Why not call it *problem solving* or *knowledge seeking?* The essential features of decision making—not just in business but in other administrative settings as well—is that the arguments concerned require one to make choices within certain limits or constraints, particularly constraints of time and limitations on resources. Where other forums for reasoning permit the search for grounds and the analysis of arguments to continue patiently, with the major focus on the quality of the outcome no matter how long it may take, managers must usually make their decisions and choices with one eye on a deadline. Of course, they are interested in the quality of the outcome among other things—after all, their jobs depend on the success of their decisions—but this success itself depends on their being able to decide in time for the decision to be effective.

Scientists, by contrast, may debate a question for years and never come to agree on any one claim enough to say that the question is decided. Art critics likewise may debate their rival interpretations indefinitely. Even lawyers, who are under pressure to reach decisions during a trial, still have the luxury of years of potential appeals and retrials. Managers have no such luxury. The questions that face them have to be decided here and now. So the managers decide. Failure to decide would itself imply a decision—to do nothing. For example, a company has the opportunity to add a new product to its line, and the responsible manager must decide whether to do this before a competitor preempts the market or the tastes of consumers change. The refusal to make a decision is, in effect, a decision to refuse. Although there may be occasional second chances in management decision making, the forum can be characterized in general terms as one requiring *prompt* decision. Business managers are normally acting not for themselves alone but in the interest of thousands of shareholders. Incorrect or tardy decisions will affect the shareholders' incomes; really bad decisions can destroy a company and so render their investments worthless.

This is not to say that for every business question there is one and only one correct decision or one and only one effective solution for every business problem. Managers do not operate as though that were the case. Rather, they have the task of recognizing several alternative courses of action and then selecting one or another on the basis of some general rules of thumb or principles. It is usually desirable, for instance, that all the managers understand and agree about the basic "objectives" of their business organization, and decisions about these basic objectives will tend to set the general principles by which other more specific decisions will be made. Even so, the question being addressed in some particular situation may still be susceptible of several responses, each of them justifiable by appeal to one or more principles relevant to the company's objectives. One decision may be justified on the ground of likely profit, and another may rest on the desirability of diversification; a third choice may be recommended on the principle of economical investment, and yet another may be defended in terms of likely future trends.

Observers of organizational operations have found a variety of patterns of decision making. Standard procedures often call for a deliberate process quite similar to that found in science, law, or other fields. Facts are sought, criteria on which the decision will be judged are set out, alternative decisions are suggested, and the best one is chosen through careful argumentation. In practice, other patterns are quite often found to be employed. What is called "satisficing," i.e., opting for the first alternative that meets minimum needs, is a common practice. Here arguments center on comparing one alternative after another in relation to a set of needs. To avoid pure satisficing, other arguments may try to show that still other alternatives meet the needs better than the first one found. "Incrementalism" is still another pattern found in practice. Instead of trying to argue about entire problems and whole solutions, those using incremental arguments break the problem into a series of smaller problems. Then arguments are directed toward relatively small decisions taken in series over time, which may not solve the entire problem until considerable time has passed. In fact, incremental decisions may stretch the argumentation over such a long period of time that it will never be possible to say the problem is solved, because by then the situation will have changed considerably.

In the course of management reasoning, the term *scanning* suggests an analogy with computers. The process involves generating many alternative claims in each situation and examining them in sequence, eliminating them one by one by reference to increasingly rigorous criteria. These criteria are chosen so as to make an optimal contribution to the company's overall objectives, and this choice of criteria requires the managers to view the whole company as an operating system with many interlocking parts. As a result, the managers from different parts of the company have to compare notes and exchange reasoning. Executives from the different departments (such as production, marketing, and personnel) will thus have to make presentations for overall decision-making groups made up of higher administrators and directors. These presentations may feature arguments that support some policy decision that the particular manager seeks to have made or, alternatively, that defend some decision she has previously made. The argumentation thus goes on in both directions. Challenge and criticism proceed both upward and downward in the organization, and the process of reasoning and deciding never ends.

THE NATURE OF MANAGEMENT ISSUES

Despite their great complexity, modern business organizations, large or small, all tend to have one singular objective: to be profitable. Certainly different businesses have different specific goals, but any business that remains in the red for any length of time will eventually cease to exist, and it will then be unable to pursue any specific goal whatever. So in characterizing the nature of management issues, we cannot ignore the central question that arises about any claim or proposal: How will this affect profitability?

Given this fundamental point, business issues naturally involve considerations of strategy rather than problems for timeless contemplation. Individual managers often move from one organization to another, one day being concerned with the sales of automobiles, the next with trying to arrange to build weapons for the Department of Defense. Although the details of each endeavor may be quite different, the manager is still faced with the same issue: How will acceptance of any proposal contribute to the economical operation of the organization? And how does it compare with other coexisting proposals? In large measure, managers are not charged to inquire about the value of selling cars or the importance of building weapons. The organization typically does not require managers to think deeply about the question, How will selling more cars (or building weapons) make better children? Just as a military leader is required to develop strategies for pursuing policies already decided by the government, rather than spending time contemplating the merits or demerits of those policies, so the business manager is required to devise strategies for operating the organization economically and profitably, within the framework of whatever organization he is serving.

Given the competitive environment of most business, this analogy with the military can be carried further. For the strategist, the primary issues concern matters of fact. The soldier needs intelligence: Where are the enemy, what is their strength, what are their plans, what is their frame of mind? The soldier also needs data about the friendly forces: What are the comparative capabilities of our weapons? What are the strengths and weaknesses of our forces? Only once reliable data are available can strategies be set. The business manager—as strategist—also deals with issues of fact: What is the position of our competitors? What are the sources of our raw materials? What is happening in new technology? What organizational problems do we have? Which markets are growing and which declining? What is the availability of capital? What new lines are our competitors developing? How well are our own products competing? Working with factual estimates about all these matters, the business manager can then turn to strategic issues:

— If we add a new product, will it sell?
— If it sells, will our competitors counter?
— If so, can we spend additional money on advertising so that sales will increase enough to make it worthwhile?
— If we invest in a new plant, will it eventually lead to greater profit?
— If we acquire a new addition to our company, will it pay off in the long run, or in the short run, or not at all?

Obviously the critical task for a manager is to make claims involving reliable projections into the future. (Such claims are comparable to a political claim that if some law is enacted, certain predictable outcomes will come to pass.) The manager, however, is required to make more specific projections than the politician, and his predictions are subject to much more immediate evaluation. When a manager argues for the adoption of any specific policy, she or he must state clearly just what the expected consequences will be for both initial and ultimate productivity, or sales, or overall performance, and just what contribution it will make to the organization as a whole.

The business manager and the legislator are comparable in one other respect. Both of them make substantive policy decisions subject to budgetary constraints. (In the running of any large-scale organization, the two ultimate scarce commodities are time and money.) These money decisions constitute the most potent measure of modalities, and the allocation of money to various elements in a business organization is a continuing management problem. Any decision to go into a new product line will initially mean less money for established lines. If the new product does not initially sell, it will be necessary to choose: Should one put still more money into advertising, packaging, marketing, and production facilities, or should one write the new line off as a loss and save the money for more successful lines? However attractive a proposal may be in technical terms, the manager must face the question of how the resulting expenditure can be justified to the board of directors or the shareholders.

Behind such day-to-day issues of fact and strategy, business managers also deal with issues involving the conception of the organization itself, its future goals and objectives, and the principles on which future strategy decisions will be made. These issues most typically confront only the top-level managers, although in some modern organizations, responsibility for considering such issues is spread more widely through the system. Such issues are generally concerned with substantive questions:

— Under what circumstances should a new business be established?
— Should it produce a new or an established product?
— Should the existing company be strengthened by a restructuring of the organization, improvement in public and customer relations, the provision of better manufacturing facilities, a focus on better management–labor relations?
— Should volume be increased?
— Should we increase the spread between cost and selling price, by reducing costs or increasing selling price?
— Should we concentrate on reducing expenses or improving quality?

In a period of diversification, certain particularly important management issues emerge from the mergers of entire businesses, and so from consideration of possible acquisitions:

— How would this acquisition serve our overall business strategy by giving us entry into a new market or protecting supply sources?
— What is there to be gained from this acquisition—brand identification or research data, patents or processes, added distribution channels or liquid assets, borrowing power or tax benefits?
— How would this new element fit into the whole organizational system—will managers be replaced or kept, will development money be granted, or would the new acquisition's assets be stripped?
— How should the success of the policy be measured—what criteria should be used to judge the acquisition?
— What are the alternatives to acquisition—to launch new brands ourselves or to relinquish this entire field?

In working through such issues, managers must ponder their conception of the whole organizational system in its relations to the entire industry, the larger marketplace, and the society as a whole.

In some of the most highly developed business organizations, various forms of "systems analysis" or "operations analysis" are employed to assist in decision making. Dealing with an organization as a system means considering the ways in which its component suborganizations are interconnected and interdependent. The use of the term *interdependency* implies a rejection of one-way cause-and-effect thinking and focuses attention instead on the mutual relations and influences between the components and on the nature of their contributions to the functioning of the entire system.

The so-called systems analysis takes many forms. In general, however, it involves evaluating systemwide interactions and the ramifications for the entire organization of a decision taken within a single department. Taking advantage of modern computer technology, one can generate a quantitative "model" of the whole enterprise, with which it is possible to estimate how all the component elements will be affected by any decision. The model is built up by the bringing together and synthesizing of the experience of those directly involved in elements of the business. The production specialist is asked what it would cost to produce a certain product; the marketing specialist is asked what price could be asked for the product that would still allow it to compete in the marketplace; financial specialists would comment quantitatively on the availability of capital for different ventures; and other managers would have to assess the likelihood that personnel problems would increase. All these elements are built into the model, which can be manipulated in many ways on the computer. Decision makers can then ask questions in terms of the model, such as:

> If we assume such-and-such market conditions, and if we take a certain action, what will be the result?

Given a full range of such alternatives, the final decisions made by managers will be based on better factual information and estimates, and to that extent, they should be more effective and reliable.

Some observers believe that systems analysis reduces the scope of management issues. This is probably untrue. On the contrary, managers who employ systems analysis methods must address a new set of issues having to do with the construction of the model itself. Computers must be fed information; they do not define it. Yet what, for instance, is to be considered "information"? Once an estimate is defined in numerical terms and put into the model, the computer will treat it with the same respect as every other piece of data. But in business, there is often some difficulty in separating "business estimates" from "sales objectives." In their enthusiasm to do ever better, business managers set goals for themselves that may be more ideals to shoot for than real possibilities. Such goals may generate support from financial backers and stockholders without justifying solid expectations about future performance. Before a computer model can be trusted to give reliable answers, managers must therefore satisfy themselves that the information being given to the computer really is the information that will support trustworthy inferences. Under such circumstances, it is easy to forget the modalities that must qualify all claims about the probability of some future occurrence. If we combine half a dozen estimates, each of which has only a 0.85 probability, we may well end up with an estimate whose reliability is well under 50 percent—which is just as likely not to happen as to happen. Once such numerical probability estimates are programmed into a computer model, one can too readily forget the many different qualifications that accompanied each claim.

Managers must also determine the underlying "values" that the model will assume. In setting up a model of a food service company, for example, they may have to ask fundamental questions about what people are ready to eat, under what circumstances they prefer to eat, and how much they are willing to pay. Thus, the "fast-food" revolution began only when people challenged the traditional concept of a restaurant—a quiet, leisurely place where well-prepared food was served in an unhurried way—and suggested that many people would appreciate quick service of marginal-quality food to be consumed elsewhere. Naturally a computer model could not come up with that observation by itself unless the proper values were programmed into it.

To summarize, management issues are heavily oriented toward questions of fact and strategy. They deal chiefly with the problems involved in the development and maintenance of an established organization in an established line of business or industry. Broader issues of policy are addressed, however, when it is necessary to present justificatory arguments to such decision-making groups as shareholders or government agencies. Like the legislator, the manager must deal with budgetary issues, which place strong constraints on all policy claims. Finally, the modern manager will have to determine how the entire "system" of the organization and its relations to the other systems with which it interacts should be conceptualized for the purpose of computer modeling.

ESSENTIALLY CONTESTED ISSUES

Evidently the business manager does not spend as much of her time facing "fundamental philosophical issues" as do her counterparts in fields such as science and law. Still, even within business organizations, there are certain essentially contested issues that emerge again and again, and their resolution greatly affects the future pattern of business decisions and behavior. Let us look at a few of these.

The best style of business leadership

Under the general term *leadership* come many basic questions in business organizations. We earlier described the old fashioned entrepreneur who created and dominated nineteenth-century business: the tycoon, autocrat, boss. Let us call this leadership of the *intuitive*. In *Challenge to Reason*, C. West Churchman speaks of the "intuitive" manager as seeing the world to be one of his own making, the product of his genius. This leader admires the great men of government and industry, "the fine gray-haired stern fathers who grace our boards of trustees."

Churchman also identifies two other prototypical leadership styles: the model-building rationalizer and the practical philosopher. The practical philosopher thinks in terms of *action:* his heroes are the doers, the people who get things done and lead the way to continuing growth and improvement. the model-building rationalizer sees the world as one that can be described *mathematically:* his heroes are the scientists and others who can understand reality and shape it to their heart's desire.

Organizational structure

Walk into the offices of most business executives and ask them about their jobs: their first response will probably be to show you a table of organization. Typically this schematic resembles a military structure, with the "chief executive" at the top, a few vice-presidents below, and then more and more people down the line. Any particular manager's location in such a table will be a mark of his or her status and power. However, from the point of view of the whole organization, the table should be directly related to the efficient functioning of the organization. This is not always the case. In fact, there is ongoing debate over the best way to structure a complex organization.

The arguments take place at various levels. If a new manager is put in charge of a department, an early task may be to restructure it. The manager will need to provide convincing arguments to top management to justify changes, and if they are approved at that level, the manager will need to make still other arguments to employees in the department to secure their enthusiastic support. Conferences at the highest levels of management may generate arguments about the structure of the entire business organization.

Contemporary theories argue for modification of the familiar military-type structure, which formally designates roles and power and can be criticized as inhibiting free-flowing communication. Some would prefer to view the organization as a system, identifying various functions and assigning people to functions. Furthermore a major value in organizations is the satisfaction and performance of workers, and worker satisfaction is increasingly recognized as a contributing factor in the continued successful functioning of the organization. It has even been argued that decision making should be shared by all the workers involved with a problem, rather than this function's being left in the hands of a few top executives. Look at the sample of the arguments that might occur:

Maintenance of organizational equilibrium. Businesses range in scale and scope from small retail stores to massive international conglomerates. Some concentrate on a few closely related products or services, and others diversify their activities widely. Some companies function in a single region, some are national, some operate around the world. So business organizations are constantly facing the question of what size and range of function is optimal. Some years ago, for example, *Life* magazine had one of the largest circulations of all such publications, yet it was discontinued as unprofitable. In a field that had always valued a large circulation as a way of keeping advertising rates and subscription revenues high, the magazine simply grew too large. Advertisers now wanted to communicate to more specific audiences; as a result, they were no longer willing to pay the high rates required by a mass circulation in order to hit their own smaller target. So *Life* has been replaced by a variety of special-subject publications that can provide advertisers with a more selected audience.

In other cases, business may fail as a result of neglecting to analyze the optimum structure for maintaining their equilibrium. For example, a company may be dependent on one product; this is true, for example, of railroad companies or weapons manufacturers. When demand drops sharply, such a company may suffer severely. To avoid this risk, some companies have moved into widely diversified fields, only to discover, on the other hand, that management success in one field did not transfer to the new one. Having invested heavily in a new venture that it did not have the means to manage, the company may suffer or die. The objective is equilibrium: a well-balanced company, with enough focus on its expertise to be able to guarantee effective management and enough diversification to guarantee continued survival in a changing market. The problem is discovering what makes for equilibrium in each case. Obviously no one argues against equilibrium. The ongoing debate centers on questions of what steps are most likely to ensure continued stability. Executives can differ sharply on the steps best designed to protect the company's successful position, and every proposed change in the organization and every significant change in the financial posture of the firm is likely to generate arguments focused on long-term equilibrium.

Division of resources between innovation and current activities. Analogous to the issue of equilibrium is the question of how much money and effort to put into innovation, and so into research and development. Over this issue, the sides are rather well drawn. On the one hand, some managers have little faith in the profitability of research and development. They favor concentrating on production, marketing, advertising, and other areas that will increase the immediate success of the current product line; research, in their view, absorbs great amounts of money that may never come back to the company in the form of increased profits. On the other hand, some managers believe in putting the maximum available effort into research and development; not only into laboratory research but into the training and development of personnel as well. The company that spends resources in these areas will, in their view, always have the most advanced products and the most efficient management, and so be assured of retaining an edge on its competitors.

Division of resources between profit-making and service activities. The immediate objective of a business organization is to gain a profit. However, in a complex society, it may be necessary for the company to devote part of its resources to activities that relate only peripherally to profit making. Determining how this division should be set is a continuing issue. In earlier years, the basic philosophy of some businesses was to pay the lowest possible wages and maintain the most economical working conditions in order to get the highest profit. The Scrooge-like boss of such a business would refuse to contribute money or service to the community on the grounds that doing so did not help his business profit.

Today all businesses are under pressure to donate money and managerial time to a wide range of worthy activities. Businesses are invited to pay for building parks and hospitals and for developing recreation areas, to assist in community affairs and support the local orchestra, and to volunteer the cost of reducing pollution from their plants and making them more attractive. All of this has only the most remote relationship to profit and is simply presented as a public responsibility of the business. Obviously a company that spent so much time and money on such projects that it became significantly less profitable would be in trouble. On the other hand, a company that concentrated on making money alone would come in, these days, for severe criticism from the public, followed even by government intervention or legal action.

Capitalism, socialism, and the "profit motive."   Before we leave the present topic, we should pay attention briefly to one final, very general issue. In these last two sections, we have been discussing management issues—both straightforward and contested—as they arise in the course of business, given the way in which "business" is currently conceived of in the United States. Within that framework, the kinds of considerations we have been looking at—profitability, efficiency, diversification, prospects for long-term growth, and so on—are all real and serious considerations. Apart from anything else, company law *requires* managements to pay prudent attention to these issues, as demanded of them by virtue of the "articles of association" (i.e., the basic document through which any business corporation is established), and in the case of such an incorporated company, the shareholders can actually sue the managers if they have evidence that they are deliberately neglecting those obligations. (There is a whole list of business malpractices—"stripping the assets" and the rest—for which business managers can be brought to court by the shareholders, whose interest in the business can be damaged by dishonest or careless manipulations on the part of the management.)

Within a socialist society, of course, the arguments and issues facing managers of large organizations are somewhat different. To the extent that the formal objectives of a business enterprise under a socialist system are not limited by the same kind of strict articles of association, for instance, there may be less in the way of a formal obligation on managers to pursue profitability first and foremost. To that extent, business management becomes much more like bureaucratic administration. Still most of the other issues around which management reasoning revolves hold good equally in any kind of economic organization. Just because a business is "nonprofit" does not mean that it can afford to ignore considerations of efficiency, long-term viability, and the rest. Even in the Soviet Union and the

People's Republic of China, profitability has intermittently been imposed on industrial enterprises—by government policy rather than by legal incorporation—as a device for increasing productivity. (Lacking such an index of effective operation, purely bureaucratic organizations are apt to become slack and unproductive.)

Still, in the most general possible way, the current status of business in the United States itself represents a *contested issue,* just as, in their own ways, the status and scope of law and science are contested issues. In all three cases, there are people who have ethical, political, or philosophical objections to the manner in which the respective enterprises of law, science, and business work out in practice in contemporary America. Some people believe, for instance, that the Supreme Court is encroaching too much on the proper business of politics and legislation; others that science is illegitimately undercutting religion; others again that business is pursuing profit to the detriment of social welfare and the environment. For these people of course, the arguments and issues that we have been discussing here are of limited significance. And if we ourselves were convinced of the need to reappraise and redefine the proper scope of each enterprise—so redrawing the boundaries between law and politics, science and religion, business and social service—then we should have to reconsider and revise many of the basic warrants and arguments in each enterprise also.

The kind of study we are engaged in here can scrutinize only the *actual* modes of reasoning within *actual* human enterprises. Other possible enterprises—or historical successors to our present enterprises—would use different, or modified, modes of reasoning appropriate to their own objectives. But what those other modes of argumentation would be cannot be decided in advance of knowing both what those new objectives were and what organizational means might be devised for achieving them.

THE NATURE OF MANAGEMENT DECISIONS

The nature of management decisions is indicated rather clearly by the material presented thus far. To summarize, management decisions fall into three categories:

1. Establishing objectives for the organization.
2. Directing the attainment of those objectives by a series of operational decisions.
3. Monitoring the results and deciding whether and where corrections of course may be needed.

More specifically, the typical business organization is divided into various activity areas, each requiring decisions of somewhat different kinds. In *research and development,* the decisions have to do with what future products or service elements should be developed and where money can be most profitably invested in potential innovations. *Production* requires decisions having to do with the use of current technology in making a product and with managing the personnel who do the work. *Marketing* brings into play decisions about the economics of the marketplace and about the tastes and habits of present and future consumers. It also deals with the problems involved in the moving of products and services from place to place and with the salesmanship needed to attract customers. *Finance and control* are self-explanatory terms. Keeping records of the money flows within a company can influence the pattern of business in many ways; a change in accounting methods, for instance, can influence other decisions throughout the company. A decision to borrow money rather than to issue more stock will influence the course of a company's operations, as will a decision to convert surplus overseas funds into particular foreign currencies. *Personnel* decisions have to do with hiring and firing and with keeping workers happy and efficient. *External relations* concern how to present the organization and its activities to other individuals and systems in a favorable light, and managers in this division have to participate in other company decisions, to assure that relations with the public are considered carefully before they have the chance of becoming problems. Finally, the *secretarial and legal branches* of the organization deal with the kinds of decisions discussed in our chapter on legal reasoning.

Upper-level managers make decisions about whether, when, and how to acquire new elements to be added to the system; notably through "taking over" entire functioning businesses. This requires them to relate the proposed acquisition to an overall business strategy in terms of its values, risks, and other available alternatives. Again they will be responsible for decisions about major capital investments; whether and when new plant and equipment should be obtained or existing facilities expanded. They must decide, similarly, whether and when to diversify into new products or even enter a new industry; whether to enter into mergers or joint ventures; or whether to participate in some form of a cartel or other collective agreement. As we have suggested earlier, one particularly tough decision is to determine just how many resources are to be put into research and development. Managers must decide how far to decentralize the organization or whether to maintain centralized control. As foreign nations tend to become more sensitive about absentee ownership, for instance, it is necessary to decide whether to get involved in foreign-based and partially owned operations or whether to retain a central base of operations.

CHARACTERISTICS OF MANAGEMENT ARGUMENTS

In characterizing management arguments, one must put particular stress on the importance of *grounds*. Because so many managerial decisions are essentially *tactical* ones—because the overall objectives of the organization are not usually in doubt—strong emphasis has to be placed on building up the necessary data base for effective decisions.

Managers need to deal with information that is evidently "factual." Frequently these grounds will be presented to them in quantitative form. With their warrants and backing often left only implied, business reports and presentations as a result will often appear unbalanced, with all the emphasis being on data and claims. However, we can illustrate some characteristics of each of our basic elements as they figure in management arguments.

Claims

Management claims, for the most part, deal with policy proposals. It is claimed, for example, that the company should produce some product or service, should adopt some personnel practice, should settle a certain labor-management contract, should acquire some new operation or modify one of its production facilities, should invest in some new equipment or retain the services of some advertising agency or law firm. More rarely, management claims go behind immediate tactics and propose new objectives for the business or new models for the analysis of its organization. At times, the claims also raise issues of evaluation: how some aspects of its operations should be assessed or how the company should react to some new law or regulation. Most often, however, the claims have a strategic or tactical character; that is, they propose ways of getting done something that the firm has already decided to do.

Grounds

Sizable businesses spend considerable amounts of attention and money on developing the data base on which management claims can be securely based. This involves collecting information both from within the organization and also by retaining outside agencies that specialize in generating relevant kinds of information. They will amass, for instance, information about social trends and consumer behavior—the effects of affluence and the spread of education and the ways in which leisure time is spent. They will study social developments: changes in family life and women's liberation, new modes of sexual behavior or levels of stress. And they need to have up-to-date information also about all relevant government regulations on advertising and packaging, environmental protection and consumer protection.

Economic information, in particular, must be collected and analyzed, so that it can provide the grounds for use in the final management arguments. The growth and distribution of wealth and income must be followed; changes in interest rates, price policy, international exchange rates, and the relative prices of capital, labor, and raw materials must be documented; activities within the industry must be thoroughly examined. Where are growth and decline occurring? What is happening in the market? What factors are influencing the supply of labor? How does the company stand alongside its competitors?

Information must be collected also about new ways of doing business. Managers need to know about new professional techniques in marketing, organization, production, and administration; they need information on distribution trends; and they need new insights into organizational communication and decision making and new modes of management reasoning.

They have to gather information about the workings of their own business also. They constantly receive reports on sales, cost of sales, gross profit, other operating costs (administrative expenses, marketing expenses, and costs of research and development), operating profit, interest costs, net profit before and after taxes, and so forth. All these data regularly serve as grounds in management arguments.

In addition to these specific sources of grounds, the typical manager will seek other kinds of information from leading newspapers, business magazines, and newsletters, from government reports and the *Congressional Record,* from statistical summaries and reports from special agencies. They will pay for advertising analyses, market studies, credit reports, and investigations of other companies in the industry. They will attend professional conventions to share information with other managers.

Estimates will be obtained from members of the organization and through specialized analyses of levels of risk and uncertainty in each phase of the business; such estimates will be expressed quantitatively, in terms of the chances of selling a certain amount of a given product, the chances of the market's increasing or decreasing by a given amount, or the chances that the supply of raw materials will change significantly. Estimates will likewise be needed of the damage that would follow if a particular product failed, including estimates of the likely response from competitors.

From a management point of view, one vital source of data and arguments consists in the consideration of all possible alternatives. Using a variety of decision-making techniques, management must set forth all the viable alternatives in any given situation. This may involve use of "brainstorming" techniques, designed to bring to light all possible claims, however unlikely they initially appear. Alternatively a potential decision will emerge from a careful analysis and discussion of the situation by those best informed about its details. Whatever the technique, the outcome of such efforts will be a relatively limited list of alternative decisions or claims.

Once this list of possible decisions is generated, the estimated outcomes and risks for each alternative will be added. The result will be a "matrix," showing all possible combinations of alternative, outcome, and risk, along with the estimated values of the different outcomes. Given a mathematical model of the organization and its objectives, these data can then sometimes be programmed into a computer,

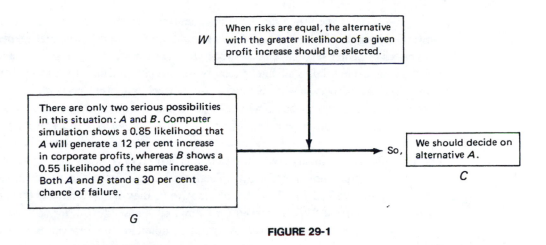

W | When risks are equal, the alternative with the greater likelihood of a given profit increase should be selected.

There are only two serious possibilities in this situation: *A* and *B*. Computer simulation shows a 0.85 likelihood that *A* will generate a 12 per cent increase in corporate profits, whereas *B* shows a 0.55 likelihood of the same increase. Both *A* and *B* stand a 30 per cent chance of failure.

G

So, | We should decide on alternative *A*.

C

FIGURE 29-1

and the various possible decisions can be displayed, along with their values and liabilities.

Although such computer manipulations do not directly *make* management decisions, they can provide powerful grounds for the claims that the managers themselves will make. Notice how such an argument might be developed (Figure 29–1).

Warrants

The fundamental *general* warrant underlying such arguments is clear enough: that which promises to increase profit, without endangering the existence of the company, should be done. Implicit in this warrant is another basic principle: the survival of the company is to be safeguarded, so that which puts the company in jeopardy should not be done. Although these statements are greatly simplified, they indicate the significance of the main core of warrants to be found in the arguments advanced in managerial contexts.

Churchman has suggested another grouping of warrants under the general rule that "a social institution becomes rational to the extent that it can be considered to function like some other institution." For example, a business organization may seek to model itself after a scientific organization, as in the use of systems analysis, and may come to rely on the warrants implied in the structure of a scientific institution. Thus, increasingly, management arguments assume, as a warrant, that whatever is the product of "scientific" analysis is reasonable and should be respected or adopted. Meanwhile, Churchman argues, a different set of warrants appeals to, and comes from, those who are more pragmatically oriented. For them, the basic warrant is to the effect that whatever "works" should be respected and continued. The implication is that the courses of action that have proved successful in the past are most likely to remain successful in the future.

Sometimes the warrants of management arguments involve appeals to the intuitive insights of some Great Man: close attention is paid to the management practices of people who have been successful in the past. If so-and-so has served with remarkable success as chief executive of one corporation, it is assumed that he or she can recognize what is needed for success in another corporation. Thus the warrant may simply be "If so-and-so says that it ought to be done, we should do it." (This is a prime example of arguing *from authority*.) But reasoning by analogy is also common in management arguments. When one is determining the serious alternatives in any given situation, it is natural to begin by looking at experience with other similar problems. When company *A* faced this problem, they did *X*, and it worked for them. So alternative *X* may be recommended on the basis of the warrant "What worked for Company *A* should work for us."

We may mention a few other warrants common in management arguments. Whatever will reduce costs will be favored, as will whatever increases efficiency. Claims that promise to improve the overall functioning of the organization or are consistent with the overall goals of the entire system will tend to be recommended. Individuals shown to be "team" players—who work well within the organization's values and expectations—will tend to be valued. A claim that does not promise substantial, immediate profits but that should produce long-term benefits to the company may be accepted.

There is a strong tendency to favor those claims that rest upon warrants of "practicality." In business parlance, the phrase *blue sky* is often used to reject a claim regarded as merely theoretical, idealistic, and unlikely to "work" in the real world. On the other hand, those claims that rest on a clear warrant of practicality ("It can be done") will be received more favorably. Given the current nature and structure of business organizations, there is indeed some reliance on the so-called technological imperative: "If it can be done, it should be done." (Certainly the reverse is a basic principle: "If it can't be done, it shouldn't be"!)

In actual business contexts, then, it is not as common to state the warrants of arguments clearly and explicitly as is the case in many other fields. Often the warrants are only implied: they are clearly understood, because all involved are intimately familiar with the organization's goals and values, which determine the operative warrants for most such arguments. The claim is framed as a strategic or tactical proposal, directly based on factual data or grounds, with the warrant unstated because of its well-understood institutional nature. This method, of course, may create serious problems when other inconsistent warrants are introduced unexpectedly. Think back to the Korean War, for example, when General Douglas MacArthur was shocked to learn that the warrant to be assumed in all his military strategy was not to the effect that total victory should be obtained at any cost. His conflict with President Harry Truman can thus be seen as a disagreement about funamental warrants. The general concept that Truman was working with at that time—"limited war"—was a novel one, whereas MacArthur still thought in terms of the "unconditional surrender" demanded in World War II.

Business managers may similarly be surprised when new warrants become operative. Having long been accustomed to working with the warrant "Whatever is good for business is good for America," many managers have been slow to recognize the need to accept, and work with, warrants concerned with protection of the environment and with preserving resources for future generations. As a result of this change, claims that would previously have been accepted as solidly based may no longer be as effective. Today managers may have to pay attention to arguments in which claims about the interests of business are warranted by concepts concerned with the larger interests of society.

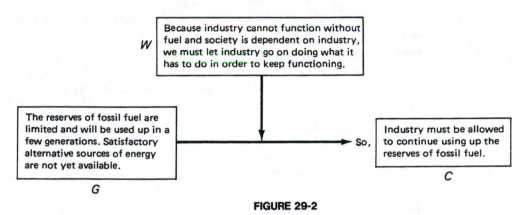

FIGURE 29-2

Notice how such a change of warrants may influence the layout of an argument (Figure 29-2).

Given only a small change of viewpoint, this argument can be reformulated (see Figure 29-3).

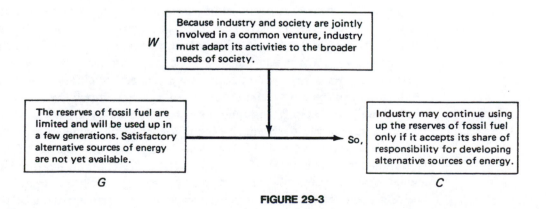

FIGURE 29-3

Although it may have many similarities to a business institution, a nonprofit organization or an arm of government cannot rest its decisions on precisely the same warrants. Just because of their very different definition, such organizations must rely on different warrants in justifying their decisions. Income may be less important than the services provided; cost may be less important than quality; during a period of underemployment, the goal may be to increase the number of people employed on a certain kind of task, in sharp contrast to a profit-oriented operation, which may rightly aim at accomplishing almost all of its production by machines alone.

Backing

While systems analysis and the result of computer modeling provide important sources of grounds for management claims, they are probably even more significant as providing backing for specific warrants. Decisions about the optimum characteristics of a business organization, its objectives and values, and its relations to other societal systems constitute the backing for the warrants that are operative in its month-to-month and day-to-day decisions about strategy and tactics. The definition of an organization as a purely profit-making enterprise validates only warrants concerned with increasing profits. Similarly, new ways of defining the roles of business and industry in society validate other kinds of management warrants. Definitions of efficiency, cost control, product effectiveness, personnel administration, and the like serve as backing for more specific warrants.

Modalities

Virtually all decisions, or claims, in business carry a price tag. Unless the organization is willing to expend some of its resources as a result of accepting a claim, that acceptance may be meaningless. Similarly an organization's willingness to go on record—to be publicly associated with a claim—is an important consideration. In complex organizations, a manager must take care to preserve status and credibility. To have been publicly associated with a claim that is soundly rejected, or that proves to be unsound when applied, is to risk one's position and future ("When a diplomat says No, he means Perhaps: when he says Perhaps, he means Yes"). So managers may differentiate clearly between their willingness to commend a claim privately and to support it publicly.

Finally, management modalities can be expressed by the use of ordinary words of reservation. A systems analyst will express his claims in quantitative terms, in degrees of probability. To present claims in this way confines to general terms one's responsibility for the content of the claim. Thus, the weather bureau tends to predict the weather in terms of "chances" by saying that there is a 60 percent chance of success; the forecaster leaves it to the manager to make a decision for or against that alternative. The manager, in turn, may express a choice using one or more of the common modal words of reservation, such as *probably* or *possibly*. (In the pragmatic world of business, however, regardless of the modality used at the time of decision, the ultimate test is success, and those associated with failures—no matter how well they protected themselves in words—may end up unemployed.)

Rebuttals

The ways in which rebuttals enter into management arguments again invites comparison with political reasoning. Management decisions function in social situations that almost always demand their acceptance by a number of different individuals or groups, and these social interactions are relied on to generate rebuttals from those holding different points of view. In any typical organization, every decision will be the concern of several people having relevant interests and experience; when claims are advanced by one person, those other interested persons are then expected to seek out weaknesses and express their reservations. Before a claim is finally accepted by a decision-making group, it will thus have to withstand the scrutiny of many people, including some who are selected precisely because of their ability to detect flaws in the reasoning involved. Such persons, furthermore, have powerful motives for finding weaknesses, if there are any, for once they have accepted a claim, they will become institutionally associated with it, and they themselves will succeed or fail as the decision itself succeeds or fails.

So questions will be put by critics to those who advance any claim, in the form of possible rebuttals, and counterclaims must be advanced to meet these rejections. As an outcome of this interaction, the final decision is expected to take all relevant rebuttals or objections into account.

AN EXAMPLE

One common type of management argument is that presented in the annual message to stockholders from the top management of a corporation. The following passage is taken from the annual report of Marriott Corporation in its report of March 7, 1983.

Mariott Corporation's strategy and attention to management fundamentals served it well in 1982, during one of the most difficult business environments in recent memory.

Real gross national product in the United States declined 1.8%—the largest drop in nearly 40 years. Unemployment reached 10.8%. Business travel declined and airlines lost over $600 million. International travel was disrupted by economic instability. Earnings of U.S. corporations, as measured by the Standard & Poor's 500 index, declined an estimated 14% during the year.

Despite these conditions, Mariott was able to increase net income by 10% and earnings per share by 8%, and to maintain its return on equity at the 20%

level. Over the last five years, the company's earnings per share have compounded at an annual rate of 27%, while return on equity has nearly doubled. We continue to believe Mariott can average 20% earning per share growth though the 1980's, increase dividends commensurately and maintain a return on equity of over 20%.

Let us examine by diagram the reasoning suggested in this portion of the Mariott report. One line of reasoning is shown in Figure 29–4.

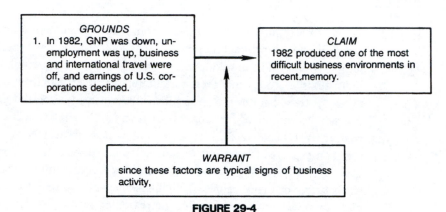

FIGURE 29-4

And, using the claim of this argument in order to reach the major claim, the reasoning proceeded as shown in Figure 29-5.

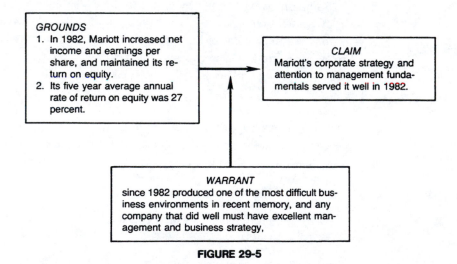

FIGURE 29-5

In another section of the Mariott report, the following argument is presented:

Our lodging business began in 1957 with one hotel in the Washington, D.C. area. Today, lodging is the company's fastest growing business, and represents more than half of Mariott's overall operating profits.

Now there are 118 Mariott hotels, resorts and franchised inns operating in 81 cities in the United States, Mexico, Central America, the Caribbean, Europe and the Middle East. These properties, which have been highly rated by the Mobil Travel Guide and other recognized authorities, make Marriott a leader among chain operators in the quality segment of the lodging industry.

The argument from authority proceeds as shown in Figure 29-6.

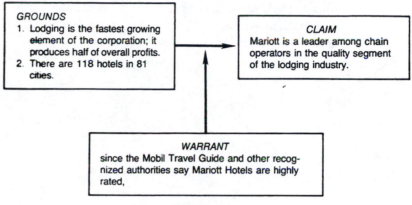

FIGURE 29-6

EXERCISES

Read the following excerpt from another annual report—Northwest Energy Company—for the 1982 year. Diagram the arguments presented and then discuss them critically.

The recessionary economy in 1982 and rising costs of natural gas have resulted in less demand for gas in the Company's market areas. Northwest Central Pipeline's gas costs under certain gas purchase contracts have continued to rise primarily as a result of price escalation provisions and take-or-pay obligations. As a result, the cost of gas now exceeds the cost of residual fuel oil and sales have been lost due to this price competition.

Since April 1982, Northwest Pipeline has reduced its cost of purchased gas by approximately $140 million or 42 cents per million Btu. This equates to a 10% reduction over the past year, primarily as a result of Northwest Pipeline increasing its proportion of lower cost domestic gas and reducing its takes of Canadian gas.

Despite this reduction, Northwest Pipeline has lost gas sales for industrial use because of the continuing high cost of Canadian natural gas included in its gas mix and the availability of residual fuel oil at lower prices.

1. What kinds of decisions are reported and justified in this report?
2. To what objectives were these decisions directed?
3. What outcomes of earlier decisions have affected, and been relevant to the justification of, current decisions?

4. How have these current decisions affected profitability?
5. What modalities figure in the report?
6. What production factors have been relevant to recent decisions?
7. What marketing factors have been relevant to recent decisions?
8. How is the equilibrium of the enterprise being maintained?

Magazines such as *Forbes* and *Business Week* contain arguments drawn from the field of management. Students should find further examples for discussion there, as well as in *The Wall Street Journal,* Sunday newspapers and other national weekly magazines.

30

Ethical reasoning

As a final illustration of our method of analysis, we shall look at the nature and roles of ethical reasoning. This is a large topic—too large for us to deal with comprehensively here. It has also, traditionally, been a contentious topic: people tend to hold their ethical views with force and warmth, and ethical disagreements generate something more than intellectual differences.

Furthermore, ethical issues themselves arise in many very different kinds of situations, so that it would be a laborious task to map out *all* the different sorts of occasions that exist for ethical discussion and *all* the varied procedures we employ for mediating and resolving those disputes in a reasonable manner. Still, much can be said to compare ethical reasoning with the other kinds of reasoning and argumentation that we have been looking at in the last four chapters.

THE OCCASIONS OF ETHICAL DEBATE

Under what circumstances do "ethical" questions arise—whether about a decision, an action, a policy, a piece of legislation, a personal life-style, or anything else? For a start, we may remark on *two* characteristic occasions for ethical argumentation. In both cases, ethical issues arise in ways that mark them off from the occasions for argumentation in the narrower, more professional areas of law, science, management, and the like.

To be specific:

1. All of the enterprises discussed in the preceding chapters are, to a greater or lesser extent, areas for "professional" expertise and analysis. In contrasting legal issues with problems of management or scientific issues, we had to begin by examining the *specialized* areas of concern and the *technical* problems that unite lawyers, scientists, or business managers within a shared professional enterprise.

Each of those enterprises provides clearly defined "roles" for those who are directly involved in it. Any particular participant has the task of performing—and reasoning—in his special capacity as, say, the defense attorney rather than the jury foreman or the chief accountant rather than the production manager. Correspondingly, each enterprise and role has its own characteristic procedures, forum of discussion, and criteria for resolving the specific problems that arise within the enterprise. The very fact that we can give a clear and simple account of the ways in which issues arise and are resolved within such professional forums of argumentation reflects the *specialization* of these different professional roles, tasks, problems, and procedures.

On the other hand, the very fact that the tasks and techniques of these professional enterprises are so narrow and specialized gives rise to a counterproblem also, for what happens when the demands of the different enterprises themselves conflict with one another? Any particular person may be—by profession—a research biochemist, a tax lawyer, or the manager of an electronics factory and so may be required to master the corresponding kinds of professional argumentation. But nobody is ever *only* a biochemist, a lawyer, or a factory manager. The research biochemist may also be a practicing physician, the tax lawyer may also be in politics. In addition to such professional role and avocations, either one of them is also likely to be a parent, a friend, a church member, and/or a voting citizen. And one characteristic point at which ethical issues arise is at *the margins between* different professional roles or at *the points where* professional and private lives meet and overlap.

2. Not only are the technical issues of these professional enterprises comparatively easy to define; in addition, the procedures for resolving such issues are usually self-contained and in many cases can lead fairly rapidly to definite results. More often than not, problems of science, law, management, or whatever can be investigated straightforwardly, and we can decide with some accuracy what can be said about the issue *from the corresponding professional standpoint.*

But no such standpoint is universal or all-embracing. So the answers we shall get to our questions will be subject to qualifying phrases:

"As far as science can tell us . . ."
"From the legal standpoint . . ."
"Financially speaking . . ."

and the like. As a result, the answers we get and give in all specialized arguments will be framed in terms of the specific standpoint whose relevance is presupposed. If the parties to any particular discussion turn out, after all, not to have shared a common professional standpoint, they will have been—in professional terms—at cross-purposes. The two parties simply did not understand one another at the outset, and the consequent discussion was fruitless.

By contrast, there are other occasions on which we are obliged to ask whether the specific, technical problems and solutions of our professional enterprises really have the power to give us the answers we need. It may be granted that they may generate solutions to our problems that are "technically correct," so far as they go. But is that the end of the matter? May not other considerations require us to *override*—and so *overrule*—these technically correct answers, however validly they were arrived at from the particular standpoint in question?

A three-year-old child is suffering from leukemia. The doctors declare that technically speaking, only a drastic course of chemotherapy has any chance of saving the child from a quick death. On the other hand, the success of the treatment is very uncertain, and the chemotherapy itself will have painful and disagreeable side effects.

The question may then be raised, "Is this technical answer the last word? May not the child's parents, acting on its behalf, elect a few short but reasonably happy months of life now, rather than subjecting the child to the sickness and misery induced by the chemotherapy, with only the slightest chance of its being cured?"

The sharply defined roles of enterprises like science, law, and medicine can thus be challenged in either of two ways: (1) on the one hand, the specialized questions we ask and the professional procedures we follow as scientists, attorneys, physicians, or whatever may conflict with one another; (2) alternatively, the technical concerns and procedures of those professional enterprises may have to be overridden in the light of broader and more general considerations having to do with the larger impact of those professional issues on human life:

1. A research biochemist who also happens to be a practicing physician finds the condition of one of his patients perplexing from a scientific standpoint. The procedures needed to investigate those puzzling features will be "scientific," whereas the procedures needed to treat the patient are "medical," and these two sets of procedures may not be compatible.

    How is he to balance off the claims of medicine and science in such a context? At what exact point will the research procedures necessary for a scientific investigation of this case encroach indefensibly on the demands of good medical treatment? In itself, that question is *neither* a medical *nor* a scientific question. The task of arbitrating between the demands of science and medicine, in such a case, is an ethical task.

Alternatively:

2. In the case of the leukemic infant, just what chance of success must the chemotherapy possess before the parents can justify subjecting the

child to all the associated miseries instead of reconciling themselves to its death and making its remaining months of life happy?

That decision, too, is not—strictly speaking—a medical decision alone. Rather, it is a decision whether or not to set aside the technical demands of professional medicine in favor of other, overriding ethical considerations.

So as contrasted with the arguments of more professional enterprises, *ethical* reasoning has at least two characteristic functions:

1. To arbitrate between the demands of different professional enterprises when these conflict.
2. To determine in what special conditions larger human concerns require us to override the technical arguments of our professional enterprises.

To go further, whereas the professional issues of science, law, and the rest are commonly faced and resolved within the correspondingly specialized professional forums—scientific meetings, law courts, and so on—*there is no special forum for ethical discussion*. To put the point more precisely, there are no situations within which ethical issues of some kind *cannot* be raised. Whatever situation we are in, our proceedings and procedures are always open to ethical questions and challenges. Whatever the immediate topic of discussion, it is always possible for our attention to be drawn either to outside, conflicting considerations that we had overlooked or else to matters of overiding human concern for which we had made no provision.

THE NATURE OF ETHICAL CONSIDERATIONS

Accordingly, at least two sets of considerations have a bearing on ethical problems and their resolution. In any group of people—any society, culture, or community—we find ethical discussions revolving around considerations of those two corresponding sets:

1. "Right" and "wrong": certain kinds of actions, proceedings, and/or consequences are recommended or ruled out as being *categorically* acceptable or unacceptable.
2. "Good" and "bad": certain kinds of actions, proceedings, and/or consequences are perceived as being desirable or preferable *to a greater or lesser degree*.

Where strong considerations of the first kind arise, they are normally seen as *overriding* other, more technical considerations as a matter of right or wrong. Where the matter at issue is, by contrast, one of weighing the respective priorities of different technical enterprises, ethical argumentation concerns itself rather with what is *preferable,* that is, with balancing different kinds of good and bad against one another. So the contrast that we have already noticed between ethics as an arbitrator between different specialized enterprises and ethics as placing definite limits on the authority of all technical considerations corresponds to the contrast between "matters of good and bad" and "matters of right and wrong." Negatively speaking, the question can always be raised of whether our actions are in accordance with—or in contravention of—right and wrong. Positively speaking, the question can always be raised whether—given the rival claims of, say, scientific research and medical treatment, or managerial efficiency and legal exactitude—we have appropriately balanced off the different kinds of good and bad open to us.

What sorts of considerations do these two headings embrace? The differences that exist between the ethical considerations carrying weight in different countries and communities are often exaggerated. In actual practice, a certain central body of ethical ideas, both about right and wrong and about good and bad, are recognized in just about all societies and communities. This ethical core is usually associated also, in each case, with other, marginal issues and considerations about which different societies, cultures, and groups display much less unanimity. For instance:

1. In just about all communities, considerations of *right and wrong* include as wrong the infliction of needless pain by one person on another. Meanwhile, every community also has its own particular, local ideas about right and wrong concerned with more marginal matters, such as clothing, smoking in public, and the precise modes of address, sexual expression, and so on.
2. In just about all communities, the scope of *good and bad,* likewise, include bodily health as good and illness as bad. Meanwhile, different communities have other rather different preferences about more marginal issues, for example, promoting baseball rather than cricket or valuing good housing over gourmet food rather than the other way around.

Right and wrong

In any society or community, one major class of ethical issues has to do with those considerations that make some decisions or courses of action intrinsically obligatory or objectionable. In any particular society, there is a clear and well-defined consensus about many of these actions and considerations. To that extent, there are correspondingly well-defined and accepted procedures for determining obligations or raising objections.

There will also be ways of recognizing ethical objections that are not meant to be universal, for example, personal scruples. Thus, given the overriding character of ethical issues, responsible individuals often perceive certain courses of action as obligatory or objectionable *for themselves,* even though others may be free not to see them in the same light.

This kind of liberty of conscience once again extends, in the first place, to marginal issues alone. We are free to have personal scruples about smoking during Lent, but we cannot suspend the ethical objections against murder to suit our own personal feelings.

So, when the question arises, "Would there be any objection to this course of action?" the general thrust of the question will normally be to inquire (1) whether any generally accepted considerations stand in its way, or (2) whether the parties concerned have more personal objections, based on private scruples and the like. For example, the statement "I ought not to join in your dinner tomorrow night" may be explained in either of two different ways:

> "I ought not to join in your dinner tomorrow night."
> "What's the objection?"
> "I have already promised to spend the evening working with a PTA study group."

(Here the implicit warrant is a *general* one: "It is wrong for anyone to break a promise.")

> "I ought not to join in your dinner tomorrow night."
> "What's the objection?"
> "As an orthodox Jew, I am bound by dietary rules that it is impracticable to maintain in gentile households."

(Here the implicit warrant is an *individual* one: "My personal religious commitments make it wrong for me to risk transgressing the orthodox Jewish dietary rules.")

Notice two things:

1. Ethical issues of right and wrong arise and are dealt with in a fairly simple *form.* Anyone who claims that some course of action is either obligatory or objectionable on ethical grounds can immediately be asked for his reasons. In most cases, he will have little difficulty in producing his grounds, that is, in saying *what it is* that makes the conduct in question either obligatory or unacceptable ("It was a promise," or "It would be against my dietary rules"). The pattern of argumentation employed is, thus, quite straightforward, as shown in Figure 30–1.
2. Nor are the *kinds* of things that different individuals and groups regard as right or wrong, obligatory or unacceptable, usually very problematic. In most cases, everybody is going to agree that murder

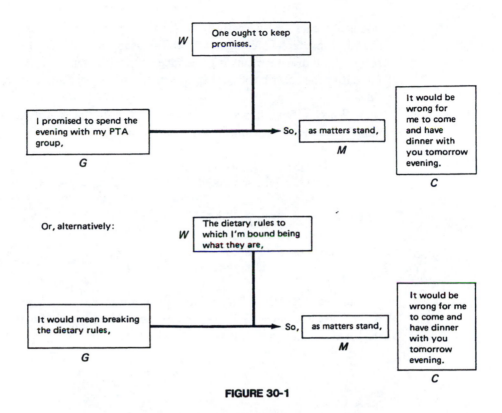

FIGURE 30-1

and inflicting needless pain are morally objectionable, whereas loyalty and keeping one's promises are morally admirable.

Serious differences of opinion arise in practice only over the contested question of just how broadly these terms apply and to what actual classes of situations:

> If a captured Palestinian commando tries to mislead or deceive his Israeli interrogators about the plans of the PLO, is that a case of loyalty (and so *obligatory*) or of lying (and so *objectionable*)?
>
> If a school principal inflicts corporal punishment on a persistently disobedient pupil, is that a piece of character building (and so *admirable*) or of cruelty (and so *unacceptable*)?
>
> If a sexually active unmarried woman who has missed a period arranges with her gynecologist for a routine D and C, does that exemplify normal health care (and so *innocent*) or possibly murdering an unborn child (and so *wicked*)?

How we shall finally *judge* any particular action from the ethical standpoint is, therefore, closely bound up with how we agree to *describe* that action. Once the Palestinian commando's actions are described as "loyally keeping a secret" or as "lying," one has already gone nine tenths of the way toward approving or disapproving them. Similarly, once a gynecological procedure is described as "routine health care" or alternatively as "denying an embryo's right to life," one has already—in effect—prejudged the ethical issues involved. So if the *substance* of these ethical disagreements is to be faced explicitly, some way must be found of presenting the issues involved that does justice to the considerations raised on both sides.

We may, for instance, pay closer attention to the *modalities and rebuttals* implicit in any such argument. Where we just said

> "lying" (and so objectionable), or
> "health care" (and so innocent),

we could perhaps have said, more exactly,

> "lying" (and so *presumably* objectionable), or
> "health care" (and so *presumably* innocent).

In each case, the force of the ethical claim advanced on the one hand has to be weighed against the possibility of contrary considerations that may serve to *rebut* the original claim (see Figures 30–2 and 30–3).

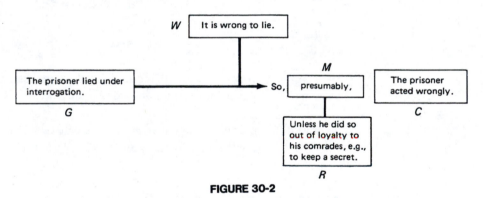

FIGURE 30-2

In the practical conduct of the ethical life, it is not enough for us to know what *particular considerations* count for or against any particular kind of action. (There is little ground for disagreement about lying and loyalty, health care and murder, so long as those terms apply without conflict or ambiguity.) In addition, we must share some clear understanding about the circumstances and manner in which such considerations can be weighed against one another in cases where they come into conflict.

Any study of actual ethical reasoning, in fact, quickly brings to light not merely the principles appealed to by the people concerned but also the general understandings governing their decisions in case of *conflict of obligation:*

1. In the ethics of war, there has been a widespread understanding that prisoners who mislead interrogators about military secrets are display-

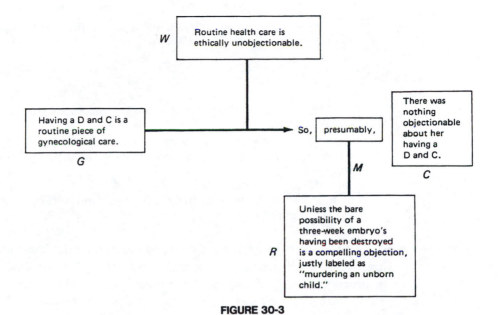

FIGURE 30-3

ing loyalty rather than lying. If there are particular difficulties in the case of Palestinian commandos, that is because the Arabs and the Israelis disagree about their status, that is, whether they are genuine soldiers and so prisoners of war when captured, or rather criminal terrorists lacking the recognized privileges of war prisoners.

2. Similarly, as the U.S. Supreme Court spelled out in *Roe v. Wade,* there has been a longstanding traditional understanding about the termination of pregnancy, namely, that gynecological procedures that displace a newly implanted embryo during the first three months of pregnancy are legitimate health-care procedures, whereas during the final trimester—after quickening—the fetus should not be aborted without grave cause.

   If first-trimester abortions have become a topic of dispute today, that is because the traditional understanding has been challenged, and the Right to Life Movement is demanding the same consideration for the embryo throughout the entire pregnancy as was traditionally reserved for the final trimester.

The point can be restated in terms of initial presumptions and burden of proof. The general understandings involved in balancing off the conflicting claims of loyalty and lying—or of health care and possible murder—represent also general understandings about where the burden of proof lies from the ethical point of view:

> "If he's a prisoner of war, you can't very well complain of his misleading you about his comrades' secrets."
>
> "But he isn't really a prisoner of war; he's just a common criminal and a terrorist."

> "That's just what is in dispute, and so is what you have to *prove* before you can fairly condemn him as a liar."

Similarly:

> "Since a D and C is a perfectly routine gynecological procedure, you really cannot object to it."
> "But if a woman chooses to have an unnecessary D and C, merely to terminate a possible pregnancy, that's tantamount to killing her unborn child, and so it is murder."
> "That's just what is not generally agreed, and so is what you have to *demonstrate,* because the fetus has traditionally been considered an unborn child only after quickening."

Accordingly, over matters of right and wrong, the current patterns of ethical argumentation are simple and straightforward unless there are serious disagreements about conflicts of obligation and the burden of proof. Conversely these matters become *essentially contested* just at the point where those general understandings are challenged. Hence questions like

> Are Palestinian commandos "soldiers" or "terrorists"?
> At what point does an embryo become an "unborn child"?

are just as much *ethical and legal* questions as they are *factual* questions. In either case, the decision whether to concede or deny the label *prisoners of war* to captured commandos—or the label *unborn children* to newly implanted embryos—is by no means a straightforward factual determination. Rather, it can be rationally justified only if we weigh the ethical and legal demands on both sides: those of civil order against those of humane interrogation, or those of a woman's autonomy against the supposed rights of a three- or four-week embryo.

Good and bad

Alongside these questions about what courses of action are—in themselves—*obligatory* or *objectionable,* there is the other set of ethical questions about the effects of consequences of decisions and actions, specifically, whether those effects are *desirable* or *regrettable.* Issues of this second kind are commonly discussed as matters of good and bad rather than of right and wrong.

Here again, of course, people are not unanimous:

> Was the resignation of President Nixon "a good thing"? There were those who cheered this event, but there were also others who deplored it, and others again who considered it, on balance, a very marginal matter.

If there is disagreement in such a case, it springs largely from the complexity of the events involved. Within the whole range of considerations arising from those events, different people are inclined to pick on different factors and to balance off the good against the bad in different ways.

Although this kind of disagreement is especially apt to arise about cases on which complex and multiple considerations can be brought to bear, it can arise in simpler cases, too. For instance:

> Is it "a good thing" to become an enthusiastic supporter of some sports team, so that you end by devoting part of every weekend to following their matches? Evidently many people regard being a loyal follower of the Raiders as a very fine thing, whereas some others would decry the whole preoccupation with a particular sports team as a childish waste of time.

In either case disagreements about good and bad, as with right and wrong, chiefly affect peripheral issues. About a certain central core of topics, there is much less disagreement, much more consensus. For example although there may not be general agreement about good or bad ways of spending Saturday afternoons, there is much less room for disagreement about fundamental issues such as health and disease. Who seriously doubts, for instance, that it is bad to have one's leg broken in an automobile accident and good to find a job that exercises one's abilities and interests to the full?

Likewise, the forms of ethical argumentation employed in discussions of *good and bad* are normally as straightforward as those employed in discussions of *right and wrong*. Suppose, for instance, that somebody says

> "It's a great life. I'm in good physical shape, I've got an interesting job, and I can watch the Redskins on television every weekend."

There is nothing problematic about the relationship between the first sentence ("It's a great life") and those that follow it. The speaker is simply drawing attention to the things that spell out the content of his initial declaration. It would be almost pedantic, indeed, to insist on presenting the implicit pattern of argumentation in detail, as in Figure 30–4.

Here, too, it is of course understood that we all have personal preferences, as well as beliefs about what is desirable for everybody. Just as one may acknowl-

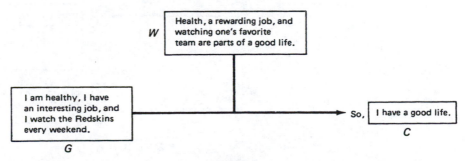

FIGURE 30-4

edge personal scruples about eating with gentiles because of one's religious affiliation, so one may develop a personal vision of "the good life" that includes being a committed Redskins supporter. We may thus commiserate with *anybody whatever* about breaking a leg or losing a job, but we can commiserate with someone about the latest Redskins defeat only if we know that he is a Redskins supporter. Conversely, however, the fact that each of us constructs "a good life" *in part* on the basis of personal tastes and preferences in no way implies that *all* matters of good and ill are personal and arbitrary. To say to a friend, "That's a great broken leg, man!" is clearly understood as a piece of grisly humor.

Accordingly, whereas ethical discussions about good and bad may vary *in substance* from individual to individual and from community to community, such discussions do nevertheless share a general *pattern or procedure*. Difficulties and disagreements arise where issues become problematic, where there are conflicting "goods" or "bads" between which a balance must be struck:

> Jack gets great satisfaction out of his work, and that's good. On the other hand, his work takes a lot out of him and he doesn't get enough exercise to stay healthy, which is a pity.
>
> The establishment of a federal system was of great benefit to the newly independent colonies because it helped them to consolidate their autonomy. At the same time, it worked against the interests of many Americans by frustrating the moves toward more effective democracy pioneered by such leaders as Samuel Adams during the Revolutionary period.

In social and political changes especially, one man's meat is always apt to be another man's poison. Yet even for individuals, every good is apt to involve a corresponding price. So in discussions of good and bad, we often end with the same sort of balancing argument—involving initial presumptions and burden of proof—that we found in the case of arguments about right and wrong (see Figure 30–5).

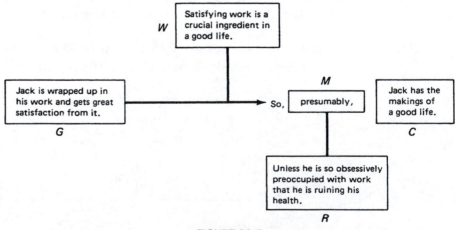

FIGURE 30-5

In studying the actual *practice* of ethical debate and decision, we need to consider not only the separate items that people find good (physical health, satisfying work, rewarding leisure, and so on) but also the manner in which they balance off the claims (or values) of these different items, when they conflict.

Notice, for instance, the implications of the remark, "Jack is a *workaholic*." The newly coined term *workaholic* makes a rhetorical point about *good and bad*, namely, that not *all* hard work is equally desirable. In this respect, the term operates in the same way as calling Palestinian commandos *soldiers* or newly implanted zygotes *babies*—words that make similar rhetorical points about *right and wrong*. Only recently was it recognized explicitly that people can become "addicted" to work and so damage their physical and psychological health. In part, no doubt, this change of attitude has sprung from a better understanding of the psychodynamics of addiction. But as always, the points at issue in such essentially contested cases are never *merely* "factual" ones. In accepting the term *workaholic* as a legitimate basis of criticism, we are also committed to rethinking our *preferences:*

> "What good does it do, in the long run, if a rising industrial manager has the short-term satisfaction of working a seventy-five-hour week *now,* only to give himself a heart attack at the age of forty-five?"

Justice and equity

Furthermore ethical discussions of good and bad require us to pay attention to the question, "*Whose* good are we talking about?" Ethics is concerned not only with considerations of *value* (e.g., with balancing the claims of good health and satisfying work) but also with considerations of *justice* (e.g., with balancing the health, education, and welfare of one group or individual against the health, education, and welfare of other groups or individuals). One terrain on which ethical issues become strongly contested is over the problem of how we are to decide what exactly "justice" and "equity" properly demand:

The debate begins in the nursery, where children are much concerned with questions of equity—"Mummy, it's not fair!" So the primary forum for the discussion of justice is the *family*. But it goes on throughout life, wherever the scarcity of necessary resources and services puts the interests of different people in conflict with one another.

This is especially so in the area of *social* justice, where ethical and political arguments most strongly overlap. To what precise extent is "robbing the rich to pay the poor" *a good thing?* To what precise extent, that is, may limits be placed on the self-enriching activities of some in order to divert resources toward others who are not wholly self-supporting?

The basic difficulty in promoting the end of social justice by the use of political means springs from the difficulty of treating an entire society as the ethical counterpart of a single family. Patterns of ethical argumentation that operate easily and unambiguously within small enough groups inevitably give rise to problems when extended to a whole state or nation. It is one thing to divide up a cake fairly among the members of a family. But on the political level, how do we determine—and measure—the size of the national "cake"? And what is the "just" way of dividing it up? (Should we begin by making sure that everybody has a decent minimum share and then leave the rest for auction or free competition? Or should we simply go for equal shares all round?) These questions are the beginning of a much longer argument than we have space for here. This is the argument associated with such ethical and political slogans as:

— To each according to his need.
— To each according to his deserts.
— To each according to his contributions.
— To each according to his talents.
— To each a fair opportunity to gain his own share.

THE ELEMENTS OF ETHICAL ARGUMENTS

"I really oughtn't to tell him that story."

"What's the objection?"

"It would be deceitful."

"You ought to give him back his wheelchair."

"What's the obligation?"

"You only borrowed it, and besides, he'll be immobilized without it."

"I really should not attend that dinner."

"Why not?"

"I can't be sure it will be kosher."

"You should think more seriously about going back to school."

"What do you have in mind?"

"Without proper professional training, you won't be able to make the most of your capacities."

"We really ought to make more effort to recruit women executives."

"Why?"

"Up to now, our hiring practices have been quite unfair, not to say sexist.

> In addition, we risk having an antidis-
> crimination suit slapped on us."

> "The way the judge ran that trial
> was a disgrace."
> "What makes you say that?"
> "He let the prosecution get away
> with murder. They played fast and loose
> with the evidence, muddled the jury with
> talk about 'conspiracy,' and intimidated
> the witnesses."

When ethical issues are introduced into the middle of a conversation about other issues, they have the effect of shifting discussion away from practical or professional matters onto another plane. When this happens, we often find the adverb *really* used to enforce this change of subject. In several of our initial examples here, for instance, what is in debate is not the *general* ethical issue—whether or no we ought to return borrowed items, develop our capacities to the full, or whatever. Rather, it is the question of whether the present *particular* situation falls within the scope of those rules or maxims. For instance:

> "I really oughtn't to tell him that story."
> "What's the objection?"
> "It would be deceitful."
> "Why worry about that? Who do you think he is, anyway? All you're required to tell an enemy interrogator is your name, rank, and number. Aside from that, you should conceal anything you can from him—that's simple loyalty. Anyway, how can you deceive a man who isn't *expecting* you to tell him the truth?"

In this case, the ethical discussion is a serious one just because the demands of truthfulness and loyalty pull in different directions. So a question is raised of whether misleading an enemy interrogator does or does not fall within the scope of the term *deceit*.

Grounds and warrants

In ethical argumentation, the interdependence of grounds and warrants is particularly apparent. The facts worth mentioning in support of any claim are those—and only those—that are relevant to the ethical maxim being invoked. Thus we cite as grounds those specific features of any situation that are seen as imposing an obligation on us. But how do we recognize and select such features? We do so always with an eye to some specific warrant. We pick out things that are apparently deceitful (or unfair, or irreligious, or whatever) precisely *because* truthfulness, fairness, piety, and the rest involve familiar ethical warrants.

In actual practice, indeed, the connection between grounds and warrants in ethical arguments is so close that we rarely trouble to spell them both out. Each implies the other. Thus, instead of saying, "I really oughtn't to tell him that story; it would be deceitful," I might have said, "I really oughtn't to tell him that story; it is wrong to be deceitful." In the first case, the claim, *C*, is apparently supported by grounds (*G*) alone and in the second case, by a warrant (*W*) alone (see Figure 30–6). Strictly speaking, of course, the same full argument is relied on in either case (see Figure 30–7). But it would be so pedantic to insist in such a case on

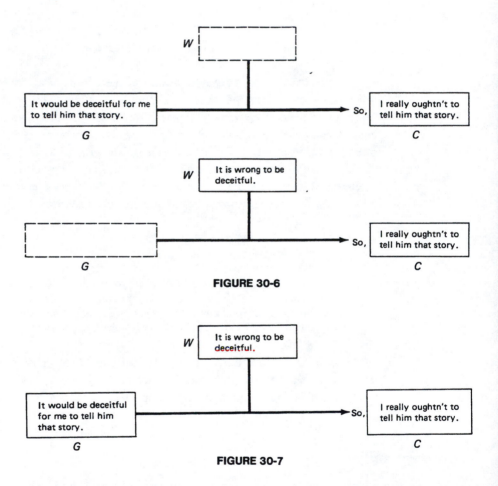

FIGURE 30-6

FIGURE 30-7

separating questions about the *relevance* of the grounds from questions about the *applicability* of the corresponding warrants, that we rarely have occasion to distinguish between them.

For instance, the question "Is it deceitful for a prisoner of war to mislead an enemy interrogator?" amounts in practice to the same as the question "Does the maxim 'It is wrong to be deceitful' apply to the interrogation of a prisoner of war by an enemy intelligence officer?" In such a case, deciding whether the behavior in dispute constitutes deceit at all—whether the matter of deceit is relevant as grounds at all—also settles the question of whether this situation falls within the scope of the corresponding warrant.

If we can jointly agree on a *description* of the situation in dispute, the ethical significance of that description will normally be apparent without more ado. Compare our prisoner-of-war example with the following examples.

> In the course of a routine physical examination, a physician detects in a patient a slight swelling that might conceivably be an early sign of cancer, and she persuades the patient to undergo additional laboratory tests but carefully avoids explaining the true purpose of those tests.
>
> A child's parents organize a surprise birthday party and conceal their plans by saying things to the child suggesting that they have something quite different in mind.

Are we to describe the behavior either of the physician or of the parents as "deceitful"?

There are two alternative ways of answering that question. On the one hand, we can say:

> "It was a bit deceitful, I admit, but it was an innocent kind of deceit—a white lie, if you will."

That is to say, we can concede the negatively toned description of the case and reserve our excuses for the rebuttal stage. Alternatively we can say:

> "You can't call that deceit. Until the additional pathology tests were done, it was pointless to worry him." Or, "Letting him guess what we were planning would have spoiled the surprise."

That is, we can narrow both the term *deceit* and the maxim "It is wrong to be deceitful" to cover only cases in which someone is given misleading information *to his detriment*. Mentioning the possibility of cancer prematurely or giving away the birthday plans would "do no good"—so the physician or the parents can defend their actions as designed to protect the interest of their "wards." Thus, once again, the ethical significance of the action in question is already decided in the acceptance or rejection of the use of the term *deceit* for describing those actions.

Backing

The difficulties involved in distinguishing ethical grounds from ethical warrants carry over to the discussion of ethical backing. In the course of everyday argumentation, we commonly take the standard ethical maxims as *not in dispute* and so as needing no explicit backing. In general, how can one call in question that health is desirable or sickness regrettable; that we are subject to the obligations of truth, loyalty, and human consideration; or that deceitfulness, injustice, and cruelty are open to objection?

Calling in question the backing for our ethical principles, as a result, has the effect of changing the subject yet again. It moves the issues in debate away from the practical level and onto a more philosophical one. For instance:

> "In a society that tolerates so much commercial dishonesty, why should the rest of us feel so strongly about being honest as individuals?"
>
> "Tell me about this pork and shellfish, meat and milk products business. What does *kosher* really signify today?"
>
> "What's all this hang-up about pain? I don't myself find a little healthy pain all that insupportable. So why ought I to worry about hurting other people?"
>
> "So far as I can see, it was never regarded as unfair in earlier times for men and women to play different parts in society, so why must we start worrying about hiring practices or feeling ashamed about paying attention to sexual differences?"

Such questions as these are normally used to blunt the original argument, not to challenge it:

> "Honesty is still a virtue, but does it still have all its old weight?"
>
> "Equity is fine in general terms, but does it really oblige us to pursue absolute equality of opportunity between the sexes?"
>
> "What point does a devout Jew see nowadays in the continuation of the kosher code?"

These are debating issues rather than practical objections. Few would question in practice the *general* soundness of the familiar ethical maxims about pain, honesty, equity, and the like, any more than the soundness of well-established laws of nature in science, statutes and precedents in law, or rules of investment strategy in business. Taking these questions seriously, therefore, means pursuing them either in rhetorical or in philosophical terms.

The overall *kinds* of actions covered by such familiar maxims as these may be justified philosophically, as generally obligatory or generally objectionable, in a variety of different respects:

— Because they are acknowledged by general consensus.
— Because their consequences would be found generally desirable or unacceptable.
— Because the chosen "way of life" of a particular community or group requires them to be regarded in this way.

But in pursuing these questions about "backing" further, we shall discover not so much the underlying set of reasons that *anyone* should accept the maxims as sound warrants as the manner in which *particular individuals* perceive them as fitting in with their own conceptions of a good and admirable life:

> "Simple honesty is, for me, the basis of all human trust: there is no reason that we should copy the vices of the commercial advertisers in our everyday personal affairs."
>
> "Respecting the kosher rules is, for me, an essential part of the Jewish tradition, something that, as a Jew, I accept as a basic expression of my personal faith."
>
> "It's not the pain as such that I worry about; it's the refusal to let others decide for themselves just how much pain they want to put up with on their own account."
>
> "If we don't respect the demands of equity between the two natural halves of the human race, I don't see how we can expect equity to be taken seriously where the interests of smaller groups are affected."

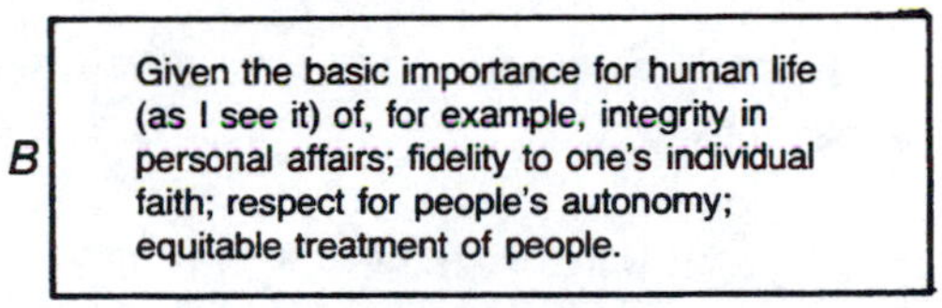

B
Given the basic importance for human life (as I see it) of, for example, integrity in personal affairs; fidelity to one's individual faith; respect for people's autonomy; equitable treatment of people.

FIGURE 30-8

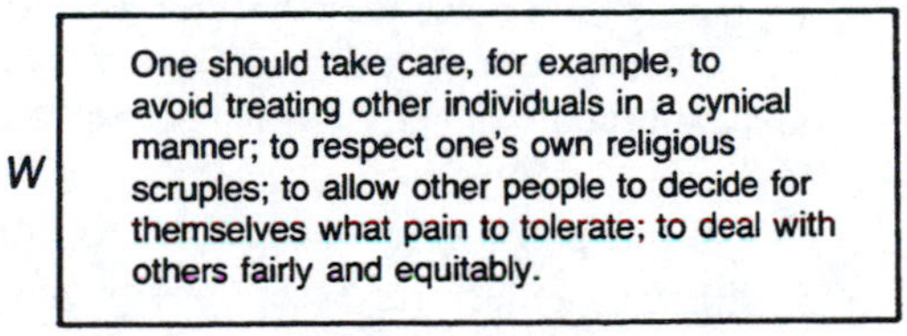

W
One should take care, for example, to avoid treating other individuals in a cynical manner; to respect one's own religious scruples; to allow other people to decide for themselves what pain to tolerate; to deal with others fairly and equitably.

FIGURE 30-9

The effect of such statements is, in each case, to produce as *backing* a general affirmation of the form seen in Figure 30–8. Such an affirmation indicates the ethical significance to be attached to the corresponding maxims, or *warrants* (Figure 30–9). And these maxims can, in turn, be cited to explain the relevance of particular factual descriptions as *grounds* for supporting the corresponding *claims*. (See Figure 30–10.)

It would be a cynical and commercial way of treating her.
It would not be kosher.
It would be a wanton disrespect of his right to choose for himself.
It would be thoroughly inequitable.
G
So, you should not act in that way.
C

FIGURE 30-10

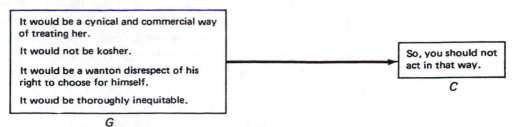

Modals and rebuttals

Whereas warrants and backing play a rather small part in ethical argumentation by comparison with *grounds*, this is much less true of *modals* and *rebuttals*. Very few ethical considerations can be put forward with any kind of absoluteness. Instead, they are almost always liable to excuses and exceptions and are subject to challenge on that account:

> "It would be deceitful to tell him that story, so *presumably* I ought not to tell him that story."
> "It would be discriminatory to retain our earlier hiring policies, so *apparently* we ought to change those policies."
> "I can't be sure that dinner will be kosher, so *unless it's unavoidable*, I ought not to attend it."

In such cases, we often recognize the need for qualifications or special dispensations:

> "It would do no good to have him worry about cancer before the tests have even been done, *so* no real question of deceit arises at this stage."
> "In this particular community, the employment opportunities for black male youths are even worse than those for women, *so* it's too soon to cry sexism."
> "Given the political importance of the dinner, you can be forgiven for putting in an appearance, *even if* it means the risking of a dietary offense."

We might prefer it if we could respect most of our ethical rules *absolutely,* that is, without the need for exceptions or qualifications. But life does not always allow us that choice. People repeatedly find themselves facing situations in which *two* such rules point in opposite directions—in which they can avoid giving serious pain to a friend, say, only at the price of dishonesty. The goal of ethical reasoning is, accordingly, to devise courses of action that, so far as is possible, tread the delicate line between the demands of rival but incompatible maxims—doing justice to the underlying spirit that animates both maxims without too gravely contravening either of them.

This being the case, it is often possible to present the same ethical dilemma in alternative ways, which emphasize different aspects of the situation as shown, for example, in Figures 30–11 and 30–12. The issues to be balanced against one another in practice are thus capable of being presented either in the form of the question, "Would failure to attend the dinner be so grave a breach of loyalty as to outweigh the dietary risks?" or, alternatively, in the form of the question, "Would the risk to my dietary scruples be so intolerable as to outweigh all the claims of party loyalty?" Whichever way the problem is posed, however, the issue is evidently the same: How is one to tread the line between the contrary claims of loyalty and scruple? How is one to order the *priorities* of different kinds of claims and obligations?

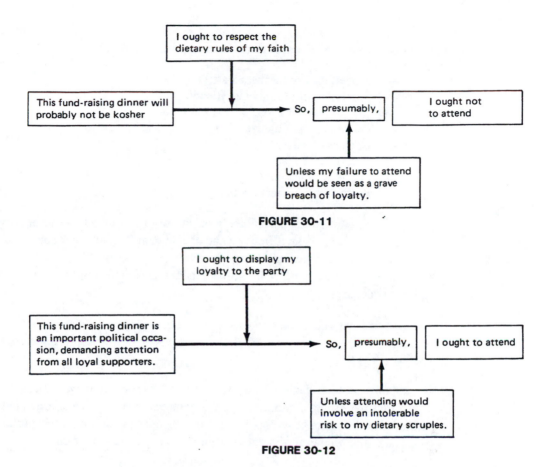

FIGURE 30-11

FIGURE 30-12

Different people will, in practice, tend to deal with such marginal decisions in different ways. One person will lean in the direction of rigid conformity to the demands of scruple, another in the direction of respect for the demands of loyalty. Much of our vocabulary for describing people's personalities and characters, in fact, reflects such tendencies—this man is fiercely orthodox, that one is loyal to a fault, a third is highly conscientious or, maybe, none too scrupulous.

THE UBIQUITY OF ETHICS

One last feature of ethics and ethical argumentation is worth remarking on in conclusion. Ethical issues, as we have noted, arise and are dealt with in situations of all kinds. There are no specific *forums* for ethical discussion, as there are for law and science. Nor are there any clear restrictions on the *classes of people* qualified to discuss and present arguments about ethical issues. (True, some religious denominations reserve the right to speak with authority about matters of morals to ordained priests or ministers, but this restriction only covers ethical discussions *within* the denomination in question, and it has no general applicability.)

Nor, for that matter, are there any formal limitations on the *topics* for ethical discussion. Ethical issues can arise equally well in relation to:

— Professional or business matters.
— Relations with family and friends.
— Past or future actions.
— Personality and motives.
— Choices of career.
— Social legislation.
— Public administration.
— Personal self-understanding.

In speaking about ethics, indeed, the problem is not so much to avoid defining it too narrowly as to prevent it from expanding and engulfing all other fields of practical reasoning and argumentation.

Taking the term *ethics* in a broad enough sense, we might be tempted to take the questions

— What ought one to do and to avoid doing?
— What good reasons are there to act or to avoid acting in any particular way?

as defining the central concerns of ethics. But such a definition would leave us no way of distinguishing ethical issues and arguments from issues and arguments of other kinds. For throughout this entire book, the central questions facing us in the discussion and appraisal of practical arguments have the same form:

— What claims ought one to accept or to avoid accepting?
— What good reasons are there to accept or to avoid accepting any particular claim?

Therefore, we must find some further way of marking off the narrower class of *specifically ethical issues and arguments* from all those issues and arguments that arise in science, law, art, management, and the like.

Drawing these further distinctions does not mean *exempting* professional conduct in such rational enterprises from ethical scrutiny. On the contrary, the conscientious performance of professional tasks and duties—as a physician, a judge, a locomotive engineer, a store manager, or whatever—can itself be regarded as a basic kind of ethical obligation. Correspondingly, any individual who occupies a position of responsibility within one of our rational enterprises—

— the editor of a scientific journal,
— a prosecuting attorney,
— a teacher in art college,
— a professional accountant

—is open to ethical criticism in the event of *failure to perform* those professional duties to some minimum standard. A careless physician, a sloppy editor, a gossiping priest, a bribed policeman, or a lazy music teacher—people who fall down on their professional tasks—not only show themselves incompetent; they should also be ashamed of their performance. Their failures are not only *professional* failures; they are also *ethical* failures.

Even so, it is often helpful to mark off the specific virtues and obligations associated with professional status and to distinguish them from ethical virtues and obligations. What is admirable or regrettable about the manner in which a physician (or a judge, or an editor, or whatever) carries out professional tasks is not the detailed character of those actions. There is nothing ethically good about prescribing tetracycline rather than penicillin for an upper respiratory infection. What is *specifically* admirable or regrettable is the physician's attitude of mind, which results in his paying—or failing to pay—adequate attention to each patient's individual peculiarities, for example, his allergy to penicillin. What is *ethically* demanded of any professional, as a result, is that he should perform in a conscientious manner *whatever professional tasks* fall to his lot in his capacity as physician, judge, editor, or the like.

So we may end this chapter as we began it. In its broader sense, the field of ethics is large enough to embrace all our rational enterprises within its scope. But in a more narrowly defined sense, the actual conduct of those enterprises gives rise to problems of ethics only in a limited range of situations. We may have to arbitrate between the professional claims of different rational enterprises. Or we may have to override professional considerations in the interests of other, broader human considerations. (1) In the former kind of case, the ethical issues to be dealt with commonly have to do with comparing the *consequences* of going in one direction or the other—taking the technologically more effective route rather than the politically acceptable one, or the other way about.

One term increasingly used in this context is *impact*. In balancing off the different *kinds* of consequences that will flow from one social decision or another, we are obliged to pay better attention to "economic impact," "environmental impact," "social impact," and all the rest. If these requirements are pressed strongly and broadly enough, the task of balancing off economics and technology, environmental protection and human rights can be carried through only with the help of some agreed standards for deciding on priorities, that is, for deciding what human claims should carry weight over others (e.g., just how the preservation of traditional Indian hunting grounds weighs in a scale against providing water supplies for the metropolis across the mountains).

(2) In the second kind of case, the ethical issues to be dealt with arise on a more personal level. They have to do with the conduct of individual, professional practitioners. It is in this second kind of context that terms such as *professional ethics* and *business ethics* are most typically encountered. They refer to the specific demands placed on practitioners in any profession as a result of their general

obligation to act conscientiously and with consideration for the interests both of their clients and of those others who are affected by their professional actions.

Whether we concern ourselves with individual or personal ethics on the one hand, or with collective or professional ethics on the other, one thing at least is clear. Either way, we can set out the *considerations* (i.e., the grounds, warrants, rebuttals, and so on) that are relevant to any *ethical* judgment or decision in a form that is open to public criticism—as a piece of practical argumentation— quite as straightforwardly and explicitly as we can with a piece of scientific or legal argumentation. Certain kinds of ethical decisions may be, perhaps, matters of individual choice or personal commitment, notably, those of religious affiliation and scruple; but that fact need not remove the associated arguments from the sphere of public criticism. Speaking as a Protestant, for instance, I may perfectly well draw the attention of a friend to ethical considerations that apply to his personal conduct rather than to mine, for example; "As a Catholic Traditionalist, you probably ought to pass up the club dinner next Friday. It will be at the steakhouse, and they don't have any fish on their menu." Thus, the *personal* character of some ethical attitudes and decisions does not make them any less open to *rational discussion and criticism*.

This point is worth bearing in mind when you hear people talking about the so-called "subjectivity" of ethical issues. No doubt ethics is concerned in part with the ways in which we *feel about* things and with our *personal reactions* to choices and actions and, for that reason, people often jump to the conclusion that ethical views are outside the scope of "rationality." But this conclusion simply does not follow, for the questions can always be raised: "Were our feelings about this action *well placed* and *appropriate*? Was our reaction *justifiable*?" And once these questions have been stated, the whole machinery of rational criticism and practical argumentation can immediately be called into play all over again.

AN EXAMPLE

Consider, for instance, the following case, as presented in a recent issue of the *Hastings Center Report* (Harvey Kushner, Daniel Callahan, Eric J. Cassell, and Robert M. Veatch, "The Homosexual Husband and Physician Confidentiality," *Hastings Center Report*, April 1977, pp. 15–17):

Case 251

David, the oldest of three children, was the son of a well-to-do manufacturer. David's father valued physical prowess and athletic accomplishments, areas in which David showed little interest. When David was twelve or thirteen years old, conflicts with his father resulted in almost nightly arguments. It was evident that David's father had become concerned about David's mannerisms and considered them to be effeminate.

David's schoolwork deteriorated considerably and he became withdrawn. His father decided to send him to a military school, but he remained there for only six months. By this time, David had told his parents that he was a homosexual, had engaged in, and was engaging in homosexual practices. He came home and completed his high school studies, but did not go on to college and continued to live at home.

He was treated for gonorrhea, asthma, and infectious hepatitis. At the age of twenty-one, to gain exemption from the draft, his physician attested to the fact that he was a homosexual.

Five years later, Joan visited her family physician for a premarital serological exam. The physician was the same physician who had treated David. She was twenty-four years old and had been under this physician's care since the age of fourteen. A close and warm relationship had developed between the physician and Joan's family, and it was normal, then, for the physician to ask about her fiancé. When he did, he learned that she was about to marry David. She had known him only briefly, but well enough, she felt, to be certain about her choice. Nothing more was said at the time.

David and Joan were married shortly thereafter and lived together for a period of six months. The marriage was annulled on the basis of nonconsummation. David told Joan that he was homosexually oriented, and she learned as well that not only did they share a physician but also that the physician was aware of David's homosexuality. She subsequently suffered a depression as a result of this experience and was angry that her physician had remained silent about David. She felt that she could have been spared this horrible episode in her life—that it was her physician's duty to inform her. His failure to do so was an act of negligence resulting in deep emotional scars.

To whom did the physician owe primary allegiance? Do the interests of one patient prevail over the requirements of confidentiality surrounding another's case?

—Harvey Kushner

by Daniel Callahan

Why is there a general rule of confidentiality? That seems to be the first question to ask before looking at the details of a case like this. I believe the rule has three purposes. The first is to establish a context that will elicit from the patient maximum disclosure of the patient's condition, a major requirement for effective diagnosis. The second is to recognize, in a working way, that patient's lives are not disconnected from their bodies, that both the causes and cures of illness have a personal and social context, and that effective diagnosis and therapy require going beyond the boundaries of the merely physical. The third purpose is the general one of maximizing patient trust and thus strengthening the bond between physician and patient. Seen in this way, the rule of confidentiality is readily justifiable.

But should it be a flat rule, admitting of no exceptions? Clearly, our society thinks not, for it has established a number of circumstances which require physicians to report their patient's condition to public authorities, e.g., dangerous communicable diseases and gunshot wounds. These are reasonable exceptions, which simply recognize that some otherwise private conditions have significant public implications. It is not just the welfare of one patient which is at stake in those situation, but the welfare of other individuals as well.

Most significantly, the conditions under which confidentiality must be violated are matters of public law and knowledge. Hence, disclosures will not represent any arbitrary imposition or expression of the physician's personal values. They are public rules, binding upon all, and simply because of that fact they are not taken to endanger the general goal of patient-physician trust (and there is no evidence they have done so).

In the case before us, there are no mandated social rules for making an exception. And yet clearly the circumstance was one in which not just the welfare of one person (David) was at stake, but also that of another (Joan). Implicitly at least, those conditions were present which in other—but publicly specified—circumstances, the welfare of one individual is allowed to be overridden by consideration for the welfare of others. So in one sense it might be said that the physician could have broken confidentiality and done so on the grounds of a non-arbitrary and otherwise justifiable principle.

Yet I would argue that the critical issue in this case is not that the physician could have brought an otherwise legitimate moral principle to bear, but that, in this particular type of case, there is no known *public* moral rule about the breaking of confidence. David would have had no complaint had he appeared with a gunshot wound; that is a well-known circumstance for violating confidentiality. No such reasoning applies in the case of homosexuality, and David could well have felt that the physician was inventing his own set of moral rules and imposing them on him.

Are we then to conclude that the rule of confidentiality should have been honored in this circumstance? I am afraid so, however disturbing the implications of honoring it were for Joan's future life. If there is to be a rule of confidentiality, then it must be a clear and flat rule, not admitting of ambiguity and unclear exceptions, much less the devising of personal and idiosyncratic interpretations. David's trust would have been betrayed, the physician would have been imposing his own private meaning on the moral rule and we the public, though minutely, would have been harmed by the breaking, in our midst, of a general principle meant to protect us.

Am I happy with such a rigid outcome? Well, not really. As a member of the wiggling and squirming school of moral reasoning, let me propose two possible solutions. The first is that there are conditions under which I would allow a physician to break confidence. If this physician had told David that his moral scruples were such that he felt he must break confidence, that he would make it openly known to others that he was doing so, and that he would be willing to take the social punishment which might result (a malpractice suit, for instance), then I think the physician would have acted in an honorable way. The point is that there can be moral reasons for breaking even the most rigid of rules, and rigid because they are so socially important. But the test of the moral rectitude when a rule is broken is that it can be done in the daylight and that the rule-breaker be prepared to pay a social penalty. It is the breaking the dark, dodging the personal consequences, which is the real threat to patient-physician trust.

The other solution is a more dangerous one, but perhaps justifiable in this case, given the special intimacy of the physician with both David and Joan. He could have asked David for permission to break confidence, and attempted by persuasion to get David to agree. Or he could have tried to persuade David to tell Joan himself. He could have gone back to Joan and asked her just how well she knew David, talking all the while in a general way about the importance of couples knowing as much as possible about each other before marriage—the vaguest of hints, that is, that she should want to know more about David. Or, finally, he could have talked with them independently of each other. This policy of deliberate but directed ambiguity involves walking a dangerous line, but I think it would have been justifiable in this case.

by Eric J. Cassell

We can no longer draw a simple distinction between moral and medical problems, at least in an internist's office. What we used to call the "medical facts" and the "personal facts" are indistinguishable. In this case, for example, David had gonorrhea and infectious hepatitis, both diseases of increased prevalence among male homosexuals; he had problems in school and job instability, also common among this group. But more important, both the medical and personal problems are in the realm of the moral, because the problems here had to do with the welfare of two individuals.

What really creates the dilemma in this case is that the physician had cared for both patients for a long time, and had an equally longstanding obligation to both. I believe that he ought to have explored all possibilities that might have led to disclosure but without, finally, breaking confidentiality.

At the very least the physician had an obligation to say to David, "Have you told Joan that you are a homosexual? If you haven't, you really should." Having done this, he might be acquitted of his obligation in much the same way a physician might ask a man who is getting married and whose family has a history of genetic disease whether the bride knew about it.

Second, I believe that the physician had an obligation to discuss her sexuality with Joan prior to the marriage, in order to get some sense of knowledge, problems, expectations, and needs. Perhaps Joan knew full well that David was a homosexual. Indeed, that knowledge may have been one of the conditions of the marriage and of its eventual failure. Just as David expressed his hostility to his father through his school and other problems, it is possible that Joan may have been acting similarly in marrying a homosexual.

In common with every other physician, I suppose, I have been stunned by finding out during my sixteen years in practice that the world and the way people manage to live in it is not at all like I thought it was when I started out. A similar case arose in my own practice. I have known a couple for fourteen years, and they are both my patients, although the wife was not originally my patient. The husband has had a series of intriguing, original, and tangled affairs. He has also had several episodes of gonorrhea, syphilis, and assorted other diseases and disasters. The family is still intact, with one child; from my point of view, it's a rather odd family, but this couple has managed to make an accommodation to this most tangled maze.

I tell couples that marriage consists of three individuals: the man, the woman, and the marriage, and that each deserves privacy and consideration. I don't like husbands or wives automatically accompanying each other into the doctor's office.

I feel the same way about parents and children. I tell parents of adolescents that it is an absolute rule in my office that a child is allowed to see me without my necessarily telling the parent what the visit was about (without the child's permission), unless I believe the child's life is in danger. If the parents can't live with this, then I don't want to be the child's physician. I have a sense that in the long run wisdom is best served by this absolute rule of confidentiality. It does keep physicians from deciding—on the basis of their own limited knowledge—what indeed is in a patient's best interest in complex matters.

by Robert M. Veatch

One principle shared by physicians and lay people is that, at least in uncomplicated cases, the physician should convey to the patient any medically relevant information that would be potentially meaningful or useful in medical decision-making. The physician's Hippocratic ethic instructs him that he should do what he thinks will benefit his patient. Lay people form similar conclusions from other systems of ethics, ones that focus on principles of antonomy and honesty.

The tradition of physician ethics on confidentiality is not at all clear. The Hippocratic Oath, marvelous in its ambiguity, says that the physician ought to keep secret things he learns in his practice that ought not to be "spread abroad." Which things those are is not specified. The World Medical Association's twentieth-century version of the Hippocratic Oath states simplistically that the physician will keep confidences entrusted in him.

On the other hand, the American Medical Association takes a quite different approach. Its principle of ethics says that the physician ought not to disclose things learned in confidence except in three cases: when disclosure is required by law, when it is in the patient's interest, or when it is in the interests of other people. The AMA insists on the physician's duty to persons other than the patient from whom the relevant information has been learned, thus taking a much more social course. But it opens the door for a wide range of disclosures.

Nowhere does traditional physician ethics say anything about resolving conflicts between duties to two patients whose interests may not be the same and whose values and interests may differ from the physician's.

By the time the physician has reached the dilemma in the case of this man and woman, there may simply be no morally acceptable resolution. If the problem of potential conflict had been faced earlier, then several solutions might have been acceptable. Had the physician as an individual, or physicians as a profession, or society as a whole adopted a policy that physicians will not disclose any information obtained in confidence unless, say, life is imminently in danger, then this problem would not have arisen. Alternatively, the AMA rule that confidence can be broken when it is in the interests of others to do so could have been adopted, also eliminating the moral conflict. If there is no good solution to the problem as it evolved, is there anything the physician can do to make the best of an impossible situation? I think there is.

Assuming that the physician is convinced that the information would be important to the woman, he could explain his perception of the situation to her future spouse, determine whether she does know about the homosexuality, and try to convince him of the importance of telling her. If he agrees, the physician's problem disappears. If he does not, the physician has three options.

First, he could continue in both physician-patient relationships without disclosing. This seems to me to be the least acceptable option, a basic violation of the implicit contract based on trust and confidence.

Second, he could disclose anyway, after explaining to the man that he has a moral obligation to do so. (Although I am convinced that such a case might arise, I am not convinced that this situation fits this description.)

Third, he could withdraw from one or both of the relationships. He might claim that his practice was so busy that he had to transfer one or both to a colleague—a blatantly deceitful explanation. He could say openly that he had to break the relationship because of information received in confidence. That would provoke so much curiosity that it might lead to violation of the confidence. He could say vaguely that conditions in his practice were such that he had to transfer one or both to colleagues. As unsatisfactory as this solution is, I believe that it may be the best moral compromise available.

In transferring the woman to another physician, he no longer has a duty to do what would benefit her as his patient. That satisfies the Hippocratic rules, but somehow to me it is still morally very unsatisfying. In fact, from my standpoint as a nonphysician, the duty to disclose is strong even if the person who may benefit from the disclosure is no longer the physician's patient. Nevertheless, breaking the relationship is preferable to continuing in a relationship that must be based on trust without disclosing.

This case shows how important it is to know clearly what the ethical ground rules are at the beginning of a relationship. I prefer openness and disclosure, even if privacies must occasionally be violated. If patients know in advance that the physician may be forced by conscience to break confidences in certain limited situations, I do not think a patient ought to object to such disclosures.

Exercises

1. Identify the factual considerations that each of the three commentators in the *Hastings Center Report* case regards as ethically relevant. State the warrants on which their arguments rely.

2. What is the basic conflict of obligations that makes this particular case a marginal and so a difficult one? Do the three commentators agree in al! respects about the nature of this conflict? If so, what leads them to resolve it in different ways? If not, how are we to analyze the differences between their respective positions?

3. Try to characterize the overall "views of life," or priorities, underlying each commentator's discussion of this case, by finding the general ethical affirmations that serve as backing for the respective arguments.

4. Show how the conflict of obligations involved in this situation can be set out, alternatively, in either of the two ways indicated in the preceding section on modals and rebuttals.

5. In what respects do the arguments presented by the three commentators seem to express the *personal feelings* of the writers? How are these feelings connected with the particular claims and arguments they present? To what extent are they obliged to "agree to differ" at the end of the discussion on account of the personal (or subjective) character of those feelings?

Index